SCIENCE FICTION SEEN FROM THE RIGHT

LENNART SVENSSON

www.manticore.press

Science Fiction Seen from the Right

Lennart Svensson

Copyright © By Lennart Svensson, 2016.

All rights reserved, no section of this book may be utilized without permission, including electronic reproductions without the permission of the author and publisher.

Published in Melbourne, Australia.

BIC Classification:
FL (Science Fiction), FM (Fantasy), JP (Politics and Government), DSK (Literary Studies - Fiction)

978-0-9942525-9-3

MANTICORE PRESS
WWW.MANTICORE.PRESS

SCIENCE FICTION SEEN FROM THE RIGHT

LENNART SVENSSON

TABLE OF CONTENTS

Introduction	7
1. Robert A. Heinlein	14
2. Frank Herbert	38
3. C. S. Lewis	51
4. J. R. R. Tolkien	62
5. Karin Boye	70
6. Orwell, Zamyatin, Huxley and von Harbou	78
7. Ernst Jünger	87
8. Filippo Tommaso Marinetti	108
9. Arthur C. Clarke	120
10. Michael Moorcock	129
11. J. G. Ballard	142
12. Three British Fantasy Novels	158
13. SF Films	166
14. SF Art and Comics	187
15. Development of the Genre	202
16. Jorge Luis Borges	218

17. Carlos Castaneda	224
18. Edgar Rice Burroughs	230
19. H. P. Lovecraft	234
20. Clark Ashton Smith	245
21. Robert E. Howard	252
22. A. E. van Vogt	262
23. Philip K. Dick	270
24. Larry Niven	287
25. Jerry Pournelle	292
26. Ray Bradbury	299
27. Ayn Rand	306
28. Three American SF Novels	314
29. History	320
30. Anarchy	324
31. Nihilism	329
32. War	335
33. Marginalia	352
34. Coda	367
Sources	372
About the Author	377

INTRODUCTION

THIS BOOK IS ABOUT SF and fantasy literature, seen from the political and existential right-wing. And my definition of "right", "a man of the right", is "a man adhering to traditional, eternal values".

These eternal values can be exemplified as: duty, honor, honesty, accountability, selflessness, modesty, fidelity, faith, courage, justice, mercy, clemency, compassion, magnanimity, equanimity – values that are in harmony with the eternal natural law, with *Dharma* and *Tao*, with *Physis* and *Lex Naturalis*.

To vindicate these ideals is what I do as a man of the right. I honor Tradition. To systematically embrace eternal values within a spiritual framework of Christianity, Hinduism and the Ancient Way of the West, of esoteric strains in Greek, Roman and Norse thought, is called traditionalism.

This is my creed. And to clarify: to merely advocate limited government, personal responsibility, moral values and productivity, the *Conservapedia* definition of a conservative, is not to be a traditionalist. It's a start but it's not enough. There has to be an esoteric element present, a connection with the causal realm in which all of existence can be anchored in the Platonic World of Ideas. Here, ultimately, the eternal values have their footing.

For instance, I haven't mentioned "willpower, truth and compassion" among the values above. To me, these have an even more basic, primordial existence than the eternal values proper.

To begin with, *Willpower*. According to esoteric theory (*q.v.* my study *Borderline*, 2015) this existed in the beginning. Will was a primeval force, outside of causality, along with Truth, Light and Dark. Then Will merged with *Truth*. And when choosing *Light* the ensuing entity, God, began his constant struggle against darkness. Now, from Will can be derived duty, accountability, fidelity and courage. And from Truth can be derived honesty and justice. And supposing that the spirit of God, Logos, was also present in the beginning, we then get *Compassion* from which can be derived mercy, clemency, magnanimity and equanimity.

As a side note, Man, as a microcosm, is a mirror of the macrocosmic God, made up of Will, Truth and Light. To have Will, Thought and Compassion, imbued by Light which is the Inner Light, is what defines us as humans. This, as my spiritual creed, may exert some presence throughout this study.

There you have my outline of traditional values and their source. So a story like Frank Herbert's *Dune*, dealing with meditation, courage and honoring your fathers, in the framework of this study, is an SF story of "the right-wing" kind, a story rooted in Tradition. My focus in this book is on conservative, right-wing SF and fantasy, of fantastic stories having the character of being based in eternal values as the ones sketched above, fantastic literature having some discernible relationship to Tradition.

For a textbook rendering of the Perennial Thought intimated above, see René Guénon (1886-1951), *The Crisis of the Modern World*, Julius Evola (1898-1974), *Revolt Against the Modern World*, or Sri Dharma Pravartaka Acharya (1963-), *The Dharma Manifesto*. Another lion of traditionalism currently alive, is Seyyed Hossein Nasr (1933-). Indeed, you might suspect that figures like Herbert, Heinlein or Lovecraft didn't live by *Dharma* in the same way as Guénon and others did. But the traditional element is notable in these and some other SF authors and in this study I'll show you why.

For that matter, I won't go into the anti-traditional attitude in this study. Only in chapter 31, treating nihilism, do I venture into "the dark side" – that of SF stories denying the existence of eternal values like self-restraint, accountability and justice. Overall, I focus on the positive side of the topic, of authors acknowledging Tradition. But I also admit that there are SF authors in this study hard to categorize. For instance, J. G. Ballard isn't an author you would think of as a traditionalist. Rather, he's some kind of a modernist. But he isn't explicitly Marxist. His authorship moves on a level of complexity that makes it fruitful to study, along with the more expressly conservative authors examined. Another such gray area figure is Michael Moorcock. In his heroic fantasy he touched on elements of Tradition, mostly degrading them, or merely glossing over the nihilist aspects of his Eternal Champion with purple prose, "marvels upon marvels" and wisecracking. But Moorcock can't be completely ignored in this study and I'll explain this in due time.

However, I do have to say this on the subject of nihilism. I may come across as excessively judgmental in labeling people nihilists, people that still maintain other, viable ideals. So I say this: *"nihil"* is Latin and means "nothing". Nihilism, to me, is the tendency of not acknowledging eternal ideals, not acknowledging the invisible, spiritual side of reality. Nihilism is to emphasize the material side of things, of seeing man and nature as machines. Nihilism is to deny the existence of a soul, of the soul as a fragment of the Eternal Light of God. *Mutatis mutandum* – this is the definition of nihilism employed in this study. Nihilism highlights a central feature of what Tradition is not: Tradition is acknowledging eternal ideals, nihilism is to deny them. Tradition is to acknowledge transcendent values, nihilism is to reduce everything into "the death of the body and the decay of matter". Authors in this study labeled as nihilists may acknowledge some fine ideals, but the crux is to anchor these ideals in an ontology worthy of its name – and more often than not – I don't see these authors espouse such a perennially viable ontological base for their views. That's why I criticize nihilism the way I do.

As for defining the concept of science fiction, you could take the easy way out. You could say, like Norman Spinrad: "Science Fiction is anything published as Science Fiction". This is seeing SF as a market label which, in itself, is fully justified.

A bit more abstract would be saying, like an author of a certain book on SF films: "'SF' in this book is what I call SF, right?" This, for a study like mine, could give you some freedom as a writer, looking at any author you choose without it having to be within the confines of a strict definition.

On the following pages I don't intend to deliver an exhaustive view on SF. Still, I think I must give the reader some sense of what I personally mean with SF. I have to delineate the territory called "SF" that I examine in this study, so here goes. The authors that I deliberate on in this book were all active in the 20th century. Their fiction is in focus. They wrote stories, contemporary, original tales with a technological-speculative element. Even if the stories weren't strictly scientific in every sense they always had a scientific feel, exploiting narratives in the fields of modern science. SF is about scientific sagas venturing Beyond the Beyond and Within the Within, trying to portray man in relation to the cosmos.

As for the fantasy stories examined in this study they are of the epic, pseudo-medieval kind (and not "magical realism" or the like, excepting Borges, Lovecraft. Bradbury and maybe Jünger). However, these archaic epics additionally have the character of "something new", a *novum*, something creatively original, along with being traditional – that is, having that medieval feel. For instance, the epic fantasies of Tolkien and Moorcock are wholly original creations. In comparison, Howard Pyle and T. H. White wrote glorified summaries of the King Arthur Saga which isn't fantasy in my sense of the word because the element of creating something original isn't there. Each and every author examined in this study was an original creator, venturing out to formulate something new within the confines of speculative literature, mapping out new lands in the process, be they dystopias, technotopias, the present with some slight alteration or a parallel world of that or the other kind.

The reader might react to some imbalances in the layout of this study. For instance, the title is "SF Seen From the Right" but it treats both SF and fantasy. I know that, but to treat the archaic epics of Tolkien along with the more modern outings of Heinlein, Clarke, and Ballard is pretty common in SF studies, such as in Aldiss' *Trillion Year Spree – The History of Science Fiction* (1986). The realm of fantastic literature I roam is rather vast, having vague borders.

Thus, the study incorporates many things, such as portraits of both European and American authors, both genre-conscious authors and others, even though SF predominantly may be an American phenomenon. But I just can't be without Boye, Huxley and Jünger in a study like this.

Then the reader might think, where's the horror, the weird fantasy? It's represented by Lovecraft and to some extent Carlos Castaneda, so I've got this covered too.

A general feature of this study is that it focuses on books, not authors. Stories are examined, not author *personae*. The majority of chapters are structured along certain authors but I'm primarily out to examine texts, not what the author may have thought when writing them. I do provide some biographical information, as this seemed feasible at times. However, I seldom or ever make any artistic claims based on a specific event in an author's life. I give biographical details when they are interesting in themselves. In this book, as a rule novels and short stories are in focus, not authors themselves.

A note on spoilers. This is an in-depth essay, not a review. Therefore there are "spoilers", I don't warn the reader of revealing of how a story might end. The study isn't entirely relying on plot summaries but while writing it I've not been hemmed in by spoilers.

The most recent works treated exhaustively in this study are from the mid-1980s. Revealing the plot of books thirty years old or more isn't exactly a spoiling activity. But to be sure, don't read this book if you're immature enough not being able to endure spoilers of any kind.

Hereby a general overview of the book. The chapters focus on authors. In this respect I start by looking at two trusted American conservatives (Heinlein, Herbert) and then treat two equally legendary British conservatives (Lewis, Tolkien). This sets the tone of the book, for this is "as traditional as it gets" – this is the benchmark of traditionalism, SF, and fantasy. Then I stay with European authors for a while, looking at dystopias, Jünger, and futurism before returning to England (Clarke, Moorcock, Ballard).

Next, I leave the specific author focus for a while, instead dedicating some chapters to SF film, SF art, and the development of the genre (chapter thirteen-fifteen).

Then the literary world tour continues, first with a sweep over Latin America (in the form of Borges and Castaneda) and then it's back to the US for a look into the traditional aspects of old stalwarts (E. R. Burroughs, Lovecraft, C. A. Smith, Howard) and some slightly younger names (van Vogt, Dick, Niven, etc.) The study is wrapped up with some thematic chapters treating History, Anarchy, Nihilism and War.

This is a conceptual look at SF: SF seen from a right-wing, traditional viewpoint – that is, *my* kind of traditional viewpoint. So please, don't come and say "this right-wing study omits trusted conservative SF author X, what a major blunder!" To this I say: I treat the authors I treat, looking into those I look into – period. Furthermore, the conceptual, essayist nature of the book means that it isn't a general history of the genre (even though I touch on generic issues too, as in chapter fifteen). Also, the focus is on 20th century authors while the stars of earlier and later years are only fleetingly observed, if at all.

That said, I still do believe in SF and fantasy as modes of expression, as serious literary strategies. For instance, I've personally published some fiction that can be labeled as SF so technically, I'm a 21st century SF author myself. I still have some hopes for this kind of literature, for "speculative fiction" in mirroring the times ahead. We're living in a period of transition, in a time of conflicting realities: the way we look upon ourselves and the world – via ontological issues – are crucial in this respect and SF is ontological-metaphysical literature by default, it can't avoid posing questions about the nature of reality, as I discuss in chapter nine. Therefore the genre, call it SF, speculative fiction, metaphysical fiction or whatever, to me implicitly seems to hold a future for us all. In mere sales the SF genre today may see a slope, as it has for many years, but stories about aliens, space travel, parallel worlds and ontology in general, stories about human reactions to conceptual changes, stories about future scenarios, will still be written and read. This, at least, is what I see in my crystal ball.

When looking at a reasonably old SF title you might ask yourself: is this book still worth reading on its own premises, beyond what it says conceptually? Is it "living literature", a book that readers still pick up and read willingly? As for the books treated in this study I'd say that they are, *mutatis mutandum*, still in the realm of living literature. So this isn't some antiquarian review of quaint oddities, it's about living, breathing classics with a still viable message – that of Tradition, that of embracing eternal values such as faith, duty, courage, and self-restraint. These values are trampled underfoot today by the liberal mainstream. At the same time, a resurgent right-wing acknowledges these values. Thus, the books treated below are rather topical and relevant to the era we live in.

Härnösand, December 29, 2015

LENNART SVENSSON

1. ROBERT A. HEINLEIN

THE MOST ICONIC right-wing SF author ever is Robert Anson Heinlein (1907-1987). Apart from acknowledging Tradition, duty and the values of the early Republic he had an immense influence on the SF field per se. He widened the attitudes and tropes of modern SF and became a force that everyone had to relate to. Even Philip K. Dick, the idol of the 1960s "new wave", reportedly saw Heinlein as the master. Therefore a closer look at Heinlein will be the opening chapter of this book. To the myopic mind, maybe Heinlein wasn't a model right-winger in every sense. Nevertheless, he remains something of a portal figure for this study. His output from 1939 through 1959 is a hidden treasure of conservative values.

TRADITION

Traditions, the ways of our fathers, the timeless values – are these compatible with spaceships, techno cities and an environment characterized by change? Even Robert A. Heinlein stressed the reality of change, how 20th century society had undergone transformations and we along with it. *Tempus mutantur, nos et mutamur in illis* (the times are changing and we along with them). But parallel to this Heinlein also did stress traditional values. Even in the 1960s, the time when he started to become somewhat libertine in the lifestyles depicted in his books, he could still praise chivalric virtues.

In *Glory Road* (1963) we meet Oscar Gordon. He has been in Vietnam, in the days when the US only had military advisors there. He has been drafted into a tour of service and in the jungle he has seen some action. It wasn't overly heroic but Gordon stood his ground since he knows what fighting is about. The whole mood of the opening chapters of this novel is Heinlein at his best, a first-person narrator wisecracking as he goes along portraying his life and times, an incomparable view from the right of the Affluent Society and the Safe Generation. Most importantly, he talks about patriotism. This wasn't a welcome subject even then, the early 60s, not among the societal elite. The anecdote of Gordon writing a school paper on patriotism and having to tone down the more radical sides of it, is the right-winger's plight *in nuce*.

After his Vietnam tour Gordon's glad that he's out of the military since this opens the road to a prosperous civilian career. But he's wary of the prospect of settling down in suburbia with a mortgage, wife and kids. He yearns for adventure, true adventure in a meaningful world and not "the tawdry, lousy, fouled-up mess" that is our world, the 20th century quagmire of super power confrontation, consumerism and nihilism.

VALUES

Gordon wants a world where values still matter. And he gets it, in the form of a mission to a parallel world. As a pupil of secondary school he had actually been taught fencing and soon he wields a sword against monsters and various foes, day in, day out. He becomes a hero. It's a bit leisurely told and incredible as such but the Heinlein narrator still manages to bring the reader along. He has something to say in all this. Like stressing traditional values.

Like this: once in his adventurous path Gordon is approached by an adolescent wishing to see his sword, a boy in need of that Heroic Presence. Gordon isn't wholly comfortable with the demand, he doesn't want to sound like a cliché, but he understands the symbolic value of giving such advice. And so he tells the lad to study hard, work hard and wait for the right moment; there's always room at the top and you might make it. The boy is also given the advice of introducing himself to women he meets, to befriend them is always a good thing. This is eminently chivalric, this the Grail stories said too. There was no rigid theme of chastity in them, as Julius Evola has shown in *The Mystery of the Grail* (1934). A knight should not be exclusively led by carnal needs but otherwise it's good to meet women and enjoy their charms; that was the advice in the Grail Stories and that's the advice given now.

In his pocket Gordon has a coin depicting George Washington and now he tells the boy of this man who always spoke the truth, fought against impossible odds and stood tall and proud. To the reader Gordon admits that it's a bit cliché but overall, when approached by a young man in this respect you have to play the part of wise man imparting traditional values, the other guy expects it. Gordon may not be a traditionalist through and through but as we've seen, back in the real world, the mid-20th century he comes from, he was a patriot and he had served in the Army, he knew the demands of the combat zone and he had a world-view yearning for more than living the petite-bourgeois life. Therefore this lecture in traditional values rings true.

IDEALS

The ideals of olden times are still viable. Self-restraint, self-reliance, responsibility and nobility of character must be remembered and imparted, again and again. And in his 1950s novels Heinlein did just that. Maybe his later books strayed off into "strange lands" for a right-winger but we must remember that Heinlein remained an anti-communist all his life, bent on opposing the most nihilistic and murderous regime there ever was, this in a time when the mainstream intellectual embraced socialism and collectivism.

Heinlein's so called juveniles aren't solely readable for youngsters. These novels, like *Starman Jones*, *Farmer in the Sky*, *Citizen of the Galaxy* etc. have young protagonists but otherwise they have become timeless classics. And they showcase traditional values, discreetly but nonetheless. It's there, it's advocated. Like in *Time for the Stars*.

This is a novel about a youngster going on an interstellar space mission. He's a telepath, he can communicate with this twin brother who remains on earth. Communication faster than light is thus assured. Along with him on the spaceflight the boy, Tom, has his uncle Steve, an experienced space navy officer. And at a certain moment Steve conveys this conservatism *in nuce*, a glorified John Wayne-comment, and it reads: "A man pays his bills, keeps himself clean, respects other people, and keeps his word. He gets no credit for this; he has to do this much just to stay even with himself."[1] This is traditional values in hands-on terms, obvious truths we have to be reminded of again and again, especially now when acting irresponsibly is a matter of course, when everybody blames someone else and "being offended" is everyone's god-given right.

Heinlein teaches the need to shape up and become a man. There's something called willpower: the will to live an authentic life, will to assume responsibility, will to be all that you can be. Take a shave and speak the truth. In his juveniles Heinlein teaches these values, *mutatis mutandum*, but persistently so. His sermons are exquisitely easy to relate to.. And original. They might seem like "typical 50s stuff" today but they aren't. As intimated patriotism wasn't topically mainstream back then, neither was the praising of speaking the truth, keeping yourself tidy and proper, standing up straight and keeping your word. Among "those who counted," the intelligentsia and the cultural pundits, it was a time of beatniks and drop-outs, of the budding counter-culture. This culture might have been right in protesting against intervention in Vietnam but it was wrong in throwing all traditional values out the window.

---

[1] Heinlein, 1973, p 126

SERVING

Heinlein served in the US Navy in the 1930s. He was a First Lieutenant with expertise in communications, serving on capital ships. He was high-tech and contemporary while still acknowledging the traditional sides of being in the military. And in *Space Cadet* (1948) Heinlein did praise the traditional aspects of the life in uniform. *Space Cadet* is a hymn to The Service Life, as such a worthy precursor of *Starship Troopers* (1959). The latter will be treated in chapter 32 of this study.

Space Cadet teaches us what it's like to be an officer, of serving in the Space Watch policing the solar system of the 2070s. First, it gives us the rhetorical, formal side of it, rather convincing. In a speech to the new recruits at the Space Academy the commander says that these are the traditional values an officer has to embody: self-restraint, responsibility and nobility of character.

As for *restraint* this is needed in an officer. He has to have ambition but he mustn't be a careerist, an egotist running a one-man show. A military man is a team player and for this self-restraint might be needed, like having to serve under officers you don't personally like.

Then there was *responsibility*. Any military leader must assume responsibility. Any soldier or sailor too; every man in a military unit has to take responsibility for his share. There's nothing such as trusting all to the leader. In the German Bundeswehr this is called *Innere Führung* (inner leadership: every soldier has to take charge of his being in the line of duty).

The responsibility of the leader, Heinlein stresses, can be of the dictatorial kind. When the commander of a vessel gives an order it mustn't be questioned. Combat is a crisis business and there can be no discussion then. Not everyone knows this in the age of "democracy, debate, I'm entitled to my opinion".

As for the last quality, *nobility of character*, we're back in the Grail Stories again, in the chivalry of the ancient times living on in modern days. The commander expressly says that an officer has to be *a true and noble knight*.

BIO

Robert Heinlein was born in 1907, in Butler, Missouri. A career in the US Navy enticed him early on and he graduated from the Annapolis Naval Academy in 1929. As a communications officer, serving on the aircraft carrier USS Lexington, he had his dream job. However, in time he contracted pulmonary tuberculosis and in 1934 was discharged on medical grounds.

From this time on Heinlein had a variety of jobs. He was also active in Upton Sinclair's "End Poverty in California" movement and took part in getting Sinclair being nominated for Democratic candidate for the governorship of California. In short, Heinlein was a man of the left in these days. He soon turned to the right, according to Isaac Asimov by being influenced by Virginia Gerstenfield. This "Ginny" was to be Heinlein's wife from 1948 to his death.

Early in 1939 Heinlein saw an ad for a competition, the magazine *Thrilling Wonder Stories* promising 50 dollars for the best debut SF short story. So he sat down and wrote a 7,000 word story. Then he saw that the top SF magazine of the day, *Astounding*, paying one cent per word, would pay 70 dollars for it if accepted, so he sent it there instead. And it got accepted and was printed as "Life-Line" in August, 1939. The same issue also saw A. E. van Vogt's first SF story in print, "The Black Destroyer". The editor of the magazine was John W. Campbell who would have some influence on the early Heinlein as he had on van Vogt and Asimov. Asimov had already started writing SF in 1938.

Heinlein started out as a writer. He also had his disability pension from the Navy to live on. The period 1939-1941 mainly saw him writing short stories, what would become his "Future History" delineating a chronicle from the present to the 2100s. But WWII loomed and the Navy again needed his services, now employing him as a civilian at the Aircraft Facility at Philadelphia Naval Shipyard, Pennsylvania. The aeronautical engineering he did there included working on pressure suits, knowledge he reportedly later could use for the novel *Have Space Suit – Will Travel* (1958). As an employee of this Shipyard Heinlein also recruited fellow SF authors L. Sprague de Camp and Isaac Asimov to work there.

After the war Heinlein's writing career took off. He continued to sell to the genre magazines like *Astounding* but he also sold stories to mainstream magazines like *The Saturday Evening Post*, *Town and Country* and *Boy's Life*. These "slicks" payed better than pulps like *Astounding* and *Unknown*; they were printed on better paper and had a wider circulation. Heinlein now also started writing SF novels in earnest, both for adult readers and for a younger audience. The latter were the above mentioned "juveniles", commissioned by the publishing house Scribner's.

In sketching the above, the framework of Heinlein's career is pretty much in place. He was married to Ginny, they lived in California, they had no kids and Heinlein kept churning out right-wing classics, at least up and until *Starship Troopers* of 1959. And in line with the traditionalist aspect, of the right-wing ideals having already been touched upon, what can be said of Heinlein's works? Apart from the ones I've already mentioned, are there some stories of his profiling reality in a way having some bearing on conservatism, spirituality, the responsible life?

THE MOON IS A HARSH MISTRESS

The Moon is a Harsh Mistress is a Heinlein novel from 1966, by some seen as his last credible performance as a writer, his last show of force. It tells the story of a future moon colony rebelling against Mother Earth, the narrative giving Heinlein the opportunity to tell an *operational* story, of tangible action within a more-or-less brainy framework, like *Sixth Column*, *The Puppet Masters* and *Starship Troopers* before it.

This operational aspect of Heinlein will be treated further in chapter 32. Hereby some other topical remarks, beginning with the just mentioned 1966 novel. At the beginning of *The Moon is a Harsh Mistress* we're met with the idea of artificial intelligence (AI) in the form of a thinking computer, Mike. His intelligence and sense of self is explained by analogy, like: man is a machine and he thinks so why wouldn't a computer, being a machine, be able to think? Heinlein here presents us with the idea that self-consciousness emerges in a man when the enough number of association webs are present. This sounds plausible but it's false. A machine has no will; he acts by human input, even though a super-computer may conduct its actions pretty fast. A man on the other hand is an organism endowed with a Self, a creature acting volitionally; man's soul precedes the physical body, the soul steers the body and as an organism mind, body and spirit functions holistically. As intimated in the Introduction Will and Thought encapsulated by Compassion is what defines us as human beings, in all the complexities of human existence, of being able to create, talk, sing, deliberate. A computer, impressive as it is, remains a machine, not endowed with either Will, Thought or sense of Self. This can't magically arise out of nothing, how complex it may be.

That said, the Mike character in the novel at hand is an enjoyable acquaintance, a super-computer in the realm of Clarke's HAL and Asimov's Multivac. Mike is the Heinlein attitude embodied in AI-form.

FREEDOM

In this novel, *The Moon Is a Harsh Mistress*, Professor Bernardo de la Paz is a memorable guru character. His freedom philosophy is spelled out like this: there may be societal rules around, you may have to follow them for the sake of practicality, but nonetheless you remain free in your essence, you can break the laws if your sense of freedom demands it – and in doing this you're still a responsible man, you're morally responsible for your acts, the very thing that makes you free. Only the responsible man can be truly free. Freedom obliges, you might say; that's the aristocracy of the soul that the best of Heinlein's heroes belong to.

Bernardo's high-profile saying in question reads like this: "I am free because I know that I alone am morally responsible for everything I do." This summarizes the conservative ideal of accountability, linking it to the timeless ideal of freedom – existential, personal freedom, from which societal freedom is derived.

SIMULTANEITY

I've just elaborated on some aspects of Heinlein's 1966 novel *The Moon Is a Harsh Mistress*. One of the aspects was a critique of Heinlein's man machine-philosophy. This gives me the urge to say something more on Heinlein's metaphysical side, which is mostly ignored by critics. For he wasn't merely a worshiper of reductionism and man-as-a-machine. He didn't shut out all metaphysical discussions; on the contrary. He went rather far out into speculative realms now and then.

For instance, again take *Time for the Stars*. It's about a pair of twins being employed in a starship venture, using telepathy to communicate. Even in ordinary, interplanetary space travel it takes several minutes for a radio signal to travel from a ship to an earth side base, as in the traffic of unmanned space probes. Now, suppose we have a manned ship going off to another star system, traveling at near light speeds as in the novel at hand; then the relativistic effects disturb and delay radio communication even more. But with telepathy as a means of communication, these problems are solved. You get instantaneous connection, faster even than the speed of light.

Already this is a rather speculative idea: that ESP could be used operationally on a journey to the stars. *Time for the Stars* is a novel in the realm of "not recognized scientific ideas" as regards the normal science of today – "normal science" in the paradigmical, Thomas Kuhn sense. Heinlein challenges the paradigm, he underlines the iconoclasm in saying that instantaneous interaction might be possible, doing it in a chapter where the traveling starship conducts an experiment specifically checking up on the temporality of the mind-reading communication. As for the role of simultaneity in physics, Heinlein by way of a crew member, Dr. Babcock, sums it up in this way:

> Son, ever since the great Doctor Einstein, "simultaneous" and "simultaneity" have been dirty words to physicists. We chucked the very concept, denied that it had meaning, and built up a glorious structure of theoretical physics without it. Then you mind readers came along and kicked it over. (...) You've split

us physicists into two schools, those who want to class you as a purely psychological phenomenon and no business of physics – these are the "close your eyes and it will go away" boys – and a second school which realizes that since measurements can be made of whatever this is you do, it is therefore the business of physics to measure it and include it... since physics is, above all, the trade of measuring things and assigning definite numerical values to them.[2]

And since the ESP works the narrator later concludes, "the concept of simultaneity was forcing a complete new look at physics".[3]

Heinlein in speculating about ESP in this way is ushering in a new physics, aligning himself with names like David Bohm, James Jeans and Alfred North Whitehead, people not afraid of seeing the universe holistically. If the universe is an organism, if it's alive, then instantaneous interaction would go with the territory. Simultaneity (and the akin concept of "action at a distance", something Einstein also disliked) is a mainstay of holistic ontology and holism is the defining character of perennial metaphysics.

LOST LEGACY

Time for the Stars was published in 1956. Heinlein was even more esoteric in the 1940s. From this era, we for instance have *The Unpleasant Profession of Jonathan Hoag*, with its parallel worlds and wavering reality. And we have the novella *Lost Legacy* (in book form in *Assignment in Eternity*, 1953), about a full-fledged ESP strike force combating the forces of evil in a future America.

"ESP strike force" might sound a little simplistic. And the story might become a wee bit streamlined at times. But the melodrama element of vicious enemies is quite right in the context. And in preparing the stage for it Heinlein gets it all right, even imbuing his psychic heroes with some lifestyle qualities. First we meet the psychology teacher Philip Huxley and the physician Dr. Coburn.

---

[2] Heinlein, 1973, p 81
[3] Ibid., p 138

In the beginning of the story Huxley complains about the current *Leitkultur* of behaviorism, the model man-machine concept of the time of writing (1941), a reductionist outlook making it hard for him to pursue academic freedom:

> You see, officially, we are supposed to be behaviorists. Any suggestion that there might be something to consciousness that can't be explained in terms of physiology and mechanics is about as welcome as a Saint Bernard in a telephone boot.[4]

This strikes the chord for this story of truly speculative fiction, ESP variety. The paradigm of reductionism is challenged. Next Coburn and Huxley meet up with one of Huxley's students, the chic Joan Freeman, and the discussions on the poverty of current psychology continues. The trio is fed up with not being able to academically speculate on the essentials of being, "what life is, what thought is, whether free will is a reality or an illusion."[5] But they soon start to develop ESP properties themselves, then, at least, proving that will is free; will by definition is free; the "bound will" is desire. They develop the power of the mind whereby Will governs Thought. Heinlein doesn't expressly phrase it thus but he intimates it.

Next the trio goes to Mt Shasta where it happens to meet legendary author Ambrose Bierce, now being part of a glorified ESP collective there. Heinlein, the supposed materialist-reductionist paragon, in this story is "really out there". True, the story was originally published under the pseudonym of "Lyle Monroe" (in *Super Science Stories*, November 1941) but ever since its book publication in *Assignment in Eternity*, 1953 it has been under Heinlein's own name.

Thus Heinlein can be seen as an informal teacher of esotericism – indeed, even better, a myth-maker for the coming golden age of spirituality, depicting as he does how the group our trio joins is embroiled in a psychic struggle all over the land, a fight between the forces of Light and Dark. This is unique – because, fiction on the theme of spiritual elevation and the fight between will-powered Light

---

[4] Heinlein, 1954, p 97
[5] Ibid., p 103

and desire-driven Darkness, is a rare thing indeed, in and out of the SF field. However, maybe Edward Bulwer-Lytton in *The Coming Race* (1871) and Frederick S. Oliver in *A Dweller on Two Planets* (1905) come close to the dramatic spirituality of *Lost Legacy*.

A nice way of connecting *Lost Legacy* to what's gone before in this chapter is the telepathy element. As in *Time for the Stars* these heroes can communicate mentally. And this quote, of Joan seeking ESP solace from her guru, encapsulates all that's admirable in *Lost Legacy* – the humanity, the drama, the esotericism. Calling her Master Ling, he answers:

> "Why are you weeping, Little Flower?" Her head jerked up. "Master Ling!" "Can that not be which has been. Is there a past or future? Have you learned my lessons so poorly? Am I not with you, as always?" She felt in the thought the vibrant timeless merriment, the gusto for living which was the hallmark of the gentle Chinese. (...) She relaxed as Ling had taught her, let her consciousness flow in the reverie which encompasses time in a single deathless now.[6]

GULF

Assignment in Eternity is a collection of novellas / novelettes / short stories. Worth mentioning too among them is *Elsewhen*, a piece about travels to other dimensions, not as profound as *Lost Legacy* but sitting fine alongside with it in its metaphysical approach. Also, we here find *Gulf*, a near-future spy story about one Joseph Gilead, out on a mission to save the moon from exploding. In the process Gilead is recruited into a private organization led by "Kettle Belly" Baldwin, a genius and expert on everything, it seems. They come to discuss the nature of thought, how to raise man mentally, how to construct a perfectly logical language and such. It all gets a bit titanic, the soul element is missing here, that which made *Lost Legacy* more convincing.

---

[6] Heinlein, 1954, p 168.

That said, *Gulf* gives us *in nuce* the Heinlein creed of rationalism, otherwise evangelized in *Stranger In a Strange Land* and implicitly in almost every Heinlein story. The ideal is to be a studied man, to take your PhD, to learn and use your mental faculties to the utmost. To destroy all the lies devised in the past and shed light over all the darkness...! Again, we also need compassion and feeling so as not to become mental titans. But the *Gulf* sermon about the other side of the coin, of the danger of the ill-informed everyman, I can fully agree with:

> If the average man thinks at all, he does silly things like generalizing from a single datum. He uses one-valued logics. If he is exceptionally bright, he may use two-valued, "either-or" logic to arrive at his wrong answers. If he is hungry, hurt, or personally interested in the answer, he can't use any sort of logic and will discard an observed fact as blithely as he will stake his life on a piece of wishful thinking. He uses the technical miracles created by superior men without wonder nor surprise, as a kitten accepts a bowl of milk. Far from aspiring to higher reasoning, he is not even aware that higher reasoning exists. He classes his own mental process as being of the same sort as the genius of an Einstein. Man is not a rational animal; he is a rationalizing animal.[7]

Baldwin (and possibly Gilead) are geniuses. They come aplenty in Heinlein's novels. And why not. The wiser the better. Contrariwise, it's a mistake to have all novel heroes being quirky and dysfunctional as is the norm in current mainstream fiction, being littered with junkies and lowlifes. They have their place too in literature but when they become the norm, as they are in the urban literature of the 20th century, something is wrong.

The literary cult of the outcast is a sign of decadence. But in Heinlein's novels we find Competent Men, people knowing their way around problems. It's a nice change from the miasma of mediocrity pervading Normal Fiction Type 1A. Here's Heinlein's take on the specificity of the genius:

---

[7] Heinlein, 1954, p 46

Geniuses are usually long lived. They are not modest, not honestly so. They have infinite capacity for taking pains.[8]

COVENTRY

A guy named MacKinnon is going over the plains of western USA in a terrain vehicle. He's in high spirits – because he's going to Coventry...! "Be sent to Coventry" is a British phrase meaning to send someone into exile and here, in the current context, it becomes a symbol of freedom. The future US this plays in, namely, consists of the Regular US in the east and, in the West, beyond an energy barrier, a supposed anarchist utopia – Coventry.

MacKinnon is in conflict with the law. In the future, placid, peace-and-prosperity-focused USA he has committed the ultimate crime: he has struck another fellow, punched a man having offended him. In his defense he rants about the system, rather efficiently as a critique of this "air-conditioned nightmare", virtually a symbol of our times:

> What is there left today? Cautious, compromising "safe" weaklings with water in their veins. You've planned your whole world so carefully that you've planned the fun and zest out of it. Nobody is ever hungry; nobody ever gets hurt. Your ships can't crack up and your crops can't fail. You even have the weather tamed so it rains politely – after midnight. Why wait till midnight, I don't know... you all go to bed at nine o'clock! If one of you safe little people should have an unpleasant emotion – perish the thought! – you'd trot right over to the nearest psychodynamics clinic and get your soft little minds readjusted. Thank God I never succumbed to that dope habit. I'll keep my own feelings, thanks, no matter how bad they taste. You won't even make love without consulting a psycho-technician. Is her mind as flat and insipid as mine? Is there any emotional instability in her family? It's enough to make a man gag. As for fighting over a woman – if anyone

---

[8] Heinlein, 1954, p 54

had the guts to do that, he'd find a proctor at his elbow in two minutes, looking for the most convenient place to paralyze him, and inquiring with sickening humility, "May I do you a service, sir?"[9]

Thus we read in Heinlein's short story *Coventry* (*Astounding*, July 1940, in book form in *Revolt in 2100*, 1953). Having quoted the above could be enough for assuring us Heinlein's keen eye for the downside of living in a well-ordered civilization reminiscent of the "control-and-consumer" societies of the current kind, ruled by liberal nihilism.

The critique stands, but in relating the rest of the story we also see a splendid example of the Heinlein "intelligence operation", of his way of shaping SF as a Gestalt of ideological debate and individual characterization, told in a relatable plot.

MacKinnon has done damage to another citizen and gets the choice of psychological treatment or being banished to the lands of the West, to Coventry. With joy MacKinnon chooses the latter, having heard rumors of them as being an anarchist utopia. A land of the free for a real man...! But he soon becomes disappointed. Not only that; when portraying MacKinnon venturing out in the wilds he, the supposed hero of individualism and self-assuredness, comes through as an ignoramus – he's a fool as regards how really to survive in the outback with only a hunting rifle as a means of adding to his stores of canned food and concentrates. And he knows nothing of how to serve his vehicle but he thinks that he could build one from scratch, given the means.

When encountering inhabited lands in this Beyond-the-Barrier realm MacKinnon becomes disappointed. There's no anarchist state there, only New America with a frontier-style ruggedness in its judicial system. He's deprived of his vehicle and jailed. His musings in jail is that of "the idealist mugged by reality": "Evidently Coventry was not quite the frontier anarchy he had expected it to be."[10] But from a figure named "Fader" Magee he gets help to escape. Then a war breaks out between New America and the Free State, another

---

[9] Heinlein, 1955, p 130
[10] Ibid., p 139

state in this beyond-the-beyond territory, this Free State actually being a dictatorship. This gives reasons for even more disappointment in the alleged preserve of freedom that Coventry was supposed to be: "Coventry was an even more complex place than MacKinnon had gathered up to this time."[11] "Magee's words demolished MacKinnon's dream of finding an anarchistic utopia within the barrier..."[12] *Realpolitik* rules, not dreams of freedom.

Eventually MacKinnon and Magee can escape in the countryside where the latter has a safe house, run by a medical doctor and her daughter. MacKinnon gets to speak with this child genius, Penelope. She sees the matter of his bar-room brawl, when he punched the other guy which got him convicted, as an overreaction. The other guy merely "made a noise with his mouth – a verbal label".[13] If the label was meaningless, why bother? And if it was right – what damage did he do? Whereas McKinnon in punching him actually hurt him.

That's rather thoughtful. Heinlein even manages to make the Eastern USA in question look good, a state respecting the freedom of its citizens, making them choose between Coventry and psychic correction. This is the US of "the Covenant", a treaty saying that a government must never be permitted to tamper with the mind of any citizen, and any citizen can reject this Covenant. Further, in the Covenant the concept of "justice" is questioned – since justice isn't empirically observable whereas damage, physical and economic, is. This is materialist utilism but still, Heinlein doesn't stack the cards altogether in depicting the idea. The future Eastern USA is a "safe" land but still with challenges to be made in science and exploration. And eventually McKinnon and Magee end up there again, Magee being in actuality a secret agent for it, a captain of the US Army espying the dealings of the lands beyond the barrier, seeing if they pose a threat to the US with their rumors of war. MacKinnon, back in his homeland, must now logically choose psychic correction for his original crime but this isn't needed. Magee says:

---

[11] Heinlein, 1955, p 142

[12] Ibid., p 143

[13] Ibid., p 161

You have cured yourself. You may not be aware of it, but four psycho-technicians have interviewed you. Their reports agree. I am authorized to tell you that your status as a free citizen has been restored, if you wish it.[14]

This might confuse the orthodox mind. Wasn't the Eastern US depicted as a caricature of a modern state? That might be, but still, please mention another SF story that in forty pages condenses a political scenario like this, with memorable figures and fast-moving action. The story spans the whole spectrum of political ideas, making it into a playing field of debate and deliberations, showing the strength of SF as a literature of ideas. Like the best of Heinlein's works it functions on several planes, as both entertainment and education, this one urging the reader to perfect his own ideas about anarchy, state and utopia. More on anarchy in chapter thirty of this study.

MUSICALITY

Heinlein had a slightly titanic character, writing as he did about triumphant heroes of space travel, war and engineering. But along with this he also had a *musical* side, an ability to give room to activities inspired by the Muses. In German we have the adjective *Musisch* covering this, being "musical" in a wider sense, affirming the power of culture at large, of song, literature and painting.

So in this respect a "musical man" is inspired by the activities protected by the Muses, the goddesses of song, lyric poetry etc. In his way Heinlein was something of a musical man, maybe not like a Keats, a Baudelaire or a Lovecraft, but in Heinlein's works the role of the artist and the artwork plays a much larger role than it does in the writings of Asimov, Clarke or van Vogt, his *Astounding* contemporaries.

For instance, we have the Heinlein novella *The Man Who Sold the Moon*, a story of the planning and executing of a trip to the moon by way of financing, R&D and advertising, focused on the character

---

[14] Heinlein, 1955, p 169

of David Delos Harriman, a rather captivating but also slightly titanic figure. Harriman is a CEO prepared to do a lot to fulfill his dream. But his mellower sides are also shown; along with being an operational pro he's a dreamer and a visionary, and an accompanying epilogue called "Requiem" tells how the aging Harriman at last can go to the moon himself. He previously was forbidden to do this because his financiers said no. He was invaluable as a figurehead for the earth side operation of it all. But finally he can go and the story aptly quotes Stevenson's "Requiem" at the beginning, the poem with the payoff: "Home is the sailor, home from the sea / and the hunter home from the hill".

This hits the spot, this is in sync with the whole story. Heinlein could sometimes play on the softer keys. True, style wise he's overall rather unrefined. Like Philip K. Dick his style first and foremost was efficient. But there were many sides to the man. Heinlein constantly had the ability to surprise the reader.

Heinlein, the politician-cum-officer-cum-astronomer, had a genuine interest in art *per se*, art as a phenomenon. Sometimes it didn't quite succeed narratively, as in "The Green Hills of Earth", a short story about a future poet, Rhysling, the bard of the space ways. It got a bit too sentimental. Still, in the musical context this is an honest effort. Our future world won't be populated solely by engineers, pilots and sergeants.

In "The Green Hills of Earth" story this, "The Green Hills of Earth", is the name of the defining poem by Rhysling, praising the beauty of our planet – "let us rest our eyes on fleecy skies / and the cool, green hills of Earth" – and it figures briefly in another Heinlein text, *Farmer in the Sky*. This novel isn't about music or poetry; it's about becoming a farmer on the Jupiter moon Ganymede. However, one single passage tells about music in a rather succinct manner. The main character, Bill, is about to leave for Ganymede. He has a musical instrument, an accordion, which makes him overweight. But as it turns out it can be shipped on the colony quota as a cultural object, thus it doesn't count in his personal maximum weight.

Lastly, to prove his ability with the accordion Bill has to play before the Culture & Science Committee, performing "The Turkey in the Straw," Nehru's Opus 81, the overture to "Dawn of the 22nd Century" and, as an encore, "The Green Hills of Earth". It's thereby approved, the instrument is shipped along to Ganymede. In brief, along with the musical element, this shows us the Heinlein attention to detail. In a quiet way I think this episode is rather hilarious.

DOUBLE STAR

A major showcase of the musical lifestyle is *Double Star*. This novel tells about a future actor, Lawrence Smythe, being hired to become a stand-in for a top-level politician in the interplanetary realities of the year 2050. That Heinlein can portray politics we already know but how about acting? Does Smythe come across credibly as an actor, a practitioner of the Thespian art? Indeed he does; in passing Heinlein gives that and the other clue on how to act. For instance, once Smythe in his role (as John Joseph Bonforte, the politician) has to deliver an impromptu speech – it's supposed to be unplanned and spontaneous and he knows what to say but he still insists on having the speech written down. But then it won't become spontaneous, his controllers complain. Wrong, Smythe says, only the prepared can improvise. This is to the point, an acting wisdom otherwise taught by film director Ingmar Bergman in his artistic memoir *Laterna Magica*.

Smythe knows everything about acting. Maybe all the acting wisdom shared in *Double Star* becomes a little too perfect at times but you can't accuse Heinlein of not knowing what he's talking about when portraying an actor. As mentioned above, Heinlein has the ability to surprise you, his ingenuity being all over the place.

Surprising indeed. The Heinlein opus from 1939-1959 is solid whether in the form of juveniles, adult novels or short stories. Even a seemingly pedestrian story like "We Also Walk Dogs" has some depth. An interplanetary conference is to take place and a consulting firm gets the task of providing living quarters for all the different alien beings taking part. How to make comfortable, livable spaces for beings used to high-gravity, low-gravity and different atmospheric conditions? The scientific challenges aside, a team of the firm eventually gets embroiled in the task of enticing a certain scientist to work on the problems. This is done by obtaining a certain Ming china bowl, the inventor's hobby being china and this particular bowl holding a certain fascination for him. It's described thus:

> It was not that it was beautiful – it *was* beauty. Its subtle simple curve had no ornamentation, decoration would have sullied it. One spoke softly in its presence, for fear of a sudden noise would shatter it.[15]

The bowl is obtained, the scientist agrees to work on the problem in question – and afterwards, the consulting team makes sure that it can come and look at the bowl when it so pleases. The beauty of the bowl has it in its power. In all, this is a fine illustration of the power of art.

ETHNICITY

No SF author willingly writes about ethnicity and race – except for Heinlein. True, the neighboring subject of genetic engineering and breeding may have been covered by others, as in *Brave New World* by Huxley. I only want to say that in this respect, Heinlein's *Beyond This Horizon* from 1948 treats the subject in some noteworthy detail. A 2080 utopia has eradicated disease, famine and war. And the pitfalls of genetic engineering are avoided; "don't breed supermen, they lack adaptability" is a lesson learned. But alongside this the art of breeding, of perfecting the gene-pool, is at the forefront of this society. Still, there are malcontents, and a return to an authoritarian regime and full-scale genetic engineering is planned by an elite group.

The main character, Hamilton Felix, is recruited to the group. But he's a double agent for the regime, the one being more moderate about the blessings of genetic engineering. The coup is averted. But still Felix is something of an outsider in this utopia, he can't seem to fit in this air-conditioned dream because he lacks an existential meaning in life. This, however, he seems to get at the end when the realities of soul transmigration, of metempsychosis, is hinted at. "Man is more

---

[15] Heinlein, 1951 I, p 105

than his genes", man's essence lives on after death. To overcome death was a persistent Heinlein theme, from his debut short story "Life-Line" in 1939 to his last novels. In *Beyond This Horizon* he actually faced the problem in a way satisfactory to an esotericist. To this, the novel in question portrays speculative aspects of economy, problem solving (how to be a generalist in an era of specialists), genetics and then some. Heinlein threw in a lot of brainy reflections in this one, an ideas novel par preference. This is an ambiguous utopia with the ordinary happy Heinlein ending. But he challenged the reader even here, like talking about breeding. This is rather taboo. That is, any man acknowledges that by selecting animals for breeding you get better offspring. But doing this with humans – how unfitting...!

As intimated, Heinlein in this novel advocates against full-scale genetic engineering. To breed supermen is a dead end. Mankind needs some bio diversity. And babies shall not be grown in vats, like in *Brave New World*. But to breed better children can be done by gene selection with,

> ... normal babies, stemming from normal germ plasm, born of normal women, in the usual fashion. They differ in one respect only from their racial predecessors: they are the *best* babies their parents can produce![16]

It's rather bold for a postwar novel to advocate breeding in this fashion. True, in the same novel Heinlein looks down on aristocratic and Aryan ways of perfecting the people. But overall he wasn't ignorant of issues of race. In *Farnham's Freehold* he writes about a group of white people coming to a future America ruled by blacks. They don't like what they see. And in *Sixth Column* America is invaded by Asians. A group of military men starts a rebellion by using a race-selective energy weapon. They conceal the power of the weapon by building a church, specifically, by camouflaging the energy weapon in the form of a priestly staff. And in their ecclesiastical appearance the team underline their white, Caucasian characteristics by wearing miters, adding to white men's taller stature, and by growing beards, all in order to alienate the Asian enemy.

---

[16] Heinlein, 2007, p 55

Sixth Column and *Farnham's Freehold* might bring a sense of aversion because of the race issues treated. But to be an author is to push the envelope, to not let the reader be able to predict what's going to happen – neither on the next page, nor in the next novel – never! Heinlein was good at this, as intimated he could surprise the reader. As for race, to sum it up: the question is, "did Heinlein discuss the specifics of race?" has to be answered in the affirmative. In mentioning race, however briefly, Heinlein was unique. Because, virtually all other SF authors ignore this issue.

TABOO BREAKING

Heinlein had the habit of breaking taboos. In many a book he challenged some "apparent truth," some holy cow. Reportedly his attitude was: when in doubt, consult a well-meaning fool and do the exact opposite...! This might sound adorable but to an author this approach might also decline into a game, to showing off, to "look at me, I'm breaking taboos". Like having elements of cannibalism and libertine social mores in the later books. But when he was in form a Heinlein challenging diverse holy principles was great to read, like criticizing universal suffrage (*Starship Troopers*), discussing race differences (*Sixth Column, Farnham's Freehold*), positing that ESP might work (*Lost Legacy*) and that heroism and patriotism are viable attitudes (*Glory Road, Channelmarkers*). All these were uncommon views at the time he presented them. His slightly pushy, daring approach, the element of Heinlein-slaughterer-of-holy-cows gained him a wide readership, appreciated by right-wingers and left-wingers alike. For instance, in *The Dreams Our Stuff Is Made Of – How Science Fiction Conquered the World* (2000), left-leaning SF author Thomas Disch appreciated *Farnham's Freehold* for its elegant breaking of a taboo. And in the pamphlet "Starship Stormtroopers" Michael Moorcock complained about his leftist allies daring to like Heinlein. That text was written in 1977 which tells us that already there were some left-leaning persons around appreciating Heinlein.

Where does this take me? I'm merely saying that Heinlein had some complexity and variety in his outlook. He's somewhat validated as an artist by being liked by left and right alike. The variegated character of his opus makes him into a classic for all times, in the sense of this Oscar Wilde quote: "Diversity of opinion about a work of art shows that the work is new, complex, and vital."

COMPLEXITY

Heinlein was a complex man and his novels mirror that. He liked to challenge his readership at times. The model right-winger might cringe at some attitudes of the late novels. And this wasn't just to challenge and provoke; for instance, the libertine mores he displayed were probably heartfelt. But having said that, Heinlein comes across as authentic in most things he said, above all in his conservative opinions. He remained a reliable, hard-right anti-communist all his life. And his adherence to traditional values still rings true; they are still needed. To assume responsibility, to "put up or shut up," to strive for nobility of character and self-reliance; to expressly preach this is artistically risky but overall the Heinlein stressing of them has, with time, elevated him into an enduring voice of reason. The ideals of duty, honor, honesty, accountability, selflessness, fidelity, courage, justice and magnanimity has to be stressed again and again. They aren't some miracle medicine that simply is there to be taken, some fuel for a serially working, single-purpose machine. Instead, they have to be acknowledged by "We, the Living" – they have to be cherished by our very natures, take root in our very souls. Only thus will they live on.

Man isn't a machine, neither is society or nature. It's true that Heinlein had some imperialist traits and he wasn't really into the Gaia aspect of nature, of earth as an organism. He had his reductionist strains. But, as we've seen, at times he championed metaphysics like no contemporary author. And overall, I'd say, in Heinlein's looking at man and his activities, he had a consistent human approach. "He has accepted membership in the human race," Henry Kuttner once said of Heinlein.[17] And this human approach expressed itself in Heinlein's conservative values, exquisitely embodied in his best writings.

---

[17] Introduction to *Revolt in 2100*, p 9

Being the portal figure of right-wing SF he is, Heinlein will be treated again in this book, in chapter 32.

LITERATURE

- *Beyond This Horizon* (1948)
- *Space Cadet* (1948)
- *Sixth Column* (1949)
- *Farmer in the Sky* (1950)
- *The Man Who Sold the Moon* (1950)
- *The Green Hills of Earth* (1951)
- *Revolt in 2100* (1953)
- *Starman Jones* (1953)
- *Assignment in Eternity* (1954)
- *Double Star* (1956)
- *Time for the Stars* (1956)
- *Citizen of the Galaxy* (1957)
- *Have Space Suit – Will Travel* (1958)
- *Starship Troopers* (1959)
- *Glory Road* (1963)
- *The Moon is a Harsh Mistress* (1966)

2. FRANK HERBERT

THE PREVIOUS CHAPTER envisioned Robert Heinlein as a sort of "lion of conservatism". This epithet perhaps would be more befitting of Frank Herbert (1920-1986). In his "ancient future" depicted in the Dune series an aura of Tradition permeates everything. Topics of spirituality, faith, honor, feudal loyalty and communion with nature are treated sincerely and affirmatively, making the opus into a rare occasion in modern SF. For this is indeed science fiction, it's about a future time, a time with space travel connecting the worlds of the galaxy. *Dune* is SF and not archaic-epic fantasy playing in some yesterday shrouded in mist. In staging this saga of spaceships and swords, Herbert is the champion of *archeofuturist* SF.

CONCEPT

A new concept makes its triumphal march through today's debate: *archeofuturism*. It basically means combining archaic traits with modern technology, fusing the old with the new. The man who coined the name was French philosopher Guillaume Faye. He said: "[F]uturism must be *tempered* with archaism; or to use a bold expression, we might say that *archaism must cleanse futurism*."[18] It's about affirming

---

[18] Faye, 1998, p 72

the future but also acknowledging ancient times – in politics, art and everything. To me, this means that technology and science can co-exist with seemingly ancient phenomena like spirituality, faith and fidelity. Faye seems to mean that we're moving towards a future that isn't linear modernist; instead, after some cataclysm, the world will be reconstructed on partly modern, partly archaic grounds. In the spiritual terms that I personally endorse this can be formulated as: until 11/11 2011 we lived in the *Kâli Yuga* of nihilism, duality and materialism, but after that we live in the emerging *Sat Yuga* of truth, holism and spirituality.

Details aside, the concept of archeofuturism is useful when looking at such a novel as Frank Herbert's *Dune* (1965, with sequels). Specifically, the impulse to label the novel thus I received from the Swedish blogger Wodinaz in an entry on the think-tank *Motpol*, in February 2010. Calling *Dune* archeofuturistic clarifies Herbert's attitude towards creating SF, refining the concept of having archaic elements in a future story. Otherwise, the co-existence of sword and feudalism in an SF story runs the risk of it being treated with contempt or ridicule. So in incorporating archeofuturism in SF a new way of looking at many works is possible, like Flash Gordon and Star Wars; a conceptual breakthrough in SF scholarship indeed.

SPACESHIPS AND SWORDS

Herbert conjures up a future of both spaceships and swords, a space empire that isn't controlled by expendable bureaucrats, but by archaic feudal counties. Computers are curiously absent (as such a relic from the 1960s enmity of all things datalogical) but otherwise there's some modern technology around, symbolized in spacecraft and everything applying to this. Parallel to this, traditional handicrafts are often mentioned in the form of interior design and clothing. This gives *Dune* a unique, rich atmosphere, freeing it from the antiseptic trait otherwise being default mode in SF environmental depiction.

But is it all believable? "Swords and spaceships" we have as intimated seen in SF before, on the screen in the Flash Gordon and Star Wars epics and in comics such as *The Trigan Empire*. But with the thorough background Herbert has construed for his future world, along with the consistent story arc of the first four novels in the series, it all has some depth and width. Conversely, Herbert does *not* assume that the future will be exclusively urban and economic; his future is based on non-economic relationships between people, grounded in feudal fidelity and personal sacrifice. The entire Herbertian galaxy breathes in ancient frenzy with sandworm worship, drug esotericism and a religious feeling along with operational pragmatics. Contrariwise, in the dyed-in-the-wool modernist future, symbolized for instance by Asimov's Foundation series, we only find sterile technocities populated by nihilists talking politics. In Herbert's future there are winds from the archaic along with the high-tech.

SAGA

The Dune Saga is truly cosmic in scope. In Book One it's already 21,000 years into the future. Then the millennia pass between some of the novels in the series. This creates depth in the picture, not directly through atmosphere and environment portrayal but by plot-related feints and trickery, artifice and structures. Among these elements we undoubtedly find spirituality. We find ourselves in a future that not only cares about building better spaceships; there's also the talk of spiritual practices, trance and meditation. As for the narrative style, it may be rather bare-bones but Herbert overcomes his stylistic limitations on a symbolic plane with his inventive background material, like depicting sandworms and the harvesting of the drug *melange*, and by populating his books with priests and abbesses along with politicians, pilots and other modern figures.

In his time Herbert was schooled in the magazine *Analog*. He was usually mentioned in the same breath as Heinlein and Asimov, Niven and Pournelle. But more than all these, Herbert had a sense of the archaic, "the olden-old". He gave his galactic future depth with the implied passing millennia – but, unlike Asimov, Niven, Clarke *et al*, who also had broad perspectives in their galactic futures, Herbert gave the whole thing an additional, idiosyncratic touch by letting spirituality permeate everything.

Spiritual *pathos*, indeed, even salvation is achieved in this saga, by taking the drug *melange* that has both mystical and practical applications. Spiritual meaning we also see in the dealings with the sandworms that pierces the sandy vistas of this desert planet, Dune or Arrakis, the main place of action. This artifice of sandworms has true symbolic character, beyond the text on the page. The sandworm has an existence that is something other than literary, something that doesn't depend on any stylistic brilliance per se. Herbert often writes like a columnist, as the journalist he started out as, but the books still have that magical touch because of its mythical elevation. Symbols and archetypes raise *Dune* from bestseller prose to myth.

SYMBOLISM

The symbolism of *Dune* is like a folk tale. For example, everyone can tell the tale of Hansel and Gretel, it doesn't depend on any specific, artistic version or configuration. It's the concreteness speaking (the forest to get lost in, the gingerbread house, the witch, the oven etc.). Similarly, any SF fan can retell the gist of *Dune* and entice others to read the books. You may mention how Paul Atreides in Book One becomes an heir to a desert planet, Arrakis, a world he becomes lord of having formed an alliance with the nomadic primitives and defeated some cainitic coalition. Then the galaxy is conquered in a veritable *jihad* and Paul becomes a religious leader. His power base is still Dune, the planet Arrakis and its special desert climate that produces the drug *melange*. This drug is needed, among other things, for space pilots to reach the trance required to navigate the light years of the galactic abysses.

Book Two (*Dune Messiah*) is something of an impasse, the ever-balancing, almost bipolar Herbert giving us a plot counter positing all that *Dune* said. Here Paul nihilistically seems to wish to tear down everything he has built up as a leader and a messiah. It becomes more intricate in Book Three, *Children of Dune*, and not least in Book Four, *God Emperor of Dune*, cleverly depicting how Paul's son, Leto II Atreides, manages to surpass his father. It isn't easy, how to beat a father having conquered the entire galaxy...? But Leto unexpectedly finds a way; with a kind of strange, minuscule life-form in the desert, he turns himself progressively into a superman, being able to run fast like the wind and having the strength of ten men – literally. In time he becomes a veritable worm creature, a humanoid sandworm which lives for thousands of years as a god-like ruler, the *God Emperor of Dune*.

This was a great achievement, to become a god, while his father was merely a messiah... Leto has beaten his father, he has assured himself a place in the history of the galaxy like no other – he's more than history – he *is* history, he *is* myth. It's truly a novel *tour de force*, a truly mythical narrative in SF form. The Dune books have a rather tiring impact with all their myopic dry bestseller prose, but as intimated, all the inventions, mysticism and other ingredients raise the whole from purely literary to timeless, fairytale-like levels. Literature can be written in ways other than this, it can be stylistically more imaginative, but this author is still impressed by the Dune Saga as an attempt at myth-making. And with the Bruce Pennington covers from the 1980s you'll get an *objet d'art* adorning its place on the bookshelf. Another artist giving the Dune world artistic vision was John Schoenherr, epitomized in *The Illustrated Dune* (1978) with eight color paintings and 33 black-and-white drawings.

QUOTES

You could try to pinpoint the right-wing, conservative nature of Herbert's Dune Saga with some quotes. This venture starts by looking at a treasure-trove in this respect, Book Four in the series, *God Emperor of Dune* with its plethora of wisdoms uttered by the main character, Leto II Atreides. As related in the synopsis given above, he has evolved into a man-god by the time of this story, a supreme ruler of the galaxy living in the shape of half man, half sandworm, a five-meter abomination of supernatural powers and in psychic rapport with all of history, all its characters, ideas and circumstances. This makes for spontaneous reflections on history, power and spirit.

God Emperor of Dune is a discreet conservative classic. While reading it you may think of another right-wing stalwart, Ernst Jünger and his novel *Eumeswil* from 1977. There we see the same seemingly unforced reflections on history, power and all from a conservative standpoint. For instance, Jünger praises the value of the gold standard. Herbert does the same in *God Emperor of Dune*; at least, the Empire in question works fairly well on similar grounds, with the rare commodity of spice taking the place of gold. Specifically, the Imperial economic system says this of usury: "... the economics of the empire, simplified in the extreme: no interest charges permitted; cash on the barrel head"[19] – this is Herbert preaching like Ezra Pound, a plot element of the truly conservative kind.

More similarities with Jünger's *Eumeswil*? In his novel Jünger once says that the liberal view of history is immanently heroic (while the conservative view is pragmatic), and Herbert with Leto II as mouthpiece says this on "liberal aristocracy":

> Liberal bigots are the ones who trouble me most. I distrust the extremes. Scratch a conservative and you find someone who prefers the past over any future. Scratch a liberal and find a close aristocrat. It's true! Liberal governments always develop into aristocracies. The bureaucracies betray the true intent of people who form such governments. Right from the first, the *little* people who formed the governments which promised to equalize the social burdens found themselves suddenly in the hands of bureaucratic aristocracies. Of course, all bureaucracies follow this pattern, but what a hypocrisy to find this even under a communized banner.[20]

GUARDS CAPTAIN

In *Eumeswil* the narrator works as a bartender in the castle of the city's military dictator. For instance, he can listen in on the conversations between this Condor and his Major Domo, the aptly named *Domo*,

---

[19] Herbert, 1982 II, p 26
[20] Ibid., p 175

the no-nonsense commander of the security of the castle, allowing the narrator to deliberate on issues of command and control. Herbert does something similar in chapter three of *God Emperor of Dune*, with Leto meeting his guards captain Duncan Idaho. This man is a clone of a figure with the same name from the novel *Dune*; by way of successive cloning there have been many Duncan Idahoes serving House Atreiedes, making him into a sort of archetypal Palace Guard Commander, in the same way as Leto becomes an archetypal despot. For instance, with Duncan Leto now discusses the nature of radicals and rebels, Leto teaching his servant that you either "co-opt them or kill them."[21] This is a terse statement rather similar of Domo in *Eumeswil*.

Aside from the similarities with *Eumeswil*, *God Emperor of Dune* has some topical aphorisms. Like this on the value of geopolitics, a discipline favored by right-wingers and shunned by liberals: "The influence of geography on history went mostly unrecognized, Leto thought. Humans tended to look more at the influence of history on geography."[22]

Then we have this, a statement summing up the specificity of being a leader of divine dignity. A rival of Leto, the Bene Gesserit order of nuns, had accused him of creating another religion, to which his answer was: "Nonsense! I have not created a religion. I *am* the religion!"[23] This is glorious rhetoric, a Faustian *hubris* quite on par with Nietzsche's Zarathustra, Heinlein's Michael Valentine Smith, and, to some extent, the final sermon of Rand's *Anthem*. And maybe Feric Jaggar in *The Iron Dream*. Someone said that the archetypal SF hero can command the Universe itself to make a somersault and Leto in this novel comes close to this. He knows everything, has seen everything; with his drug-induced trances he can see, feel and know everything that has gone before. Truly, a God Emperor.

Leto conducts his Empire "... as a musical conductor guides a symphony through its movements."[24] The Dune Saga isn't a clear-

---

[21] Herbert, 1982 II, p 28
[22] Ibid., p 86
[23] Ibid., p 86
[24] Ibid., p 155

cut preachment for old-school, feudal government; instead, Herbert has a way of balancing his narrative, of even making Leto critical of tyranny, religion and all. This is the bipolar trait of the Herbert prose. But overall Herbert has put himself in the role of an observer in an archeofuturist gray area, giving room for traditional perspectives on power and spirit. There are also modern strains to the Dune Saga, there are progressive free kicks inlaid here and there (religion is bad, tyranny is bad). But in terms of publishing Herbert's *Dune* first did appear in the expressly modernist, Campbellian magazine *Analog*. And among SF authors of the 20th century I know of no other who, like Herbert, can put in passages like this, unpretentiously making History and Tradition present in the future. The House Atreides ruling the Empire since the days of Paul in *Dune* stems from some earthly bloodline, making Leto II the heir of Middle Eastern rulers of the past. Thus he can muse:

> Our ancestor, Assur-nasir-apli, who was known as the cruelest of the cruel, seized the throne by slaying his own father and starting the reign of the sword. His conquests included the Urumia Lake region, which led him to Commagene and Khabur. His son received tribute from the Shuites, from Tyre, Sidon, Gebel and even from Jehu, son of Omri, whose very name struck terror into thousands. The conquests which began with Assur-nasir-apli carried arms into Media and later into Israel, Damascus, Edom, Arpad, Babylon and Umlias. Does anyone remember these names and places now?[25]

SUPERMAN

In Book One of the Dune series Paul Atreides ventures out in the desert, has a spiritual experience and becomes a prophet. In Book Three, *Children of Dune*, there's some repetition of this with Paul's son going through the same process. Nevertheless, there's a timeless grandeur in the portrait of Leto II Atreides emerging as a Prophet of Prophets, a superman of mind and body. The following preaching by

---

[25] Herbert, 1982 II, p 138

Leto II is *not* standard fare in fantastic literature or even 20th century literature at large:

> I am your spirit. I am the only life you can realize. I am the house of your spirit in the land which is nowhere, the land which is your only remaining home. Without me, the intelligible universe reverts to chaos. Creative and abysmal are inextricably linked in me; only I can mediate between them. Without me, mankind will sink into the mire and vanity of *knowing*. Through me, you and they will find the only way out of chaos: *understanding by living*.[26]

This is beautifully ambiguous. Leto is a gray area character, seemingly beset by hubris but with flashes of wisdom. For instance, the above mentioned "understanding by living" versus mere "knowing" is the crux of the Existential school of thought, namely, the idea of life and thought being inseparable, an illustration of the essential unity of Will and Thought. And hubris aside, if you indeed have supernatural powers like the strength of ten men and having second sight, being able to foresee the future of man and is about to live for a thousand years as Leto will, then some hubris might seem natural. He's an emerging man-god. In depicting the transformation of Leto, Herbert tries to answer the question, "what is a superman, how does he think" even better than van Vogt in *Slan*. As will be mentioned in chapter fifteen van Vogt's forte in *Slan* was having the superman come through as a little slow and dumb before he has realized all of his powers. Fair enough, but other than that van Vogt's superman figure Gilbert Gosseyn is rather flat. Not so Leto II Atreides, his thought is something out of the extraordinary; he's "a living glyph to write out changes which must come to pass," he's "the son of Muad'Dib, able to see the future".[27]

Leto II treads the same prophetic lands as Zarathustra in *Thus Spake Zarathustra*, with a spate of Jesus, Moses and other desert prophets thrown in. Herbert's way of storytelling might seem a bit

---

[26] Herbert, 1984, p 264-265
[27] Ibid., p 266, 267

over-meticulous and pedantic. And the fantasy setting with all its invented terms (*kralizec, fremen, sietch*...), along with words borrowed from actual historic contexts (*umma, mahdi, hajj*...), creates a miasma of mystique, making Dune into a gray area of both being with and without meaning. In the craze for specificity everything gets its special concept but the concepts *per se* tend to become *simulacrum*, signs only referring to themselves. There's a certain "myth-making meaninglessness" that threatens to invade the Dune universe. But this is true of every epic fantasy: works that you can make a veritable dictionary over, listing and explaining terms specific to the myth in question, these dictionaries have that exquisite character of being totally sane (as a guide to Opus X) and totally insane, being a collection of in themselves meaningless terms.

Having said that, in instances like the development of Leto II, the Dune Saga has an enduring allure. *Children of Dune* also has the previously mentioned scene of the superman Leto meeting his father Paul, the latter now a blind figure called the Preacher. This desert meeting expresses much in the way of father and son relationship, humility and hubris, self-restraint and self-aggrandizement, responsibility and personal comfort, history and destiny. As for the father-son-relationship we have this unique feature, intimated above: Paul was just a prophet, Leto is an emerging god; I've surpassed you, father... The best of speculative literature has a way of portraying things that are incredible but still may say us one thing or two.

DENOUEMENT

As we've seen, the relationship between the ruler and his guards captain is well covered in *God Emperor of Dune* with the Leto-Duncan dialogs. And as intimated, this Duncan figure was present already in Book One, *Dune*, where he got killed rather early. But the role of military adviser to the ruler is then taken over by the bard Gurney Halleck; he comes to represent the loyal military man. Duty, honor and loyalty to House Atreides are his guiding principles.

Halleck is Paul Atreides' personal combat instructor, teaching him to fight with a sword. Later, when Paul has encountered and mastered the

Fremen tribes of Arrakis, he learns how to fight with a *crysknife*, made from the tooth of a sandworm. In the final denouement of *Dune* Paul has to duel against the master fighter Feyd-Rautha of House Harkonnen. The way the duel proceeds is an example of martial arts philosophy. For instance, we have this, right from the heart of the traditional way of the warrior, whether Eastern or Western or general. Both before and during the dual Feyd-Rautha is boisterous which Paul takes as a sign of weakness. Then Paul has this thought, rather Bushido-like:

> Expect only what happens in the fight. That way you'll never be surprised."[28]

And this was a wisdom he had gotten from the self-same Duncan Idaho.

What more can be said of traditional wisdom and mores, presented in *Dune*? Book One is permeated with the feudal spirit: we see this in the portrait of the duke Leto I, Paul's father, his entourage of loyal servants (and the disloyal Dr. Yueh who assassinates the duke, becoming the symbol of treason) and his relation with his concubine, the Lady Jessica. Then there are spiritual ponderings, and the way of the native Fremen where the archaic version of "duty, honor, country" is ever-present. In all, a showcase of Tradition like nothing in modern SF. For again, this wasn't presented as a fantasy piece; *Dune* was published slightly before the epic fantasy wave which started only in the 1970s when *The Lord of the Rings* was published in paperback. *Dune* is a rare instant of SF traditionalism, clothed in partly modern, partly ancient garb: spaceships and swords, mentats and spice fiber, lasguns and cloaks.

SLOTH AND LECHERY

The above mentioned Dr. Yueh was employed by the Harkonnens, the family battling the Atreides over the possession of Arrakis. The Harkonnens, symbolized in the Baron Vladimir Harkonnen, is a paragon of anti-tradition, embodying sloth, lechery, indulgence, lust,

---

[28] Herbert, 1982 I, p 459

envy and deceit. The Atreides, on the other hand, symbolized by Leto I and his successor Paul, stand for duty, honor, honesty, selflessness, modesty, courage, justice, mercy and magnanimity.

Herbert's Dune Saga has some spiritual elevation. For instance, the religion depicted might be a critical portrait but still, there's some real piety in it all. A sign of Herbert's appreciation of things spiritual is found in the appendix to *Dune*. There it says:

> Religion must remain an outlet for people who say to themselves, 'I am not the kind of person I want to be.' It must never sink into an assemblage of the self-satisfied.[29]

Again, this is the Existentialism way of thought: change your life with willpower. And seek out the teachers and the texts giving you advice on how to do this.

Herbert was a man of small gestures, in the case of poetry uttered in tangible, down-to-earth phrases. And a certain mantra repeated by the characters of the Dune universe, when trying to calm down in their operations, has some allure in its terse style, beyond the choice wisdom displayed in it. The idea of facing your fear in this way stems from Krishnamurti (1895-1986). I can't give the source for it now, it has evaded me, but an essay I once read about this Indian philosopher contained a train of thought in some ways similar to Herbert's "Litany of Fear":

> I must not fear.
> Fear is the mind-killer.
> Fear is the little-death that brings total obliteration.
> I will face my fear.
> I will permit it to pass over me and through me.
> And when it has gone past I will turn the inner eye to see its path.
> Where the fear has gone there will be nothing.
> Only I will remain.

This is self-restraint, this is the *apateia* of stoics, this is the *samatva* of Bhagavad-Gîtâ – traditional wisdom brought to the masses by way of *Dune*, the greatest SF bestseller ever.

---

[29] Herbert, 1982 I, p 480

LITERATURE

- *Dune* (1965)
- *Dune Messiah* (1969)
- *Children of Dune* (1976)
- *God Emperor of Dune* (1981)

3. C. S. LEWIS

THE STUDY WILL now leave America for a while and go to Europe and England in search of right-wing SF. The first stop is Great Britain where we find Clive Staples Lewis (1898-1963) as a fine example of a conservative fantasist. He knew what Tradition meant, he believed in God and he showed it in poignant stories. His was an integral mind, unifying the timeless tradition of a cosmos ruled by God with a keen sense for modern times. His stories include space travel, parallel worlds, medieval chivalry and faith, all related to 20th century man. The fiction of C. S. Lewis is eminently relatable while at the same time being firmly footed in Tradition.

ODD THINGS

The first SF novel C. S. Lewis wrote was *Out of the Silent Planet* (1938). It's a peculiar version of an SF adventure with the hero being a professor of linguistics. In the mood and attitude this is worlds apart from the American approach to space exploration. I mean, I appreciate American SF as a whole, especially in vitalizing SF from about 1940 and on, but Lewis' humanist-cum-space explorer is a welcome break from the slightly titanic, larger-than-life characters that until then had conquered the stars, like Kim Kinnison, John Ulnar and John Carter.

Elwin Ransom is shanghaied onto a spaceship bound for Mars. Having arrived he escapes from his captors and explores the planet on his own, meeting odd but heartwarming inhabitants of both the animal and humanoid type. The overall strength of this book is the efficient yet free narrative; for instance, the Lewis vision of the Martian landscape is that of a totally different world – the colors, the distances, the shapes, everything is unfamiliar to a terrestrial eye. And yet he doesn't indulge in the "otherness" like some late-romantic poet. Lewis once said, "describing odd things in an odd language is about one oddity too much" and *Out of the Silent Planet* highlights this in being totally relatable, even when the author describes the most peculiar phenomena.

There's some moral depth to this story too. Ransom is the humanistic hero, his captors a titanic duo of a politician and a nihilist scientist. This outline is fair but not overly original. That's also the impact of the whole story: overall not extremely original, there had been cultured space-farers before Lewis (in stories by Wells, Stapledon, Lindsay) but as intimated Lewis comes through as highly relatable and human and *Out of the Silent Planet* deserves the label of minor classic.

The follow-up, *Perelandra* (1943) sees Ransom going off to Venus for more spiritual adventures and glorious indulging in exotic nature. Like Book One in this Space Trilogy the charm comes from the relatable tone of the narrative, here executed in the first person by Mr Lewis himself, starting out to tell us how he went to meet Ransom in his countryside cottage and intimating the stories Ransom has already told him of his trip to Mars, this distraught professor of a hero. Then the run-up to Ransom's next voyage is described and when the man finally returns he himself, Ransom, gets to relate it all. As Book One this is charming and personal and perhaps even profound but to me this is merely a build-up to Book Three in the series, one of the greatest SF novels of all time. *That Hideous Strength* (1947) stands in line with *Nineteen Eighty-Four*, *Anthem* and *Brave New World* as a critic of our times, a warning against the forces of nihilism and leveling and an apology for spiritual values and humanity, all the more efficient by being set in contemporary England but still having fantastic elements. And by stressing the need for the spiritual dimension, for individuals to acknowledge the Inner Light, the spark of the Divine Light, the soul-light that essentially makes us human.

HYGIEN

Part one of the Space Trilogy introduced the hero, Dr. Elwin Ransom. One of the villains was the physicist, Prof. Edward Rolles Weston; Ransom chanced into Weston again in Book Two, Weston meeting his fate there. In Book One we also met the politician Dick Devine, now, in Book Three, *That Hideous Strength*, ennobled as Lord Feverstone.

In this story Lord Feverstone is a leading figure of a titanic endeavor, a company that will create total happiness with social engineering. The goal is to create a new humanity with liquidation of bad elements, then selectively breed the new generation and condition it biochemically and psychologically, manipulating peoples' brains with "pragmatometrics". That's what the evil grouping in this novel plans – NICE, National Institute of Co-Ordinated Experiments, led by ideals of hygien and efficiency.

NICE is a symbol of nihilism, the scourge of our times. Again, "*nihil*" is Latin and means "nothing". Nihilism is the tendency of not acknowledging eternal ideals, not acknowledging the invisible, spiritual side of reality. Nihilism is to worship the material side of things, of seeing man and nature as machines. Nihilism is to deny the existence of a soul, of the soul as a fragment of the Eternal Light of God. Nihilism highlights a central feature of what Tradition is not: Tradition is acknowledging eternal ideals, nihilism is to deny them. Tradition is to acknowledge transcendent values, nihilism is to reduce everything into "the death of the body and the decay of matter". Authors in this study labeled as nihilists may acknowledge some Fine Ideals but the crux is to anchor these ideals in an ontology worthy of its name – and, more often than not, I don't see these authors espouse such a perennially viable ontological base for their views.

At the center of *That Hideous Strength* is a pair of academics, Mark and Jane Studdock. When the novel opens Jane has been haunted by a nightmare; she has dreamed lucidly, truthfully; she has preconceived things that will happen, like the digging up of a corpse that is reanimated, all jumbled but essentially true. We get other indication of Jane being a precog, like her dreaming details of the murder of a certain Will Hingest before hearing of it. Hingest is a scientist eventually found dead after he decided to leave NICE. Jane's dreams are deemed precognitive by a Mrs. Ironwood, an ally of Ransom that Jane visits in order to get help. Returning from Venus, the eternal paradise, Ransom was rejuvenated and is now some sort of golden age Leader, sporting a golden beard and a undefinable aura of sunlit climes. As a glorified Fisher King he leads a spiritual Society, the only force that may counter the deeds of NICE.

RIOT

NICE has its own police force. NICE is virtually an army bent on taking power by means of propaganda and expropriation, and some selective use of force, as in the disturbances in the town of Edgestow. By provocation it triggers a crisis. Nationally NICE controls both left and right.

For instance, NICE wants to redirect river Wynd. The once heartwarming flow giving character to Edgestow is in the process transformed into a muddy ditch littered with trash. By this development the university college of Bracton is itself threatened.

Disturbances in Edgestow become a leverage to control the town. Specifically, it's effectuated by the many workers deployed in the project of building a new NICE research facility; 100,000 workers are employed and they come into everyday conflict with the townspeople. Then the NICE police handle a riot that breaks out, proclaiming martial law. Jane's husband, Mark, is hired by NICE to write a news story in advance, giving the correct spin of the event.

THE LEADER

At a certain estate, the manor of St Anne's, Jane meets The Leader of the good guys who says she can't be a member of his society as long as Mark works for NICE. The Leader, for his part, the transformed Elwin Ransom, is a symbol of a Golden Age ruler, associated with gold in every aspect of his appearance, humanely so but nonetheless different. He and his estate is called Pendragon of Lordes; Lordes was King Arthur's realm, now seen as a spiritual England, the England of figures like the poet John Milton while the titanic, materialistic England is symbolized by figures like Cromwell, the republican Lord Protector of the 17th century.

Jane eventually sees in a vision what NICE seeks in Brandon Wood, the alleged place of a future NICE HQ. It's a case of the modern powers of NICE looking for the old, magical powers of the figure of Merlin buried in Brandon Wood. When this unification occurs Lordes, in fact all of mankind, will be encircled and lost. Therefore, Ransom says, this must be prevented. They have to dig out the body of Merlin before NICE does.

The NICE project is ultimately about making a god of man by uniting natural science with magic – a modern science having by the mid-20th century become nihilistic by denying the existence of a transcendental order and eternal ethical values. Fallen man would thus finally shake off the limitation of his powers that Providence had imbued him with in order to alleviate the consequences of that Fall. If this succeeds Hell on Earth will be realized. Men would rule the Earth as demigods to the end of time...!

MARK

In chapter ten Mark, for his part, is visibly evolving, becoming a whole man, a complete human being. He questions his involvement with NICE, learning the hard way what is essential in life: compassion, willpower and an inherent sense of nobility.

Eventually the reanimated Merlin is won over to the side of The Good Guys, its agent Dimble having been instructed by Ransom to have gun in hand, a prayer on his lips and the mind focused on the Forces of Light. Merlin must be bound by a spell by Dimble saying, "I come in the name of The Lord and all the angels and by the power of the planets from the one who now sits on the throne of Pendragon; I command you to follow me". Dimble is also advised to keep his will anchored in God's will, having been told that he can't lose his soul if he mobilizes his will to keep it.

Merlin, having joined The Good Side, speaking with Ransom, then gives a traditionalist view on society when comparing his world with the modern world. Then the Society go off to chase away NICE from Edgestow. In summation, this is Tradition in popular, fictional form.

LANGUAGE

Beyond the main plot, *That Hideous Strength* has some clever discussions, like the one on the use of language as a tool, how the right words can trigger the right effect. Like, how to sell the public certain new ideas, for instance wording it, not in the form of "experimenting on criminals" but of "readaption of misfits", not "experiment on kids" but "free education in experimental school". In the plot proper the same syndrome of language packaging is seen when the item of selling Brandon Wood is brought forth. Because, NICE by way of its agent at the college council meeting has not labeled it as "selling of Brandon Wood" instead, it's put under the headline of, "sale of college land", and there forming a point called, "questions about Brandon Wood" where the agenda primarily is about renovation of the wall enclosing it. By this opening move the goal of selling it is concealed and the actual sell of the land to NICE is soon effectuated without resistance.

Above was mentioned the way of selling new opinions to the educated public and the novel has more examples of this. First it's the instance of a paper, *Weekly Question*, which first accepted the notion of Basic English as a progressive invention but when a conservative PM got in on the idea Basic English at once became "a threat against the purity of our language". Example two; for long monarchy was an expensive absurdity but when the Duke of Windsor abdicated Weekly Question became 100% royalist and legalistic in fourteen days. The studied reader is hooked to memes likes this, he must get his daily feed of opinions, keeping on being led. This is like how Orwell in *Nineteen Eighty-Four* described how language is used to control people, only here, by Lewis, set in a more relatable narrative – one that isn't totally painful and depressing in every line.

That Hideous Strength may artistically balance on a ledge sometimes, like the final chapters bringing along Merlin the Magician on the side of the good guys. And having Elwin Ransom transforming into some Arthurian leader of royal-spiritual nobility. But Lewis' aim is true and his relative lack of painterly prowess is balanced by the pragmatical strength of the book – "that hideous strength" of human Willpower, united with Truth and Light, impossible to defeat even for darkness.

So if it's allowed to compare, as intimated I hold *That Hideous Strength* above *Nineteen Eighty-Four* and *Brave New World*. These two tend to indulge in the evil, antagonistic sides of the plot while Lewis's novel along with showing us evil shows us a way out. Lewis has balanced the incredible with the eminently relatable. Orwell's and Huxley's novels were dramatically credible in stressing how "the enemy is well organized" but Lewis, in showing the power of The Common People, of the echo in medieval vaults and of acknowledging the Light, is more relevant to the era of the *Sat Yuga* we live in today, the Era of Truth following on the Iron Age of *Kâli Yuga* having just ended.

NARNIA

Then what about Lewis' fantasy series, Narnia? It's decidedly less artistic than Tolkien's *The Lord of the Rings*. However, other things equal, Lewis' opus is also viable. And sometimes he even beats Tolkien as regards poignancy. That is, Tolkien has mythologized evil almost into a Black Hole of Evil, resting Beyond the Beyond, so repulsive it almost becomes a primal force beyond moral deliberations. That may be a mythical strength but it's also an ethical weakness. But Lewis, with his less ambitious narrative style, can go along a bit more freely. He can have evil represented in a Wicked Witch – an approachable figure, you can converse with her, but still she walks in mysterious ways. The simple is sometimes the best.

Simple but not simplistic, that's Lewis' artistry to me. Narnia is a masterpiece of naive art, it would seem. Naive art of the Western, 20th century kind was sometimes made by artists who mastered the formal, educated style but consciously chose naivism as a way of expression, like Swedish painter Bror Hjort (1894-1968). I wouldn't say that Lewis could have written a *Lord of the Rings* if he wanted to, but he was a skilled author who knew his style levels. He knew how to make sense to his readers. Narnia, in its seeming simplicity, is to the point and arresting. The narrative approach is loose and casual, it moves on several levels, winking at the reader. Some might resent this "breaking of the fourth wall," perhaps seeing it as standard children's books jargon, but to me this attitude is just right.

Narnia isn't merely about self-irony, cute animals and precocious children. It's about "having something to say" – in this instance, to present a sterling creed. Lewis's Christian-traditional world-view permeates everything spontaneously. He goes playfully along, like Tolkien in *Bilbo*. But Lewis had more proportion in his religious outlook; Tolkien, God bless him, has a sort of mazdaic, Old Testament world-view. That is, Good against evil, Light against darkness is certainly a reality, but to convey this ontology to modern readers you need some sort of entry level, something which invites. Tolkien had his Hobbits for this. Lewis had a different approach conceptually: a lighthearted narrative tone.

And he had *Aslan*. Portraying evil is easy, Dostoyevsky said; portraying good is much harder. Where is the goodness in the Ring trilogy? There's a certain light falling on the things, there's Elves and Gandalf, but in my eyes, the lion Aslan in the Narnia cycle is a more succinct symbol of goodness. A talking lion, a vital force, a moral preaching guru: it works!

DIVINE

Portraying goodness is hard, portraying the divine is even more difficult. Philip K. Dick perhaps touched on it in *Eye in the Sky* where two of the characters in some parallel world meets a big eye in the sky. It was meant as a parody but also having a serious under text, if you have Dick's later fate in memory. When Dick had become a believer, he would promptly have God along as a fictional character (*q.v. The Divine Invasion*) but this wasn't so successful. However, the Glimmung from *Galactic Pot-Healer* was rather complex and convincing as a god archetype. Dick later denigrated this effort in *The Exegesis*; don't listen to him in that respect.

Gods in modern art: we saw them on stage in Wagner's Ring. Sometimes successfully so, sometimes not. And in Michael Moorcock's fantasy epics gods play a part, maybe even credibly so; more on this in chapter ten. But they are generally of the demonic kind. With Lewis' Narnia it's a different affair. Aslan is wholly convincing as a god archetype. It's not merely an allegory of Christ. Reportedly, Lewis with Aslan wanted to portray how God would appear to men in a world where the development and history was totally different from that of our world.

That's why the following passage from the first book in the Narnia suite, *The Magician's Nephew*, to me seems rather striking. Aslan has just held his farewell sermon. It's before the kids get to go home to their own world, to the England of the 1800s, and the lion has given some warnings about the ways of the world. And then this:

> Both the children were looking up into the Lion's face as he spoke these words. And all at once (they never knew exactly how it happened) the face seemed to be a sea of tossing gold in which they were floating, and such a sweetness and power rolled about them and over them and entered them that they felt they had never really been happy or wise or good, or even alive and awake, before. And the memory of that moment stayed with them always, so that as long as they both lived, if they were sad or afraid or angry, the thought of all that golden goodness, and the feeling that it was still there, quite close, just round the corner or just behind some door, would come back and make them sure, deep down inside, that all was well.[30]

---

[30] Lewis, 1989, p 165

Quite some scene...! It *is* possible to depict genuine goodness, metaphysical goodness, in fantasy form – well, maybe particularly there. Fantasy needs not be mechanical battles between perceived good and evil; you can also describe the good in such a way that it gets human dimensions, humanly conceivable and relatable, and this in symbolic form – as in a talking lion. Kudos to you, Mr. Lewis!

PASSIVE IDEALISM

Lewis is a color on the palate of traditionalist SF. He does remain a strong voice for faith and hope but pragmatically somethings lacking. His essays on faith (*Christian Reflections, The Screwtape Letters* etc.) are worth reading, they can inspire the esotericist, but as such, as a willpower-driven esotericist, I lack *Will* in Lewis' spiritual outfit. To me, he comes forth as a *passive idealist*. And my personal ideal is Active Idealism, built in the intersection between Plotinus, Nietzsche, Goethe, Evola, Castaneda and Ernst Jünger.

Lewis, and the latter-day Christian faith he espoused, rather often advocates a passive idealism. As individuals we can't do anything, we're vessels waiting to be filled with grace. This "faith alone, only by grace" may have been needed as an antidote to the orthodoxy of The Holy Land by the year zero. But today, people need to know about Will – the force that by its nature seeks Light. The reverse, desire, leads to the dark.

Will is a neglected value today. And Lewis never or seldom mentions it in his pragmatical essays.

Put differently, the Lewis creed like the overall Christian creed, the "mere Christianity" he preached, is *exoteric*. The divine Light is seen as an exterior, outer phenomenon: O God look down upon us, let us enter your heaven, I am but a sinner etc. This we hear in every psalm, in every orthodox sermon – and in Lewis' essays. Conversely, you never hear him talking about affirming your Inner Light, of realizing your divine nature, of the will-driven acknowledging of interior forces.

In short, Lewis was no esotericist, lacking some of that holistic strain. A holistic mind has gone beyond the duality of God and man, body and soul; a pious man of the Church like Lewis may still have some of that dualism left. In all, be forewarned of this and the passive idealism and old-school exotericism he advocates.

LITERATURE

- *Out of the Silent Planet* (1938)
- *Perelandra* (1943)
- *That Hideous Strength* (1947)
- *The Lion, the Witch and the Wardrobe* (1950)
- *The Magician's Nephew* (1955)

4. J. R. R. TOLKIEN

THE PREVIOUS CHAPTER was about C. S. Lewis, taking the battle of good versus evil to a 20th century audience. Lewis was a close friend of John Ronald Reuel Tolkien (1892-1973). And Tolkien also gave us a relatable myth about good fighting evil, an archaic epic on the grand scale, a trilogy whose influence has only grown with time.

CURRENT BATTLE

The battle is still raging. Good still opposes evil. J. R. R. Tolkien's *The Lord of the Rings* is still topical, even more so than when it was first published in the 1950s.

Case in point: there's a film out called *Arrivals*, a sort of philosophical documentary of our times and its ills, suggesting that Tolkien's trilogy is a symbol of the rejuvenated mythical forces about. The film says: Sauron is the Anti-Christ, Aragorn is the reborn Christ and Gandalf is the Mahdi...!

As we all know, the Anti-Christ is the essence of evil, mentioned in the Bible. Further, the rebirth of Christ is about Christ-consciousness being acknowledged in our hearts and minds. And the Mahdi is a concept among Shia Muslims, the Twelfth Imam who will come and bring peace. Then it may be argued that Gandalf is not an imam, he's a Nordic-style magician whose name derives from the *Poetic Edda*. True, but in terms of art there's no definite answer as to what figures are, different interpretations must be allowed to be discussed.

Details aside, this shows the ambiguous, resilient nature of Tolkien's epic. It can be interpreted in many ways and now it may even be seen as a prophecy. For indeed, we all know who wins in the end in the Middle-Earth Saga. And now, having read the Trilogy or seen Peter Jackson's movie version, we may go strengthened into the battle in the real world, fighting the nihilism of the NWO and defending every people's right to exist – exist *überhaupt*, exist in its place of origin. What is needed in this battle is Willpower, a vision of the Light and a conception of the Good, embodied in eternal values like duty, honor, faith, courage, justice, clemency and magnanimity.

Tolkien was a conservative Christian, steeped in traditional values. His heroes fight the evil, enslaving empire of Sauron by employing willpower, faith and courage, and by being loyal to The True King of Gondor, Aragorn. This clear-cut plot structure is of enormous value. You might think that any fantasy story is about Good Fighting Evil, the heroes adhering to eternal values like the above, but that's not the case. Many fantasy epics seem to be steeped in nihilism, like those of Michael Moorcock. Many fantasy authors are wary of having good winning over evil, maybe thus wishing to alter the dramatic outcome for the sake of originality. In view of this you must praise Tolkien and Lewis for being so "unoriginal" to take the side of the Light against the Dark.

20th century epic fantasy is a quagmire of nihilism, treason, indulgence and debauchery. Above them all shines the beacon of Tolkien and Lewis, champions of Tradition, Law and Light versus the hordes of chaos, confusion and banality.

GOD

This chapter is about J. R. R. Tolkien. And some fine samples of his traditional creed is found on the Swedish blog Café Exposé. For instance, there I've found this saying of Tolkien from 1969 about God

– an elliptical quote, not in itself profound, but it really tells it how it is to live with God in your everyday: "The chief purpose of life is... to increase according to our capacity our knowledge of God by all the means we have, and to be moved by it to promise and thanks."

Tolkien was a pious man and it showed in his works, his drawings and his stories. God is real, the Light combating darkness is real, and man can muster his own Will and unite it with the Will of God, in the process being moved to thanksgiving.

Another poignant Tolkien saying is this, in a letter to his son Christopher in 1943: "I will not bow before the Iron Crown, nor cast my own small golden scepter down". This speaks for itself. And further, think about G. R. R. Martin's *A Song of Fire and Ice* with its iron throne: to sit on such a throne or bow before it to me seems the very definition of nihilism. And maybe that's Martin's point with this symbolism. Anyhow, Tolkien was no nihilist, he could display poignant symbols of Faith and Hope along with the iron symbolism, like the white spires of Gondor, the wonder of Lothlórien and the winged mithril-helmet Aragorn is crowned with after the War of the Ring.

There's a certain, unmistakable light falling over Tolkien's Middle Earth. In *Silmarillion* he outlined a mythology for this battle between the Dark and the Light. Like telling how the Big Dipper or Valacirca, "The Scythe of Valar", was placed on heaven by the vala-archangel Varda as a promise of victory over Melkor, an early incarnation of evil. Varda was then celebrated as *Elbereth Giltoniel* (The Star Lighter) in the elven hymns.

Then we have the story of the half-elven Earendil sailing to the land of Valar with a certain gem, the silmaril, on his forehead, in order to gain help in the battle against Melkor. Later, Earendil was also elevated into a star, a true apotheosis.

The same light we see in the starry luster of the elven queen Galadriel in *The Lord of the Rings* proper, a true counter-force against the evil archetype of Sauron. In her as well as in the silmaril gems is a spark of Lux Aeterna from Varda, the star lighter. She has the light of the all-father Ilúvatar upon her face.

This I've learned from Café Exposé. The site also quotes a saying of Aragorn to his comrade Boromir, when they stop by in

Lothlórien: "Only the evil has something to fear, or the one carrying something evil inside". So indeed, evil isn't just some elemental, far-away force in the Ring Trilogy (as intimated in the previous chapter), the individuals also have to battle it inside of themselves. And evil becomes relatable in figures like Saruman the wizard and Gollum, the latter a creature hooked to the power of the Ring like a junkie to his fix, as someone likened it to.

The Lord of the Rings has it all: alluring scenes, sublime nature descriptions, archaic interiors and the whole gamut of names, names and names, construed by a philologist versed in Celtic and Germanic languages as well as Latin and Greek, names that also have their melodic quality, like Lothlórien, Gondor and Orthanc, to name but a few. All this, then, is structured by the battle between good and evil in an earnest, real way. Idealism versus nihilism, freedom-fighters against the NWO, remember...!

ARMY SERVICE

Tolkien enlisted in the British Army a year after the First World War started, he became a Second Lieutenant in the Lancashire Fusiliers and was sent to the front in the spring of 1916. He was a signals officer. In the autumn of the same year he participated in the Somme battle, a British attempt to break through the German lines. By this time Tolkien had already begun writing drafts of what was to become Silmarillion, in dirty underground shelters by candlelight during the shelling.

After four months in the combat zone Tolkien incurred typhoid fever, a common syndrome in the trenches. In early November, he was sent back to England. The rest of his army service he spent at home, well enough to be promoted to First Lieutenant before the war was over.

The influence of the military life itself, can this be detected in Tolkien's opus? Indeed: as an officer, he once had an adjutant, a hefty cockney type with both feet on the ground. His good relationship with him is reflected in the relationship between Frodo and Sam Gamgee. This we read in Humphrey Carpenter's biography. And the military science, history and tactics aspirant Tolkien may have gathered, could have been of some use when he would portray the Battle of Five Armies in *The Hobbit* and all the clashes of the trilogy, the Battle of Helm's Deep and so on.

GODS

In the previous chapter I mentioned the phenomenon of depicting gods in 20th century fiction: the hardest thing there is. Tolkien for his part has some success in this – when he sneaked in this and that peculiar figure that isn't presented as a god, but for all intents and purposes must be regarded as divine. Like Gandalf, the seemingly human wizard who in *Silmarillion* appears as an angelical *maia*. And the figure of Tom Bombadil, a forest-dwelling geezer, a Nordic Pan. The divine nature of him is hinted at when he says, "Tom was here before the river and the trees; Tom remembers the first raindrop and the first acorn", he remembers the rise and fall of generations and much more. A primeval creature, an avatar of the godhead, a fertility god of the Nordic type.

Gods aside, another captivating mythologism of the Tolkien narrative is the elves' waning power, the species at the end of the saga departing for better countries to prepare a place for man's dominion. This might be seen as a successful portrayal of how the world is "decharmed", a case of "*die Entzauberung der Welt*" that Max Weber spoke of. That this motive itself, that of elves shying away from the world of men, is borrowed from the Celtic fairy treasure doesn't diminish Tolkien's greatness. On the contrary, it's symbolic of his ability to take archaic, legendary stuff and incorporate it in a story relatable to modern man – a pastiche of old epics with a deep sense of meaning, that of how the forces of nihilism still are threatening everything that's worth living for.

STYLE

Tolkien's style was simple but not simplistic. He avoided vague constructions and relied on the power of the symbol. In the following quote from the Ring Trilogy the charms of the elven forest Lothlórien is described by the elf Legolas:

> There lie the woods of Lothlórien! (...) That is the fairest of all the dwellings of my people. There are no trees like the trees of that land. For in the autumn their leaves fall not, but turn to gold. Not till the spring comes and the new green opens do they fall, and then the boughs are laden with yellow flowers; and the floor of the wood is golden, and golden is the roof, and its pillars are of silver, for the bark of the trees is smooth and gray. So still our songs in Mirkwood say. My heart would be glad if I were beneath the eaves of that wood, and it were springtime![31]

To showcase the mastership of Tolkien's style, hereby another idyll, this time with the dwarf Gimli telling Legolas of some wondrous caves, the caves of Helm's Deep. Again, it shows the power of the symbol but also something more; this is an author writing on the edge of his ability, gaining a deathless splendor when describing "immeasurable halls, filled with an everlasting music of water that tinkles into pools":

> And, Legolas, when the torches are kindled and men walk on the sandy floors under the echoing domes, ah! Then, Legolas, gems and crystals and veins of precious ore glint in the polished walls; and the light glows through folded marbles, shell-like, translucent as the living hands of Queen Galadriel. There are columns of white and saffron and dawn-rose, Legolas, fluted and twisted into dreamlike forms; they spring up from many-colored floors to meet the glistening pendants of the roof: wings, ropes, curtains fine as frozen clouds; spears, banners, pinnacles of suspended palaces! Still lakes mirror them: a glimmering world looks up from dark pools covered with clear glass; cities, such as the mind of Durin could scarce have imagined in his sleep, stretch on through avenues and pillared courts, on into the dark recesses where no light can come, And plink! A silver drop falls, and the round wrinkles in the glass make all the towers bend

---

[31] Tolkien, 1988, I p 434

and waver like weeds and corals in a grotto of the sea. Then evening comes: they fade and twinkle out; the torches pass on into another chamber and another dream. There is chamber after chamber, Legolas; hall opening out of hall, dome after dome, stair beyond stair; and still the winding paths lead on into the mountain's heart.[32]

Tolkien knew how to paint, how to let the symbols play in vivid imagery. However, he also had some psychological insight of the rather "realistic" kind. He could give renderings like the following, capturing the essence of the evil sorcerer Saruman by describing his voice:

Suddenly another voice spoke, low and melodious, its very sound an enchantment. Those who listened unwarily to that voice could seldom report the words that they heard; and if they did, they wondered, for little power remained in them. Mostly they remembered only that it was a delight to hear the voice speaking, all that it said seemed wise and reasonable, and desire awoke in them by swift agreement to seem wise themselves. When others spoke they seemed harsh and uncouth by contrast; and if they gainsaid the voice, anger was kindled in the hearts of those under the spell. For some the spell lasted only while the voice spoke to them, and when it spoke to another they smiled, as men do who see through a juggler's trick while others gape at it. For many the sound of the voice alone was enough to hold them enthralled; but for those whom it conquered the spell endured when they were far away, and ever they heard that soft voice whispering and urging them. But none were unmoved; none rejected its pleas and its commands without an effort of mind and will, so long as its master had control of it.[33]

The Saruman figure is sorely needed in The Ring. He's an evil character that's also relatable, almost like Lucifer in Milton's *Paradise Lost*. The other dark-side characters in The Ring are so elementally

---

[32] Tolkien, 1988 II, p 194
[33] Ibid., p 234

evil that it becomes rather incredible. The Ring is a fairy tale, Tolkien mythologizes everything and this is often a strength, however, sometimes it gets a bit too much. Then a figure like Saruman can give proportions to the fantasy: his human traits, his ambiguous character does much to give the story depth.

There will be more Tolkien material later in this study, in chapter thirteen, when Peter Jackson's film *The Lord of the Rings* is examined.

LITERATURE

- *Bilbo* (1937)
- *The Fellowship of the Ring* (1954)
- *The Two Towers* (1954)
- *The Return of the King* (1955)
- *Silmarillion* (1977)

5. KARIN BOYE

C. S. LEWIS' *That Hideous Strength* was examined in chapter three, a novel about the forces of nihilism combating the forces of Tradition in a modern setting. In the two following chapters we'll take a look at some kindred works, some classics of societal, European SF. The overview begins with *Kallocain* by Karin Boye (1900-1941). Like *Nineteen Eighty-Four* this is a dystopia of a future totalitarian state with an official starting to doubt the regime. Overall, *Nineteen Eighty-Four* might have a more poignant quality than *Kallocain* but Boye's novel has some additional artistic allure compared to Orwell's. Boye was a poet along with her novel-writing and this gives *Kallocain* an aesthetically pleasing quality, if only moderately so. Also, in the ambiguous approach to the depicted totalitarian state Boye comes through as a closet rigorist, discreetly giving kudos to a nation structured along military lines.

LEFT-LEANING

Karin Boye was a left-leaning intellectual. But she still fits into this survey. Why? Because she wasn't expressly anti-tradition. When looking at her poetry we see a lot of approvingly traditional themes. For instance, she hailed courage and willpower, determination and self-sacrifice, conceptualizing a latter-day Valkyrie lifestyle: "Rest is only possible in battle, / only between the shields there is peace". And: "You must carry armor / in the heavy-handed game of life". Swords and armor abound in her lyrics.

The Valkyrie strain in her character has been criticized, even by herself (as in "I Want to Meet..."). She struggled with the hard, warrior-like side of her nature. That's human. You might get enough of the rigorous attitude at times. But a traditional spirit also has to know the ideal of balance and integration, of both being able to stand firm in battle and to embrace compassion and modesty. Boye didn't quite reach that integration in her mindset. Having said that, her warrior spirit mustn't be totally ignored by today's readership. Like Edith Södergran she knew the truth in the line, "the spirit of song is war". The freedom and joy of the warrior determined to die, this Boye knew. Again: "Rest only awaits you in battle, / only between the shields there is peace". She wanted to be like the blade of a rapier, both flexible and strong.

TRIUMPH

Boye's novel *Kallocain* is the prime interest of this chapter. This novel was Boye's artistic triumph, published in 1940. For as long as I can remember *Kallocain* has been lauded as a classic. It has almost been "hugged to death" by the Swedish elite. So then, has it stood the test of time? Short answer: it has. It isn't perfect but it has some depth and allure, even artistically.

In *Kallocain* you're not blown away by some explicit stylistic mastership, as in Yevgeny Zamyatin's *We* or Aldous Huxley's *Brave New World*. *Kallocain* at first comes through as rather dull, page up page down giving us the monotonous lecturing of the main character, chemist Leo Kall. First he's a supporter of the totalitarian regime. But when he finally becomes a lion of freedom he sounds equally dull. And even though Boye was a poet, capable of some *mimesis*, we don't see much of it in this novel. Then again, a future-like atmosphere indeed is created, not by sublime word-painting but by certain keywords like "police eyes and police ears", "metro" (subway) and "granite gray and meadow green tarpaulins", the latter giving obli against air raids. And then the *paternoster elevator*, existing in the real world in 1940 and here incorporated as the epitome of high-tech. This might seem meager compared to American SF of the day with its engineering spree but still, the futuristic markers in Boye's novel strike me as just enough to create that other-worldly atmosphere. Also, the inclusion of outlandish personal names such as Edo Rissen, Kalipso Lavris and Hung Paipho is the work of a skilled poet. In the way of SF Boye only wrote this but she had a clear talent for creating SF-like names. It's the same pleasure you get by reading, for instance, Asimov's *Foundation* with names like Hober Mallow, Bel Riose and Hari Seldon. Boye's name flora is of the same high standard, having the same atmosphere-creating ability.

As for *Kallocain's* structure and intent, I guess Yevgeny Zamyatin's *We* from 1921 was the model for this approach with the official in the future dictatorship beginning to doubt it. That another dystopian master, Orwell, had read Zamyatin is proved beyond doubt; he reviewed the Russian's book in 1946. Before that Zamyatin's novel was available in German and this language Boye knew. Zamyatin's novel is alive in every sentence with poignant similes and metaphors. And Orwell's book grabs you in no uncertain fashion: the totalitarian state in question is evil in modern form, period. Also, the consistent analysis on how the dictatorship, above and beyond ruling with an iron rod, uses language and brainwashing to control its citizens, makes his novel reminiscent of our contemporary regime of Political Correctness. In comparison, Boye's novel becomes more of a mirror of the 1930s with Nazism versus Communism, a symbol of an openly totalitarian society. The World State, the country where Leo Kall lives, tends to become the center of attention of the story.

RIGORISM

In *Kallocain* The World State in some aspects becomes the "hero", this land with its equality where everyone eats the same food, all live in the same apartments and all have the same salary. Only the insignias of the various guilds become status markers, and Leo Kall makes it all seem rather appealing:

The standard uniform – one for work, one for leisure and one for military and police service – was the same for everyone, for man and woman and for high and low, except for the insignia. Even the latter was actually no fancier for the one than for the other. The desirability of higher insignia lay purely in what it symbolized. So highly spiritualized, I thought happily, is actually every fellow soldier in the World State, that he feels that life's highest value hardly can have a more concrete expression than in the three black chevrons on the sleeve – three black chevrons being the token both of his self-respect and the respect of others. Of material pleasures you certainly can get enough and more than enough – and because of this, I suspect that the old civilian-capitalistic societies with their twelve-room apartments were hardly nothing more than a symbol – but the most subtle of all, as pursued in the shape of insignias, this can never be measured. No one can have so much respect and so much self-respect, that he doesn't want more. In the most sublime, most airy and sought after way, our solid social system is resting secure for all time. [34]

On all accounts this is a sharp analysis of Boye, how a leveled society allows the individual's upward striving to find an outlet in uniform insignia. Also, when Boye portrays an official of a censorship bureau, Djin Kakumita, and reflects his ideas on how propaganda films should be, it's equally telling. He says that effective dramas mustn't shy away from showing the hero dying. Dying is not what the better part of the audience is afraid of. Instead, the movie goers who are susceptible to such films are afraid of being "cowardly, dishonorable, ugly in the internal sense"; this is "a driving force of the heroic nature" which is what the films must target [chapter eleven]. And this is true for all dramas, not only dictatorship propaganda films. Boye had some psychological insight and such findings make the book worth getting through.

---

[34] Boye, 1992, p 131-132, translated by the author

PROPAGANDA

In the Swedish reception you always hear that *Kallocain* is such a classic, it's so necessary, it must be read to warn against looming dictatorship tendencies. And indeed, even today we live in a society that is something of a dictatorship functioning with propaganda, brainwashing, rigged languages and branding of government critics, those daring to criticize mass-immigration and the multicultural society. Orwell depicted that kind of dictatorship. Boye is more into a hands-on control state, it seems to me. For instance, each family has a government employed housekeeper who is also an informer. She keeps a watching eye so that nobody says anything hostile about the state. It seems to me a somewhat primitive form of control. Orwell's dictatorship rules by the language itself being emptied of content and making opposition impossible. Opposition itself becomes taboo. Like in the PC regimes of today. Criticism of immigration is considered immoral. You're not considered a humanist if you don't want to allow mass-immigration. Nationalists are fascists and fascists are racists. They shouldn't even be heard. They are taboo, they are lepers; outside the camp, they shall have their abode.

Boye's hero has no such internal battle to fight. He doesn't see through the regime's exercise of power through the language. From reasons of pure state loyalty, he invents a truth drug (the Kallocain of the title, its name modeled after the analgesic ointment Xylocain launched by Swedish company Astra at the time). With it, he finds that people don't want a society of control, they want freedom. What a surprise. *Kallocain* lacks some depth in this respect.

As intimated Boye was a poet of some renown, at least in Swedish. She was fierce: "I dreamed of blood last night, I dreamed of death last night". And "rest only awaits you in battle, / only between the shields there is peace". This fierce side is also displayed in *Kallocain*, like the praise of dictatorship that the seemingly misled Kall delivers. On the surface the novel has the theme of "freedom before dictatorship" but beyond this goes a silent shout of approval for marching in line, wearing a uniform and eating the same food as everyone else. *Kallocain* has a hard surface that the author wants to counteract with clear, sometimes too clear, signals.

This is also shown in Boye's poetry. She said no to being a knight in armor, but the way she rejected it is telling.

LAGERCRANTZ'S CRITIQUE

Boye had many strings to her bow. She could both praise the sunshine and have an interest in "death and night and blood". True, to some extent she tried to suppress the darker sides. Olof Lagercrantz uncovers some discrepancies in Boyes works in the study *Tretton poeter och Fågeltruppen*. Even in praising life she sounds a bit rough.

> "'Be quiet. Have faith", Boye cries, the words sounding like a command. (...) 'Pull the shoe off your foot. Be still, keep guard', it reads in a famous poem, sounding as if it were the case of a relaxation exercise in gymnastics".[35]

Lagercrantz is on to something here. He touches on how *Kallocain* with its supposedly critical depiction of a dictatorship government still shows a sort of silent sympathy for its Spartan sides, much like I've indicated above. A not inconsiderable part of Boye's essence was at home in an archaic world of asceticism, sacrifice and discipline, courtly love and dedication. All or nothing, victory or death. When she affirmed these traits she wrote with force. When she denied them it became a waffle and "scholarship prose," texts that want to be good but between the lines scream of unreleased rigorism. "Rigorism" doesn't mean downright death wish even if Boye also had that feature (*q.v.* "The Quiet Steps Behind"). It means devotion, sacrifice, idealism of a combative nature.

As a whole Boye's opus contains some bland and superficial moral sermons, fine ideals rolled out in a pedantic spirit. Her "death poems" are more authentic. It's true that "The Quiet Steps Behind" worships death itself in a strange way. Strange, because in essence death is just a transition, not a state. But of course, death is also a symbolic figure and it isn't emotionally strange to worship it; this phenomenon isn't a riddle as such. And I will always pay tribute to

---

[35] Lagercrantz, 1973, p 71

Boye for a poem like "The Amazon". Its lines are unique, harder than even the martial Edith Södergran could write: "I dreamed of blood last night. I dreamed of death last night. (...) I dreamed my death was fair and good. / Thus I dreamed last night."

These are true lines, delivering the essence of the Nordic shield maiden, capturing her condition. It's a sincere portrayal of a longing for "death and night and blood" in the spirit of Yukio Mishima.

OBSERVER

Boye understood the soldier psyche. We saw this in some of the poetry quoted. And as intimated, when she in *Kallocain's* first chapter depicts the state practice that everyone should wear a uniform, she lets her narrator, chemist Leo Kall, show appreciation for this. Possibly this will showcase his of propaganda deluded mind but in itself this is an accurate observation of the nature of grade insignia. Here Boye saw how the leveling still can let people vent their quest to become something more, to rise above their status and to make this endeavor a spiritual practice. This is a universally viable observation, a reflection that reveals a spiritually insightful intellect. Not even in the leveled Soviet Union did a general have the same salary as a private soldier, Boye's future has gone further and it all has some credibility on its own premises.

Boye was a sharp observer generally. She had, for example, once seen a portrait of Adolf Hitler in Vienna in 1938. To a friend she wrote: "Thus it is, this is true, not all the caricatures, nor the usual stereotyped idealized idealizations, but this ascetic, grim, consecrated, dedicated face, and at the same time strained even to the utmost limit of power..."[36] All else being equal, she noted the radiation in this portrait; she was honest, she was able to express herself bluntly, even in things that were not *comme il faut*, especially not for the left-leaning intellectual she was.

Boye ventured inside the totalitarian psyche and mysteriously thrived there. Openly she said that writing this novel scared her.

---

[36] Boye quoted after Lagercrantz, p 82

Kallocain depicts freedom against slavery and light against darkness, but often it all moves in a gray area where the peculiarities and characteristics of the World State takes on a strange life of its own. It's like a life in the moonlight, maybe even in the artificial moonlight *á la* 1944 when the Wehrmacht directed searchlights towards the undersides of clouds to illuminate the battlefield. Boye has vividly portrayed her world and her future. In comparison, Orwell's *Nineteen Eighty-Four* makes you scream for mercy, Zamyatin is amusing, von Harbou is melodramatic and Huxley is partly annoying but overall Boye is more complex.

SWEDISH INTERIORS

Just so that we're in agreement: of course Boye the person was sincere in her being against the dictatorship. And personally, neither do I want a government where kids are encouraged to play war games, where they're enrolled in a pseudo-military corps and all families have a maid with parallel operation as informer. This and other things in the novel, as the injection of a truth serum and a life in underground cities as a natural mode of living, is somewhat frightening. This I admit. For although today's society with a brainwashing media, a propagandistic regime and the slavery of materialism is no holiday, you mustn't let it overshadow that the regimes of WWII also were harsh to live under, seen from a strictly humanitarian view.

Boye captures the distinctive nature of the Russian and German dictatorships she knew, with a spate of the Swedish War Preparedness regimen added. The result was the fictional world of *Kallocain*. But she realized this world with all the design you can demand of a novel, so much so that the interiors and scenes acquire more meaning than a mere "warning". This is what makes a great writer: to let some ambiguity prevail, not putting things right in every sense, letting the novel's reality exist on its own terms.

LITERATURE

- *Kallocain* (1940)
- *Complete Poems* (1994, translated by David McDuff)

6. ORWELL, ZAMYATIN, HUXLEY AND VON HARBOU

In this chapter we'll take a closer look on European dystopias, stemming from the former half of the 20th century. They are *Nineteen Eighty-Four* by George Orwell (1903-1950), *We* by Yevgeny Zamyatin (1884-1937), *Brave New World* by Aldous Huxley (1894-1963) and *Metropolis* by Thea von Harbou (1888-1954). First they're examined one by one, and then an attempt is made to see them all together, trying to reach a conceptual conclusion.

ORWELL

The number one controversial, politically oriented SF-novel of all times is George Orwell's *Nineteen Eighty-Four* (1948). It's got this towering, iconic quality to it. They say: if your author name becomes a label, like Lovecraftian, Dickensian or Dantesque, then you've succeed. And we all know what "Orwellian" is.

Not least our times, the 2010s, are truly Orwellian. We live in an Empire with seemingly perpetual, peripheral wars and we have our equivalents to Newspeak and Two Minutes Hate. "Freedom is Slavery" (since eating, watching TV and fornicating is the "true" freedom) and "Ignorance is Strength" (since castigating opposing voices in the media is the highest form of good).

Orwell's book has been read as an assault against both Communist Russia and Capitalist America. But in the changing times the novel has metamorphosed once again, now becoming useful in decoding the governing techniques of the current nihilistic, "liberal", multicultural establishment. It isn't hard to find preachers sounding like the O'Brien character in 1984. Just substitute "white man" for "man" in what Orwell's O'Brien says, and you find the jargon that until recently was viable in "polite society" in the West:

> "If you are a man, Winston, you are the last man. Your kind is extinct; we are the inheritors. Do you understand that you are alone? You are outside history; you are non-existent."

Nihilism is threatening us, then and now. But how to fight it? With idealism of course, by stressing Will, Thought and Compassion and the ideals derived from them; see the Introduction.

PREDECESSOR

Orwell is an all-time classic in the dystopian genre but he had a predecessor: Yevgeny Zamyatin's *We* (1921). In the previous chapter I noted that the Englishman had read Zamyatin's novel. And in *Nineteen Eighty-Four* as in *We*, it's all there: a man in a future dictatorship caught between the official demands of power and the longing for love. The protagonist starts to doubt the propaganda and gets caught up in the state's repressive apparatus, in the end emerging as a brainwashed robot. These are the superficial similarities between *We* and *Nineteen Eighty-Four* and they're interesting to note.

What more do I have to say about *Nineteen Eighty-Four*? Nothing, actually. While I acknowledge its status as a classic, shaping our view on the kinship between Bolshevik Russia and the Politically Correct regimes of the current Westworld, I have a hard time enduring the passive nihilism of its outlook. I mean, the novel is tight and well told, it makes perfect sense all the way, but as a viable take on nihilism vs. idealism I'd rather read Lewis' *That Hideous Strength* or Boye's *Kallocain*. Orwell isn't idealistic enough for my tastes, he shows no viable alternative rooted in eternal values. It isn't enough to put your hope in the proles. Orwell was a man striving for decency but mere decency isn't enough to fight nihilism.

WE

The Russian Yevgeny Zamyatin wrote the novel *We*, about a Bolshevik-style dictatorship dominating a future world. What immediately falls into mind is the constructivist style and playful language of the story. I here think of the author's inventiveness in creating his future city landscape with its Accumulator Tower, the Music Factory and the spaceship Integral made out of copper and glass, "about to integrate the endless equation of the universe".

Artistically this is on another level than Orwell, maybe even beyond Boye's *Kallocain* and Huxley's *Brave New World*. As for narrative style, von Harbou's *Metropolis* seemingly rivals it; the problem is that her story stylistically comes through as pretentious and vague, Zamyatin on the other hand is perfectly understandable all the way with his narrative brinkmanship. His story also rewards the reader with clever observations and off the cuff-reflections about this and that. In comparison, Orwell (God bless him) is less of an artist and more of a reporter, a common man driven by indignation and fear. As intimated he is, if you will, a nihilist – like O'Brien, his chief villain...! Zamyatin on the other hand has a different, more diversified outlook on life. This hints at what is needed for a dystopia to work, namely, a counterpoint, a counter-image of what the dictatorship is not. More on this below.

The narrator of *We*, the Head Engineer, in the text expressly says that "We" shall be the name of his story (compare *Anthem* by Ayn Rand, *q.v.* chapter twenty seven, which also has this "we"- narrator). To say "we" instead of "I" is an example of a basic element of the collectivist dictatorship, of the vocabulary shaping your thoughts. It could remind you of Samuel Delany's novel *Babel-17* where you automatically become a traitor by using a certain language. That's an important point to make, now and forever. Conversely, if you want to fight a regime bent on mind control like this you have to create your own vocabulary and make the opponent use it.

HUXLEY

Aldous Huxley's *Brave New World* is a dystopian story focusing on biology, physiology and psychology. The programmatic side of the dictatorship in question, this World State 600 years in the future, is a sort of glorified, internalized utilism. This is a subtle form of slavery; people are brought to love the dictatorial lifestyle, not by being coerced but by being conditioned from birth.

That's the difference between this story and *Nineteen Eighty-Four*. Orwell's book, along with showing brainwashing techniques in the form of a rigged language, also told us about physical torture in no uncertain way. *Brave New World* treads more subtle lands and in doing so is even more reminiscent of the current dictatorship of mass media, consumerism and social control as means of maintaining the regime of nihilism.

In a preface written fifteen years after the first publishing, Huxley mentions that in states where the economic and political freedom goes down the sexual freedom tends to go up, as a compensation. This is true for Soviet Russia at least, with its "sexual Bolshevism", and maybe even for our over-sexed times ruled by the PC dictatorship.

Brave New World tells about a world without freedom, spirituality or a concept of God. Eventually a man grown up outside of this regime is presented, called The Wildman. He hasn't been submitted to conditioning and psychic tinkering; he has read books and roamed the wilderness. And he wants freedom and spirituality. But he's deemed insane because the old world, which had this, also had diseases and insecurity. This a teacher of the World State tells him. Now I wonder: do Politically Correct operators of today still maintain such things, warning against the supposed medical deficiencies of the World of Tradition, or have they formally given up the fight against the reflected life...?

SOMA

Brave New World is a profiling and dramatization of a life devoid of love and spirituality. It's about a society where everyone constantly is drugged by taking something called *soma*, with people never doing things like reading or thinking but instead being occupied with sensory entertainment, being hypnotically educated. To this, promiscuity is an ideal. No ordinary families exist; children instead being reared in state nurseries.

So I say: I get the picture. This is a warning and rather efficient. But I have to add, perhaps frivolously: the world of today, of the 2010s, isn't totally like *Brave New World*. It has some similarities but along with the attempted conditioning of people, the propaganda and some cloning techniques around we still have people willingly reading old, supposedly outdated books on esotericism and spirituality; they meditate, they have real feelings and heartfelt relationships. Huxley's vison of "machine technology applied to human society" from eighty years ago is still valid but overall I'm an optimist since this technocracy hasn't won yet and never will. Since 11/11 2011 we live in the *Sat Yuga* of harmony and order. This has to be taken into account when we today read dystopian stories like Huxley's, written during the *Kâli Yuga* of dualism and nihilism.

Brave New World was published in 1932. After this Huxley even wrote a book on esotericist philosophy, *The Perennial Philosophy* (1946), a comparative study of quotes from documents of Eastern and Western mysticism. So instead of reading *Brave New World* and being indignant on how bad everything is, my advice would be to read up on books like the just mentioned and cherish the *Philosophia Perennis*. Essentially, it's about following the Law of Attraction and seeing how "like attracts like": as you sow, so you shall reap. Willpower is of essence, the Will to Light; contrariwise, the lack of Will drags you down in darkness and despair.

REWARD

Brave New World can, at times, reward the reader. For instance, chapter three mixes lines from different voices in different circumstances, those of a private person, a scientist and a politician of this future world. The narrative thread thus becomes loosened up, if only for a chapter, and that's a peculiar trait. Everything is symbolized by the mere lines of the three separate speakers, the gist of the novel thus being conveyed conceptually. So if you want this novel condensed into a few pages, read chapter three.

The current, real-world PC regime is bent on eradicating indigenous peoples via mass-immigration and multiculturalism. This is hinted at even in *Brave New World*, in names like Jean-Jaques Habibullah, Bokanovsky Jones and Mustapha Mond, although the main characters like Lenina Crowne etc. are "common" Brits living in London.

Brave New World depicts a caste society: *alpha* and *beta* persons rule the society while *gamma*, *delta* and *epsilon* people do routine work. Huxley has cleverly constructed his future world, both detail-wise and as for the big picture.

SUNNY STYLE

Brave New World is a rather curious dystopia, a book giving you a warm-cold feeling. We're met with a wholly sterile future with propaganda, conditioning, cloning and rigid castes, but told in a sort of sunny narrative with puns and witticisms. The novel deserves its status as a classic and it's nice with a dystopia without the harshness and drama of *Kallocain* and *Nineteen Eighty-Four*. That is, *Brave New World* is dramatic enough but overall it's kind of more civil. It's a dystopia of the "air-conditioned nightmare" type.

Huxley was a skilled, self-conscious author by the time he wrote this; strangely he never wrote anything similar again, he never got so speculative and futuristic. And maybe the narrative gets a little too self-conscious at times, maybe Huxley could have cut down a little on the irony. It's all over the place, even in the title.

VON HARBOU

Thea von Harbou's *Metropolis*, as a novel, is too much and too little. There's too much melodrama, excessive metaphors, *pathetique* and sentimentality. And too little of ideas, ideology and conceptualization.

Metropolis isn't essential reading for the right-winger. It's primarily of interest for the history of SF and for the history of film. The movie from 1927 was a masterpiece through and through, von Harbou writing the script based on her own novel (more on the film in chapter thirteen). The film script streamlines the narrative. A lot may be "lost in translation" this way – the better, I say...! Because the novel *Metropolis* is an effort to read for the style-conscious reader. Everything is excessive; the city roars not like a beast but "like a thousand beasts", the machines are evil gods and a certain foreman swears "like a hundred demons" and so on and so forth.

Having said this, the cityscape and its underground may have its alluring aspects even in the novel, the form-loving aesthete may have some fun exploring this – if, indeed, the reader can stand the hyperboles, the "exciting" storytelling and the metaphors, these mainly being of the disappointing kind. Seen from the right this is a tale of a rebellion in a future techno-city. At the end the factions of workers and employers unite, maybe foreshadowing Nazism's deemphasizing of the class struggle concept.

Metropolis is the least refined of the novels treated in this chapter. But you shouldn't be too harsh; overall it stands rather well along the others. The ideological, conceptual element is rather absent. But a symbolic trait of the dystopia is exquisitely represented in the form of the "counter-image to the dictatorship" that the other novels treated also have. In this respect, *We* has an Ancient House still standing outside the right-angled future city, *Nineteen Eighty-Four* has a special apartment the hero and heroine occupy in order to cultivate their resistance to the regime, and *Kallocain* has an elaboration of a dream one of the drug-induced patients has, a dream of a desert city. And *Brave New World* has The Wildman, born outside of the modern world and steeped in the plays of Shakespeare. And *Metropolis*, finally, in the realm of "counter-image to nihilism", in the cityscape has a cathedral still standing in spite of the atheistic governance. This building and its interior of statues of saints occurs several times in the novel, making it an effectual counter-image to the modernistic squareness of the city at large.

I said that *Metropolis* had its elements of sentimentality. But of course, some sentiment must be allowed in a novel. And as yet another counter-image to the techno-world may be seen the love incorporated in Maria – the human Maria, in contrast to the robot made in her image. Maria is a saintly figure caring for children, oppressed workers and for Freder, the son of the city's ruler and her love interest.

Although melodramatic and vague at times *Metropolis* conveys the traditional values of spirituality, motherly love and caring as a counter-image to a technocity of perfect machines and regimentation. Man isn't a machine and if we learn that from a dystopia, that man has a heart serving as mediator between head and hand, then it's still conceptually viable.

CODA

In depicting the battle of nihilism vs. idealism, which one of the above novels does it best? I'd say, none of the above. Lewis' *That Hideous Strength* is overall more efficient in this respect.

The reception of the dystopias is a bit smothering. In my schooldays and in the media of those years we were fed with *Nineteen Eighty-Four* and *Kallocain* with the hint that "you know that this awaits you around the corner, don't you, with all the data programming, police state tendencies and wars we see around us...?" It's true that at the time of writing we do live in a sort of dictatorship with traits of *Nineteen Eighty-Four, Kallocain* and *Brave New World* but still, The Powers That Be haven't triumphed overall. There's still meditation courses, edifying books and culture to be found; there's still friendships to cultivate and a time to be alone. An *active idealism* can still be performed as a counterforce to the forces of nihilism. Therefore I'd say that these novels are classics in the realm of prophesy and warning, and they can sometimes be read even for enjoyment. But Lewis' book is a more triumphant document as a counterforce to nihilism. SF mustn't always be about indignantly looking at worse-case scenarios. There's also the individual and his self-reliance to look at, as in Lewis' *That Hideous Strength* and *Lost Legacy* by Heinlein. Conceptually, such stories are the future, not *Nineteen Eighty-Four*.

Acknowledge your inner powers and don't be occupied with visions of despair and darkness. Don't go backwards into the future.

LITERATURE

- Evegeny Zamyatin: *We* (1921)
- Thea von Harbou: *Metropolis* (1926)
- Aldous Huxley: *Brave New World* (1932)
- George Orwell: *Nineteen Eighty-Four* (1948)

7. ERNST JÜNGER

EVERYONE KNOWS THAT Ernst Jünger (1895-1998) was a man of the right, in his youth a radical conservative, in his late years a more mainstream conservative. But throughout his life, he fought for Tradition. And this is clearly visible in his fantastic fiction.

GEOGRAPHY

To the north lies the Forest, a mossy dark expanse spreading fumes and mists, devilry and weirdness, the residence of the Forester General and his irregulars. This is where the Pied Piper of Hamelin is said to finally have gone, as it also became the refuge for Villon after the judgment and for scattered bands of robbers, heretics and troglodytes.

South of it lies the Campagna, a free pasture with archaic farms, crowded with faithful figures like Belovar, a shepherd among shepherds; a man to trust, both in drinking and in battle, the latter preferably with an element of blood revenge.

South of the Campagna rises the Marble Cliffs, a ridge overgrown with broom and snapdragon, lupine and thyme and populated by lizards basking on the rocks during midday. Here also lives Otho with his brother, two flower-collecting, studied and experienced men of the world; they have contacts both in the Campagna and down in the towns, the port cities of the Great Marina. Beyond this you can sense the rich lands of Burgundy and, turning to the north, you can see mountains and glaciers.

Thus the geography of Ernst Jünger's *On the Marble Cliffs* (1939), a rather delightful fantasy land I've never seen depicted on a map in any issue of the book. This had probably been too down-market. But Jünger's SF novel from 1949, *Heliopolis*, indeed had a hand-drawn and colored map in the original German edition, a map signed Werner Höll. Far to the south you can see the prison island the boat passes in the beginning chapter, sailing the strait between this and the happier island next door that once had summer houses but now only serves as the goal for excursions of youths who light fires on the marble floors of the ruins and dance in Dionysian frenzy until the sun rises.

The main part of this map of course included the city of Heliopolis, a burgh endowed with two capes, two "land spurs" framing the harbor *à la* Genoa. As for the city proper, from the middle of the harbor you can go north, traveling the length of the city up to the church, walking along the Corso which divides the city in two; on the left hand you have an organic street layout as well as a palace, the classic habitation of the Proconsul and his legitimate rule in the form of the army. On the right hand you have a regular grid of blocks and the Land Marshall's pentagonal stronghold, a nihilistic bureaucracy exerting power in a more invisible way.

Pentagonal was the word, and at the same time as the book was written the Americans built the Pentagon defense headquarters in Washington. In its original plan the building would have lacked windows which would have made it a well-protected bunker in the war then looming – but as things stood the builders decided to have windows anyway. The idea as such was still rather appealing in a titanic way and Jünger immortalized it in this tetrarch temple.

As for Jünger's fantasy geography we can also look at *Eumeswil* of 1977, playing in another future city, but this had no map on the inside of the cover. It wasn't needed; the narrative style is highly subjective and a timeline there isn't, some vivid views of the environment as cityscape aren't given. But there are certainly details like the castle of the Condor, his Casbah on a crest outside the city, and bird-rich lands on the river Sus, and the bourgeois city proper and a port. And the surroundings of the mythical Woods in the south and the realms of the Yellow Khan in the east. And, below the city, the Catacombs, technological caves of factual and titanic schemes.

Then, why this overview? The thing of it is, as novels *On the Marble Cliffs*, *Heliopolis* and *Eumeswil* are all classics of traditionally minded fantasy, each one sketching the battle between idealism and nihilism from slightly different points of view, like a kaleidoscope slightly turned for each time.

TRADITION

In *On the Marble Cliffs* the narrator lives with his brother Otho on the Marble Cliffs, the two spending their days with flower collection, studies in ancient scriptures and excursions into the woods. In the nearby towns of the Great Marina they thrive in the bosom of Tradition, of a life celebrating spring and autumn festivals in traditional garb, of castles and hunting parties, of churches and monks, of commerce and husbandry giving prosperity to all.

But this idyll is threatened by the forces of nihilism. The gangs of the Forester General exert an invisible presence with their torture nests and haunts, a presence poisoning even the well-ordered cities of the Marina. Eventually, the gangs form alliances with people in the cities and civil strife erupts on the streets, the contesting gangs killing each other surreptitiously. In the process, a poignant image is this: the cities still have a burial ceremony on the Roman pattern, releasing an eagle above the closed grave to symbolize the deification of the dead, the ascent of his soul to happier realms. But now this custom has degenerated: "Otherwise, when the eagle took off, there was silence but nowadays a wild cheer rose. This commotion made us and many others sad, because now we felt that the good ancestral spirit of the Marina had been lost."[37]

---

[37] Jünger, 2006 p 45, translated by the author

The bands of thieves and mutineers, of stranglers and poachers, torturers and blood-suckers advance. And against this the forces of Tradition have to make a stand. This they do, in the form of the narrator and his brother along with Belovar and his clan plus the mercenary captain Biedenhorn. To this, esoteric faith in the form of Father Lampros is brought along. We also have the prince Sunmyra venturing out into the woods and making a stand against the Forester General, Sunmyra being a symbol of the aristocracy.

This evolves into a symbolical drama, a gripping display of the battle against chaos and confusion. It's like a slightly more intellectual *Lord of the Rings* – but only slightly since both of them convince by its imagery. They're a field day for symbolism and a certain ambiguity. Neither of them is a clear-cut allegory. It's about fairy tales with an adult feel, a sense of urgency.

Jünger depicts his battle as that of order and harmony, the quaint bourgeois cities, being threatened by Forces From the Woods. As a side note, Jünger formally was a paragon of transparency, of orderliness. The meme "keep it vague" wasn't sported by him, at least not expressly. He had the ideals of the Enlightenment, of French *moralistes* and Voltaire, along with his right-wing character of glory to the brave, Duty, Honor, Country and having the Army as a spiritual home, seeing the baptism of fire in World War I as a second birth. Jünger was a glorified militarist but he wasn't much for romanticist yearnings for the Germany of olden days, of the Edda and Asatru. He knew the tradition as such but his mindset and cultural profile was one of southern climes, Romanism and well-ordered parks, not the murky Wagnerian woods where things are shrouded in mist. In comparing Jünger with Tolkien you could say that Jünger would never had thought up a figure like Tom Bombadil, this archaic divinity roaming the woods. Unless, of course, the shepherd Belovar of *On the Marble Cliffs* is to be taken as such a paragon of archaism.

LENNART SVENSSON

HELIOPOLIS

Moving on to *Heliopolis,* here the forces of Tradition battle with nihilism, presented as the struggle for power over a city. The Central Department rules with terror and bureaucracy in conflict with the Army exerting its time-honored power based on duty and honor. Actually, the city is ruled by a prince but he's not present, he's on the Islands of the Hesperides or somewhere. The function of the viceroy and deputy is performed by the Proconsul. When he deliberates on what makes his body politic fit to rule he delivers a sermon of Tradition like nothing on earth, delineating patriarchy and its roots. In ancient times belligerent nomads migrated into lands ruled by matriarchs bent on ecstasy and dark rites, worshiping deities of the woods; to this the wind-blown nomads, born under the open sky, brought order and livestock culture, caste society and a sense of direction, leading ultimately to the modern world.

But we need more than the *Auctoritas* and *Potestas* of the Army to make the world go round. We need art, symbolized in de Geer's friends, the painter Halder and the author Ortner. And we need the discreet forces of life, symbolized in bees. In *On the Marble Cliffs* Father Lampros had beehives and so has Pater Foelix in *Heliopolis.* The following quote gives a telling picture of the subtle forces giving life to everything, spiritual life uttered in the activity of bees. Bees, in gathering nectar, don't work, not in the ordinary sense of the word; instead they're driven by an indescribable joy. Pater Foelix says:

> We could learn from the bees what work is. No enterprise can bear fruit if there isn't a sparkle of love in it. The joy of life keeps it all together, much stronger than the economy or the brute force. It's like a farmer plowing in the morning sun or a blacksmith standing at his anvil or the fisher lowering his nets: in all of them we can surmise a sense of satisfaction that's unmeasurable. You can notice it even in the marketplace and the hubbub of the city. In this sense of satisfaction lies the true treasure of the world, the solid gold, the harvests and the profits being merely the yield.

This is also true for the industry – no economy can blossom if it isn't founded on love. Benevolence has a golden hand.[38]

As a city to live in Heliopolis has its advantages. It's a splendid city in the sun with some opportunity for idealism, Tradition and the good life. But in the plot Captain de Geer, the novel's main protagonist, ends up in trouble in the battle between the Palace of the Proconsul and the Central Department. He has let the daughter of a Farsi bookbinder stay with him in the palace, as a protection from persecutions of this minority. This noble move, this responsible act by a True and Noble Knight, is misinterpreted by de Geer's superiors so he has to apply for resignation. But a splendid career is offered in the form of space travel, a newly begun endeavor in the future scenario at hand. Several spaceships are already out, roaming the spatial vistas to seek out new worlds, and in the end de Geer and his female friend, Budur Peri, can sign on as cadets on a rocket ship.

This aspect of space travel really anchors *Heliopolis* in the SF mode, although its generic quality at large is rather absent. To use T. S. Eliot's vocabulary, it's a self-conscious artwork, not a genre-conscious work of craftsmanship. But as it stands, the view on space travel in *Heliopolis* makes it a much needed commentary on the specificity of this phenomenon. Here is touched upon what Norman Spinrad saw as the unique character of space travel stories.

SPACE

According to Holmberg (2003) Norman Spinrad had this view on the specificity of the SF genre: that SF was special in expressing intellectual progress in romantic terms. This can be exemplified with stories of space travel, a central theme for SF from the mid-19th century to the mid-20th century and beyond.

Spinrad's train of thought is this: traveling into outer space with ships employing some technical innovation isn't merely about faster communication, it's a mind-bending achievement, a striking

---

[38] Jünger, 1954, p 209, translated by the author

experience and a challenge towards existence itself. You could say that it's a metaphysical feat, not just a physical. It's about reaching another level of reality, a higher dimension. In this vein, Spinrad talks about "the romance of progress and increasing insight" as the dominating feeling of SF literature.

Thus Spinrad. And Jünger, in delineating the specificity of "the promise of space", says that the spacefarers found what they dreamed of,

> a realm where the earth was transformed into a treasure trove and knowledge into power. They found more than they had been looking for. Knowledge was like a drill in the rock having at last reached a plenteous vein. They had increased their speed to the point where it either becomes extinction or rest. The memory of that triumph remained with them...[39]

Jünger, in *Heliopolis*, gave a unique vision of the essence of space travel and space exploration: that it's a spiritual endeavor. This attitude is viable also for the development of space travel in the real world, in the 21st century. *Heliopolis* mirrors the prevailing, at-the-time-of-writing enthusiasm when the West gathered itself to enter space and go to the moon. Then a backlash came. The Apollo project went to the moon, a much sought-after event, only to bring home a sample of rocks. In his diary Jünger wrote about this: "They only found a desert because they had the desert inside."

That's a sounding memento for the rest of the space age. The way to space goes inward. We have to raise ourselves mentally and spiritually in order to go to space. We have to have an inner mind able to mirror the higher levels of reality that space essentially is. That is, we're not just bound for Inner Space, meditating. We are, indeed, going to space in solid ships. But that way, to outer space, goes by way of inner space, by way of man reaching a higher level in his mental and spiritual development.

The Apollo project era saw man embroiled in war, strife and a focus on economic growth and material affluence. The project's

---

[39] Jünger, 1954, p 368, translated by the author

outcome mirrored this: a handful of dust. As for the future, when a lasting peace is here, reached by the consent of all people, secure in their places of origin, when spiritual aspects are hailed along with prosperity for all, then mankind can go into space for real. Like Captain de Geer and Budur Peri in *Heliopolis*, joining the Blue Pilot, Phares, on his journey to the stars.

> The signals sounded for the second time. Figures appeared in front of the blue shadow of the ship, hurriedly going about their tasks. Now they were standing alone. Phares took their hands. They crossed the dark borderline and entered the area. Even though they were prepared they felt a tinge of pain, as if being touched by a flame. But Phares smiled at them. Then they put on the golden masks.[40]

EUMESWIL

Heliopolis is stylistically rather "out there", a bit like Thea von Harbou's *Metropolis*, with intentionally "captivating" passages, a style aiming at the sublime. The only difference is that Jünger has some control of his language. He wrote "a hard and lucid prose" (Chatwin). And in *Heliopolis* the rhetorical sweeps take in everything. In *Eumeswil* (1977) the style is more low-key, however, still being able to take in "everything": history, tradition, art, politics and the Jünger experience *per se*. The forte of this novel is that the narrator, Manuel Venator, thematically tells about his world, of the future city of Eumeswil and his work as an historian, his teachers and his situation. Thus he can elaborate on everything that he pleases, not expressly having to tell an exciting, linear story as in *Heliopolis* and *Marble Cliffs*.

Manuel Venator is an historian, steeped in ancient times. But he gets perspective on his conceptual outings by working as a bartender in the city-state castle, the Casbah. The city has some character of the Moroccan town of Agadir that Jünger visited some times in the post war era. But in essence Eumeswil is a city that's nowhere

---

[40] Jünger, 1954, p 382, translated by the author

and everywhere, the literary playground for Jünger's musings on "everything".

For instance, *Eumeswil* demonstrates that Jünger was something of an esotericist. He carried along the Primordial Tradition from Plato, Aristotle and Plotinus, that of the idea carrying the essence of things. The tangible objects are symbolical expressions of the idea. Nature tells us in symbolical terms of the presence of God. In *Eumeswil* this is exemplified in the following praise of birdwatching:

> Ornithology has its peculiar magic, a profound sense of observation connecting the native place with the infinite. Also, it acknowledges the glory and fullness of life. The eye resting on the palette having its fill, not in some distant hope but in a "here and now": *universalia in re*.[41]

In stressing the eidetic nature of reality Jünger carried on the tradition from Plotinus, Goethe and Schopenhauer. Jünger's idealistic worldview is formally presented in his study *Typus, Name, Gestalt* from 1963 and in Gisbert Kranz's *Ernst Jünger's symbolische Weltschau* (1968).

POLITICS

What about the politics of *Eumeswil*? For instance, we're presented with a refined form of Anarchism, symbolized in the Anarch; this is Manuel Venator's designation of himself, a counterforce to the Monarch symbol of the Condor. The difference between the Anarch and the Anarchist is that the latter *has to* kill the Monarch; the Anarch, for his part, can do it but essentially he's more free, he isn't so automatically disposed towards the deed as his nihilist kinsman. The Anarch can also live life to the full, enjoying his god-given freedom. He's free and has always been it, he doesn't have to "fight for freedom" in the political sense.

More on the theme of anarchy in chapter thirty of this study. Otherwise, *Eumeswil* tells us of a future city under a military government, the patriarchal Condor having seized power in a coup

---

[41] Jünger, 1981, p 171, translated by the author

and ruling the city from his castle just outside town. In the city proper a clerical body of Magistrates rule, a governance with ideals of liberality, formality and propaganda while the Condor rules with ideals of authority and responsibility. The pattern from *Heliopolis* is repeated but with some variation, that of armed power with archaic, traditional foundations and modern, nihilistic power directed solely towards prosperity and safety. But here Jünger's enthusiasm even for traditional power is limited, the Condor essentially being yet another ruler in the succession of coups and counter-coups.

Still, Manuel Venator has chosen sides and he will stand and fall by the Condor. Manuel's father and brother side with the Magistrates. Thus, in this novelistic pattern, the narrator – Manuel – can elaborate on the power of the sword and the power of the pen, on military rule and the rule of mass democracy, and he can put himself in the equation too – "himself" as a figure that is in some way Jünger. In an existential authorship the author figure is always present and Jünger sometimes solves this elegantly, like here. Namely, Manuel Venator, as an historian, has access to the Luminary, a sort of glorified internet with sources to all times and all places. If you play it right, you can experience history more or less directly. And so Jünger places himself in these historic visions, like mentioning how he, as Manuel Venator playing on the Luminary archive of pictures and sceneries, marched along Unter den Linden under monarchist, dictatorial and democratic banners. It all results in a peculiar form of double exposure, having the Jünger figure in the form of the Kaiserstadt, Reichswehr and Nazi era soldier playing along in a fictional narrative.

NIGHTBAR

The narrator of *Eumeswil* alternates his duties between the university and the casbah, the seat of power. Here he tends the nightbar listening in on the governing clique's discussions in this post-war, post-debacle future. As such, *Eumeswil* is a rich novel, echoing Jünger's other utopian / dystopian novels. Hereby some topical subjects in *Eumeswil*, possibly relevant for current debates:

- Precious metals: "The powers that be always rob the common man of his gold." All throughout history those in power have diverted gold from the people, either by diminishing the gold content of coins or by issuing paper money. A common investing tip of the 2010s is, "buying gold as a hedge against a crashing dollar", and there's a rebellious trait to this, in the common man exchanging dollars for gold and storing it in his private cache. In discussing the role of gold in the economy Jünger was ahead of his times, stressing the everlasting quality of that yellow metal.
- Survivalism: what to do if there's an upheaval, an interregnum? The narrator concludes that the best is to furnish a dug-out in the woods to use as a safe haven. This is like a miniature of the mega-crisis some think we face today. "Stock up on food, water, ammunition...": we all read that on the internet today but Jünger was way ahead of these "preppers" too.
- Spiritual values: We can't do without myths, legends, dreams. Having food on the table isn't enough. Many prophets have said that throughout history so having Jünger propagating the same isn't original in itself. However, since no one listened last time it has to be said again and again.

VENTURE OUT

At the end of *On the Marble Cliffs* the narrator and his brother leave the burning Marina and seek a haven in Burgundy. At the end of *Heliopolis* Lucius de Geer leaves the city to roam the spatial vistas. And at the end of *Eumeswil* Manuel Venator leaves the city to accompany the Condor on a hunting expedition. They are set to explore the Woods to the south, enigmatic hunting grounds transformed by the cataclysmic events of the recent past. They are setting off into Myth itself, possibly even encountering Leviathan, the bird Roc, the Chimera and the Unicorn. All throughout the novel these woods have been mentioned, a place of dreams and astral reality, in contrast to the Catacombs beneath the city, vaults and chambers storing data and technical information in a nihilistic way.

Manuel Venator leaves the city with the hunting expedition of the Condor, joining him, his chief of staff Domo and his personal physician Attila. The visions of the Woods are rather mind-blowing; as always Jünger's style is lucid and transparent but with the themes of expressing the reality of dream and myth it can get rather "spaced out", in a sort of magical realism. Attila, sitting in the night bar and speaking of his private experiences in the Woods, transcends the *Eumeswil* narrative to sublime levels, a transformational vision of genetic experiments, mutations in the wake of the Bomb and mythical revelations:

> The road back from the tree of knowledge to the tree of life is creepy. But there was no way of going back into the desert lying behind me. There, death was certain. Despite the dangers I must cross the Woods to reach the sea. [In the forests he sees snakes, which seemed to be] neither gliding nor flying; flaps of the skin fluttered. Apparently, this demonstrated the transition from the snake to the dragon. The snakes merged with the trunks that they embraced. Ruddy resin or resinous blood trickled from the cracks their claws had ripped up in the bark. I didn't miss my binoculars; every scale was engraved in me. [A certain tree has a kind of winged fruits leaving the branches,] the fruits not sliding to the ground but flapping. A swarm of miniature bats celebrated its wedding around the trunk. Here you could take root and become a tree. In a glade a ray of sunshine fell on a figure with a ram's head. The creature supported his left hand on a lamb with a human face. Both were dissolved in light, as if the vision was too strong.[42]

GLASS BEES

Any Jünger book can be an alluring read, giving you succinct reflections on Tradition, history, modern times and all. But if I should stay on topic – SF novels – there is another such by Jünger to highlight, one from 1957, once translated into English (all of the above novels except *Heliopolis* are translated): *The Glass Bees*. Artistically this

---

[42] Jünger 1981, p 368-369, translated by the author

is hardly a novel at all, it's merely "the typical Jünger narrator" telling you of this and that. Practically nothing tangible happens in the form of scenes and action. That said, in dribs and drabs this novel tells a rather fascinating story of a cavalry man enjoying a model pre-war, Victorian existence of safety and predictability. Then the World War breaks out, here telescoping the events of WWI and WWII by having the cavalry men dismount and become armored troops. Then the post war world ensues, a world of technical marvels, symbolized by the industrialist Zapparoni, a sort of combined Walt Disney, Howard Hughes and Edison: a technical genius enchanting the world with FX films and miniature robots.

These robots are the glass bees of the title. They come to symbolize the hurtful nature of technology, these glass bees when sucking nectar actually killing the flowers in contrast to the operation of live bees. Here we can compare the Pater Foelix figure from Heliopolis and his praise of bees. As a novel *The Glass Bees* is a bit faulty. Also, it was supposed to be a series but only came to this one part. But the text, as it stands, still has a lot of clever reflections on the titanic nature of technology.

Titanic nature: in his late diary (*Siebzig verweht*, 1965-1996) Jünger often reflected on how the 20th century seemed to be ruled by Titans, the ancient elemental gods bent on work and war, blind to the charms of wine and song that the Olympian gods enjoyed. As for gods Jünger prophesied that in the 21st century the gods would return – higher gods, gods of spiritual splendor and might. Will this be then? I'd say, it's up to us, as with acknowledging the way to space by inner space, as I told of above. If we raise ourselves spiritually, making ourselves worthy of meeting the gods, then they will return: "Build a temple and the gods will come".

Thus: first "make your body into a temple and your heart into an altar". When this spreads, when sufficiently many people are spiritually evolved and harmonious, the gods might come. But only then. Conversely, it won't do looking at the skies with a worried mind, waiting for the gods to arrive and fix things.

JÜNGER LIFE

I've written a biography on Ernst Jünger, entitled *Ernst Jünger – A Portrait* (2014). In that book I deliberate further on the Jünger fiction, from aspects of spirituality, artistry and Jüngerian specificity. I also give a rather thorough account of Jünger's life, his essays and his role as a nationalist, esoteric teacher and diarist. Below I'll give you a shorter bio, focusing on the tangible events of Jünger's life.

Ernst Jünger lived an eventful life. Moreover, he lived a long life. He was 102 years old when he died. He was throughout his career the subject of controversy, from his time as a nationalist in the 1920s, as part of the opposition against Hitler in 1944 as well as a conservative author in the postwar period. True, he constantly issued books and many appreciated him. But just as many considered him to be a relic from the empire and the Nazi era which ought to be silenced.

Ernst Jünger was born March 29, 1895 in Heidelberg, Baden-Wurtemberg, the German Empire. His father was a chemist and pharmacist named Ernst Georg Jünger. The mother's name was Catherine, called Lily.

Ernst grew up in the Lower Saxon city of Rehburg. Early on he began to collect beetles and butterflies, a hobby he would keep for life. He read adventure books and joined *Die Vandervögel*, a German scouting movement. In 1911 in their journal he published a poem called "Unser Leben" (Our Life). This was the first text he published, telling about the healthy life of this movement with hikes, campfires and songs.

Jünger was an adventurous lad. For example, in the fall of 1913, he escaped from home to join the French Foreign Legion. He succeeded and came to a camp in North Africa. But life there was hardly adventurous. Finally, through his father's efforts, he managed to be free.

When Jünger was in secondary school First World War broke out, in the autumn of 1914. Germany simultaneously attacked France in the west and Russia in the east. Thus, it was also at war with England, which was allied with these powers. Jünger at once volunteered. After a simplified matriculation he ended up in the 73rd

Hanoverian Infantry Regiment. When he came to the Western Front at the end of 1914 there was a lull. He experienced the everyday of the ranker with guard mount, digging trenches and the like. During his baptism of fire at Les Éparges in Lorraine, he was wounded. At home, on convalescent leave, his father advised him to apply for officer training. In November 1915 Jünger graduated as Second Lieutenant.

During 1916-1917 Jünger was in the line of fire pretty much. He was wounded a couple of times, he was promoted First Lieutenant and he became a company commander. The main event of 1918 was that the German General Staff began planning a major offensive. This they could do because they had closed the Eastern Front in 1917 by knocking out Russia from the war. Jünger's company would take the lead during the spring offensive. It all began on March 21. The prep fire was intense. The English lines were set on fire and burned for several hours. When Jünger and the shock infantry were sent forward they took trench after trench, well depicted at the end of *Storm of Steel*, its *sine qua non* chapter entitled "The Great Battle".

After a few days was reached the climax of the attack. Englishmen, Americans and Frenchmen held their positions. The Germans had to retreat. Jünger participated in several battles during the summer. Finally, he was wounded and sent back. When he in November 1918 was in hospital in Hannover, he learned that the war was over. Germany had surrendered to France, England and the US. In connection with this, the Emperor abdicated and Germany became a republic. It was called the "Weimar Republic" because the capital for a few years was located in the city of Weimar in Thuringia. On a personal level Jünger could rejoice in the fact that he in September 1918 received the finest award of the German empire, *Pour le Mérite*.

END OF WAR

The period just after the war Jünger lived in Hanover. In the wake of his recent war wounds he experimented with drugs to ease the pain. He chose opium drops. Later in life he took drugs like chloroform and LSD but it was only for experimental purposes (*q.v. Annäherungen:*

Drogen und Rausch, 1970). As for his career Jünger's regiment had been decommissioned in 1918 and he was relegated to the Army reserve. In 1919 he got a permanent job at the 16th Hanoverian Infantry Regiment. It was part of the newly established *Reichswehr,* the 100,000-man army that Germany was allowed to have after the war. The neighboring countries France and Poland had significantly larger armies. In addition, it was decided that Germany would pay a huge reparation to the Western powers. The Nazis would later come to play on the discontent with these conditions.

The service in the *Reichswehr* eventually brought Jünger to Berlin where he took part in writing a new set of infantry regulations. Later, he received permission to edit his diary from the war, doing it during his regular working hours. The result became the front memoir *Storm of Steel* that was released on his own label Gibraltar. Later the same year, in 1920, a regular publisher took on the book and in time it became a classic, this no-nonsense book of trench warfare by a western samurai.

Jünger was unhappy in the peacetime army. Also, the three years when he studied zoology, geology, biology and philosophy in Leipzig was something of a dead end. However, his books on war were selling rather well so in May 1926, he interrupted his studies without graduating and became a freelance writer. Apart from writing war books (like *Der Kampf als inneres Erlebnis, Feuer und Blut* and *Copse 125*) he contributed to nationalistic papers like *Die Kommenden* and *Stalhelm.* He was a radical conservative who wanted to abolish the Treaty of Versailles and replace democracy with a military-style leadership.

MARRIAGE

In 1925 Jünger married Gretha von Jeinesen. The next year they had a son, Ernst, called Ernstel ("Little Ernst"). The same year, 1926, Jünger had planned to meet Adolf Hitler. But Hitler had to cancel. He was at this time to build up his Nazi party again, it having virtually collapsed after Hitler received a one-year prison sentence for the Beer Hall coup in Munich in 1923. Despite some differences of opinion Jünger supported Hitler at that time, indeed, even after the Nazi takeover in 1933 and some of what followed. It was above all the resistance against the Treaty of Versailles that united them. Hitler for his part admired Jünger, this is testified; *Storm of Steel* made an impression on him, as the front-veteran he himself was. Even towards the end of the Second World War, when Jünger was persecuted by his connection to the July 20, 1944 plot, Hitler ordered his Culture Minister Goebbels to let Jünger be.

Jünger in those years wrote the book *Der Arbeiter* (1932). It was about the world being reshaped into an industrial landscape, and how the entire society is directed to produce and consume. It's a cold world, free from the budding forces of life. But Jünger felt that this was his most important book, seen as a depiction of modernization and industrialization. Jünger also began his travels at this time. It was done by trips to Dalmatia, Italy, Spain, the Balearic Islands and France; apparently, southern climes attracted him. An interesting book by Jünger from this period is *The Adventurous Heart* (1929; version 2, 1938). With its diary entries, nature observations, dreams and reflections, and everything in between, it's a book difficult to classify. Like Jünger himself. *The Adventurous Heart* even contains some short stories of a dreamy nature. The SF reader eager for some magical realism, unorthodox fantasy and speculative musings should look up this book, newly issued in English by Telos Press (2012).

PRE-WAR

In 1927, and again in 1933, Jünger was offered a Nazi parliamentary mandate. He declined. The latter year he also refused to enter the newly formed Goebbelsian German Academy, *Deutsche Akademie der Dichtung*. The secret police plagued Jünger at this time, because of his friendship with the anarchist Erich Mühsam and because of his contact with the National Revolutionary Ernst Niekisch. The police wanted to find suspicious papers about them in Jünger's home.

To avoid more acute searches Jünger moved south. The years 1936-39 the Jünger family lived in Überlingen on Lake Constance. Lake Constance (Ger. *Bodensee*) is Germany's largest lake, bordering both Switzerland and Austria, a lake giving impetus to the Grand Marina where *On the Marble Cliffs* (1939) takes place.

In the spring of 1939, the Jünger family moved to Kirchhorst, a community north-east of Hanover. Both Jünger and his wife had their roots there in Lower Saxony. An old rectory was purchased where the family remained during the war. In July of the same year Jünger finished writing *On the Marble Cliffs*, how an idyll is invaded by the forces of nihilism. In September World War II broke out. Jünger as a Lieutenant in the reserve was called up but the service at the Western Front wasn't so burdensome. So while being deployed at the *Westwall* he could sit down and edit the novel. The book came out later in the autumn on Hanseatische Verlagsanstalt and sold rather well. It became a kind of code word among people who were against the Hitler regime. Goebbels' Ministry of Culture had indeed approved the book and it remained in circulation but influential voices meant that it should be withdrawn.

Specifically, Jünger was called up on August 26, 1939. He had been in the Army reserve since his dismissal from service in 1923. Now he was promoted Captain. Then war broke out with the German attack on Poland on September 1, 1939. Germany attacked and overpowered Poland in just over a month-long campaign. Soviet Russia, having entered a treaty with Germany, invaded and took over eastern Poland. Then there was a lull in the war. Germany had mobilized even along its border with France and the Benelux countries but nothing happened here for a while. Jünger was stationed on this front, the German bank of the Rhine.

FRANCE

The German attack on France and the Benelux countries began May 10, 1940. Shortly a breakthrough was effected on the Meuse River, in the towns of Sedan, Monthermé and Dinant. Jünger's company advanced in the queue and cleaned up. It wasn't much in the way of actual combat. The unit marched in the wake of the armored spearheads and most of the resistance was broken when they arrived. In the summer, France surrendered. A year later Jünger was transferred from field duty to staff duty. By June 1941 he was commanded to the military governor's staff in Paris, located in various luxury hotels.

In the Paris HQ Jünger worked under Hans Speidel, the role model for *Der Chef* in *Heliopolis*, commander of the army rivaling the reign of the nihilistic Central Department. Among other things, Speidel had Jünger work with planning for *Unternehmen Seelöwe*, Operation Sea Lion, the invasion of England that never came to pass. Jünger remained stationed in the Paris HQ during all of the occupation, until August 1944. His was an unusual army career. The natural thing was to let staff services alternate with commissions to the front, in Russia or in North Africa. But Jünger was protected by his chief, the military governor Karl-Heinrich von Stülpnagel.

In 1944 Jünger worked privately on a peace pamphlet, a call for peace to the world's youth. The book was published in 1946 in Holland as *Der Friede*. Before this it had led an adventurous life. During the war in Nazi Germany, it was to say the least forbidden to preach peace. The pamphlet circulated in manuscript form and Rommel himself thought that it could be used as a *pronunciamento* after an attack against Hitler.

As a captain in the army of occupation Jünger met the rich and famous, people of the cultural elite like film and theater director Sacha Guitry and the authors Marcel Johandeau, Jean Cocteau, Paul Léautaud and Céline. Jünger briefly knew about the plans to assassinate Hitler but he wasn't involved too deep. Also, on the day of the event, July 20, he was off duty. Then came the Allied breakout from the Normandy beachhead. Jünger and the Army HQ left before Paris fell on August 25. Next Jünger was dismissed from the army, having to serve in the Home Guard.

ERNSTEL

Earlier in 1944 Jünger's eldest son, Ernstel, had been arrested for having formed a resistance group against the Nazi regime. Ernstel had his penalty converted to army duty and was sent to the Italian front. There, he fell as a *panzer* grenadier in November 1944. It was symbolically on the marble cliffs, in the quarry Massa at the Carrara marble mountains, Tuscany.

As Home Guard officer Jünger ordered his unit to surrender to the Americans. It was pointless to fight with old men and boys against armored spearheads. The Yanks did arrive in April and so a time of tangible occupation followed. An American unit settled down and formed a motley camp on the Kirchhorst parsonage. When they had left Jünger could sum it all up with: "Here people have passed" (war diary, April 13, 1945). This can be seen as finding that the Yanks behaved properly. Some abuse occurred but it was basically an ordered occupation. Worse, it would have been if you lived in East Germany and experienced a Soviet Russian liberation.

Nazi Germany being defeated called for a semi-judicial review of Nazism. For instance, any person being suspect of anything politically incriminating could be ideologically acquitted, being "denazified". Jünger however refused to denazified. The reason he gave was that he had never been a Nazi.

This resulted in Jünger being left out in the cold. Added to this was that during the war he wrote his peace pamphlet, *Der Friede*, which circulated as a manuscript. Reportedly the allied rulers were reached by a rumor that the Nazis liked its contents. Thus a press campaign started against Jünger. This contributed to a publication ban for him, effective until 1949.

The Jünger family now moved to southern Germany, to the city of Ravensburg, Swabia where they lived 1948-50. The latter year Jünger moved to his last place of residence, the village Wilflingen at the foot of the Swabian Alps on the border to Switzerland. The home became the forester mansion to the family von Stauffenberg's Castle. Before the war, in *On the Marble Cliffs*, Jünger had portrayed a Claus von Stauffenberg-type figure in prince Sunmyra.

When the publishing ban lifted Jünger could issue books like *Heliopolis*, his war diary and travel books and essays. In postwar Germany he became something of a conservative icon but the Left hated him. In France, his popularity grew slightly in the 80s. In 1981 the English writer Bruce Chatwin had a relatively appreciative article about Jünger in the *New York Review of Books*. As for Jünger's life story proper he became a widower in 1960 when Gretha died. Later he married the editor Liselotte Lohrer. In 1982 he received the Goethe Prize, Germany's finest literary award.

On the official side Jünger participated in the 1984 German-French reconciliation ceremony at Verdun. The following year, President Mitterrand visited him in Wilflingen. The reason for the visit was Jünger 90th birthday.

In January, 1988, for that matter, Jünger and German *Reichskanzler* Helmuth Kohl went to Paris. They would attend the celebration of the French-German friendship pact, established in 1948. Finally, Jünger died on February 17, 1998, 102 years old. The funeral was attended by a thousand people and five generals of the German *Bundeswehr*.

LITERATURE

- *Storm of Steel* (1920)
- *The Adventurous Heart* (1938)
- *On the Marble Cliffs* (1939)
- *Heliopolis* (1949)
- *The Glass Bees* (1957)
- *Eumeswil* (1977)

8. FILIPPO TOMMASO MARINETTI

WHERE DID SCIENCE FICTION as a self-conscious genre take off? In America in the late 1920s. What were its icons? Machines, techno cities and flying vessels. Where had these things been worshiped before? In Italy, by the Futurist movement. The man who created Futurism was Filippo Tommaso Marinetti (1876-1944). He later became a co-founder of Fascism. He was rather anti-tradition but he was a speculative mind, a right-winger concocting his special brew of SF.

THE MAN

Futurism is a mix of several things: skyscrapers, abstract paintings, concrete poetry and techno-heroic visions. The futurists despised traditional art but worshiped airplanes, cars and war. As for futurist art per se, it may not always have succeeded. "Futurist painting was something of a grand failure", Folke Edwards said in 1972. But futurist art was fresh and vital; indeed, it was never boring. Futurism and its creator, Filippo Tommaso Marinetti, was partly an art movement, partly a literary movement. Marinetti was a poet preaching the creed of futurism, bringing artists along. And in his Futurist Manifesto from 1909 he painted a stylish science fictional painting of techno-heroic qualities. More on this later. First a bio of Marinetti.

Filippo Tommaso Marinetti was born in 1876 in Alexandria, Egypt, of Italian parents. He acquired higher education in Paris and Pavia, graduating as a lawyer in 1894. He came to work as a poet, playwright, entertainer and war correspondent.

When Marinetti wrote his futurist manifesto in 1909 he lived in Milan. In 1910 he published the novel *Mafarka il futurista*. It was accused of obscenity, then acquitted. The same year Matinetti met the painters Umberto Boccioni, Carlo Carrà and Luigi Russolo, all becoming co-workers on the futurist venture, stared by Marinetti having published his futurist manifesto in the French Newspaper *Le Figaro* in 1909, on the first page and everything. At that time, when print media was big, such things made an impression. Artistically speaking futurism became something of a movement, not only in Italy but also in continental Europe. Among other things seeds were sown in England.

In 1911 Marinetti was a war correspondent in the Italo-Turkish War. For example, he reported from the Battle of Tripoli. When World War I broke out in 1914 Italy wasn't involved, but Marinetti urged that Italy would go to war against Austria, which Italy formally was allied to at the time. Marinetti wanted to regain some Italian lands to the east. In 1915, when his country finally went to war with France, England and Russia against Germany-Austria, Marinetti enrolled as a volunteer in the Lombard cycle battalion. This was in July.

Having participated in the battles at Trentino, Marinetti got wounded. The rest of the war he seems to have continued with his futuristic agitation. After losing the battle of Caporetto in 1917 the general Italian enthusiasm for the war was at a nadir. When the war ended the next autumn Italy was in social and political chaos. The development can be described as follows: The Communists tried to seize power but the Fascists prevented it.

In 1923 Marinetti married Benedetta Cappa (1897-1977). She was also an artist. And as you can see she was about 20 years younger than her husband. They eventually had three daughters. This might be interesting for those who believe that Marinetti was a misogynist. Indeed, in the futurist manifesto he advocated "contempt for women" as a noble motivation. However, what he was against was the rather traditional, passive female, it's been said. Marinetti was complex: for example, he was an atheist, but later on he was to some extent reconciled with the church, and his attitude towards Tradition in general may be seen in his relationship to Fascism.

DEGENERATE ART

Marinetti had radical political views. In 1918 he founded a futurist political party. Its ideas were socialist, however without the element of class struggle (without Marxism). The platform sported ideas such as tear down the old, build up an industrial state, implement social legislation. It was like the Labor Party or Scandinavian Social Democracy, but with humor: for example, he wanted to reduce the minimum age for members of parliament from 22 to 12.

His futurist party having left no mark Marinetti next joined the Fascist Party; indeed, he co-wrote its first manifesto of 1919. The following year he left the party, it having become too reactionary he thought. But he continued to be close to the regime, for better or worse. He could, for example, in 1938 persuade Mussolini to refuse the Italian entry for the Nazi exhibition of degenerate art. Futurist art was considred degenerate by the Nazis.

Mussolini for his part recruited quite a few artists like Marinetti for the Fascist cause, including many pictorial artists of the advanced, abstract kind. Mussolini as a person probably was less artistically inclined than Hitler, but as a government head he rallied his country's artists on a much broader front than Hitler. This is widely acknowledged. All forms of modern art were considered degenerate in the Third Reich. One might say: The Nazi regime was formally-industrially bent on modernization, employing new technology and new means of construction, but in Nazi *beaux arts* this wasn't reflected at all. Archaic and ancient styles were emphasized in sculpture, painting and architecture, like houses built in medieval style (while at the same time the construction method was thoroughly modern). Mussolini's Italy on the other hand had many futurists and modernists aboard, artists given a freer reign than in Germany at the time.

Marinetti eventually moved from Milan to Rome to be closer to the regime. He soon became a war correspondent again, particularly on the Eastern Front during World War II. He then moved further north as a supporter of Mussolini's Salo Republic. He died of a heart attack in 1944 while he was editing a collection of poems celebrating the attack divers of the *Decima Flottiglia MAS*.

PAINTING

As for futurism it was rather prominent in painting, the visual art being the most striking, and most enduring manifestation of it. True, futurism also occupied itself with stage performances, concrete poetry, noise music and other things, but they are of mere historical interest and won't be treated here. In his later manifesto writings (he wrote several) Marinetti had the painters Carrà, Boccioni and Russolo as co-workers, plus the architect Antonio Sant'Elia. All seem to have been living in Milan and they are the mainstay of futurism – they, along with the literary landmark in the form of the 1909 manifesto. The manifesto will be treated at the end of this chapter.

In Italy many futuristic works were painted in 1910-1914. This was the heroic phase. The paintings wanted to capture movement, abstractly and without disturbing people in the picture. To say, like Folke Edwards (see preamble), that futurism failed in its ambition is a bit bold. But he's on the trail of something, meaning that the painters themselves admitted that they rarely found the successful expression of their goals, like the ambition of *an in itself static image capturing motion*. But today we have such things as cartoons, in which it's quite easy to give the impression of motion in formally stationary images (with things such as motion lines, action lines or speed lines). The reading itself of the comic, the movement through successive series of frames, gives the impression of motion. And in photography such elements as a blurred background to a vehicle reasonably well captures the essence of movement, making it look as if the vehicle's moving though the photo itself is stationary. I'd say that futurism gave the impetus to such things. It's been called "trickle-down modernism", like the terse, experimental prose of Gertrude Stein leading to Dashiell Hammetts hardboiled detective prose. Then it isn't so far-fetched to see futurist painting affecting car commercials and adventure comics.

Futurist paintings are experiments that sometimes are successful, sometimes not. It's true that the images can be difficult to understand, perhaps missing something, but there is still a sense of life in the works. They say that art can be anything except boring, and boring the futuristic visual arts certainly are not. It's true that these images are a bit messy, "the movement is intense at the expense of substance" as Jünger said in a different context. And of course, personally I'm more into the artwork that the mentioned Carrà painted later; he started painting tranquil motives rooted in Tradition, precisely what the Futurists wanted to smash.

SANT'ELIA

The futurists were against Tradition, and Tradition is something that I espouse as a radical conservative, not least in this study. Marinetti said: down with museums and academies...! Italy shouldn't be a vacation colony for English misses and German professors...! Venice's canals should be filled and the paintings of Venice masters sold to fund the rearmament of Italy...! You could say: Marinetti revolted against a stagnant, stifling Tradition. He was a nihilist and an atheist but he had more strings than that to his bow. He revitalized the Italian art scene. And the just mentioned Carrà who originally was a futurist, the Carrà who Marinetti inspired with his manifesto, later became an interesting metaphysical painter. He and Giorgio de Chirico could (1) paint so you could see what it represented (2) still gave the image mystery and depth. de Chirico and Carrà are firmly rooted in Italian art history. In particular, the former painted abandoned cities with colonnades, piazzas and palaces. And I personally think this is a more interesting school of painting than the futurist alarm.

So futurist visual art isn't always my favorite art. But it was as I said vital: it shifted the focus from solidified academicia and a yearning museum cult to innovation. It allowed art to also occupy itself with factories, cars and airplanes. This was taboo before 1909. Art meant painting portraits and landscapes. Nothing more. Well possibly still lives.

True, there were at the same time innovative ideas around from men like George Braque and Pablo Picasso (cubism), but putting technology at the core of artistic expression was Marinetti's original idea. He gave technology artistic and formal status. He gave technology artistic right of domicile. And as for a striking, easily accessible side of it – in the form of architecture – there was in Europe already applied art movements and architects that welcomed new technology into forming a functional style (Adolf Loos, Otto Wagner). But the Italian Antonio Sant'Elia (1888-1916) who became a futurist took it one step further.

It's true that Sant'Elia's towers often resemble house blocks that we in Sweden have seen enough of, built in the 1960s and 1970s: sterile towers without surrounding greenery. Freestanding towers are by nature misanthropic with, among other things, the great vertical bodies creating unpleasant downward winds. Systems with low houses create a better shelter in this respect. A pleasant micro climate is for example generated by quadrangle courtyards.

Thus it is. But Sant'Elia is still worth his salt. As in his sketch of a power station, with chimneys and pylons in classical style: this to me is the symbol of the urge to give artistic shape to power plants and factories. This we actually do in the West: even factories and hydroelectric plants are designed and given a special external form, an aesthetically pleasing shape. It certainly isn't just rows of turbines and rows of windows, laid out according to the requirements of necessity. Aesthetics is often aboard these functional projects and Sant'Elia to me personifies this.

Furthermore, when you mention *futurism* and *futuristic* Sant'Elia's drawings mostly come to mind. His images are relatable. He has given a lot of impetus to the archetypal SF city *à la* the film *Metropolis*. The concept of "the city as a machine" isn't humane, it shouldn't be realized straight off, but it has its allure as a vision and a symbol. That is, you can't just stamp "fascism" on Sant'Elias drawings and think this solves it all. Also, the American SF artist Frank Paul was reportedly inspired by Sant'Elia's drawings for his own techno city visions, displayed on the covers of *Amazing Stories*. According to Lundwall (1981) Paul plagiarized Sant'Elia's futurist cityscapes. More on Paul in chapter fourteen.

SEVERINI

If you should mention a futurist work that really stands out, you may pick Gino Severini's *Armoured Trains in Action* from 1915. It's very stylized, with blue-gray soldiers and cannons firing from an armored train, the soldiers losing their human shape and morphing into the technological form of it all, underlined by the square forms. At the same time the picture is softened with the appearance of circular smoke clouds and greenery on the flanks.

The inspiration for this picture was Marinetti. Now, I know that you shouldn't glorify war. Marinetti did, however: "We salute the world's only hygiene, war," he wrote in the manifesto of 1909. I for one don't salute war *per se*. As a Swede, at the same time I embrace the fact that Sweden historically has been prepared to defend itself (and it's well known that it's the small state that must choose war, the conqueror choosing to present himself as a "liberator"). In the 100 years between 1890 and 1990 Sweden was prepared to go to war to defend itself. I myself was a soldier in the Swedish Army, being prepared to defend the country with weapon in hand.

Personally I don't eulogize war as an adventure. To me as a Swede "war" is equivalent to armed defense, which I support. That said, artists must also be allowed to depict war. And as for Marinetti, in 1914 he said this to the currently Paris residing Severini: "Try to live the war in pictures, studying it in all its wonderful mechanical forms (military trains, fortifications, wounded men, ambulances, hospitals, parades, etc." I quote this after Humpreys.[43] And Humphreys continues:

> Severini followed Marinetti's advice and although he hardly was a belligerent war enthusiast, he produced a series of images of

---

[43] p 65, my translation

armored trains and hospital trains on their way through Paris. His intention was to create what he called "war symbols".[44]

Severini (1883-1966) captured the war in emblems and symbols, distinct hieroglyphs of the ongoing European struggle. So this art was a kind of symbolism, and symbolism as an art form Marinetti didn't really like. He envisioned a completely abstract art where Motion, Speed and Power in themselves would be expressed. But Severini's war images may be said to exist in the intersection of a new art where previously neglected subjects such as technology and violence became parts of a new synthesis. You can also note how Severini in his paintings inserts people, which seldom occurred in futurism pictures.

War having begun in 1914 of course led to artists beginning to portray it, with or without futurism in their luggage. But with impulses from futurists and others (like Wyndham Lewis in England, partly inspired by futurism) artists began to see things in a new way, refining the forms to constitute works of timeless beauty.

FUTURISMS

According to the history books "futurism" can mean much. It can be pre-war poets standing on stage in ridiculous costumes reading incomprehensible poems. And it may be the futile attempt of capturing how a person moves in a statuette. And it can be chaotic, messy paintings. And it can be an architectural sketch depicting a railway station with an airport on the roof.

As I said futurism was never dull. It was also contrary to much of what I hold as essential; it was anti-spiritual, anti-tradition and anti-individual. The gist of futurism can be expressed as the desire to go from man to nature, from a humanistic art to a scientific art. This I deem stillborn. And in poetic terms, I think that Marinetti's later writing experiments (such as dissolved syntax, pre-Dadaism with text freely flying over the side) was a dead end. Then it was better to, like T. S. Eliot and Ezra Pound, recognize Tradition but express it in new

---

[44] Humphreys, ibid.

forms. Eliot and Pound were a kind of *archeofuturists:* well-grounded in the history of literature from antiquity onwards, at the same time intent on countering the romantic rhetoric and artificially polished language.

Futurism was nihilist. But it was still commendable. As hinted, Italy's artistic and cultural life in the beginning of the century had atrophied. Italy was being turned into a museum, a tourist environment for upper-class Europeans, old ladies and snobs who were expected to say oooh and aaah when seeing the past masterpieces of Florence, Rome and Venice.

Marinetti's demand to wipe out all of this, all the Italian art of the Roman Empire, the Middle Ages through the Renaissance and Romanticism, was excessive. But as a kick in the butt to contemporaries his manifestos, his *soirées* and his preachments were necessary. Tradition namely could survive after this, revitalized. As in Italian art during and after the First World War. A certain Julius Evola indeed coined his traditionalist credo under the pressure of modernism, of futurism and dada, art forms that he himself was occupied with for a while. And the art world in Europe flourished thanks to Marinetti stressing the heroic, pictorial qualities of technology.

Now, at the beginning of the century there already was an avant-garde, such as Picasso and the Cubists. But Marinetti had more energy and he traveled and preached eloquently for his cause. He didn't just say, "paint so and not so"; he was a poet and made the events into artworks in themselves. For example, he visited England in 1910 and Russia in January 1914. In addition, he published his manifesto in the Paris newspaper *Le Figaro* in 1909; he wrote the manifesto in French, having studied at the University of Paris as a young man and being well versed in French culture.

Marinetti's ideas were received in different ways. The Englishmen where among Lewis and the expatriate American Ezra Pound were hostile on the surface, but probably these "vorticists" adopted parts of the message. Wyndham Lewis and his group Art Center are said to have stood in contrast to the Bloomsbury Group of *salon* Marxists, with the artist group Omega Workshops, and that for one was a good thing. Furthermore, the Russians tended to interpret Marinetti's ideas in their own way. A number of things to them became futurism, like the silliness and the performance element. Still, we also had Russians like Malevich, Kandinsky, Mayakovsky, Tatlin and other venerable artists, more or less inspired by futurism. Together they created vital art that (after the revolution) would drag the Republic out of the mire.

MYTHOLOGY

An interesting aspect of Marinetti is that he hailed technology on mythological grounds. He said that in terms of the myth now having been *overcome*, but you might as well say *confirmed*. In his 1909 manifesto he said that we will see centaurs and angels:

> We're ascending, I say, we're setting off, my friends! We travel! Finally, we have overcome mythology and the mythic ideal has found its match. We witness the birth of the centaur and we shall soon see the first angels fly![45]

With that, I think Marinetti meant something very concrete, giving us the image that a man in a car is like a centaur, the mythical being who is a man's torso on a horse. The man-in-the car, then, is a new (or old-new, or archeofuturistic) creature, partly anthropoid but in that case a stronger anthropoid. A man in a car doesn't just place himself in a carriage to be carried off; he more or less *assumes* the vehicle and controls it as a manifestation of his will. This is the centaurian element Marinetti wanted to capture in his wording. And the angels can be seen as men in the aircraft. It's an apt image: again, it's not just people sitting in sky chariots and allowing themselves to be transported here and there, it's a consciously controllable journey in a new way, a new design of life. Pilots aren't supermen but men in a new mode.

I appreciate this techno heroism of Marinetti's first manifesto. The same trait is to be seen in other texts of his. In describing the music of tomorrow Marinetti for example meant that it would express "nature's new metamorphoses" as they were shown by science and by,

---

[45] All translations from the 1909 manifesto in this chapter are by the author.

the musical soul of the masses, the big factories, trains, Atlantic steamers, armored boats, automobiles and airplanes. Finally, add to these theme songs for the musical poem the glorification of the Machine and the victorious rule of Electricity.[46]

And when Marinetti wanted to create a new poetry, freed from traditional typography, the new typography would go in "all speeds, those of the stars, the clouds, the aeroplanes, the trains, the waves, the explosions, the bubbles in the sea foam, the molecules and atoms."[47]

Marinetti elevates technology into poetry. In the 1909 manifesto he does so eloquently, maybe going a bit too far stylistically, but who am I to complain about this Faustian Song of Songs. He talks about everything futurism wants to glorify, such as "... the vibrant night time heat from the shipyards and factories, inflamed by violent electric moons; the gluttonous railway stations devouring smoking serpents; industries that are suspended from the clouds by the twisted threads of smoke; bridges like mighty athletes descending upon the rivers, flashing in the sun like knives; adventurous steamers scenting the horizon; broad-chested locomotives stomping on the rails like enormous steel horses with long tubes for bridle, and the gliding flight of aircraft, whose propellers sound like banners in the wind and the applause of an enthusiastic crowd."[48]

This isn't just a poet playing with words. It's the description of a new lifestyle, since seen by many others. In the modern era "technological constructs took the place of revelation", Alexander Dugin for example writes in *The Fourth Political Theory* (2012). And Arthur C. Clarke's saying, "any sufficiently advanced technology is indistinguishable from magic", is in the same spirit. All this can be a fruitful vein to explore. Technology certainly is more than simple objects. That is, motorism and titanic technique certainly needs to be checked by human forces, however, human interaction with technology can't simply be branded as unhealthy. As Spengler said, the mere movement pattern of predator is a form of technique; the

---

[46] Quoted after Edwards, 1972, p 84
[47] Ibid., p 81
[48] After Edwards, 1987

animal uses this way and that way to proceed through the landscape. All beings are involved in technology, even man living in God's free nature. And today we interact with computers, raising ourselves mentally online.

Properly used technology can be liberating. This, you might say, is what futurism learned. It's the vein Marinetti began to explore and one that we still, today, can explore and generate wealth from.

9. ARTHUR C. CLARKE

ARTHUR CHARLES CLARKE (1917-2008) may have been an orderly, "Victorian" author in that there's no emotion, no color, just constructs of engineering and technology playing the lead. In an artistic sense Clarke these days may not set my soul on fire. But there was a peculiar zest to his narratives and symbolically his stories of space travel are rather unique.

SINGLE TRAVELER

There isn't *one* way of going to space. There isn't one way of conducting a space journey.

Consider Robert Heinlein. His space travels were as a rule *communal* affairs: big ships, large crews. Further, it was about venturing out from Earth, seeing adventure, seeing the worlds, and then returning to Earth (*q.v. Methuselah's Children, Time for the Stars, Citizen of the Galaxy*).

Now consider Arthur C. Clarke. His typical space trips had *one* participant (*A Meeting with Medusa, Against the Fall of Night*, last part of *2001*), a single traveler going out into the unknown, challenging, as it were, the whole cosmos.

Clarke was a slightly unrefined author. A lot of his fiction are safe musings on technology and space exploration. But often enough he stepped out of his comfort zone and gave us deathless epics of space, time and man. In about a handful of his novels he "boldly goes where no man has gone before", seeking an answer to man's place in the universe in a time when man had only begun to master space travel.

Clarke's debut novel was *Against the Fall of Night*. Despite a somewhat over-elaborate background the narrative style is very distinct and alluring, telling about a future city and a man, Alvin of Loronei, questioning his utopian everyday and seeking answers to Life, Universe and Everything. He eventually finds a buried spaceship, a remnant from man's space-faring days, and with this makes a journey into space. He goes alone, only accompanied by two unobtrusive robots. It's about going Beyond the Beyond, a Faustian hero out on his own, seeking an answer that no one else dares find.

It's a quiet sort of heroism, a Columbian-quietist journey of the space age. Finally, the ship arrives at a planet in the center of the galaxy. The robot ship steers to a landing next to a column of snow-white rock, twenty times as high as a human being, standing in a circle of metal rising over the surrounding plain. This unadorned pillar had once been the zero point for all astronomical measures by the culture in question, the author tells us.

Such a detail is rather Clarksian, maybe even typical of the best SF: to have something relatable in the midst of all the marvels. The novel in question tells of many more things but as intimated, it's very charming and to the point and with a stupendous background of millennium having passed, of man having both conquered and retreated from space when the story begins. It also has a needless intro, a text supposed to be "arresting, sublime, atmospheric" that comes through as rather incomprehensible. However, you can write this up on the beginners account. In this novel Clarke tried his way as a fiction author and this slip can be forgiven. It still has value, showing that he had ambitions going beyond the bare-bones style of then mainstream SF. Clarke left out these "sublime intros" later on but maybe he should have continued in this vein, refining his style. But the SF-style of the times was Campbellian – "no story should begin with atmosphere" – and Clarke adapted.

The bulk of *Against the Fall of Night* is wholly intelligible, brimming over with quaint details of the high-tech city Diaspar, the low-tech neighbor Lys, a scientific recluse living in a ruin and, as intimated, the space journey giving answers to man's retreat from his space empire. There are two versions of this story. The revised is called *The City and the Stars,* issued in 1956. The early one was magazine-published in 1948 and only slightly revised for its novelization in 1953. I read this original version and I guess this is the better, having a fresher, original style, a more non-Campbellian approach style-wise. As a side note, it's a story of slightly more than 40,000 words, a rough estimate from a Swedish translation. And that indication and the scope and structure of the work to me makes it into a novel and not a novella, as some classify it. For the record, the SFWA (Science Fiction Writers of America) categories of stories are: a story of less than 7,500 words is a *short story,* a *novelette* has between 7,500 and 17,500 words, a *novella* has between 17,500 and 39,999 words and a *novel* is a story of 40,000 words and above.

END

Next among Clarke's noteworthy novels is *Childhood's End.* It might retain its status as a classic but it's severely flawed. The theme of "superior aliens arrive and take control, giving man peace and prosperity, what's not to like" is insufficient. Ethically, it's rather upsetting; this ignores one necessary prerequisite, namely, man's consent. Man's free Will has to be brought along in the equation. To merely have aliens come and give us peace-and-prosperity by force is totally unacceptable.

The idea is well-meaning. But the way Clarke glosses over human resistance against the aliens is revolting. Along with the slightly priggish tone of "Clarke narrative style type 1A" this becomes rather unbearable. Then we have ESP evolving in mankind and all things earthly just fade away. It's too much and too little.

That said, *Childhood's End* deserves praise for staging a cosmic drama in relatable form. The initial chapters with man being on the threshold of space, about to launch manned space rockets and then seeing the alien armada in the sky, has some symbolic power. And the subsequent development of the UN leader dealing with the aliens, with cosmic politics being a matter of course for a future politician, is commendable in form if not content.

As far as I'm concerned *Childhood's End* should rest in peace. A certain high-profile event reached the same conclusion, when in the 1960s movie director Stanley Kubrick approached Clarke and wanted to make a movie of it. It soon became clear that it was unsuited for this, if only for dramatic reasons; overall, the novel is lacking in coherence. But the Kubrick-Clarke cooperation evolved and soon they came up with the most iconic space travel story ever, *2001: A Space Odyssey*.

2001

As for *2001* the movie and the novel were developed concurrently, the book released after the film but still in the same year, 1968 (more on the film specifically in chapter thirteen). To make a long story short, this is breathtaking. I mean, while it's true that both the film and the book goes along a bit slow and pedantically this is rectified on a symbolic plane. Conceptually this is really out there: a beginning showing primitive hominids being visited by aliens, present only as a monolith showing them images on how to evolve. Then the primitives do learn, like beginning to use the hip bone of an antelope as a weapon, making them invincible as hunters and killers. This leads to man's development as a tool-using species, eventually taking him into space.

As explorer of the moon man detects another monolith, which in turn points to yet another such orbiting Saturn. A space expedition is launched and eventually only one astronaut of three remains, going off to approach the monolith and then finding that it's a stargate, a portal to a higher dimension.

This is more than literature, this is an initiation, a raising of man to a higher level – the next level, the space-faring, alien-encountering level. Again, the Clarke style telling this is slightly pedantic and not overly alluring in itself but the symbolic quality of this is beyond words, Beyond the Beyond. In *Against the Fall of Night* Alvin of Loronei made a first Clarksian journey into the unknown, and David Bowman in 2001 going through the stargate really tops it off. This is the space trip of space trips, actually a journey not in space proper but in a higher dimension, taking – as it were – man to a higher level of development.

What made *Childhood's End* fail is here rectified; *2001* intimates that man has to be on a higher mental level, on par with the space-faring aliens, to be able to meet them, encounter them and meaningfully communicate with them. This, at least, is hinted at. 2001 is a symbolical, yet fully relatable, rendering of man's meeting with aliens. Not a word with them is exchanged, no image of them is conveyed; Bowman only comes to a strange, humanly furnished room at the end of his trip. And again the monolith appears teaching him, changing him – into a starchild. And this child then goes back to earth, to do *what* we don't know, neither in the book nor in the movie. In the latter it's merely accompanied by Strauss' "Also Sprach Zarathustra". And I won't go into Nietzschean attitudes now, exploiting some rigorous nonsense for the fire-eating part of my audience. I merely want to say that this is beyond everything seen or read before.

2001 is about the raising of mankind, with or without the help of aliens. *2001* a classic for all times and a proof of the specificity of the Clarksian way to fly.

SHERVANE

A peculiar Clarke short story is "The Wall of Darkness" from 1949. It's a highly advanced piece of *math fiction*, conceptualizing the geometry of the Moebius band – a surface having only one side. I freely admit that the discussions pertaining to this concept are beyond me; you can find them on the internet. But the story, as it stands, again shows the Clarkisan adventurer going out there, Beyond the Beyond, on his own. In the story a certain Shervane lives on a planet with a mysterious wall in the south. He builds a staircase to the top of it and having reached it he can venture out into the unknown, eventually coming back to where he started from.

This is intriguing and enigmatic, yet told in an easy, transparent style, a conceptual illustration of the Clarksian spirit of boldly going where no man has gone before. And a fine illustration of the ontological nature of SF. I mean, take a crime story, a classic whodunnit. This kind of detective story is *epistemological*. Epistemology has to do with knowledge and understanding, it's the "theory of knowledge". For instance, how to acquire justified knowledge is a core aspect of epistemology. And detective stories function epistemologically in that a mystery is presented, a criminal case must be resolved. This is done by facts being gathered and interpreted. And in the end we are given the correct answer, the only answer. The riddle is solved, the offender is caught.

The science fiction story, on the other hand, is *ontological*. It deals with a wider topic, the very nature of reality. We again meet some mystery that apparently is solved during the story. However, an unambiguous, tangible answer can't always be given – because questions about the nature of reality are harder to answer than the more concrete, everyday questions posed in a detective story. A story playing in a future galactic empire, or being about a first contact with aliens, or containing what today is fictional science; all this is based on assumptions about our reality, a different reality than everyday reality.

SF has its strains of metaphysics, elements of asking the question "what is real". If we encounter aliens we may for instance wonder what this means for our reality, like how the aliens look at their reality and how this will affect our world-view. And if, say, a new planet sails into view, this also affects the way we look at reality. And a trip into space isn't just a journey from point A to point B, it's a mental elevation and a journey through a psychological landscape.

True, even realistic stories pose metaphysical questions. But SF makes it immanently; it can't avoid it. The very framework of an SF story compels ontological statements.

RAMA

This chapter has already touched on the elemental nature of the Clarke fiction, like *2001*. We'll even return to the movie that was made of the novel later, in chapter thirteen, noting its character of initiation into a higher dimension: metaphysical indeed.

But there are metaphysical traits to other Clarke stories. Like the novel *Rendezvous with Rama* (1973). In this, a gigantic alien spaceship, a cosmic cylinder, 50 km long, sails into the solar system. Man sends out an expedition to land on it and get inside. Then they examine it. It seems to be the creation of an alien civilization; for instance, there's a circumventing, band-shaped sea in there, there's a town on an island in the sea etc.

When this inverted world, this cosmic beer can, is about to leave the solar system, the expedition leaves the object and sees it sail off into deep space. They have solved some questions about this artifact but as many remain. This is ontological, it's about the nature of reality: we get some answers but the whole is rather impossible to give a description of. Because then you would be God. However, an omniscient god, this is what the above mentioned detective story narrator becomes. He, the elevated judge, is giving an answer, the only answer. The SF author, for his part, may also have claims for omniscience, he may indeed approach the role of a Divine Master of Ceremony, but immanently he tends to pose as many questions as he gives the answer to. And that's in sync with the spirit of the times we're heading towards: towards new worlds, suggesting us to speculate about the nature of reality, letting a thousand world-views compete. We're moving away from the zero-sum game of duality: the detective against the criminal, one man's gain being the other man's loss. SF, I believe, is about holism: it becomes a game with many possibilities, a kaleidoscopic play of opportunities.

All SF stories pose metaphysical questions. Even seemingly realistic SF makes you wonder. Like, Asimov's galactic empire in *Foundation* with its bare-bones *Realpolitik* still gives you an elemental sense of wonder, forcing you when you look up at the stars to conceive what a galaxy-spanning civilization would be like. And Haldeman's no-nonsense combat heroes deal with Einsteinian relativity effects that change their timeline out of the ordinary. Asimov and Haldeman were both printed in John W. Campbell's *Astounding / Analog*, a magazine containing a lot of metaphysical speculation despite its testified conservative scientific approach. The unorthodox science Campbell advocated was such as Dianetics, the Dean machine and the Hieronymus machine. It was no coincidence that Campbell became SF writer and editor, I would say, even with this alleged "fringe science" in mind. All SF worthy of its name induces sense of wonder: a romantic sense of the sublime, of worlds unseen next door, of reality being more wonderful than we might imagine. Philosophy begins in wonder, Aristotle said.

Rama: an alien artifact comes drifting and a team of astronauts is asked to check it out. Once inside the drum, the party sees a deserted techno world with a weird band farther away, a ring of ice. When the cylinder approaches the sun it thaws, proving to be a lake. And in the lake is a city. Like the rest of Rama the city is seen to be empty but it contains some surprises.

Because the cylinder rotates there's gravity. Much doesn't happen in the novel, they just go in there in the drum, looking upon stuff, finding the one and the other thing. It's been said that the artist is eminently present in the deserted studio and the same applies to the aliens who created Rama. Spontaneously you wonder: those who created this artifact, how do they look, where do they live, what, essentially *are* they? You never get the answer but the question is implicit on each and every page. And this is the specific, ontological feature of this novel.

NASA

I'll round off this chapter with various anecdotes, gathered from Clarke's science fictional memoir *Astounding Days* (1990).

Arthur C. Clarke lived 1917-2008. For a time, he worked at the Treasury Department in merry old England where he was born, grew up and made his career. The ministry working hours were 10-5 during the winter months and 9-4 during the summer months. Further, he took his driver's license at one time, in Australia, perhaps because it was easier there due to the absence of heavy traffic. But when he had received the certificate he never sat himself behind the wheel again, unknown why.

As a scientist, Clarke, among other things, came up with the idea of communications satellites. The concept was published in 1945 in the venerable magazine *Wireless World*, a publication lying on the coffee tables of every aspiring radio enthusiast at the time. Then Clarke corresponded diligently with the experts at NASA, in such matters as the possibility of flying manta rays being able to live in Jupiter's atmosphere, of sending messages to aliens by radio telescopes, and so on. From this avid communicating with NASA you could get the idea that he was working for them. But to this, Clarke responded: "I don't work for NASA, NASA works for me".

Clarke subsequently settled down in Ceylon. There he was once visited by the Swedish journalist Börje Crona, with camera and everything. "No pictures!" Clarke shouted when he saw Crona. But when the interview was over, he said:

"Shouldn't you take some pictures?"

LITERATURE

- *Against the Fall of Night* (1953)
- *Childhood's End* (1953)
- *2001: A Space Odyssey* (1968)
- *Rendezvous with Rama* (1973)

10. MICHAEL MOORCOCK

MICHAEL MOORCOCK (1939-) was the man writing the novella *Behold the Man* in the 1960s, elaborating on the role of Christ. And in his fantasy novels his heroes sought the salvation of Tanelorn, city of heavenly calm. Curiously enough, Moorcock also had room for dandy nihilism, even in his epic fantasy. But *mutatis mutandum* and all things considered, the co-existence of dark and light, of chaos and order and nihilism and idealism, makes Moorcock's opus into an alluring tapestry for modern man. Traditional traits are to be found there, themes of the will to light and the desire of the dark within a framework of integral esotericism.

COUNT BRASS

It's true that the praising of Tradition and the virtues of old don't occupy center stage in Michael Moorcock's novels. But it's there, it's possible to find passages in this left-leaning author's work that seem rather conservative. Just take this portrait of Count Brass, the stalwart champion of Kamarg in its battle against the imperialist schemes of Gran Bretan in the Runestaff quadrology. In Book 1, *The Jewel in the Skull*, Count Brass is presented thus:

> The sky was a light gray, carrying rain, and from it shone sunlight of watery gold, touching the Count's armor of burnished brass and making it glow like flame. The Count wore a huge broadsword

at his hip, and a plain helmet, also of brass, was on his head. His whole body was sheathed in heavy brass, and even his gloves and boots were of brass links sewn upon leather. The Count's body was broad, sturdy and tall, and he had a great, strong head on his shoulders, with a tanned face that might also have been molded of brass. From this head stared two steady eyes of golden brown. His heavy mustache was red, as was his hair. In the Kamarg, as well as beyond it, it was not unusual to hear the legend that the Count was, in fact, not a true man at all but a living statue in brass, a Titan, invincible, indestructible, immortal. But those who knew Count Brass well enough knew that he was a man in every sense – a loyal friend, a terrible foe, given much to laughter yet capable of ferocious anger, a drinker of enormous capacity, a trencherman of not indiscriminate tastes, a wit, a swordsman and a horseman without par, a sage in the ways of men and history, a lover at once tender and savage. Count Brass, with his rolling, warm voice and his rich vitality, could not help but be a legend, for if the man was exceptional, then so were his deeds.[49]

In terms of structure, it doesn't get any more heroic, Faustian and traditional than this – not in fantasy, not even in all of Western literature. Then it's no matter that Moorcock is an intellectual having written pamphlets for the Liberal Party, that he was anti-Heinlein (*q.v.* "Starship Stormtroopers") and that he didn't "mean" things like the above, merely writing it as entertainment. For in this study I don't examine what might or might not be in the author's head at the time of writing; I see the text. And the quoted text to me is a paean to Traditional Man.

Whatever Moorcock himself meant or didn't mean with his stories, his fantasy epics do have some notion of heroism. The plots have suspense and drama. Moorcock doesn't just waste away the instances of courage, willpower, endurance and adventure that his stories offer. They are true on their premises of latter-day versions of quest stories. Then, of course, there's something called nihilism forever lurking upon the Moorcockian heroes, and sometimes it's

---

[49] Moorcock, 1973 I, p 7-8

even embraced by them. I mention this to any right-winger having just gotten the urge to read a Moorcock fantasy. So I'd say, be warned; in a structural sense this isn't essential reading like Tolkien's trilogy. But Moorcock's opus has some depth which I'll try to examine in this chapter.

NIHILISM

The Moorcock fantasy saga, the Eternal Champion cycle, has nihilism present explicitly and implicitly. As represented in Elric, the supposed most popular figure in the ensemble, who wields a sword he can't control, a sword sucking up and absorbing the souls of the men it has just slain. The sword has its own will, it can even leave its scabbard and kill without Elric being able to stop it. Nihilist indeed: the hero lacking will to control his weapon, virtually being its slave.

In the end Elric himself is killed by his sword. And Corum, hero of another Eternal Champion sub series, ever so pre-Rafaelite in its rendering of a Celtic-flavored land, sees a similar fate, meeting his end by his own device. And the hero of the Runestaff Saga, Dorian Hawkmoon, has a black jewel implanted in his forehead, put there by his enemies but he decides to keep it as a stigmata of power. But to even invent such a device seems to be decidedly anti-spiritual, since the *ajna* spot where Hawkmoon has the jewel is the place of the famed third eye, accessing the pineal gland of supposed visionary powers. So in this respect I'd rather read *The Third Eye* (1956) by Lobsang Rampa, an allegedly fictional rendering of how to open that third eye and not sealing and closing it as is Dorian Hawkmoon's fate, how commendable his adventures otherwise might be.

WAR HOUND

Moorcock's Eternal Champion Saga consists of four heroes. I've mentioned three. And even the fourth, Erekosë, has a nihilist bent. In *The Eternal Champion* (1970) Erekosë finds himself in a parallel world engulfed in a deadly battle, waged between humans and a race called

Eldren. Erekosë takes the side of the Eldren and eventually kills all of humanity in this world. Within the framework of a fantasy it doesn't get any more nihilist than this. And still I persist in having Moorcock along in this study of eternal values; why?

It's like this: Moorcock's fantasy opus inhabits a gray area in many respects. But, to me, the saga is gloriously completed by *The War Hound and the World's Pain* from 1981. This isn't formally seen as a conclusion of the Eternal Champion Saga (that place goes to *The Quest for Tanelorn*) but personally I see the War Hound novel as the logical, final summation of Moorcock's take on heroism.

The Eternal Champion veered off into nihilism but in the form of the War Hound a way out of this gray area was indicated.

> It was in that year when the fashion in cruelty demanded not only the crucifixion of peasant children, but a similar fate for their pets, that I first met Lucifer and was transported into Hell; for the Prince of Darkness wished to strike a bargain with me.[50]

Thus begins the novel *The War Hound and the World's Pain* by Moorcock. It's about a soldier during the Thirty Years' War who receives a mission from the devil to find the Holy Grail to cure the world's pain.

This, in short, is the plot. But with this very little is said of the specificity of this novel.

WAR HOUND

In spite of the beginnings in "our world," the real world of 17th century Europe, *The War Hound and the World's Pain* eventually evolves into a fantasy in a parallel world. But the presence of the real world is still there for in the confluence of the Multiverse of parallel worlds the main character now finds himself in the fairy world, now in the war-torn world of the 1600s. But the hero knows his way through this Multiverse, implicitly he's the reincarnated Eternal Champion who intuitively finds his way through this multitude of

---

[50] Moorcock, 1983, p 7

dimensions to fulfill his quest – the Quest to end them all, the quest for the Holy Grail.

He's Graf Ulrich von Bek, a scarred veteran and a nihilist of his times. And so he gladly comes to serve Lucifer? But this is a remorseful Lucifer we meet, with viable traits of the ambiguous main character of Milton's *Paradise Lost*. Lucifer wants to again get in touch with his father, God, and if the Grail is found a rapprochement can be made, the beginning of such a reconciliation. This is eminent gray-area fiction, Moorcock masterfully depicting a Miltonesque Lucifer and a human hero, von Bek, being tired of carnage and wishing to have some meaning in his life. And to find the Grail and reconcile Heaven with Hell, what better mission can there be?

Previous Moorcock heroes like Elric also had this ambiguous character. But his adventures never had this unmistakable light shining over it that we find in *The War Hound and the World's Pain*. Elric also served Hell but in a more sinister way, ending up in dejection and darkness. von Bek in his quest actually finds the Grail and at the end sees a glimpse of heaven, in the form of a meadow stretching out and then rising vertically to the sky. And from the heights a feeling emerges, a sense of understanding.

This is Moorcock's finest hour, ever. This redeems and gives added meaning to all of the Eternal Champion Saga. In all of fantasy literature this is unique thanks to the ambiguous-but-predominantly-positive character of it all, the soul-searching of von Bek being shaped in symbolic terms, in a quest where he meets diverse fantastic characters. For instance, there's an euhemerized Odin in form of "Wildgrave, Lord of the Hunt," there's Cornelius Groot, a sort of Descartes figure, and there's an adversary in the form of Johannes Klosterheim, leading the forces of Hell trying to stop *der Krieghund*. In all, a classic of fantasy and a future classic of Western literature. As we saw in the quote at the beginning of this chapter, the one from *The Jewel in the Skull*, Moorcock has some knowledge of classic literary style and in the War Hound novel this really works for him, a succinct narrative with that traditional feeling implicit. The beginning has the mythical elevation of Dante's *Divina Commedia*, Part I: Hell.

LIGHT

Reading the Eternal Champion Saga, the books about Elric, Corum, Hawkmoon and Erekosë, becomes bearable when knowing that Moorcock indeed is capable of shedding light on his heroes too, as in *The War Hound and the World's Pain*, and not just letting it end in darkness and death as in many of the other novels. That said, not even in the adventures of Corum and Elric it's about nihilist outings all the time. As intimated they can seek Tanelorn, the neutral, peaceful city. There is epic outings and dramatic interiors, narrated in exquisite style, not self-consciously stylish (as Moorcock's Jerry Cornelius stories sometimes were) but elaborate and rewarding for the educated reader. Just listen to these lines of *The Sailor on the Seas of Fate*, an Elric novel. The hero is in some unfamiliar land approaching his next adventure and in the run-up to this Moorcock depicts a land in a way that only he can, a psychological landscape of the inimitable kind:

> Up the steep sides of small mountains, whose slopes consisted of gray, crumbling slate, which made a clatter to be heard a mile or more away, the white-faced one [Elric, being an albino] had ridden. Along dales all but grassless and whose river-bottoms had seen no water for scores of years, through cave-tunnels bare of even a stalactite, over plateaux from which rose cairns of stones erected by a forgotten folk, he had sought to escape his pursuers, and soon it seemed to him that he had left the world he knew forever, that he had crossed a supernatural frontier and had arrived in one of those bleak places of which he had read in the legends of his people, where once Law and Chaos had fought each other to a stalemate, leaving their battle-ground empty of life and the possibility of life.[51]

In the Multiverse Chaos and Order battles – forever, in a nihilist take on ontology. But there are also some clever aspects showcased in this, as in the Balance that is sometimes mentioned. That would make the Eternal Champion Saga into a hallmark traditional epic of wholeness,

---

[51] Moorcock, 1981, p 10

of integrating the opposites in Jungian fashion. I've already intimated this in the anti-hero von Bek who finds himself in the service of Good, though hired by the devil. Because, this von Bek is seeking the Grail. "Do you the devil's work, and you shall reach heaven sooner than your master" is the pay-off in the War Hound novel, another glorious instance of ambiguity. The Elric at the beginning of his adventures serving Chaos but at the end serving Order is another such.

The Eternal Champion is a tapestry of adventure, ontology and moral. The main purpose is entertainment but the saga has a way of sneaking up at you and delivering some profound wisdom. And, to this, some bare-bones nihilism, as in the just mentioned *The Sailor on the Seas of Fate* where all four Eternal Champions has joined forces, literally joined to form a Heroic Gestalt of four faces, four arms, four swords and eight legs to fight an energy sucking monster threatening to destroy all of the world, perhaps all of the Multiverse...! This is told in a controlled, yet breath-taking way, an indescribable action scene if there ever was one. At the end the Universe is saved – but having accomplished this the heroes are just as dejected as ever. Elric only wants to forget it, he can feel nothing, no joy, no triumph.

This is the nihilism you have to live with in the Moorcock lands. Personally I'm more into the classical world of the *Mabinogion*, *Parsifal* and *Le Morte d'Arthur* these days. These classic epics are more gratifying to the reader, giving you adventure, heroes and villains, arresting scenery *and* a sense of meaning. In Moorcock's fantasy the sense of meaning is often lacking and this might prevent them from being reread.

But I shouldn't be too harsh. They sometimes do have meaning; see above. And as for entertaining yarns with a traditional atmosphere they can be recommended. For instance, a redeeming quality is the short length of the individual stories. The Elric Saga for its part began as short stories, published in the 1960s British Magazine *Science Fantasy*. They're collected in book form in *The Weird of the White Wolf* and *The Bane of the Black Sword*.

Then some Elric novels were written. As for their accessibility they're often in themselves short, about 160 pages or so. Today the series are often bound together in volumes of 400 pages or thereabouts. This, in my mind, takes away their specificity. Instead, having the Eternal Champion books as separate, slim novels makes the saga into a *random access myth*, an epic where you can begin where you want, merely reading one book or two and then leave it with a sense of having seen an aspect of Multiverse, the whole mirrored in a facet, as it were. I know of only one other fantasy author writing short installments like this: Roger Zelazny and his Amber Chronicles. Otherwise the ideal of the fantasy novel is always "thick as a brick" and this will not engender classics in itself. Only Tolkien is thus redeemed in my eyes because he (1) invented the genre and (2) couldn't help but writing his opus in this monolithic fashion, depicting a struggle of light vs. dark in the form of an archaic epic.

MOORCOCK AND DICK

As I just said, the Moorcock novels are fairly short. This can make you think of Philip K. Dick who also wrote rather short novels, like the ones for Ace and DAW Books, usually wrapping the story up after the minimum eight printing sheets of a standard pocket had been filled up, resulting in a book of about 150 pages.

Come to think of it, there are more aspects Dick and Moorcock have in common:

- Being Men of the Left but not letting this influence dominate their fiction as a whole, making their respective fiction into a tapestry of Life, the Universe and Everything.
- Formally anti-tradition and anti-spiritual but artistically having room for these aspects also.
- As writers sometimes said to suffer from the hectic pattern of "having to write another paperback in an instant" but as a mere result the novels seldom came out bad.
- The novels having a slightly repetitive pattern, a kaleidoscope slightly turned around for each new opus, seemingly new and perfectly recognizable at the same time.
- Their novels tend to focus on *one* hero, venturing out by way of Fire and Movement, the sky's the limit.

ELEMENTAL

The Eternal Champion is an elemental force. When the hero rides out on a quest, be he von Bek of that novel, Elric of *The Sleeping Sorceress* or Corum of "The Swords Trilogy", he drags everything along with him. He's the focus of all the world, of the Universe, of the Multiverse, holding, as it were, the fate of everything in his hands. In the Moorcock fantasies it's always about The Hero, never about a collective, never about the ways of a community. The Hero as an Archetype is exquisitely conveyed in the Eternal Champion Saga, as in this portrait of Corum in *The Knight of the Swords*, his every garb and piece of equipment becoming symbolic (the Vadhagh and Nhadragh mentioned are advanced races of people):

> Prince Corum (...) wore a conical silver helm which had his full name carved in three characters above the short peak – Corum Jhaelen Irsei – which meant Corum, the Prince in the Scarlet Robe. It was the custom of the Vadhagh to choose a robe of distinctive color and identify themselves by means of it, as the Nhadragh used crests and banners of greater complication. Corum wore that robe now. It had long, wide sleeves, a full skirt that was spread back over his horse's rump, and it was open at the front. At the shoulders was fixed a hood large enough to go over his helmet. It had been made from the fine, thin skin of a creature that was thought to dwell in another plane, forgotten even by the Vadhagh. Beneath the coat was a double byrnie made up of a million tiny links. The upper layer of this byrnie was silver and the lower was made of brass. For weapons other than bow and lance, Corum bore a long-hafted Vadhagh war-axe of delicate and intricate workmanship, a long, strong sword of a nameless metal manufactured on a different plane of the Earth, with pommel and guard worked in silver and both red and black onyx. His shirt was of blue samite and his breeks and boots were of soft brushed leather, as was his saddle, which was finished in silver.[52]

---

[52] Moorcock, 1973 II, p 15

EPICS

I need to say a word or two about Moorcock's *Wizardry and Wild Romance* (1987), his study of the fantasy genre. Moorcock isn't exactly a traditionally minded scholar, he doesn't hold pre-modern literature as an ideal by way of its embracing of eternal values, but he does know what he's talking about when discussing the nature of fantasy. His pragmatic attitude is rather refreshing. He has no illusions about what fantasy is: it's about books written for a contemporary audience, books with a map at the beginning. His study is about epic fantasy, mock-archaic adventures of the kind he writes himself, books like *The Lord of the Rings,* Howard's Conan, Leiber's Fafhrd and the Gray Mouser stories, Dunsany's *The King of Elfland's Daughter* and Morris' *The Well at World's End.* Conversely, medieval epics like *Le Morte d'Arthur, Niebelungenlied, Völsunga Saga* and *Beowulf* are not to be seen as fantasy (as some other scholars do). Instead, Moorcock maintains, the direct predecessor of fantasy are the Amadis novels that flourished in the 16th century, stories with all the paraphernalia of knightly adventures but with their essence, their sense of urgency and meaning that the Arthurian sagas and the old German epics had, gone.

Instead, the Amadis novels give the reader marvels upon marvels, very much like a modern fantasy novel. Moorcock in maintaining this has a point. Most fantasy novels are indeed empty of meaning. Not that Moorcock seems to mean that fantasy can't have serious messages and aspects but the very character of what we call "fantasy" today is one of construction and make-believe, for better or worse. Therefore, *Wizardry and Wild Romance* may be worth looking up.

It's true that it doesn't say much about Moorcock's own opus. Instead, he for instance dedicates a chapter to downgrade Tolkien's writings on mostly stylistic grounds ("Epic Pooh"). In contrast to this, the – shall we say – "cozy conservatism" of Tolkien, Moorcock for his part favors the rougher and tougher attitude of Robert E. Howard's Conan. This difference in attitude has to be noted but as you can all understand, I personally praise both Moorcock and Tolkien. As for an insight into Moorcock's writings I recommend the site Wikiverse, dedicated to the

Multiverse of Moorcock with plot summaries, quotes from interviews, samples of covers etc.

GODS

"As flies to wanton boys are we to the gods – they kill us for their sport" (Shakespeare, *King Lear*). This perception of gods is implicitly to be found in the Eternal Champion Saga. I admit that I'm a little bit annoyed by this attitude, a self-righteous way of denigrating the divine realm in all respects, even the fruitful. "All gods are evil," then displaying this in a story; QED. Ursula Le Guin has the same attitude in *The Tombs of Atuan* (1971), the nihilist way of approaching godhead.

To me as an estoericist, God, singular, is an elemental force, a dyad of Will and Thought of which we, as individuals also endowed with Will and Thought, are a mirror. Our inner light is a fragment of the divine light. This is my perception of God so I can't support the atheist vein in denigrating all gods. But I also have to admit that there are lesser gods below God and that some of these may be good, some evil. And in dealing with these lesser gods, these Chaos Creatures, Moorcock often gives us plausible scenarios.

For instance, in part three of *The Sailor on the Seas of Fate* we are told of primeval times when the gods came to earth to decide the rules of their cosmic struggle, the battle between Chaos and Order. They settled in an ancient city in the southwest, R'lin K'ren A'a, whose inhabitants fled. Only one human being remained to spy on the gods. However, he was detected by the gods and therefore, as a punishment, given eternal life. Thus he became J'osui C'rein Reyr, the Creature Doomed to Live. "Doomed to live" might seem a bit nihilistic; when in this condition, why not take the chance to become a Hermes figure, a god in human form, a benign god showing people the way...? But the scenario itself with gods being spied upon and then this revenge, is credible in itself, from an esoteric point of view. It's plausible on its premises.

In this story one of the Chaos gods was Arioch, Elric's patron god. We meet him again in *The Sleeping Sorceress*. In chapter six Elric comes to the city of Nadsokor on some business. In the palace of the king he sees a demon sitting on the throne, a fearsome monstrosity. After some interesting action the figure morphs into something else:

> There was a humming sound and black smoke coiled over the throne and then another figure was sitting there, its legs crossed. It had the shape of a man but it was more beautiful than any mortal. It was a being of intense and majestic beauty – unearthly beauty. "Arioch!" Elric bowed his head before the Lord of Chaos.[53]

Again, this is a plausible depiction of a lesser god. As for this devil being beautiful we can think of the William Blake renderings of Lucifer from Milton's *Paradise Lost*, an image I also seem to find in the very Lucifer that Graf Ulrich von Bek meets in *The War Hound and the World's Pain*.

Moorcock started his career as a comic book magazine editor, working on *Tarzan Adventures*. He was only seventeen when he landed this job. Later, he wrote scripts for Marvel Comics. One such story has Elric meeting Conan: "The Sword Stormbringer". My reading of this is based on a Swedish version from 1979. Here the gods again play with men, gods like Arioch and Arkyn and whatnot, leaving death and destruction in their path. A member of Conan's and Elric's team in the particular quest, Zephra, dies in the denouement. In a moving scene Conan says that she's dead and we will live on, to which Elric, turned to the sky, says: "But for how long, Lord Arkyn? HOW LONG?"

All things considered – things like "the difficulty in staging real tragedy in fantasy" and "telling about gods in a 20th century story" – this is brilliant. It's credible as a story depicting gods and men.

SUNSHINE

Overall, the Eternal Champion Saga is a Taostic display of idealism struggling with nihilism, balanced by the artistry of the author. Michael Moorcock is the Philip K. Dick of fantasy.

---

[53] Moorcock, 1975, p 110

Now I'm off to listen to "The Great Sun Jester," the best song Moorcock wrote for Blue Öyster Cult. The other two, though fine efforts in many respects, veered off into dejected nihilism ("Black Blade" and "Veteran of the Psychic Wars") but the "Jester" song is just perfect for the times ahead, that sunny, victorious feeling, shining with "the eternal sunshine of the spotless mind," as it were. Fire and movement!

LITERATURE

- *The Jewel in the Skull* (1967)
- *The Eternal Champion* (1970)
- *The Knight of the Swords* (1971)
- *The Sleeping Sorceress* (1971)
- *The Sailor on the Seas of Fate* (1976)
- *The Bane of the Black Sword* (1977)
- *The Weird of the White Wolf* (1977)
- *The War Hound and the World's Pain* (1982)
- *Wizardry and Wild Romance* (1987)

11. J. G. BALLARD

James Graham Ballard (1930-2009) is a key figure of our times, not only in 20th century SF but in Western literature at large. Ballard, having for a while served in the RAF, brought the airman's view to the modern vistas of industries, parking lots and derelict space age objects. How, then, does this translate to a right-wing world-view?

NIHILISM

What can the fiction of J. G. Ballard teach a traditionalist mind? What does Ballard have to say to a radical conservative?

Superficially, nothing. In our times, "J. G. Ballard" has become a tool of liberal nihilism to show how meaningless and hollow our times are. "Vulnerability, alienation, urban paranoia" and other clichés are stacked in the essays about Ballard. Ballard is a recurring figure in the contemporary analysis, at least for Normal Interpretation Type 1A: that of Liberal Nihilism & Moronic Materialism. Our world is accused of being meaningless but at the same time no meaning must be found, other than possibly feeling satisfied with The Progress of Democracy.

But there are features of Ballard's opus pointing beyond this. I'm here thinking of Ballard's freedom of illusion, his freedom from liberal clichés about progress and tolerance. There's a hard core of credibility in his books. And he went to a hard school: as an eleven-year-old he met the Japanese occupation of Shanghai in 1941 and was put in a prison camp.

In reality, he sat in a camp with his parents. In the reality-based novel *Empire of the Sun* (1984) he's separated from them. However, the depiction of the transition from the safe, bourgeois world of peace to the reality of occupation and detention is credible. From a belief in the British Empire and eternal progress to humiliation and Japanese captivity: it's a model story of "a liberal mugged by reality", which is said to be a definition of "conservative".

Ballard wasn't a conservative. But he became a skeptic, one who saw through the prevailing rhetoric. For instance, when the war in 1941 devastated Shanghai Ballard found that the city became more real, like a certain casino telling him more when bombed out than tip-top and functioning. This experience eventually enabled Ballard to portray the postwar landscape with its air bases, research institutes, factories and clinics, its cold-war scare and celebrities, its murder and adultery, with an original point of view. He was a contemporary teller of fairy tales, stories rich in modern symbols like satellites, computers, televisions and, not to forget, airplanes, these eternal hieroglyphs of the sky.

The aircraft is namely an ever-present point of reference in Ballard's world. He was for a while an officer candidate in the RAF and flew the trainer North American Harvard. He dropped out after a while but you must admit that Ballard, in this and other activities, was able to "keep it real". He was an active nihilist conducting operations, not a smug intellectual complacently smiling under his tea cozy. Ballard had "torn his nails bloody against the wall of reality," having cut his lessons in the RAF, in the prison camp, in med school and journalism before he became the author of works such as *The Atrocity Exhibition*, *Empire of the Sun* and "The Terminal Beach".

IVORY TOWER

Authors must come out of their ivory towers. You sometimes get the impression that the normal, ideal writer of today starts by reading books as young, studies literature at university and then writes his Excellent Novel or Brilliant Thesis of some liberal icon and there you go, straight to mainstream media, some nihilist think-tank or the Academy. It's an environment where everyone is middle-classily kind to one another, a life devoid of the "show no weakness" of the military and criminal world. And if these normal-type authors write about reality it will only be with a left-liberal bias: pity the common people, servicemen are stupid and three cheers for multiculturalism. We need, in this sense, writers devoid of these illusions, true-minded and with more of an operational spirit. More reports from war bases and research institutes, less of coffee talk and salon nihilism. There are beautiful traits of the modern world also, the dangerous and unpleasant can reward you as experiences, and not only in the form of indulging in angst. There's beauty in the Ballardian urban landscapes and the Jüngerian Marble Cliffs. This we sorely need, anything except the left-liberal chewing of General Buzzword No. 1: pity the weak...

Exactly this cardinal sin Ballard has avoided throughout his writing. And the strategy he used is called "Death of Affect as an approach to character". Because, in the usual prose story the reader is manipulated to sympathize with the protagonist. Syrup is smeared over the dish. Ballard, in contrast, is disconnecting such sentimentality. He portrays his characters with some emotional distance but thus manages, paradoxically, to have them come closer. He doesn't manipulate, he portrays.

For this and other reasons, Ballard is a breath of fresh air. He lacks the polish of the salon and puts us in the middle of the techno landscape, our reality – a reality few other writers seem to see. Works like *The Atrocity Exhibition*, *Running Wild* and *The Kindness of Women* to me seem to convey the image of Ballard as the unsentimental but dreamy portrayer of highways, suburbs, crashing aircraft and other items of our "bomb-saturated, media-crazed environment".

THE KINDNESS OF WOMEN

Empire of the Sun was a semi-documentary novel about Ballard's life in a Japanese prison camp 1941-1945. *The Kindness of Women* (1991) returned in part to the same environment, to Shanghai and the war and all that, but now, he wrote in the first and not third person – writing, simply, "I" and not "Jim". And the emphasis in the book lay on his postwar life of medical school and being a married man, then a widower and an author, all with the Lunghua camp as an ever-present reference.

The Kindness of Women offers a lot to the reader tired of the standard autobiographic novel. Ballard has, for example, a female acquaintance who becomes a medical doctor, and of her middle classiness he means that "common sense, tolerance and understanding" had ruined her, a scathing critique of the latter-day, nihilist bourgeoisie – because, tolerance can be a kind of disguised nihilism. If everything can be tolerated, in the end, nothing can tolerated. Remember Chesterton: "Tolerance is the virtue of the man without convictions". You must have ideals, more subtle than "tolerance, understanding and common sense". You must have ideals footed in Tradition, like accountability, courage, modesty, faith, justice and equanimity.

In the same novel Ballard relates how he on a visit to Los Angeles hires a car and drives around among the houses and shops, the structures and buildings stretching along endless roads, "the scenery of a film waiting to be made". It's his first visit to the city, in conjunction with the premiere of the film *Empire of the Sun* in 1987, and about his excursion he says that he loved every inch of it and immediately felt at home. It's the feeling of falling into a trance when you saunter in half-deserted urban environments, of movement as a state.

A little contemplative tranquility Ballard also invites us to, for the first time ever, when he talks about being a writer in the 70s and 80s, of the joy of leaving the typewriter in the afternoon and devoting an hour to see a spider weaving his web. In walking along the Thames in Shepperton's sweet nature he discovered the mystery and beauty of the leaves and the trees and the wisdom inherent in the light. Truly traditional words to come from the urban nihilist Ballard.

CAMBRIDGE

In the 50s Ballard studied medicine at Cambridge and his contempt for this university town may be worth mentioning: he says that it was only a bicycle rack in front of a Gothic backdrop... This reminds me of my days at Uppsala university. You could appreciate the atmosphere of Tradition and learning but at the same time no one lived it, it was just this aura of education factory decorated with Student Community flags, parades and choral singing, the most watered down form of Tradition imaginable. It's true that Tradition is to be nurtured by us, the living, but at the same time it doesn't hurt to heckle old bastions of tradition that doesn't essentially embrace any eternally viable ideals.

Ballard gave nothing for the common image of Cambridge. A truer Cambridge was to be found at the nearby US air base with its concrete runways and landing lights, among the institutions and the modern architecture of Cambridge – again, a phenomenon I personally savored while visiting my alma mater, of going beyond the common landmarks of Uppsala and admire old military barracks, long stretches of institutions and factories, industrial areas waiting for their mythologist. The Gothic character shouldn't be denied but Uppsala is so much more than what's seen on the postcards.

RAF

In *The Kindness of Women* Ballard details his time in the RAF, after med school but before the writing career. He learned to fly the Harvard plane, a propeller engine stalwart giving him the true feeling of being a pilot. Many a later Ballard story is based on this experience, like "Low-Flying Aircraft", "Myths of the Near Future", *The Unlimited Dream Company* and "My Dream of Flying to Wake Island". He went into the RAF to experience World War III from ringside, he said, he wanted to fly the Vulcan bomber with "pieces of the sun" in the bomb bay...

If Ballard had he been a little older, he had probably been a RAF pilot in the Battle of Britain, he says, not without genuine pathos. He fights long to find a narrative of the war, an appropriate way to tell about World War II and the bomb and everything. But when he speaks to war veterans he's only served with clichés and jargon.

He must acquire a new language, his own language. And this we see in "The Terminal Beach" from 1964, of a castaway on the nuclear testing island of Eniwetok that becomes a psychological landscape, a projection of his psyche, and partly in *Empire of the Sun* that, after a gestating period of forty years, sums up his own war experiences. On the surface, this is one of many stories of prisoners of the Japanese (*q.v. Guests of the Emperor, Bridge on the River Kwai, Merry Christmas, Mr. Lawrence*), but beyond that it captured a landscape of immortal hieroglyphs. WWII in the east had never been depicted on this stylistically intense level before.

A comprehensive synthesis of Ballard's war fixation, his "Lunghua-gaze" and love-hate relationship with the B-29s, Vietnam and everything, we get at the end of *The Kindness of Women* when a Spitfire wreck from WWII is discovered in an English river bed and Ballard and friends excavate it. The corpse of the pilot is still there and a proper funeral will be held; participating in it is a Korean airliner pilot who in Ballard's eyes will symbolize Japan. The whole breathes reconciliation – reconciliation with enemies, reconciliation with the old demons, reconciliation with the past.

SENSE

Ballard's fiction still makes sense, all the way from the mid-1960s until the 1990s. And in the 21st century he published his memoirs: *Miracles of Life – Shanghai to Shepperton*, a comprehensive and down-to-earth version of things he had told about previously, plus filling in some gaps.

As for fiction, in the rest of this chapter I'll take a closer look at the Ballard works *War Fever, Empire of the Sun, The Atrocity Exhibition* and "The Terminal Beach". First, a look into the novel *Super-Cannes*, issued in 2000.

As you've noticed in this chapter Ballard is seen as a writer of SF. But the more common SF themes of "aliens, future, outer space" are absent. "Planet Earth is the only alien planet" he once said and in the context of his authorship this makes sense. The fantastic and uncanny properties of everyday reality are in Ballard's stories examined to the full, in a symbolic fashion similar to some SF but at the same time totally original.

Like *Super-Cannes*. This is a book looking into the nature of nihilism, somewhat akin to Lewis' *That Hideous Strength*, with the forces of nihilism being present here and now, in our midst. However, *Super-Cannes* lacks the redeeming quality of Lewis's novel by not putting up a credible counter-image to the forces of evil. In *Super-Cannes* we read about people living in a rich men's enclave, a gated community in southern France. But they go mad by the perfect, air-conditioned lifestyle and therefore has to go on robbing expeditions to ease the tension; they have to make break-ins and steal stuff. These expeditions are carefully orchestrated by the in-house psychologist. The discussions between the narrator, a common upper-middle class man coming to live in this "Super-Cannes" and the psychologist, have their points. The narrator criticizes the nihilist lifestyle with some efficiency. But he has no credible alternative, only 1930s British neighborhoods with their sense of community. Heartwarming, but not enough to place *Super-Cannes* in the realm of memorable socio-political novels.

That said, on the symbolic plane the novel has its moments. Ballard sees the captivating in the everyday, with metaphor-rich renderings of swimming pools, shopping malls and luxury villas, the archetypal "air-conditioned nightmare". Metaphors are a risky way of depicting reality but with Ballard they hit their target in 99 times out of 100. As for SF authors, he's in the artistic realm of Samuel Delany, Ray Bradbury, William Gibson and beyond.

An example of the rewarding style of Super-Cannes is this, of a visit to the nearby film festival, the event becoming a sugar-coated symbol of our media-saturated, titanic times:

> Helicopters circled the Palm Beach headland, waiting to land at the heliport, like paramilitary gunships about to strafe the beach-side crowds. Their white-suited passengers, faces masked by huge shades, stared down with the gaze of gangster generals in a Central American republic surveying a popular uprising. An

armada of yachts and motor cruisers strained at their anchors two hundred yards from the beach, so heavily freighted with bodyguards and television equipment that they seemed to raise the sea.[54]

WAR FEVER

Ballard excels as a short story writer. An example of this we see in the collection *War Fever* from 1990. Again, nihilism is put on trial in an amusing way – specifically, in "The Air Disaster" where a journalist on vacation in Mexico hears of a plane crash. The circumstances awaken the hunting instinct in him, believing himself to be on the trail of a big deal, perhaps he'll be the first report of a jumbo jet crash. He ends up in a backwater mountain region, asking questions to the people about traces of the supposed crash, at the end resorting into crying out loud for dead, for corpses.

Eventually he finds the origin of the supposed crash, the wreck of a small sports plane. The story of the big plane crash was a rumor having grown out of control, a mere figment of the mind. But when returning down the mountain through the villages the journalist sees how the people have heeded his call for "dead", having put forth coffins with their dead in the hope of selling them to this hustling Westerner, the one desperately calling out for dead... That's an elegant take on the nihilist nature of current mainstream media.

Another amusing story of *War Fever* is "The Index", telling the story of a postwar career by a fictitious index. The story of this "Henry Rhodes Hamilton" could be interesting in itself but Ballard goes for condensing the action into an index and thus scoring even more points:

> Hemingway, Earnest, First African safari with HRH, 234; at the Battle of the Ebro with HRH, 244; introduces HRH to James Joyce, 256; portrays HRH in *The Old Man and the Sea*, 453 (...)
> Hitler, Adolf, invites HRH to Berchtesgaden, 166; divulges

---
[54]Ballard, 2000, p 275

Russia invasion plans, 172; impresses HRH, 179; disappoints HRH, 181
(...)
Oswald, Lee Harvey, befriended by HRH, 350; inspired by HRH, 354; discusses failure of the Presidency with HRH, 357-61; invites HRH to Dallas, 372[55]

HRH has met all of the century's greats, this we get to know through this register: Einstein, Gandhi, André Malraux etc. It also provides entries like "Vogue Magazine","Lord Byron", "Perfect Light Movement, conceived by HRH", indeed a whole thick-as-a-brick biography summarized in five pages, a condensed variety of the genre "fictional documentary". Stuff like this gives back to you the faith in literature: "Hey, literature can be fun too, you know..."

Further in *War Fever*, "Answers to a Questionnaire" is partly more of the same, on the surface merely giving the answers of a questionnaire, with dry, numbered lines on blood test, the return of Jesus, the head of IBM and other Ballardiana being interspersed with "My greatest ambition is to turn into a TV programme"[56] and "He announced that Princess Diana is immortal",[57] the whole of it becoming more than fragments, more than the mere sum of its parts. It tells a story. This sounds simple but it isn't; the simple is difficult, as Clausewitz said.

SPACE

Above I quoted the Ballard wisdom of earth being the only alien planet, Ballard in this vein having confined his fiction to this realm and ignoring the vistas of outer space. But in *War Fever* there actually is a Ballard story playing in space: "Report on an Unidentified Space Station". The twist is that this report by a space team, having landed on an empty station to investigate it, in time finds that it's impossible

---

[55] Ballard, 2001, p 943-944
[56] Ibid., p 1101
[57] Ibid., p 1103

to identify, impossible to fathom: successively they try to measure its size, going round and round in the corridors until they draw the conclusion that the station is the universe itself.

A similar phenomenon is examined in "The Enormous Space": a guy decides to stay inside his house and the isolated living makes him lose perspective, literally. Everything seems to grow to his look. This, in its turn, is reminiscent of Ballard's short story "Manhole 69" from 1957. And the difficulty in mapping the infinite you also meet in "The Concentration City" from the same year.

MOON

Back to *War Fever*, where "The Man Who Walked on the Moon" finds my appreciation: a man looking for a former astronaut, supposedly living in a tourist haunt as an attraction, the astronaut having people pay him to talk of his lunar memories, but he doesn't find the guy – so he himself decides on becoming that person. For instance, he practices a special moon walk, the groping gait of stranded astronauts, accustomed to the lighter gravity of the moon... This is a story of becoming someone else, like the phenomenon of Elvis impersonators.

The piece de résistance of *War Fever* is "The Object of the Attack". It has the rewarding Ballard marque of paragraphs separated by captions, a trait both facilitating the reading of the dense prose and adding poetry by the alluring captions themselves (like "The Dream of Death by Air" and "The Astro Messiah"). The story is about an assassination attempt on an astronaut having become a fanatical politician. Among other things, it analyzes what the archetypal assassin wants – and this isn't only to change the present, no, it's to change reality itself. By taking down a main target like a president the assassin wants to, like a child smashing his toys, take control over existence at large, wishing to affect the daily lives of everyone and everything, putting Reality itself out of gear. We know for example how the Kennedy assassination and the killing of Olof Palme affected people, all who experienced it remembered where they were when they got the news, "The world changed".

If we look at the assailant of the Ballard story in question we eventually see him escaping from his mental hospital by an optical illusion, an *Ames Room*. From a look through a loophole everything in this room seems to be okay but everything is in fact suspended backdrops behind which he can escape. The assailant then stages an Ames Room on a larger scale, he eludes his pursuers through a series of illusion tricks that finally changes our view of reality. This is ontological SF at its best, in other words: "Was Matthew Young dismantling and reassembling the elements of his own mind as if they were the constituents of an Ames Room?"[58]

EMPIRE OF THE SUN

In 1984 Ballard published *Empire of the Sun*, a third-person narrative fictionalizing his experiences as a boy in WWII, living in Shanghai, China with his parents and in 1941, after the Japanese attack on Pearl Harbor and all of the colonial Pacific, being imprisoned by the Japanese. In reality he sat in the same camp as them but in the novel he gets separated from them during the detention in the Lunghua camp.

This is a WWII novel focusing on symbols, like airplanes in the sky – like Boeing B-29s dropping canisters over the neighborhood, canisters with canned food, chocolate bars and copies of Reader's Digest. In the later part of the novel the hungry Jim throws himself over the content, having his fill in his aimless wandering in the no man's land of the rice paddies, in the no-time between the Japanese having left the area and the Americans about to occupy it. Then he sees a light in the distance and then it is the same kind of B-29 having dropped the atomic bomb on Hiroshima: life and death, mission as mission, same-same...

Even before Pearl Harbor and the Japanese entry into the Shanghai European enclave this Jim is interested in aviation. And interested in war: the presence of Japanese soldiers, due to the Japan-China war started in 1937, just feels exotic. Then comes December

---

[58] Ballard, 2001, p 1098

7, 1941, and life falls apart, it will be a time of separation from the parents and drifting in Shanghai, the struggle for existence – and finally detention. But war still has an allure to the 10-year-old Jim, he likes to see the planes start from the air base next door, cheering both Zero pilots and Mustangs attacking the base.

LUNGHUA

The Lunghua camp means security: you get roof over your head and one meal per day, better than nothing. So when the Japanese finally leave in the summer of 1945 the internees fall on tougher days: wandering in the gray area of the rice paddies, an externalized psyche, a timeless geography. Death is lurking among expropriated cars in a stadium, in the canals and in the holds of the overflying B-29s, the same B-29s who drop supplies. A paradox, a symbolic oxymoron, like "heavy lightness", "movement as a state", "a sadness in rosy red"...

Symbols abound, arresting hieroglyphs. Like the burnt-out shell of a B-29, its tailfin like a billboard advertising its own squadron emblem. And the incomparable haze over the pale fields, antitank ditches and mounds, the same light seen after the dropping of the bomb, heralding the end of the war and the beginning of the next. And the reaction to news of the war in Europe, a different world symbolized by emblems such as Patton, Eisenhower, Himmler, AWOL, Utah Beach, von Rundstedt...

The transition is difficult, the insecurity of the interregnum. In the summer of 1945, the Shanghai surroundings is a never-never land, its inhabitants not knowing if the war is over or if a new just started, if the atomic bomb has created a new world or just a new war. Civilization collapses, albeit for only a few weeks; there's chaos and anarchy, exciting to read about but less pleasant to be exposed to as a 15-year-old boy in a strange land.

Stories from Japanese prison camps, for their part, is a veritable sub-genre. Titles such as *Guests of the Emperor*, *Bridge on the River*

Kwai and Clavell's *King Rat* immediately springs into mind, as well as the films *Merry Christmas, Mr. Lawrence* and *A Town Like Alice* (and even the film adaption of *Empire of the Sun* itself, Spielberg's rather fine effort from 1987). Ballard's book lives at a more advanced level than these, the style is relatively concentrated and rich in metaphors. Actually, the Ballard prose is best in short story format but in this novel the Ballard epic comes into its own, the literary pirouettes giving a finishing touch to the succinct narrative.

THE TERMINAL BEACH

Speaking of WWII, the Pacific and the bomb, a particular Ballard short story must be mentioned: "The Terminal Beach". It was published in 1964 and more or less "made" him, it meant the exploring of new symbolic lands for Ballard, it meant a new sincerity, a new credibility, a new sense of urgency compared to his earlier fiction. In his early novels he nihilistically played with the idea of apocalypse and natural disaster, or he looked into more or less profound aspects of modern life and science. But when he went east again, when he faced the demons of WWII in symbolic fashion, it became memorable in a way even different from *Empire of the Sun*.

> At night, as he lay asleep on the floor of the ruined bunker, Traven heard the waves breaking along the shore of the lagoon, like the sounds of giant aircraft warming up at the ends of their runways. This memory of the great night raids against the Japanese mainland had filled his first months on the island with images of burning bombers falling through the air around him. Later, with the attacks of beri-beri, the nightmare passed and the waves began to remind him of the deep Atlantic rollers on the beach at Dakar, where he had been born, and of watching from the window in the evenings for his parents to drive home along the corniche road from the airport. Overcome by this long forgotten memory, he woke uncertainly from the bed of old magazines on which he slept and went out to the dunes that screened the lagoon.[59]

---

[59] Ballard, 2002, p 589

This is dense, this is packed with information, with indicators of where the story is heading: of memories of WWII and of Traven's personal memories, all embodied in the psychological landscape of Eniwetok, the nuclear testing island in the Pacific Ocean. Especially gripping is the mention of aircraft engines warming up and Japanese air raids: it's all there, in a sentence, the tragic and the drama, the drama and the tragic of the US Air Force bombing Japan with TNT and phosphorous and, lastly, Little Boy and Fat Man.

So, another WWII story? No, not by far. This is the new kind of SF the 1960s sometimes gave us: "speculative fiction", a free rendering of the modern world with all its symbols and attitudes, condensed into a more urgent narrative. For his part, Ballard was always into SF in the generic way, he was never a snob saying that he wrote mainstream, highbrow fiction; however, by 1964 his literary attitude had gained a sense of necessity and tragedy not reached by any other contemporary author, inside or outside the field.

"The Terminal Beach" captures the tragedy of war. Other novels have done that too, like *The Unknown Soldier* (1957) by Väinö Linna. But Ballard condenses it all into a higher amalgam of symbols. This is an embryonic condensed novel: short story in length, novel in effect because of the dense narrative, the absence of jargon and the idiosyncratic focus on milieu, painting a psychological landscape, an externalized mind:

> As he entered the first of the long aisles [of concrete blocks], Traven felt the sense of fatigue that had dogged him for so many months begin to lift. With their geometric regularity and finish, the blocks seemed to occupy more than their own volumes of space, imposing on him a mood of absolute calm and order. He walked on into the center of the maze, eager to shut out the rest of the island. After a few random turns to left and right, he found himself alone, the vistas to the sea, lagoon and island closed.[60]

---

[60] Ballard, 2001, p 595

NOT ALONE

Traven isn't alone on the island. A doctor comes visiting, a naval search party tries to rescue him – and then there's some crash test dummies, some human plastic figures used in the experiments which Traven now employs for projecting his memories of his dead family on. And there's the corpse of a Japanese soldier that Traven mounts in a chair, having a dialogue with it. In all, this is a restrained narrative of mental and physical breakdown. Symbolically we see Traven dying there on his gray area of an island, wandering off into his inner mind, the sought after Inner Space that Ballard so meticulously mapped in his best fiction.

CONDENSED

I said that "The Terminal Beach" was an embryonic condensed novel. Because, this form, "condensed novel," essentially saw light of day only two years later, when Ballard published "You and Me and the Continuum" in 1966. This, along with other shorts with fragmented plot, consisting of seemingly random paragraphs, each with some authoritative caption, finally made up *The Atrocity Exhibition* (1970). The title of this "novel" might signal horror and revulsion but Ballard reins it in, these are images of the modern world telling us something – symbols with meaning, symbols upon symbols, gloriously unhindered by dialogue, psychological empathy and plot development, the things you usually find in a novel.

The Atrocity Exhibition hasn't got much to say about Tradition, the theme of this study. But taken for itself this is a great read. For instance, it isn't anything close to "incomprehensible", "difficult" or "enigmatic". As long as you buy the idea of merely presenting symbolic images of the postwar world, of characters venturing into this land of externalized inner minds, of non-existent plots, only scenes and reflections, only snapshots of intriguing clarity and beauty – then this is a book to return to, to be fascinated by again and again.

There are many aspects to this book but I'll mention just one: the fusing of anatomy and landscape. *The Atrocity Exhibition* examines the geographical landscape and the female anatomy with the same intent. Ballard was a med school student and he knew his anatomy, its terms and vocabulary. And his fascination with the female body may seem ludicrous and suspect to some. But as I said, he reins it in. He sees the body with the eyes of an anatomist, not a pornographer. This kind of self-restraint is commendable, in man at large and in authors specifically. "In der Beschränkung zeigt sich der Meister" (restraint is the mark of the master) as Goethe said.

Despite the ostentation intimated in the title, *The Atrocity Exhibition* is something of an Eric Satie piece. It's about scenes centered in themselves, passages portraying nothing but themselves. The absence of development, psychology and plot could make it unreadable but this isn't the case. Put briefly, it works.

LITERATURE

- *The Atrocity Exhibition* (1970)
- *Empire of the Sun* (1984)
- *Running Wild* (1988)
- *The Kindness of Women* (1991)
- *Super-Cannes* (2000)
- *The Complete Short Stories* (2001)

12. THREE BRITISH FANTASY NOVELS

In the virtual journey described by this study we'll soon leave Europe and return to the New World. But before we'll make that Atlantic crossing we have to take a look at three stand-alone British novels, fantasies that are alluring and thought-provoking in a way more or less related to Tradition.

MYTHAGO WOOD

Myths and legends aren't just fascinating stories. They are symbols encapsulating meaning – a meaning saying something about ourselves and the world, symbols expressing esoteric truths. So how about a fantasy that examines this aspect of myths, a fantasy of ideas? *Mythago Wood* (1984) by Robert Holdstock is exactly this, "a fantasy told in a science fictional mode".[61] *Mythago Wood* poses serious questions about what myths mean to us. It brings the reader literally into the heart of the myth, symbolized by a forest.

England 1946. After the war Stephen Huxley returns to his childhood home Oak Lodge, located on the outskirts of Ryhope Wood where his brother Christian lives. Their parents are dead. The

---
[61] Aldiss, p 441

father, for his part, used to explore mythical dimension of the forest and Christian has continued with this. He has written to Stephen explaining their research and that's why the latter has returned.

The two meet and discuss the situation. Then the brother disappears into the forest and Stephen begins to go through his father's posthumous papers. There he reads how he has wandered around in Ryhope Wood meeting archaic figures, mythical characters, including a woman named Guiwenneth. Stephen decides to venture into the woods himself and sound out its mythical depth. And he finds what he seeks, encountering myth with a capital M. He meets fairytale figures in archaic backdrop, legendary figures in a rich environment.

Ryhope Wood is, one might say, a dimensional crossroads. It's like the Abyss Nietzsche spoke of: "The deeper you look into it the deeper it looks into you". The deeper you wander into the forest, the deeper you walk into your psyche, in Jungian fashion encountering avatars of archetypes from Robin Hood to the First World War "good buddy in No Man's Land", Harry Hellfire – and Pan, Merlin, King Arthur and whatnot.

Stephen goes into the woods seeing energies, energies then embodied into one or other figure by his imagination. If he's predisposed to see Robin Hood wearing a green hat, tights and pointed shoes then this is the form he will take. In the mythic force field of Ryhope Wood this is how the intent is realized.

MENTAL IMAGE

You might say: your own mental image interacts with the mythical energy in question, your Will-Thought co-creating the actual Gestalt. A "brownie-energy" tends to show itself in "hood, beard and frock" to facilitate the visualization, because we humans are accustomed to seeing gnomes in this way. This I once read in a text about the gardens of Findhorn, a place exploiting the same ontological force field intimated in *Mythago Wood*.

For its part, Findhorn is located in the everyday world, in Scotland, created by Helen and Peter Caddy in the 1960s. And in this chapter the topic is fiction, the novel *Mythago Wood*. The novel character Stephen goes into the forest: he follows in his father's and brother's footsteps, leaving the known countries behind and meeting winds from the archaic. Like a Södergran he can exclaim: "What has happened in the fairytale will happen to me too!"

As intimated, *Mythago Wood* is a nice mixture of story and ideas, a serious fantasy. Fantasy as a genre isn't always so structurally creative; it can be adventure, suggestive ccenes and fairy-tale brilliance but ideas, either of Jungian or other kinds, are rarely found. To me, Mythago Wood seems to be in the top class in terms of conceptual strength. The forest as psychological landscape, as the scene of myth, history and our interaction with it, here gets an incomparable portrait.

INTERACTION

It's about interaction with the astral world, the world of dreams and images. Venturing out into Ryhope Wood you meet figures out of myth (*Myth Imagos* = Mythagos). From the novel itself hereby an example of the science imagined, in the form of notes by Stephen's brother:

> The mythogenetic process is not only complex, it is reluctant. I am too old! The equipment helps, but a younger mind could accomplish the task unaided, I'm sure. I dread the thought! Also, my mind is not at rest and as Wynne-Jones has explained, it is likely that my human consideration, my worries, form an effective barrier between the mythopoetic energy flows in my cortex – the form from the right brain, the reality from the left. The pre-mythago zone is not sufficiently enriched by my own life for it to interact in the oak vortex.[62]

You have to receive the mythopoetic energy through a calm mind, only thus interaction is possible. As an esotericist I nod affirmatively at this. Volitional mental calm is the way when practicing these matters. This is also about Jungian racial memory. From the wood

---

[62] From chapter four, quoted after Aldiss, 1986, p 442

comes Mythagos, apparently tangible figures but essentially rooted in the human mind and the racial memory. In the process, going into the wood equals going into the subconscious. And in the heartland of the wood you meet the most primitive images of the Self.

Mythagos are seemingly solid creatures made up by the human mind. Again, this is a fantasy in a science fictional mode, mixing the fantasy with realism, making the familiar "crossing over to the fairyland", the "passing from our world to the other" enticingly ambiguous and spiritually scientific. This is spirit science in popular form. I can't vouch for everything Holdstock has come up with, for example, the "cerebrospinal" part is a bit materialist but what do I know.

As for speculative fiction at large, this story shows the way to inner space literature of an authoritative, esoteric kind, going beyond the trauma and angst of the 60s "Ballardian" inner space-concept. Holdstock's novel is serious and constructive inner space fiction, devoid of New Wave nihilism. Aldiss: "its rigorous logical explanations of its themes makes it one of the most intelligent examinations of the human myth-making faculty ever published."[63]

MALACIA TAPESTRY

I have indeed read the novel *Mythago Wood* from beginning to end. But by the time of writing this I didn't have an actual copy so Brian Aldiss' quotes and summary were of some help (along with my personal notes like the Findhorn excursion; Aldiss surely didn't mention *that*). Aldiss' work in question is *Trillion Year Spree: The History of Science Fiction*. In brief, this 1986 overview is a treat. While I don't agree with everything in it I have to recommend it as a whole since Aldiss, in speaking about SF from Mary Shelley to William Gibson, has a sounding board in his knowledge of literature at large. Antiquity, Shakespeare, Romanticism etc.; all this is implicit in his takes on Verne, Wells, dystopias, Gernsback and Campbell, all the way to the 1980s situation in Anglo-American SF.

---

[63] Aldiss, p 443

I mean, today there are many scholars around knowing this and that about the SF field. But can they write, can they convey a sense of "easily shared education" in their overviews? Aldiss can, this pioneer of SF scholarship, this man born in 1925 and making his debut as an author in the 50s.

This chapter was to be about fantasy and Aldiss has written an endearing fantasy novel. I'm thinking of *The Malacia Tapestry* (1976), a tale of a "Ruritanian" city, a town in that kind of parallel-world Europe intimated by Shakespeare plays, of "Sicily, Illyria, Bohemia", all of which take the form of imaginary lands, a timeless, early modern realm of horse carriages, windmills and environmental friendly living.

All this and musicality too. In this study I've highlighted the musical mood (chapter one, at the beginning of chapter twenty) and *The Malacia Tapestry* conveys this rather fine, the main character being an actor.

The gist of Aldiss musicality in this way can be shown by a quote from a comparable text of his, "The Day We Embarked for Cythera", seemingly inspired by the Watteau painting, that of a group of people going down to a harbor for a resplendent journey. Aldiss delivers the payoff, in effortless musical style:

> And there was the ferry, screened by tall cypresses and so rather gloomy. But already lanterns twinkled along the shore, and I heard the sound of music and singing aboard. Back at the tavern, our sweethearts would be waiting for us, and the new play would open at midnight. I had my rôle by heart, I knew every word, I longed to walk out of the wings into the glittering lights, cynosure of all eyes...[64]

DUNSANY

The Irishman Lord Dunsany (1878-1957) wrote the novel *The King of Elfland's Daughter* (1924). It's about elves. Not those tiny, miniature fellows of Edmund Spencer fame; this is about "Nordic" elves,

---

[64] Aldiss, 1971, p 121-122

humanoid in stature. A man, a prince sees the mirage of Elfland and goes out to search it. He indeed finds it and he gains the royal daughter whom he weds. After a happy time in the land of men she disappears and the prince goes out to find her but she's lost to him now, gone to the elven lands which now are inaccessible. But in the end Elfland itself virtually, conceptually, invades his realm and so everything becomes enchanted and he can again be united with his elven princess, happily ever after.

Dunsany is rather "beyond category". He's fully readable and relatable but the visions he brings are indeed "out of this world". His prose is dreamy and airy yet delivered within a tight framework. This isn't a madman's ravings, this is transparent and structured and yet artistic and musical:

> At the beauty of these lawns Alveric stood gazing as they shone through twilight and dew, surrounded by the mauve and ruddy glory of the massed flowers of Elfland, beside which our sunsets pale and our orchids droop; and beyond them lay like night the magical wood. And jutting from that wood, with glittering portals all open wide to the lawns, with windows more blue than our sky on Summer's nights; as though built of starlight; shone that palace that may be only told of in song.[65]

SHORT STORIES

Thus the style of *The King of Elfland's Daughter*. It's an incomparable work, the prose poetry is rewarding and the sometime ironic attitude of the narrator is just right, but as a story it's lacking some pace in the middle part. All things considered, maybe Dunsany's style and outlook came more into its own in his short stories, collected in *The Book of Wonder* (1912). These tales are about going off into lands unseen, lands bordering on ours; just venture out in the woods next to your apartment building; turn right on that special path and see how everything starts to become a bit foggy and fairy-tale like. Now

---

[65] Dunsany, 1969, p 20-21

you're in the gray area, in the twilight zone. But fear not, just carry on, and see how the objects emerge out of their veils and everything becomes symbolic. And before you know it, you've seen Pan, the Dream Caravan, Odin's fortress and the Emerald City in the distance.

This is Dunsany's world: sailing with dream argosies, searching the diamonds of Zachrontia, debating with the genie in the bottle, eating the apples of the sun and interacting with the bramble beasts in the rustling copses. In short: change your level of consciousness, travel by different paths and set sail for the lands of wonder. This is Dunsany's uniqueness, a fairy-tale like but adult world with charm and finesse.

One of the short stories in the current book is "The Madness of Andelsprutz", about a desert where the souls of dead cities go. There you can hear the street noise from ancient Rome, the shouts from the Constantinople vendors and the city guard's cries of medieval London. This was conceptually rather quaint. Another story is about a palace where you see dawn through one window and dusk through another, like on a planet with helio stationary orbit. As such, it's reminiscent of my own short story "The Middle Zone," printed in *Morpheus Tales: The Best Weird Fiction 3* (2013).

DOGS

Authors who like cats (Heinlein, Lovecraft) are considered fine and good. But Edward John Moreton Drax Plunkett, Baron of Dunsany, liked dogs. How strange: this ethereal dream writer, a dog person...? But in reality Dunsany wasn't so ethereal and dreamy, for example, he had served in WWI as a Captain of the Royal Inniskilling Fusiliers. Here you might say "but Tolkien also served in the Great War as an officer". To this I say, true that and kudos to him, but as for psychological profiles I perceive Dunsany as a more officer-like type than the good JRR.

Dunsany was one of H. P. Lovecraft's literary models; see for example "The White Ship", "The Dream-Quest of Unknown Kadath" and "The High House in the Mist", Lovecraft stories mirroring

Dunsany's elegant, dreamlike qualities. Lovecraft is said to have attended a lecture by Dunsany when the lord visited America once. Lovecraft then wrote an essay about Dunsany, noting his literary modus operandi as "conscious unreality". Dunsany (like Lovecraft) took the wonderful seriously, he didn't just laugh it off in the nihilist fashion. You're tempted to say that they both had *seen* what they wrote about, there's an essential authenticity to it all: "Behold, the caravans start"...

Apropos of nothing, I now come to think of an anecdote about Dunsany. It's said that on his estate when he returned from the hunt, he took a shot at the clock so that it rang. Then the butler knew that the lord was home.

As for anecdotes, here's another one. In *Astounding Days,* Arthur C. Clarke's science fictional memoir, the author tells of a meeting with Lord Dunsany. It was in 1951. Clarke had with him a copy of *The Charwoman's Shadow* (1926) to get it signed – and this he got, with quill and everything, the lord's usual writing instrument. Simultaneously with the signing Dunsany made a change in his book; the phrase "The Country Towards Moon's Rising" became "The Country Beyond Moon's Rising" because this sounded better. True, but isn't this the height of pedantry, scribbling in a printed book, destroying its aura...? Because it's said that "the print ennobles". And Luther: "das Wort sollen sie lassen stehen". Misses *in nuance* like these settle with time, as it were, they fade and are absorbed by the whole. No one except for the author notices them.

LITERATURE

- Lord Dunsany: *The King of Elfland's Daughter* (1924) - *The Book of Wonder* (1912)
- Brian Aldiss: *The Malacia Tapestry* (1976)
- Robert Holdstock: *Mythago Wood* (1984)

13. SF FILMS

Are there sf and fantasy films of interest to the radical conservative? Indeed there are. Below the study will give you some examples of this. The overview starts at the perceived beginning, with Fritz Lang's *Metropolis* from 1927 and then moves forward in time. Along with *Metropolis* the films treated are *2001, Star Wars, Blade Runner, Dune, Brazil* and *Lord of the Rings*, plus the speculative works of Andrei Tarkovsky.

METROPOLIS

Fritz Lang's *Metropolis* premiered at the Ufa-Palast in Berlin on January 10, 1927. The film was enthusiastically received by the audience. But already in this version it appears to have been shortened. It was just under two hours long. When the film was shown in the USA it was even more truncated. Parts lifted out included such things as the inventor Rotwang adoring the woman Hel in the form of a bust, a giant head in neo-classical style.

In this American version the film was 115 minutes long. But even in Germany it was to be cut up and slimmed even more. When the film company Ufa soon became insolvent the businessman and right-wing politician Alfred Hugenberg took command of the firm.

The shortening of *Metropolis* he undertook is supposed to have taken away some of the film's radical left sub-theme and part of the religious imagery. The reason may have been rationalized into getting a more commercially viable version. This 91-minute version remained in circulation for a long time.

Then came the restoration attempts. Like Giorgio Moroder's 1984 version which added color here and there, and a modern soundtrack with artists such as Freddie Mercury, Adam Ant and Pat Benatar. This sounds like sacrilege. But I can't completely condemn this version. Firstly, I dislike the original music of *Metropolis*, which was thunderous orchestral music. Secondly, to give the 1980s film audience, overfed on routinely made Hollywood SF, a black-and-white German SF film from the 20s, was a noble cause in itself. But the true restoration attempts gained some momentum in 2008, when German film experts announced that they had found a 16 mm "reduction negative" of the entire original film in Argentina. With this, plus restorations made in 1986 and 2002, you can now say that *Metropolis* is 99% restored. The version I've personally seen, has German text plates and perfect image quality, along with insertions from the somewhat blurred South American copy.

This 2.5 hours movie is quite a treat. *Metropolis* was judged a bit parsimoniously by critics when it arrived but over time this film has triumphed. The film has become a concept for a future city in early 1900s style, with machines, highways, skyscrapers and social unrest. This city lives forever as a symbol and an emblem. We've all been in Metropolis. The script may have its inconsistencies. But as regards cinematography and iconography *Metropolis* is a landmark movie. No one had made such a film before. Movie audiences all over the Western world were astonished and applauded spontaneously at what they saw. The film made an impression in the industry, even in the US.

STREETSCAPES

Metropolis arose as a vision in the form of Thea von Harbou's novel from 1926. Reportedly, it was written with the intent to become a film but it also works as a novel; see chapter six. von Harbou's then-husband Fritz Lang was in the 1920s a renowned silent film director and he shared the novel's vision of the modern city. He had for example been in New York and been captured by the sight of the skyscrapers and the deep, canyon-like streetscapes. And the finished film can be said to be von Harbou's and Lang's communal vision. Lang went energetically ahead in the task to transfer the script to film. The special effects were cutting edge for their times.

Technically, the film is convincing. Artistically then? It may be that the acting style is a bit excessively expressionistic sometimes. Strong expressions, eyes wide...! This can be seen in Gustav Fröhlich (he plays Freder, the young hero), Brigitte Helm (Maria) and Rudolf Klein-Rogge (the inventor Rotwang). But Alfred Abel playing the city's creator and ruler, Joh Fredersen, is a miracle of restraint in his acting style. There's no "silent film manners," no expressionism in his firm countenance. His authoritative, calm figure gives balance to the collection of frantic, fast-moving characters that otherwise populate the film.

Then we have the true star, the scenography. The city of Metropolis has come to life with marvelous clarity, depth and variation. Later in this chapter I will look at Ridley Scott's *Blade Runner* from 1982. Scott is said to have been inspired by *Metropolis* and that you can understand – in seeing the streetscapes, the highrises etc., all this with a sense of genuine depth in the picture, this *Metropolis* had already established as an immortal symbol. And we see a reflection of it in *Blade Runner*. But to get to that depth isn't always easy. I think that Tim Burton's *Batman* (1989), another film inspired by *Metropolis*, had its Metropolis-influence remaining on the surface. The depth in the image, the alluring scenery was missing when Batman directed by Burton would struggle with the Joker.

However, Scott and Lang nailed it. Scott also has a scene directly inspired by Metropolis, from a scene in Fredersen's office. Here I think of such a thing as "overlooking a city landscape with a pyramidal complex" (it's there in the restored *Metropolis* version, and in *Blade Runner* this becomes an emblem). And in "the curtain of the panoramic window is closed with remote control". This last is hard to describe the beauty of but it looks striking in both Lang's and Scott's versions.

For the stage design in *Metropolis* nothing was spared: large models with traffic, trains and planes, striking interiors (scenes of the city's industrial, underground regions, Rotwang's laboratory, Yoshiwara's entertainment districts etc.). Additionally, we have the robot Futura, sculpted with an early form of plastic, polished and painted with the illusion of metallic shimmer.

A telling scene in every respect is when Maria tells the workers how the Tower of Babel was built. For this five-minute scene a model of the Tower of Babel was constructed, several crowd scenes with the workers were filmed and special costumes for Babel clergy were made, figuring ever so briefly. Lang left nothing to chance. This recap, the Babel sequence, depicted how a fateful distance can arise between a society's leadership and its grassroots. The Tower of Babel fell because of rebellion, this is von Harbou's interpretation, they couldn't communicate. The elite government lacked feedback from the workers. The confusion of tongues begun even before the tower fell. For in government, the brain in the form of leaders must have contact with the workers, the hand, and this with the mediation of the heart, the symbol of feeling and understanding. "The mediator between head and hand must be the heart."

This Maria says to the workers. She leads an opposition movement against the tightly run industrial regime. The workers toil underground, the upper class lives well in their skyscrapers. Maria doesn't expressly want a rebellion, she wants a peaceful reformation of "heart uniting head and hand". But the city's leader, Fredersen, impels the inventor Rotwang to build a robot with Maria's looks, a robot to incite the workers to rebel. This will then be the cause for countermeasures resulting in an even tighter dictatorship.

BABYLON

The plan is implemented and an uprising breaks out. The workers sabotage the machines and eventually get up in the daylight. The film has many crowd scenes and they are efficient. As mentioned, there was a look back at the Biblical Babylon. There we have a scene showing a priest king standing and talking to the tower's workforce from the crest of a flight of steps. But the workers have revolt in mind and rush up to him, in wedge formation, and overwhelm him. This is very cinematographically apt. And this scene is later repeated in the Metropolis setting proper, at the end. It's when the workers, in perfect sync, with a rigid marching pace, go forward in a wedge-shaped mass against the lone Joh Fredersen, outside the cathedral as it happens to be.

Others than Ridley Scott and Tim Burton have been inspired by *Metropolis*. Myself, for example. In the novel *Antropolis* (2009, in Swedish only), I sketched a plot with a city in the future, plagued by social unrest. Technology and spirituality confront each other but they are united at last in the form of art. The Engineer and the Preacher must be united by the Musical Man. The ancient Muses, the goddesses of artistic inspiration, must be present in the soul of every state. Our times has forgotten this. Materialism prevails, technology is worshiped and the spirituality that may sprout is often stiff and rigid in its appearance, lacking zest and pizazz. Technology *per se* is needed but it must be spiritually led, that's what my novel emphasizes. The public life must be imbued with the magic power of art, inspiration and compassion. Musical joy must permeate everything. This is my version of "*Der Mittler zwischen Hirn und Hand muss das Herz sein*" "The mediator between head and hand must be the heart", the final message of *Metropolis*.

Above I mentioned that the inventor Rotwang worships the woman Hel. Her name is the same as the Norse deity, the goddess of hell. But this Hel is only the woman Rotwang once loved. However, she abandoned him in favor of Fredersen. With Hel Fredersen eventually had the son Freder. When Joh Fredersen then asks Rotwang for help to crush Maria's opposition movement Rotwang sees his chance for revenge: Maria loves Freder, the son of Rotwang's rival, Fredersen, so if the robot Futura is given Maria's traits she can drag him down to perdition! This plot move is one that becomes clear only with the restored version. Earlier, the plot was mainly concerned with the rebellion, with robot-Maria as an instrument for this and not much more.

The uprising rolls on but everything is reconciled at the end. Outside the cathedral Joh Fredersen is eventually trying to shake hands with a foreman who had come to symbolize the working community. But it doesn't come easy. Then Maria again preaches about the heart having to be the mediator between head and hand. And it will be John Fredersens' son, Freder, who unites the two men, and completes the handshake. This final scene has its power and it has a bearing still today. For example, in the interpretation of spirituality (head) and technology (hand) having to be united by artistry (heart).

2001: A SPACE ODYSSEY

2001: A Space Odyssey premiered in 1968. As an enterprise it went against the then, Western movie trend. No one made lavish SF films during this time. SF, space and fantasy were considered odd themes in the 60s film industry. Two high-profile SF films from the 1950s might be mentioned, *War of the Worlds* (1953) and *Forbidden Planet* (1956). Also, we had *Planet of the Apes* in 1968. But otherwise the rule was that of great budgets only being given to historical films, westerns and musicals.

But then it befell in England that a filmmaker teamed up with an SF author. Reportedly, director Stanley Kubrick (1928-1999) phoned Arthur C. Clarke, and said: "Let's create the most epic SF movie ever." This was an odd duo but a competent one. Kubrick had made personal, headstrong films like *Dr. Strangelove*. And Clarke had written SF stories with scientific rigor, and some kind of spiritual depth, like *Against the Fall of Night* and *Childhood's End*, which I told about in chapter nine. When Clarke and Kubrick got together the result was a classic for all times.

When looking at the finished product, you may ask: how much "Kubrick" and how much "Clarke" is it? I'd say that it's more than 60% Kubrick. But Clarke's involvement was of course absolutely necessary. When the duo had rejected the novel *Childhood's End* as unfilmable, Clarke browsed his back catalogue and found the short story "The Sentinel" from 1951. Here we find the theme of advanced aliens triggering the next stage of human development, by having built a pyramid on the moon millions of years ago and the structure setting off a cosmic alarm when space-faring, 20th century man discovers it and examines it. The aliens in question are only hinted at. You never know how they look. And the same would be the case in *2001*: primitive man, for 100,000s of years ago, will in the film be elevated by what he sees in a certain artifact, a black monolith. This should then, according to Clarke's screenplay, bring the apeman on the road to higher development, like learning how to use weapons. The femur of an antelope, used as a club in the hand of a primitive man, represents a step forward in his mastery of nature. You can with this weapon hunt more efficiently, you can bring down big game, and with more proteins in the diet you get more stamina etc.

This vision *per se* is signed Arthur C. Clarke. Like the gist of the rest of the film, where it's present time / near future. I've intimated the plot in an earlier chapter and here I'll repeat it. Human practical intelligence and mastery of nature has led to space technology and a base on the moon. Once there is discovered yet another monolith, similar to the one the primitive people met. And when this new monolith is dug up, it emits a signal to yet another monolith, circling in orbit around Jupiter. This can be rationalized into a glorified test: the intelligent aliens who once raised man have placed the moon-monolith as a control along the path of man in his development. He has reached the moon, he should find it and he has found it; thus he should be able to perform the next step, to equip a ship and get to the monolith by Jupiter.

DISCOVERY

A ship is equipped. It's called Discovery. Eventually it reaches the Jupiter monolith (in the novel it orbited Saturn). An astronaut mans a capsule to investigate the monolith – but then he gets the surprise of his life. The monolith isn't massive, it's hollow. It's a gateway to a parallel universe, a higher reality.

This is absolutely unique in the history of cinema. No film had previously described the transition from our world to another world in this way. True, there are dream-like dimensional passages in movies like *The 5,000 Fingers of Dr. T* and *The Wizard of Oz*. But this is all on a higher, more pathos-filled level, everything takes place within a broader, more conceptual framework, encompassing themes like the course of history and the spiritual development of man.

What the astronaut finds beyond the gate is hard to describe. He encounters absolutely indescribable sights and landscapes: colors, distorted forms, light and patterns. The special effects guys had a fine challenge to get to this right and they succeeded. It was about portraying a higher reality.

After seeing a series of strange impressions, scenes and landscapes the astronaut lands his capsule into a room, a locale that seems to be adapted to a human. The alien intelligence has brought it about. Why? In order to bring man to further developments. Then, after due scenes, admirably restrained and yet captivating (the man walking around the rooms, he gets older, he lies down and encounters the monolith soaring above him) the astronaut returns to earth as a glorified fetus, a Star Child. And then the film ends as it began: with the intro of Richard Strauss' "Also Sprach Zarathustra". This title refers to Friedrich Nietzsche's book about man reaching a higher step in development by willpower. In the film, man is elevated with the help of aliens.

Nietzsche had his points, Kubrick / Clarke likewise. It's highly plausible that aliens in some or other form have given humanity pointers during its course of development. They are in religious contexts called angels, devas and gods. *2001* suggests this in an exemplary manner. The alien intelligence is never shown, it conducts a mystical existence in the background, in a higher dimension. But this higher dimension is indeed reached by the space capsule entering the stargate. Again, this is quite unique. The film is like an initiation, a latter-day mystery play. Someone said that the cinema screen itself plays the role of a stargate in "the stargate scene".

The message is clear: man must raise himself mentally to reach the next stage of development. Developing mentally and spiritually, that's the true theme song for the man in the space age. Materialism and duality are passing modes of thinking. Now we must raise our eyes – to the stars. And at the same time, inwardly. "Brain building" must now be conducted along with "bodybuilding". Outer space is reached by inner space.

2001 is a ceremony on these themes. Kubrick came with the artistic impulse and he was assisted by Clarke to realize the vision. Additionally, Kubrick was shrewd in his incorporation of classical music into the opus. Like the introduction, with earth seen from orbit and the sun becoming visible above the sphere's curvature, to the accompaniment of Strauss' "Also Sprach Zarathustra", which was a stroke of genius. No one played this piece at the time, it was more or less forgotten. Since 1968 and *2001* it's a signature of the space age.

For the rest of the classical, but already composed, more or less unknown music in the movie, you could mention the György Ligeti's (1923-2006) compositions. Allowing the anguished "Requiem" to accompany the journey beyond the stargate was another stroke of genius. A more banal director had perhaps portrayed it with happy or peaceful music. But Kubrick with this score portrays the mental strain of going Beyond the Beyond. The astronaut is seen to more or less break down in the process and the music is, for its part, indescribable; it's not triumphant, not languishing, instead a trying storm of key shifts. But not merely trying; it has its own beauty too.

The same applies to some other Ligeti music pieces incorporated in the film. For example, when the hovercraft on the Moon goes to the artifact to where it's been dug up, it's done to the tune of Ligeti's "Lux Aeterna". And it gives the scene a strange, evocative atmosphere, completely indescribable. This is far beyond the usual score for a Hollywood movie. Actually, a customary soundtrack to this film was also made, a traditional orchestration signed Alex North. But this music was never used, thankfully. North had, for example, made the soundtrack to Kubrick's major film *Spartacus* (1960). Traditional film music would have made *2001* a banal. The old-school classical plus the way-out modern orchestral music that Kubrick finally chose, are a contributing part to *2001s* grandeur.

In a previous chapter I've mentioned the novel version of *2001*, the one Clarke wrote and published in the same year as the film premiered. Much as I am a literary *aficionado* I must say that the film version is better. As is the case of two other items in this chapter, *Metropolis* and *Blade Runner*. It's true that the Dick story the latter is based on – *Do Androids Dream of Electric Sheep?* – is rather grand and convincing but since Dick wrote so many masterpieces I'd say, you haven't missed much if you don't read this particular novel, *Do Androids Dream of Electric Sheep*. But I might be unfair now since compared to SF in general this novel is a stand-out piece in most respects. Just don't expect *Do Androids Dream of Electric Sheep* to convey "that particular Blade Runner feeling".

STAR WARS SAGA

George Lucas (1944-) created the Star Wars Saga, a unique mix of modern legend and Jungian myth. The films in this series are, in order of creation: *Star Wars* (1977), *The Empire Strikes Back* (1980), *Return of the Jedi* (1983), *The Phantom Menace* (1999), *Attack of the Clones* (2002) and *Revenge of the Sith* (2005).

The plot aside (and the fact that the three last made films plot wise are precursors to the three first made), what mostly impresses me is that it all coheres – and that's the theme of good fighting against evil, but the evil is here not some mysterious force from nowhere. It's embodied by some of the people, like Darth Vader. That said, the evil isn't real, it's "storybook evil", but still, Lucas showed some courage in depicting how the hero figure of Annakin Skywalker develops into the villain of Darth Vader.

We also have the development of Senator Palpatine in the same direction, from a common politician to a deformed monster, rather convincing (see the 2005 movie). Within a science fantasy framework, the evil in Star Wars works well. So maybe my labeling of it as mere "storybook evil" is a bit too harsh.

I just mentioned the 2005 movie, *Revenge of the Sith*. This lastly completed film in the suite is for me the crowning work. It's not the best in the series (this title goes to the 1977 movie), but with the 2005 film Lucas managed to get out of the slump that *The Phantom Menace* and *Attack of the Clones* formed. Overall, *Revenge of the Sith* had more energy and consistency; it had a sense of urgency in tying up all the loose plot ends, doing so in a masterful manner.

In this film, it was both Vader / Annakin's and Palpatine's transition to the evil side that created interest. There was some power in the scene of the deformed Palpatine in Parliament announcing that the Republic is hereby abolished, now we introduce the Empire...! Popular rule must always be defended. Today, we need to safeguard the rule "for, by and with the people". We can't hand it over to the 24/7 propaganda of mainstream media. Who in this context is Palpatine and who will become Skywalker is still written in the stars.

Critics have said that the three last-made films lack much of what the first three had. Like memorable casting. This, I can agree with. Between Mark Hamill, Carrie Fischer and Harrison Ford there was chemistry, there was life. In contrast, the actors of the 1999-2005 trilogy were somewhat pallid. Lucas is no original director as such, it often comes down to remaking on screen what has gone before in film history (like the Christiansen-Portman romance mirroring the Plummer-Andrews romance of *Sound of Music*). But I don't demand that Lucas should be another Scorsese or Sean Penn, I'm just noting his limitations.

That said, maybe the scenography also got a little overwrought in the last-made trilogy. Then again, as a fantasy filmmaker you have to invent new scenes and planets galore, you can't just have a starcruiser and a space planet once again, as in the 1977 film. Therefore, the somewhat overripe scenography. The first three films were simple without being simplistic. The 1977-1983 trilogy had a mix of functionalism with a fairy tale aspect that felt fresh. The last made trilogy tended to give us more of everything until it became difficult to grasp. But I still like to see the 1999-2005 trilogy and study set designs, costumes and spaceships. The opening scene in *Revenge of the Sith*, with Annakin and Obi-Wan Kenobi in two pursuit spacecraft on their way to board a cruiser from which to abduct Palpatine, is rather grandiose. Lucas made it work in this movie. The work was crowned, the whole of it cohered.

JUNGIAN PATTERN

From the beginning Lucas sounded out some depth with his work. When he had written his first screenplay draft in the 70s he reportedly consulted Joseph Campbell's *The Hero with a Thousand Faces* (1949). This study, influenced by the psychologist Carl Jung, among other things, states that the archetypal hero must face his shadow, the symbol of evil. The hero can't just wipe it out, he must integrate it into his own being in some way. Thus spiritual wholeness and sanity is accomplished. And this philosophical depth to a certain extent characterizes the entire Star Wars Saga. It's there in the beginning, in the 1977 film implied by the bond between Luke and Vader, and it's also present in the last-made film.

You can say: Star Wars has some of the same depth as Peter Jackson's *The Lord of the Rings*, an epic work that can be said to belong to the tradition Lucas founded with his project: fantasy films with big budgets. Such films didn't exist before the 1970s. SF and fantasy weren't mainstream in the film industry before *Star Wars* came in 1977. Fantastic movies occurred but they were usually low budget. *2001* had somewhat opened up for serious SF films but they were often dismal in outlook (*Soylent Green, THX 1138, Silent Running...*), not as overall grand as *2001*. But today, for better or worse, the big, expensive SF or fantasy yarn is always viable on film, it seems.

The Star Wars Saga has its depth. It is not just about spacecraft design and merchandising of plastic figures; far from it. But the design is of course important in this context. Already the first-made film had something new: functionalism and antiquity at the same time. This was not the impression of sterile and antiseptic interiors and landscapes, like in the Star Trek TV series of the 60s. In the 1977 *Star Wars* there were no shiny surfaces in chromed steel; instead, it was rust and worn surfaces in the midst of all high technology. This, plus the fairytale-related but believable aliens, the stylish costumes (which felt both modern and old (timeless / archeofuturistic)) and especially "The Mos Eisley Cantina Scene" with its calypso band: it captivated me personally when, as an 11-year-old, I saw the 1977 movie the year it premiered. The scene in question seemed both familiar and strange.

And as for the music touches you must also mention the r'n'b band in Jabba the Hutt's cave in the 1983 film, "Max Rebo Band" with its catchy soul refrain. I miss the keys on my keyboard to describe the geniality of this scene. Cinematically, here a certain childishness interacts with the joy of forms and shapes to create a scene of immortal humor and exoticism. The scene may have been created by specially hired designers; Lucas didn't draw and construct any aliens, interiors and ships per se, as far as I know. But bringing all this talent together sure takes some kind of genius, structuring it all in the framework intimated above. Fairy tale like and a bit silly at times but with an enduring quality nonetheless; this is the Star Wars Saga, now an indelible part of the human collective consciousness.

BLADE RUNNER

In 1982 Ridley Scott (1937-) made *Blade Runner*. The script was based on Philip K. Dick's *Do Androids Dream of Electric Sheep?* It took the middle part of the novel and elaborated it artistically, in the interiors and exteriors. Dick was a lot but he couldn't really convey scenes in this way, scenes of impressionist sublimity. But can any SF author do this, aren't they all "draughtsmen but not painters" in this sense? I'd say, indeed there are SF authors around with the ability to paint, to render atmosphere (Bradbury, Delany, Vance, Lovecraft) – so, long story short, the movie goer should rejoice in this 1982 film, a work of art taking the Dick mythos to the realm of sublime beauty.

The star of the movie is the scenography. I know, the casting was fine too but I'll bypass it here. I'll spend the major part of this section talking about how the scenes were made in terms of props, milieus and filming locations.

To create the image of "Los Angeles 2019" the film team built a model, a significant scale model that would evoke a scattered urban landscape, a bit jumbled like Japanese cityscapes or any suburban sprawl. With light, smoke and models of modern, pyramidal towers in the background, were created a suggestive picture of the whole. You must see the opening scene with its bird's view of the future Los Angeles in order to understand what I mean.

This is the elite class of scenography. The art of film has always worked to create illusions, to create the image of something with the help of theatrical effects. *Blade Runner's* urban landscape might "merely" be a model with light effects, imprinted images of oil refineries and edited-in soaring craft, but it's more than that, more than the sum of its parts. This is artistry, the ability to paint, to convey the image of a different world.

Generally, in American films they work hard to create these kinds of illusions. Each frame tends to have "that diorama feeling". And this we also see in *Blade Runner's* other scenes. Here is also the retro-feeling part of the equation. We're not given a pristine version Los Angeles with shiny high-rises, monorails and functionalist architecture. Instead, the scenographers built some smaller, modern sceneries with conventional high-tech elements, parallel to filming in existing Los Angeles houses from the early 1900s, like the railway station Union Station (in the movie it's the Police Headquarters), the Bradbury Building (an apartment house where Batty's and Deckard's final duel takes place), "The 2nd Street Tunnel" with its glazed tiles as well as Frank Lloyd Wright's Ennis House. The last is a luxury villa in Los Angeles, built in 1924, pioneering in modern architecture by Wright having been inspired by Native American / Aztec forms. In the film we see interiors of the house, rather sparingly so that it looks like being part of an apartment building. This restraint is very apt in this context. "Restraint is the mark of the master", as Goethe said.

ATMOSPHERE

Blade Runner creates an indescribable atmosphere: again, like *Star Wars*, it's familiar and unfamiliar at the same time. Ernst Jünger once said, speaking of science fiction, for the amazing to stand out better you must put it next to something familiar. This applies eminently well for *Blade Runner*. Instead of having Harrison Ford go through high-tech environment after high-tech environment we see him living in a diverse future, now going in a modern "quibble" craft over the city, now searching through a pretty normal, furnished apartment of the 20th century kind, now sitting in his sofa in his Ennis House interior with Aztec patterns on the wall, now visiting a surgical agency with incomprehensible apparatus. And all this he does in a restrained garb: jacket and shirt with a tie, while his love interest Rachel has a rather elaborate hair-do and a costume looking like a creation of Chanel vintage 1937.

This passion for the early 1900s, especially the 30s and 40s, is always rewarding for a filmmaker. Things were better looking then, more stylish, quite simply. But as Goethe said, there has to be restraint – mastership is about showing restraint – you have to balance the well-designed art deco with more neutral objects if you, as in *Blade Runner* and *Brazil*, are making a future movie. You don't have to shout "future" in every frame. More on *Brazil* soon.

Blade Runner has some existential depth. For example, the question "what is a man?" is answered by showcasing a human-like machine, a non-human: the android. Here, in Batty's and others' shape (the movie is about how police officer Deckard must terminate an entire group of fugitive androids), this problem is symbolized in a perhaps captivating way. Along with this *Blade Runner* creates an atmosphere by recalling old detective films from the 1940s, "film noir" like *The Big Heat*, *The Maltese Falcon* and *The Ministry of Fear*.

Sean Young in a golden brown apartment, with the Los Angeles urban landscape behind, is the symbol for this. It's timeless. Thanks to what? Thanks to Ridley Scott's artistic genius, Dick's futuristic humanism, the meticulous and open-minded set design – and Vangelis' music. "Rachel's Song" and "Memories of Green" sounds like something you've heard a thousand times but it's original compositions, seductively simple but mesmerizing in their melancholy magic.

DUNE

David Lynch is an American film director, born in 1946. And in 1984 he made *Dune*, an archeofuturist film classic. I treated the book *per se* in chapter two and here I'll only say that Lynch's version is very rewarding. Just as Scott in *Blade Runner* took the Dick narrative to new heights, Lynch in *Dune* took Herbert's bare-bones prose and gave us alluring scenes, vivid imagery, the incidents are cinematographic genius. While it's true that Herbert did outline his world in some detail his prose style sometimes becomes a bit pedestrian. Therefore Lynch's *Dune* is worth seeing, adding "that artistic touch" to the whole.

Dune suffers a bit from having to be edited down to a format suitable for theaters. But not much. If you want a longer Dune film then we have John Harrison's version from 2000 – not a bad movie *per se* but artistically not on the same level as Lynch's *Dune*.

BRAZIL

On the surface *Brazil* (1985) is a *retro movie*, archeofuturism focusing on outdated modern design and technology; a film excelling in 20th century paraphernalia like pneumatic tube mail, Bakelite telephones and a vehicle like the German *Kabinenroller*, a three-wheel one-man car powered by a motorcycle engine built in the 1950s. *Brazil* was one of the first in the genre: the presence of some *passé*, high-profile technology are key elements of the vision for the future. It shows a "future perfect": an outmoded future, a future like people in the past, say in the early 1900s, could have imagined it.

There are many unwritten laws for a retro movie. Among other things, the stage design is important. Fairly old but well-designed objects, products and houses become the central element of the whole. This idea can be interpreted as part of a political conservatism: you don't always have to "make it new", in the way that modernism always tries to do. Old forms and ideas are also welcome when we'll build the future.

Brazil is a complex film. But first and foremost it's entertaining. It's cinematic: the director Terry Gilliam (1940-) has created the whole basis of images, striking scenes and symbols. But it isn't just a display of design and scenography. The story as such has some pathos. The inspiration for it all was George Orwell's novel *Nineteen Eighty-Four*, about a man trapped in a dictatorship state. The book is still alive as a classic; see chapter six. But the film adaptation made by Michael Radford in *1984* doesn't add so much to the concept.

Better then with Gilliam's *Brazil* asking questions about bureaucracy and the extinction of the individual in the technical systems, adding to these aspects about dreaming, about becoming someone else, about the necessity of having visions. It's that counter-image so necessary for dystopias that I spoke of in chapter six. The protagonist Sam Lowry's daydreams are woven into his life as a civil servant in a "velvet dictatorship", a modern control state which is vaguely similar to today's media-controlled PC society. Dreams interact with reality and the end is wonderfully ambiguous. As in *Nineteen Eighty-Four* it seems the protagonist has been crushed by the system but there's an opening here, you can interpret it as if Lowry did indeed win, taking an escape route through his inner mind, his fantasy and imagination. Such complexity is difficult to portray on film but Gilliam succeed.

Brazil is about more than this. It is about love, about problems with craftsmen fixing your apartment, and it's about the old samba song "Aquarela do Brasil" from 1939, which in different varieties make up the film's soundtrack. In the West this song is simply known as "Brazil", made popular by Frank Sinatra and others. Reportedly, the original impetus for making the film was Gilliam having a vision of a transistor radio, standing on a deserted beach playing this song. This is a musical way of creating movies which deserves praise.

LORD OF THE RINGS

In 2001-2004 Peter Jackson (1961-) took Tolkien's Lord of the Rings Saga and brought it to the movies, credibly so. The look and feel of it was artistically satisfactory, sometimes brilliant. Sometimes it got a little bit overwrought, as in "Galadriel with pig-ears in a Hollywoodish Lothlórien". In this respect the overall-not-so-successful *Lord of the Rings* by Ralph Bakshi from 1978 did it better. His Galadriel was elegant and Lothlórien didn't look like a bazaar.

It seems that Jackson doesn't fully understand the designer dictum, "go all the way, then step back". But I shouldn't be picky.

His film trilogy has an impressive cinematic quality. Nowadays, some people even like the films better than the books. I can understand that, even though I personally am an avid Tolkien fan since reading the trilogy in the early 1980s.

Jackson's version is an interpretation, one of many possible. But having said that, Jackson's Ring as it stands is worthy of its praise. The three films are called *The Fellowship of the Ring* (2001), *The Two Towers* (2002) and *The Return of the King* (2003). I must say I was a bit worried when in the 1990s I heard that they were going to film Tolkien in New Zealand. I got visions of "The New Adventures of Hercules" and Kevin Sorbo in studs and leather among palms and ferns. But I didn't have to worry. Jackson may have used New Zealand for many scenes but overall the feeling is still harshly Nordic. They have, for example, even in this antipodean archipelago *conifers*, the arboreal symbol of the North.

The project was grand. Jackson's film has the format required for an established literary classic like this, a tale rich in environments, characters and fantasies. As hinted: Jackson delivered. It may be that such a film is more about production than about artistic merit but there's also room for the latter here. Jackson has taken some liberties, a brave thing considering the dedication of some Tolkien fans. These liberties include such things as having the warriors of the good side donned in plate armor. Tolkien, for his part, only mentions chain mail. This presence of shiny plate is wholesome, it makes the impression of "a knight in shining armor", reflecting the spiritual dimension of the work. It's the struggle against evil, a struggle going on even now. The Mordor of Globalism casts its shadow over the world but still resistance is made.

Inspiration for the scenography was drawn from traditional sources, making a good portion of the history of art ending up on the screen. For instance, the elven city Rivendell was reportedly inspired by the architecture style of Art Nouveau with flowing, organic forms. Then we had the throne room of Minas Tirith in Romanesque style, rather excellent. And the City of the Dead in Dune Harrow was inspired by the rock temple Petra in Jordan. Finally, the Gray Havens from where Frodo departs at the end are inspired by the 1800 century painter William Turner's visions of ancient ruins. Especially his "Decline of the Carthaginian Empire" from 1817 seems to have guided the scenographers, of a harbor inlet flanked by classical buildings.

The film is classy. True, sometimes it's also grotesque. From the 1980s and on there were Tolkien renderings in fantasy art, in role playing games, coffee table books and such. Jackson's team looked at this art world and used some of it, which might have been a fitting gesture in the process. But these modern time Tolkien artworks often border on the grotesque and thankfully, the film is not just a show of such fantasies. The film has style, it has class, thanks to the team having incorporated a subtle but noticeable strain of classic design in it. It gave Midgard a scent of ancient, medieval and more recent traditional art and this contributes to the film's status as a classic. It's a well-designed movie, it's not ugly. It's aesthetically pleasing because of its resonance in Western art as a whole.

POLITICAL SIGNIFICANCE

I have nothing more to say about the film itself. Instead, I'll mention something about its significance for the contemporary debate. I said above that the film series' theme with the struggle against evil is topical even today. In the current Westworld the enemy is globalism. It threatens us like Sauron's hordes that engulf countries and people, lowering people mentally and pulling down everything into materialism and nihilism. In this sense, Mordor is real.

Generally speaking, I'm glad of the fact that the Tolkien films are around, depicting as they do the struggle between good and evil. Not all fantasy stories do. There are many SF and fantasy films done in the Hollywood of today but not all of them speak as plainly as *The Lord of the Rings*: evil does exist, darkness threatens us, but if we only see the Light within us, if we exercise the Will to power over ourselves and decide to fight the darkness, we can persevere and realize the Sat Yuga of spirituality, peace and harmony. Creativity, inspiration and co-nationalism, letting each people live in its place of origin; that's the way of the future. And of lauding the ideals of honor and glory, of free debate and discussions; this is the weapon against globalism's agenda of negativity, regimentation and sterility.

Not all modern films are about oppression, debauchery, nihilism and materialism. To do as the Ring trilogy film does, to demonstrate how the power of darkness is defeated by the Light, this has eternal validity – and not only that, this battle is raging now. Every freedom-fighter should know this. And the Ring films show how the Light will prevail. It certainly requires determination from us, this the movie also shows. The Ring will not destroy itself. Frodo must go on foot all the way to Mordor and cast it in the Doomsday gap. Now, you mustn't over-interpret contemporary life in mythical terms. You mustn't overheat and begin to see elves, hobbits and orcs in the street corners or expect Gandalf come riding on the clouds. But the attitudes and the struggle that Tolkien portrays is essentially true. And this is why the films in question are topical even as I write this, more than a decade after their creation.

TARKOVSKY

I'll end this chapter with a brief look at the SF films of Andrei Tarkovsky (1932-1986). Here we have a filmmaker with a strong sense of Tradition: faith and esotericism play central roles in his works. A feel for Tradition *per se* is always present, as in the presence of traditional music and artworks. As for the latter, take the panning of a Brueghel painting in *Solaris* (1972), this old-school picture really standing out in the clinical atmosphere of the space station where the action takes place. In the same vein the focusing on a book with traditional artworks, given as a gift to the main character in *The Sacrifice* (1986), serves to remind us of the archaic, of olden times and attitudes co-existing with the present.

These might be naive gestures, to merely film an old artwork. For filming is about movement and action, right? But Tarkovsky was a naive artist in the best sense of the word. Like *The Sacrifice*, with a man staving off the end of the world by visiting a Holy Woman and making love to her: a simple plot but not simplistic, not in

Tarkovsky's hands. As I say in chapter 31, I can't relate to stories about nuclear war, but this film is the glorious exception. Why? Because of the depth, the sense of artistry. A nuclear tale told by a nihilist is unbearable. A similar story told by a man of faith is something completely different, as *The Sacrifice* shows us.

Tarkovsky portrays his Christian faith, maybe it gets a little odd and bent at times, but compared to all the rest of 20th century filmmakers, SF and mainstream alike, he's head and shoulders above them. Focusing on top-notch names like Bergman, Antonioni and Fellini they were all nihilists; deft and honest, but nihilist nonetheless. In comparison, Tarkovsky had faith and this elevates him.

The Sacrifice tells of the paranoia a supposed nuclear attack evokes. It gives us the Swedish island of Gotland, a barren land with its own peculiar charm, as a psychological landscape. The end is ambiguous but an added note at the very end, a plaque saying that the director dedicates this to his son in a sense of hope, carries the day. Normally, as an artist, you shouldn't add pointers like this but in high-level artworks it's allowed, as in the notes at the end of Eliot's "The Waste Land".

A film that's rather captivating graphically but at the same time a bit odd, a bit "Dostoyevskyan cellar-dwelling", is *Stalker* (1979). Based on a Strugatsky Brothers novel this, again, takes us to a psychological landscape, now in the form of derelict industries, taking us on a quest seemingly ending in nothing. It's downcast and a bit indulgent but still worth seeing: the sense of urgency of a camera panning objects drowned in water is beyond description.

As for the already mentioned *Solaris* this is based on a novel by Stanislaw Lem (1921-2006), his best, about a station on the alien planet *Solaris* where the surroundings take the shape of your inner mind; again, it's the psychological landscape haunting us, the land of dreams, the adopted land of Lovecraft, Castaneda and Jünger, to mention some other expert dreamers of this study.

Frivolously I say, all the Tarkovsky films are worth seeing. If you have some patience and don't need to have action and marvel in every frame they're rewarding indeed. And as for Tarkovsky's SF films they function both as speculative stories and as timeless human documents.

14. SF ART

THIS STUDY WILL now make an outing into the realm of SF art, deliberating on the illustrators making the covers of SF magazines and books, in the US and in Britain. The main source for the following is Steve Holland's *Sci-Fi Art – A Graphic History* (2009). The chapter is concluded with some lines about SF comics, aiming for a praise of the *archeofuturist* strain.

FRANK R. PAUL

I start this survey of SF art in 20th century America. You could say: there had been illustrators conjuring up visions of spaceships, alien creatures and alien worlds before the 1920s, both in the US and Europe. But in this review of SF artists I'll start with focusing on Frank R. Paul (1884-1963). He contributed to the first issue of *Amazing Stories*, "the first devoted SF magazine", in April 1926. And for the following 20 or so years Paul made an indelible impression with his renderings of aliens and SF hardware. True, there were other SF illustrators around in the 20s and 30s but Paul in this context will be the symbol of the pulp era.

Primarily, Paul's cityscapes are memorable; they have something of the futurist architect Sant'Elia in them. And Paul had a background in architecture, at least in his schooling. Born in Austria and later moving to the US, Paul was working for a provincial American newspaper when the editor Hugo Gernsback discovered him. This was in 1914. Paul subsequently illustrated covers and interiors for Gernsback magazines like *Electrical Experimenter, Amazing Stories* and *Science Wonder Stories.*

In *Amazing* Paul contributed with intriguing visions of alien worlds and their inhabitants, having both some sort of scientific plausibility (from the standards of the day) and a sense of proportion and beauty. For instance, this can be seen in the back covers entitled "Serenis, Water City of Callisto" (sybarite aliens reclining by a bay with Jupiter stupendously in the sky) "City of the Future" (in the vein of Sant'Elia) and "Quartz City on Mercury" (a hexagonal structure of kaleidoscopic intricacy).

As for striving for beauty and avoiding the grotesque, Paul said this when he was guest of honor at the first SF Worldcon:

> I have always tried to interpret what the author had in mind, but you'll admit I have never tried to scare you with the purely grotesque.[66]

RICHARD POWERS

Richard Powers (1921-1996) took SF art into new realms of abstraction. In capturing his specificity, a reproduction in Holland's book comes in handy: the cover to a Frederik Pohl anthology from 1955, *Star Science Fiction Stories No. 3.*

This painting is partitioned in three background fields, from top to bottom yellow, dark green and red, and the scene displayed over these fields shows some strange artifacts, some human figures and a rocket. Holland: "Powers summarizes various concepts of science fiction in one image – alien architecture is incidental to the three main elements: a man looking towards a rocket aimed at a planet clearly not Earth".[67]

---

[66] Paul after Holland, p 31
[67] Ibid., p 51

Powers could paint realistically. But his defining feature was surrealism, abstract images representing a feeling or an emotion. From 1953 Powers illustrated many American book covers, the ones from Ballantine Books being what defined him, like books for Clarke, Heinlein, Sturgeon and Blish and Pohl's *Star Science Fiction* anthology series. By 1970 a more realistic approach was favored and by that time the Powers wave was over.

Powers' art combines the abstract with the figurative. Powers didn't invent abstract painting; in this, artists like Picasso, Delaunay and the Italian futurists had gone before him. In taking abstract art into SF illustrations Powers can be seen as a form of "trickle-down modernism", like the hard-boiled prose of Dashiell Hammett and Sherwood Anderson is said to be a popular version of the reduced style of Gertrude Stein, the minimalist poetry pioneer.

PAUL LEHR

Paul Lehr (1930-1998) was a prolific book cover artist from the 1960s and on. Starting out in a realistic vein ("realistic" within the framework of the fantastic character of SF) this American artist soon ventured out into symbolic lands, verging on the abstract. His alien landscapes with spherical and other intriguing, aesthetically pleasing shapes have a true borderline quality, speaking to the viewer's subconscious. Never entirely abstract as Powers could be, but mapping the same mental vistas as he did, Paul is a discreet master of symbolic art.

Bob Eggleton described the Lehr project as "the true embodiment of SF 'art' and not just 'illustration' as his incomparable work allowed the viewer to return for multiple times and walk away having been told a new story each instance."[68]

FRANK KELLY FREAS

Frank Kelly Freas (1922-2005) debuted as a fantasist illustrator in 1950. He went on to adorn SF books and magazines for many years. Freas could paint both people and hardware. For the latter, see for example

---
[68] Eggleton after Holland, p 46

the cover of the Queen Album *News of the World* (1977), based on a Freas painting of a startled, giant robot. See also the spaceship cover on *Analog* of June 1972 (the one with Haldeman's "Hero", the story itself is treated in chapter 32).

But it was as a painter of people, of faces, of the human Gestalt that Freas excelled. See for example his February, 1956 *Astounding* cover with the first installment of Heinlein's *Double Star*. This conveys rather well the situation of the novel, with a passerby in the street at the bottom of the picture and above him, a poster of a politician: the no-no and the man of power, the subject and the ruler, the pawn and the king. But they also have similar features, the very thing that makes this Lorenzo Smythe able to take on the role of the politician in question, John Joseph Bonforte.

Freas is an example, in the realm of SF art, of having a human element to give life to grand-but-titanic settings.

JOHN SCHOENHERR

An artist putting his stamp on 1960s *Analog* was John Schoenherr (1935-). In chapter two I mentioned his *The Illustrated Dune*, having a true feeling for the archaic world of Frank Herbert. Schoenherr even used archaic painting methods sometimes, like egg tempera where you mix colored pigment with egg yolk, giving the resulting painting a rather unique texture. He was also good at creating otherworldly animals, like the ape-man on the cover of *Analog* for July 1975. This figure is said to have inspired the Star Wars character Chewbacca.

FOSS

A central name in the history of SF art is Chris Foss. Chris Foss was born in Devon, England, in 1946. He was inspired by "rustling railway tracks and disused mines of the West Country and semi-derelict shipyards at Poole".[69] Also, the remains of Nazi German forts on the island of Guernsey made an impression on the young Foss visiting the place.

---

[69] Holland, p 60

One of the first Chris Foss covers was of Arthur C. Clarke's *The Coming of the Space Age* (1970): a detailed rendering of a spaceship behemoth, functional yet intriguing. This was something else than "the concentration camps of the soul" that NASA's spaceships played the role of, according to Jodorowsky. Foss also did covers for war novels and thrillers but eventually the SF side took over. Foss took SF illustrations to a new level, with his almost photo realistic renderings of future hardware. Plus an ability to give the space vistas depth by way of combining airbrush with oil painting techniques.

> Foss' space hardware became the style that dominated British paperback designs for the next decade. (...) Working for Sphere, Panther, Coronet, Arrow and Futura paperbacks, Foss was the artistic spearhead of a paperback boom for science fiction in Britain.[70]

Foss soon got many followers. "A group of artists represented by the Young Artists Agency in London were especially associated with the Foss School of spaceship cover designs – intricately detailed, sharply delineated star ships, majestic planetary backgrounds, and airbrushed spacescapes."[71] Painters of the Chris Foss school were Peter Elson and Colin Hay, as well as Peter Jones, Angus McKie, Bob Layzell and Tony Roberts. For the latter, see his *Double Star* cover for Panther 1976, an asymmetric "Salvador Dali" spaceship, giving a surrealist effect within a realistic framework. Holland:

> Stewart Crowley's *Spacecraft 2000-2100 A.D.* (1978) reused cover art by linking the images via a newly created future history of mankind and presenting the various craft as a kind of Jane's Fighting Ships of the future. Further volumes in the *Terran Trade Authority* series by Crowley and a number of similar styled books reused dozens of cover images.[72]

This might sound a bit down-market but the venture as such was conceptually bold, an example of image preceding idea. In most other cases SF puts the idea first and the image comes in as an afterthought.

---

[70] Holland, ibid.
[71] Ibid., p 63
[72] Ibid.

Around 1980 demand for these covers started to go down. British paperback publishing in general went down by this time, if only temporarily. As for the covers new styles developed but still, space hardware in striking spatial vistas remains a mainstay of SF art.

20TH CENTURY FOSS

A delightful collection of Foss art is *20th Century Foss,* issued by Dragon's Dream in 1979. Here you can enjoy paintings of spaceships, planets and alien perspectives with that special Foss touch. On the surface these are detailed images of machines but beyond that something else is present: hieroglyphs in the sky and technical archetypes, visions in the gray area between surrealism and realism.

The depicted ships may be functional but their form doesn't merely follow function. They are machines but not machines with just one function. Like American cars of the 50s they are symbols loaded with meaning, ambiguous forms being more than just vessels transporting you from point A to point B.

Judging by *20th Century Foss* the Foss art is airbrush, intriguing color patterns, in-depth vistas and psychedelic skies. Especially fun is when the images are accompanied by a book title, like when a painting has been a book cover, such as "The Watering Place of Good Peace", "The New Improved Sun" and "A Frontier of Going". The text affects the image and the image the text, in an eternal, positive two-way flow.

Sometimes in *20th Century Foss* there's just a dry description of the picture at hand, *à la* "spaceship in a flying dock" or "train passing an abandoned building". Over time this becomes poetic too – because over the years I've personally checked out and devoured this book, reading the images as if they were hieroglyphs – like a child reading a picture book. And the child's gaze is incomparable.

As a child himself, Foss was fascinated by abandoned mines and old railroad tracks. He also liked tracks still in service; at the time (England in the 1940s and 50s), there were still plenty of steam engines, and *steam* you see a lot of in his paintings. This seemingly archaic element creates a specific atmosphere in Foss' futures. An interstellar spaceship with some odd, functional whiff of steam, like a smoke swirl from a Biggin Hill locomotive over a yard in the London suburbs...! The one eventually becomes just as fascinating as the other, fact and fiction merging in a glorious marriage, a *hieros gamos* in the name of art.

As intimated above, Foss as a young man visited the Channel Island of Guernsey and studied the German fortifications from the war. This titanic technological poetry you can see traces of in his paintings, you can see it instinctively inserted among spacecraft, future machines and enameled technology: a successful marriage, an archeofuturistic fiesta.

PENNINGTON

In the 1970s British scene we also had Bruce Pennington (1944-), doing covers for New English Library. Books by Aldiss, van Vogt and Herbert were adorned by his often sublime artistry, classically trained in oil on canvas. In 1982 he won the BSFA award for Best Artist and then he went on to other projects than covers. Holland: "His artwork was luminous, often featuring multiple objects or creatures against sparse skies and low horizons with a large, dominant, often alien figure in the foreground".[73]

The epitome of Pennington's art, to me, is the 1980s cover of Herbert's *Dune Messiah* for NEL. A wraparound illustration, on the front cover it shows Paul Atreides being hailed by his guard in resplendent attire and on the back cover we see flying discs with additional courtiers, the picture trailing off into the distance with rosy hues along with golden desert and hazy blues. This is oil painting at its very best, this is Western art, this is Tradition in SF form.

---

[73] Holland, p 59

ALDISS FOREWORD

The foreword to the overview I've used in this chapter, Steve Holland's *Sci-Fi Art – A Graphic History,* is written by British author and SF scholar Brian Wilson Aldiss (1925-). There, Aldiss for instance tells us that his ideal is SF in the serious vein, avoiding comedy, an attitude I sympathize with. Aldiss:

> My personal taste is against funny aliens. The writing and production of SF is important business. By the same token, I feel that SF should stay clear of the comics. That it is a serious matter (...) which concerns the future, the planet on which we so far live, and the enigma of human consciousness itself. In other words (...), humanity. The enigma of human life.[74]

Indeed; there's a place for satire and fun in SF but the classics of the genre are serious works of art, elevated by some sort of idealism. Conversely, satire is married to nihilism and this will never render immortal classics. More on nihilism in chapter 31.

Further:

> Those unfortunates who cannot read SF complain that SF lacks characters; yet so often a vital character is the environment. Man faces alien nature. The environment is as strong a matter of characterization as you could wish for."[75]

This is in sync with my discussion on psychological landscapes (*q.v.* Ballard, Tarkovsky, Lovecraft).

In the Holland overview Aldiss notes that SF art often lacks the presence of humans, but the deserted vistas in themselves combine desolation and grandeur in a striking way. They are examples of the symbolical quality inherent in SF. This symbolic, metaphysical nature of SF Aldiss also delves upon in a footnote in *Billion Year Spree,* his history of the SF genre. The passage in question treats what the painter Giorgio de Chirico (1888-1978) wrote in a 1919 essay, "On Metaphysical

---

[74] Holland, ibid.
[75] Ibid.

Art", reprinted in Massimo Carrà's *Metaphysical Art*, 1971. de Chirico's words seem to capture the very essence of SF, as it were:

> Joyful but involuntary movements of the metaphysical can be observed both in painters and writers, and speaking of writers I would like to remember here an old French provincial who we will call, for clarity's sake, the armchair explorer. I refer to Jules Verne, who wrote travel and adventure novels, and who is considered to be a writer for children. But who was more gifted than [Jules Verne] in capturing the metaphysical element of a city like London, with its houses, streets, clubs, squares and open spaces; the ghostliness of a Sunday afternoon in London, the melancholy of a man, a real walking phantom, as Phineas Fogg appears in *Around the World in Eighty Days*? The work of Jules Verne is full of these joyous and most consoling moments; I still remember the description of the departure of a steamship from Liverpool in his novel *The Floating City*.[76]

As for de Chirico the painter, he was fleetingly mentioned in chapter eight of the book you're currently reading, the chapter on futurism.

GIGER

SF needs plausibility to work. But if the plausibility leads off into the grotesque, like creating all too ugly aliens, I'd say, tone down the plausibility and go for the cliché instead. Rather a wholesome cliché than a repulsive plausibility. Like, a human looking alien; that's "cliché" but still plausible. Because, according to esoteric theory the human form is rather common in the universe.

Hans Rudolf Giger (1940-2014) once received a human skull, a gift from his pharmacist father. That was some symbolic gesture: did this gift put young Giger on the path to become an artist interested in the grotesque and the arabesque? He did, anyway, and the rest

---

[76] de Chirico quoted after Aldiss, 1986, p 461-462

is history as they say. However, you can't merely label Giger as a grotesque artist. There's a sense of beauty in his visions.

This is important. Many SF creators envisioning aliens construct them scientifically, more often than not ending up in the downright ugly. As for Giger it's true that his SF visions are uncanny and revolting at times but there's also a sense of proportion, a "sensible sense" in most of them. The borderline character of Giger's art is captured in this quote by the man himself:

> I always have two elements in my paintings – the horrible things and the nice things. I mean, I like elegance, I like art nouveau; a stretched line or a curve. These things are very much in the foreground of my work.[77]

A successful design by Giger is "the Harkonnen chair". It looks organic, a bit like ribs, but still in a tasteful manner. It comes in the form of a swivel chair, a glorified office chair, a "CEO chair" – something worthy of an executive in the Harkonnen sense. This item was developed in connection with the *Dune* film.

COMICS

Now's the time to move on to another graphic SF subject, that of comics. As intimated, the following view of the subject will have a certain slant towards the archeofuturistic.

In chapter two of this study I treated Herbert's *Dune*, the epitome of the archeofuturist strain: that of new and old conceptually coexisting, symbolized in "swords and spaceships". In SF literature this might have begun with E. R. Burrough's John Carter stories. And in comics the archeofuturism really took off with Alex Raymond's *Flash Gordon* from 1934 and on. In this yarn we had a contemporary earthman going off into space encountering a civilization, Mongo, ruled by an emperor and characterized by spaceships and ray guns. And swords, most importantly. Gordon continued to explore the archeofuturist field even in the 50s when Dan Barry (1923-1997) took

---

[77] Quoted after Holland, p 138.

over the pencil from Raymond. The mix of high tech and ancient ways, of spaceships and medieval looking interiors of planet Mongo, was conceptualized for a new audience, adding relatability in the form of the entourage of the Microbe, Ray Carson, Percival "Boom Boom" Dunn and Worriless Willie, plus the regulars Dale Arden, Prince Barin and Emperor Ming. Compared to other 50s SF comics this element of "human interest" gave Flash Gordon grace and allure. In SF it's not enough to have monster plots and stupendous vistas, you have to put humans in there too.

As for British SF comics with some archeofuturist attitude you might think of *Trigan Empire*, written by Mike Butterworth and drawn by Don Lawrence. Created in 1965, this was an epic of a remote planet, Elekton, developing from a Roman style civilization to high tech interstellar, keeping the togas and swords in the process. While not conceptually profound the *Trigan Empire* drawings had painterly depth, not merely being monochrome color fields lined with ink. This style pointed forward to the works of Richard Corben (1940-), star of the 1980s *Heavy Metal* magazine.

Another fine British SF comic was *Jeff Hawke*, written and drawn by Sydney Jordan (1928-). This story of a near-future pilot and spaceman sometimes had "ordinary" futuristic plots, sometimes archeofuturist ones. The latter for instance was the case in *The Book of the Worlds* (1970), with elements such as an amulet with a hawk (*c.f.* the hero's given name, Hawke), a space princess, a South American monument with carved colossal images of Hawke and the princess, a structure where the intimated Book of the Worlds was also to be found. Toned down but exquisite black-and-white drawings underlined the pathos of all Jeff Hawke stories.

SUPERMAN

Now for a look into a later comic episode having some of that archeofuturist strain, a mind-boggling *Superman* story. This attitude of mixing old times with new, merging archaic elements with futuristic, indeed permeates all of the SF field, especially comics.

If a story has scenes in ancient Rome and 15th century Spain along with scenes in stupendous future vistas, then, to me, the story would count as archeofuturistic. And this is what a certain DC Comics adventure brought us. DC's universe of superheroes – Superman, Batman etc. – started to form in the 1930s. Then, in the 60s, the rival Marvel universe came along, with Spiderman, Hulk, Fantastic Four etc. The main drift of the stories was futuristic-scientistic but there were older strains along too, at least plot wise. Like in DC's *World's Fastest Race,* as seen in the comic book World's Finest 198-199, 1970.

The DC heroes Flash and Superman had challenged each other to cosmic races before, deciding who was the fastest man alive. Their third attempt was spawned by a cosmic crisis, by the presence of certain Anachronids, robots that exist near the speed of light. These machines were causing disruptions in the time stream, sending people randomly back and forth in time. This is masterfully shown at the beginning, when Superman's journalist friend Jimmy Olsen walks out into his bathroom – only to fall into nothingness, ending up in a court in ancient Rome. He's accused of witchcraft for appearing thus, out of nothing.

How to mend these ruptures in time? The Guardians of the Galaxy, godlike watchers of the cosmic show, have the answer in the form of two individuals traveling at the speed of light in parallel to the Anachronids, this might counteract the chaos they're creating. So Flash asks Superman if he wants to make this into yet another race, and he agrees. Flash, who can't fly, gets a certain medallion in order to even race with Superman in space, the medallion projecting a path he can run along. Other than that, this is an objective test of strength. In their cosmic race the pair encounters a fair share of challenges – human, heroic, elemental. Alongside with this, Jimmy Olsen is translocated to successive historic scenes, each one of them posing a lethal challenge to him.

At the end the heroes reach a Cosmic Power Switch having to be shut off. It sounds ridiculous when being retold like this it but it works; the story has pace, rhythm and plausibility. The robots are rendered powerless, the ruptures in time cease, Jimmy Olsen comes back to his own time. And the specific race is won by Flash. In all, rather elaborate for a superhero story. And with the earth side time travel element, and the elevated, godlike Guardians, as a graphic and dramatic plus.

Superman combated ancient threats even later, as a certain Asian demon from the dimension of Quarrm in another early 1970s story. In defeating this ancient monstrosity Superman was helped by a double. But then the pair started to fight each other, seemingly destroying the whole world in the process. To this you might say: superhero comics are storybook material, they never get tragic in the authentic sense, but to be sure, Superman's tears when realizing that he had destroyed the world – that made an impression on this author when he first read this. Later Superman learned that this was only make believe, he and the double had been hypnotized by a wise man, I Ching, before the duel to get a lesson: use your powers wisely...! This is a lesson in line with Tradition, stressing self-restraint. The braver the hero the humbler he must be.

FRANCE

In France fantastic comics led an obscure existence until the 1960s. Because, in postwar times America led the development of SF, in literature and comics, but in the 60s Europe came to the fore in graphic SF art. We saw it above in artists such as Foss and Giger. These, along with Jean Giraud, came to influence American SF films like *Dune*, *Superman* and *Alien*.

SF films are treated elsewhere in this study, not expressly focusing on this, 1970s graphic development. Anyhow, as for French fantastic comics you first have to mention the figure of Philippe Druillet (1944-). In his comics we saw things like striking splash panels, a clouded narrative and mysticism, the latter specifically in the heroic fantasy *Yragaël*, created in 1973 and written by Michel Demuth. In tone this was to some extent influenced by Moorcock's Elric stories (*q.v.* chapter ten): chaos and order, pathos and heroism, gods and men, all in the "incandescent apotheosis of a cosmic copulation".

Actually, this quote is from another noteworthy French SF comic, living in the gray area between futuristic and ancient: Caza's

"The Ark" (1983). With a poetic prose narration this is the story of an artifact, an ark, going through an elemental influence of water, earth, air and fire, eventually surviving the demise of its planet and the whole cosmos, becoming the nucleus of the reborn universe. "The Ark" is a forever viable artistic endeavor, fine art in popular form. It was published in the February 1983 issue of *Heavy Metal*, an American version of the French *Metal Hurlant*, created in 1974 by Druillet and Jean Giraud. For the record, "Caza" is the pseudonym of Philippe Cazaumayou, a Frenchman born in 1941.

Jean Giraud (1938-), for his part, has created many SF comics. Here you can mention "The Long Tomorrow", scripted by Dan O'Bannon, the man after this going on to write the script for groundbreaking SF film *Alien* (1979). According to Steve Holland, "The Long Tomorrow" would serve as "a visual reference" for this film – which could mean the dirty realism and intriguing quality in futures looking old, a "future perfect", akin to the archeofuturist strain. Future perfect, for its part, is a verb form of things that are surmised to happen in the future, things that theoretically can be seen in perfect tense, "have finished" – like "I will have finished by tomorrow".

Druillet and Giraud made comics for adults; then we had *Valérian* by Jean-Claude Mézières and Pierre Christin (both 1938-), created in 1967, which was more juvenile in tone. At least in the beginning. This comic series to me is a stand-out since along with the artistry it's got a relatable tone, a human dimension, which sometimes is lacking in Giraud's and Druillet's comics. In discussing French comics SF historians like to point out how groundbreaking Jean-Claude Forest's *Barbarella* was, a comic created in 1962. The, for the time, outspoken sexuality was hip and right on the money, is the common opinion. And true, "good girl art" sells and the marginally more chaste Laureline character in Valérian is also an eye catcher with her good looks; Laureline is the step-daughter of Barbarella. Long story short, the *Valérian* series soon outgrew the juvenile classification and with its first ten albums went on to make an indelible impression on the SF field as a whole.

To stay with a certain sub-theme of the comic's section of this chapter, let's look at the archeofuturist character of *Valérian*. This series has always had a spontaneous relation to ancient times and climes, to archaic forms and vistas. The Laureline character was even living in medieval France before Valérian brought her along to the future world of Galaxity in the 28th century, the center of a vast Terran Galactic Empire. In their subsequent adventures Valérian and Laureline often met archaic cultures, like the inner planet realm of *Land Without Stars*, complete with airships, crossbows and swords, *Birds of the Master*, with a rebellion on a medieval planet, and *Heroes of the Equinox*, with a quest-story on another ancient-culture planet with participants in the form of a sword-wielding hero, a technocratic Soviet-style worker, a new age wise man and Valérian himself. All this archaism, along with the framework of a high-tech future galaxy with space ships, space suits and techno cities, results in archeofuturism at its best, a graphic extravaganza mixing old and new in an authoritative manner. Star Wars might have learned one thing or two from it.

J. C. Mézières, for his part, seems born for the SF mode. He artistically roams the spatial vistas, free and structured at the same time; the grotesque is held in check. As for Pierre Christin, it's true that he's a man of the Left but overall his outlook is constructive, not nihilist as most other leftists of today. In his prime he never did less that tell a good story. Christin, along with Mézières and the colorist Evelyn Tran-Lé, with *Valérian* has created the best SF comic ever: artistic, fun, thought-provoking and relatable, at least in the first ten albums.

15. DEVELOPMENT OF THE GENRE

IN A FORMAL SENSE, science fiction was created in 1926. Hugo Gernsback, in launching his new magazine *Amazing Stories,* devoted to stories about fictional science, baptized the genre "scientifiction", later made into "science fiction". Thus was born a literary mode of telling speculative stories of science, a conceptualization of a storytelling previously tried by authors like Jules Verne and H. G. Wells, both of which were liberally reprinted in Gernsback's magazine. While you must praise this European origin of scientific sagas it's also true that the American way of receiving them and developing them for a new era was rather invigorating. Because, although generally well-crafted and complex, the European SF after WWI was a bit dismal and gloomy in outlook.

In labeling the genre Gernsback created a viable, modern myth. Apart from the term itself Gernsback's magazine was the first paper devoted solely to this new kind of genre fiction. Therefore, the American contribution to the genre can't be overvalued. This chapter is dedicated to some aspects of mainly American SF in the 20th century, looking at things such as the pulps, the editor John W. Campbell and the Golden Age and what followed. Campbell, for his part, can be seen as a right-wing intellectual but he had no discernible relationship to Tradition so therefore he won't get his own chapter in this study; his contribution is primarily discussed within the framework of this chapter, chapter fifteen. However, a topical, traditional aspect will be demonstrated below with outlining what way ahead SF must take to still be a viable literary force. The watchword is *spirituality*.

MAGAZINES

And so Hugo Gernsback created science fiction: the Birth of a Notion, a conceptual breakthrough. And while the previous, European SF had been published both in books and magazines, the American kind of SF at first was relegated purely to the magazines.

With the main sources in the form of Holmberg 2002 and Ashley 2000, 2005, the following can be said of the magazine phenomenon. In the 19th century there was fiction to be read in American periodical magazines (and British ones too but here we'll concentrate on the American scene). They were printed on rather fine, "glossy" paper, the normal venue for publishing short stories being this kind of magazines – and with a possible, subsequent collection of the stories in book form. High-end American monthly magazines by the late 19th century were *Harper's Monthly*, *Putnam's Monthly* and *Atlantic Monthly*. These magazines sometimes printed SF stories. Then, in the 1890s, the *pulps* were born, printed on less expensive paper. The standard format was 24.5 x 35 centimeter, called "bedsheet", rather large for today's standards – and this much I know from personal experience, that the mass-market magazine *Life* still had this size in the 1960s. (And the paper quality in *Life* made it into a glossy magazine, like *Harper's* and the rest.)

As for size, many pulps later switched to the smaller "pulp magazine format," about the size of a comic book – or, better, of *National Geographic*. This magazine is famous for its square spine and this feature was also part of the pulp magazine format. If you have a problem visualizing a "square spine", I'd say: the ordinary periodical magazine has a folded, stapled spine; thicker magazines like *National*

Geographic and pocket books have square spines with the cover glued on.

From about the 1950s and on the "digest format" became standard for the SF magazines. It was around even earlier; *Astounding* changed to this format in 1943. The size is, roughly, 14 x 20 cm, with the inner part glued to the cover forming a square spine. For the rest of the 20th century this was the normal SF magazine format.

So much for format and size. But I digress, back to the pulps. A pioneering American pulp focusing on stories was *Argosy*; the word "argosy" per se denotes a kind of ship. Then, in the 1910s, genre specific pulps were born, like *Detective Story Magazine* and *Western Story Magazine*. In 1923 *Weird Tales* came around, printing weird fantasy and sometimes even SF. Finally, in 1926, a magazine focusing entirely on SF saw the light of day: *Amazing Stories*. Editor was the Luxemburgian immigrant Hugo Gernsback (1884-1967), previously active as editor of magazines dedicated to science and technology.

Early on, Hugo Gernsback was interested in space and things Beyond, like reading Jules Verne. According to Holmberg,[78] a nine-year old Gernsback after having read a book about intelligent life on Mars got a fever and hallucinated about Martian landscapes. This "SF as a way of trance" could otherwise make you think of Bob Shaw, who at the age of eleven read a van Vogt story in *Astounding;* he later compared the experience to taking LSD.[79]

Gernsback launched *Amazing* and it was a success, quickly getting over 100,000 subscribers. In the 1930s there eventually were three American SF pulps around: *Amazing, Thrilling Wonder Stories* and *Astounding*. The latter was founded in January 1930 and the full title was, "Astounding Stories of Super Science". High-profile serials in the 1930s *Astounding* were *The Legion of Space* by Jack Williamson, *The Skylark of Valeron* by E. E. Smith and *The Mightiest Machine* by John Wood Campbell (1910-1971). By the late thirties the selfsame Campbell became the editor of *Astounding*.

---

[78] 2002, p 64
[79] Stableford, 1995, p 22

CAMPBELL

Campbell was to have a profound influence on the genre. True, he didn't invent the wheel but he did raise the American form of SF to a level previously unseen. You can say that he re-established a modicum of style present in a classic SF author like H. G. Wells. It wouldn't be possible any longer to just write bare-bones lecturing of the "tell me professor" – kind that Gernsback had favored. An element of "human interest" and relatable plot was needed for a fiction story. According to Alexei Panshin Campbell also demanded "universal operating principles" by his authors, i.e., plausibility, coherence and logic.

In the words of Isaac Asimov, "[t]here had to be real science *and* real story, with neither one dominating the other."[80] Campbell started out as an author himself, making his literary debut in *Amazing*, January 1930, with "When the Atoms Failed". He had a BA in physics but now he concentrated on writing SF, coming up with stories like *The Mightiest Machine* and *Islands of Space.* In these yarns the machine was the hero, it was super-science and effects and little of literary craftsmanship.

"In 1934, Campbell changed his approach."[81] Now he allowed an emotional, human element into his stories – like "Twilight", about a future when man's zest and curiosity are spent forces. The story demonstrates a, shall we say, crypto-religious piety for science in which the author sees "the salvation, the raising of mankind."[82] Compared to the ordinary SF of the day the story had pathos and depth. Aldiss notes the Wells influence of the dying earth (from *The Time Machine*) but in itself "Twilight" was an important impulse for the renewal of the SF field along with Campbell's subsequent role as editor.

Campbell wrote "Twilight" under the pseudonym of "Don A. Stuart". And his writing career continued with this and that story, like "Who Goes There" which became the movie *The Thing,* remade in the 1980s with Kurt Russell in the lead. But most importantly, in 1937

---

[80] Asimov, 1975, p X
[81] Aldiss, 1986, p 215
[82] Campbell after Aldiss, p 215

Campbell became the editor of *Astounding*, an SF magazine started in 1930 to compete with *Amazing*. Fifty issues had been published by the time of Campbell's employment. Campbell now established a regime of demanding more of his authors – and less. More scientific plausibility, less atmosphere and make-believe. But as intimated, an element of human interest was required to give the future vistas depth and life, much like H. G. Wells had in his day.

The July, 1939 issue was a road mark, having debut stories by A. E. van Vogt and Robert Heinlein, with "The Black Destroyer" and "Life-Line" respectively. The same issue saw the first story by Isaac Asimov in *Astounding*, "Trends". Asimov had his first meeting with Campbell in June 1938 and Asimov soon became an *Astounding* regular along with Heinlein and van Vogt. Through his magazine Campbell would influence this trio along with writers like Arthur C. Clarke, Henry Kuttner, Clifford D. Simak, Theodore Sturgeon and Poul Anderson.

INFLUENCE

Asimov once said that Campbell was "the most powerful force in science fiction ever, and for the first ten years of his editorship he dominated the field completely". Campbell pitched ideas to his authors, challenging them to write things they had never imagined. For instance, Campbell and Asimov once discussed this Emerson quote: "If the stars should appear one night in a thousand years, how would men believe and adore, and preserve for many generations the remembrance of the city of God!" Campbell, for his part, doubted the pious dimension of it all, thinking that men instead would go mad. Then he asked Asimov to write a story along those lines. It eventually became the classic "Nightfall". And in discussing how a superman might actually be Campbell gave an impulse for van Vogt to write *Slan*. Campbell suggested the concept but van Vogt's angle was that a superman at the beginning of his development might seem less than perfect, coming through as dumb before he had realized his abilities.[83] Campbell also had some influence on the early writings of Heinlein. See Panshin's "Heinlein and the Golden Age" for more of this.[84] Heinlein and Campbell both were hard-right conservatives – but Heinlein was more than that, he was an iconoclast, a synthesist and a jack of all trades. Campbell, God bless him, in the 50s and 60s came through as a right-winger and not much else. That said, it has to be stressed that Campbell wasn't a Communist, he was an American patriot and this was of enormous importance in a time when quite many of the American and European intelligentsia looked up to the Soviet Union and China as some kind of role model and ideal.

GRAPHIC APPEARANCE

Astounding had a rather stylish appearance. Let me quote a passage from Aldiss *Trillion Year Spree* that says a lot about the image of the magazine in Campbell's day:

> The exciting developments under Campbell may be read in the covers of the magazine. Symbolism always precedes actuality, just as a belief in space travel preceded the space programs. A concept must be visualized before it can be realized. So the art side often flies ahead of the contents. The 1938 covers of *Astounding* span a wide range of subjects, are interesting but have no unity. From 1939, a kind of coherence appears. The Campbell orchestra tunes up. (...) The Canadian artist Hubert Rogers was ideal for Campbell's purposes, his somber scenes and muted colors, coupled with modern *sans serif* lettering, formed *Astounding* covers into a new generic proclamation of intent.[85]

An example of this strain is seen on *Astounding*, May 1947. Here we find a cover illustration by Hubert Rogers for Lawrence O'Donnell's *Fury* (O'Donnel was a pseudonym for Henry Kuttner): majestic in scope and towering in outlook, this future display of a destroyed earth.

---

[83] Source: Panshin's essay "Man and Superman", http://www.panshin.com/articles/vanvogt/vanvogt1.html

[84] http://www.panshin.com/critics/Golden/goldenage1.html

[85] Aldiss, 1986, p 221-222

TITLES

Campbell said that if you can't think of a title for a story you've written "then it is probably a lousy story".[86] Also, Campbell favored one-word titles, like *Nightfall, Reason, Slan, Coventry, Misfit, Arena, Fireproof*. This is very significant of the *Astounding* era, I figure. Or maybe of the American style on the whole. For instance, in films the one-word title early on was a US trademark: *Intolerance, Wings, Greed, Temptation, Manslaughter, Triumph, Dynamite*.

In line with this hard-hitting attitude, Campbell emphasized to his authors not to waste time on wordy first paragraphs:

> I hate a story that begins with *atmosphere*. Get right into the story, never mind the *atmosphere*.[87]

SPACE

In a foreword to the Signet issue of Heinlein's *The Man Who Sold the Moon* Campbell spoke about space travel as the endeavor of endeavors: "the highest of all adventures – the conquest of the stars!"[88] He was right in saying this. I mean, I don't support all aspects of the space program as it came to be – the Apollo project etc. – but I agree with the Campbell crowd in that space is something to be explored and investigated and man has to go there as a matter of course. Earth is a fine planet and there's a future for man on this world but to enter space just has to be done, space travel being the ultimate symbol of adventure and the raising of man.

Aldiss notes the same trait in Campbell, seeing the prospect of space travel as something of a spiritual idea:

> One thing *Astounding* had which can never be recaptured. It had faith. The peculiar faith that space travel was possible and would

---

[86] Aldiss quoted after Holland, p 6
[87] Campbell quoted after Aldiss, p 207
[88] Campbell, p XI

come about. To be part of Campbell's audience was to feel oneself a member of a privileged minority who knew in their bones what was going to happen in the future.[89]

ODDITIES

Now for a further look at the development of the SF genre. For the moment I'll stay with the world of magazines. The postwar era saw an explosion of SF magazines, this for a while being the main venue of SF publishing. And in the history of SF magazines there are indeed many titles, many writers and many editors around to delve on. According to Aldiss in *Trillion Year Spree*, "you can get lost forever in the mountain ranges of the SF magazines". However, as for some oddities in this field I have to note the following.

For instance, Holmberg[90] reproduces the cover of *Famous Fantastic Mysteries* from June 1953, the last issue of a certain large format pulp. The caption notes that this issue sported the novellas *Anthem* (1938) by Ayn Rand and *The Transformation* (1915) by Franz Kafka. These stories are indeed varieties of speculative fiction and presenting them thus, in a pulp with a flashy cover, gives something of the specificity of SF: serious fiction in popular form.

Another pulp was *Planet Stories*, founded in 1939. It published space opera and adventurous SF, for example, an early Mars story by Ray Bradbury. The lesson of this is that not all the magazines of the era had the demand of "engineering precision" in style and content, of stories exerting a rationalist outlook, as the then prevalent Campbellian *Leitkultur* of SF can be described as.

Oddities: the venerable *Amazing* saw a rather odd development with the so-called "Shaver Mystery", 1945-48. Under the editorship of Ray Palmer it published stories portraying an alleged truth, that of evil Deros affecting earth and earth history from their subterranean dwellings. As an esotericist I'm not completely against opening up the SF genre to this kind of material, and the last word isn't yet said on

---

[89] Aldiss, 1986, p 221

[90] 2002, p 89

the stories Richard Shaver wrote. But overall, SF is about *fiction* and the labeling gets confused when you have material maintaining that it's factual truth. SF mustn't be dragged down into reports, programs and formulas, it's about artistry and inspiration, essentially about conveying a vision in a musical mood. As for the development of the SF genre, with Gernsback "the Engineer" tended to be in charge and with Ray Palmer "the Mystic," both of them overshadowing the role of "the Creative Author".

LITERARY FORAYS

There were other magazines around than *Amazing* and *Astounding*. For instance, we had *The Magazine of Fantasy and Science Fiction (F&SF)*, started in the autumn of 1949 and still published. *F&SF* had a tendency to broaden the confines of the genre, having "fantastic" material by mainstream authors along with more acknowledged SF authors. It was soon followed by another new magazine from another company: *Galaxy*, existing until 1980. *Galaxy* was edited by Horace L. Gold, and then Frederik Pohl, publishing authors like Ray Bradbury, Philip K. Dick, Alfred Bester, Fritz Leiber and Jack Vance. It was a more style-conscious magazine than *Astounding*, more musical and cultured than the somewhat bare-bones character of Campbell's universe.

The rest of this section will look at some commercial aspects of the magazine world and SF at large. Then I will deliberate on the conceptual and artistic development of SF in the 1960s and on. The focus is on the USA but the UK also figures to some extent. *F&SF* and *Galaxy* along with *Astounding* were the three leading magazines in the field for decades. If you replace *Galaxy* with *Isaac Asimov's SF Magazine*, you have the three still published monthly SF magazines in the 2010s. *Astounding* changed its name to *Analog* in 1960.

According to Holmberg[91] the 1950s was the last decade when the SF magazines led the development in the field. From the mid 1920s and on the magazines had been the main venue for publishing new

---

[91] 2002, p 105

SF, both short stories and novels. In the 1950s original publishing of novels in book form became more prominent. Then, in the 1960s, the original anthology also saw the light of day: collections in book form of short stories never before published. An example of this form was Damon Knight's *Orbit* series, 21 volumes 1966-1980. Another high profile original anthology was Harlan Ellsion's *Dangerous Visions* in 1967.

That said, the SF magazines are still alive. In 2002 there were four professional monthly magazines; as I write this there are three: *Analog, Asimov's* and *F&SF*. Add to this at least a dozen semi-professional ones and it becomes clear that the short story lives on in the SF idiom. Commercially the SF genre, as a reasonably cutting-edge literary phenomenon, isn't as bristling as before but it does seem to have some staying power.

ROLL COUNT

Counting the number of existing SF magazines, at various times, is no exact science. Anyhow, with the guidance of Wikipedia info I've tried to make a sort of statistical overview. The question is: what is an SF magazine in this context? My criteria are (1) professional and (2) high circulation. "Professional" means paying their contributors. "High circulation" means that along with subscribing to them you can (or could) buy these magazines in newsstands all over America.

Thus, according to these criteria, in 1946 there were eight SF magazines. In 1953 there were 28. In 1960 there were six, a rather substantial dip. In 1970 there were seven. In 1980 there were five. In 1990 there were four. In 2000 there were three.

In writing this in 2015 these three still remain. They are:

- *Analog*, founded in 1930
- *F&SF*, founded in 1949
- *Asimov's*, founded in 1977

As for high-end, defunct magazines, these are noteworthy:

- *Galaxy*, 1950-1980
- *If*, 1952-1974

- *Fantastic*, 1952-1980
- *Omni*, 1978-1995
- *Amazing*, 1926-2005

NEW WORLDS

Now let's go to England for a closer look at a noteworthy object in this context. *New Worlds* was a British SF magazine, launched in professional form in 1946. In the beginning it was edited by John Carnell. For instance, he printed stories by J. G. Ballard in the 1950s and early 1960s. Then, in 1964, Michael Moorcock (1939-) took over. He both switched the format from pulp size to slick magazine (larger format, better paper) and he did away with genre limitations. *New Words* under his aegis wouldn't expressly print SF, it would be defined merely by its content, an editorial statement by Moorcock according to Holmberg.[92]

Ballard for his part was encouraged by this to go wild and experiment, as in "You and Me and the Continuum" from 1966, his first condensed novel. Some loved this "new wave of SF," like American editor Judith Merril who made the anthology *England Swings SF* in 1968, collecting 25 experimental works from *New Worlds*. In addition to Ballard the magazine printed stories by Thomas M. Disch, Norman Spinrad and Samuel R. Delany, the latter with "Time Considered as a Helix of Semi-Precious Stones" in December 1968, a rather fine forerunner of cyberpunk with a criminal operator in a jumbled future.

New Worlds did prove itself as an avant-garde literary magazine. However, the editor Moorcock, by stressing that the genre of SF was dead, did sail into conceptually troublesome waters. In the long run, not all of its authors had the originality to carry a story without support from the genre, as regards themes, tropes and jargon. Sometimes generic atmosphere and attitude is a necessary meeting ground for authors and readers.

---

[92] 2002, p 151

INNER SPACE

The ideal of SF, according to Holmberg,[93] is this: man exploring nature with science and technology, thus conquering and understanding his universe, and in the process gaining insights leading to some kind of transcendence. As an esotericist I fully embrace this definition of SF. It's about venturing out Beyond the Beyond and Within the Within.

Additionally: as Spinrad once said (*q.v.* chapter seven), the one, big myth of SF is space travel, and in this we have to acknowledge its transcendental, esoteric, inner qualities. According to me, the way to space and alien contact goes through inner space. When all of mankind is peaceful in and out, the aliens will make contact. This is simple. But "the simple is difficult", as any crucial matter.

Acknowledging inner qualities, inner space, man's mental dimension: this was one of the hobby-horses of the 1960s New Wave. Along with this mental, immaterial emphasis (as opposed to the tangibility of engineering and machine building) came a lot of literary experimentation. For example, reading the more speculative, outré texts of William Burroughs, Ballard, Delany, Farmer, Ellison, Spinrad and Leiber indeed wasn't boring. But did they contribute to the development of the genre *per se*? In retrospect and seen from the right, the most influential SF authors of the 60s-early 70s were authors like Frank Herbert and Larry Niven. They left a tangible mark on the genre; Herbert, in portraying an alien world with a spiritual, traditional feel and a previously unseen attention to detail (*q.v.* for instance the ecology of *Dune*) and Niven in taking the big science of E. E. Smith and Arthur C. Clarke to a new level of plausibility *and* giving it a contemporary feel.

To this must be mentioned authors like Gordon Dickson and Jerry Pournelle, making the field of military SF an enduring character of speculative fiction. Taking the figure of Competent Man (Heinlein) and sublimating it into Responsible Man (Dickson) was the defining feature, showing that the eternal virtues of "duty, honor, courage" can and must play a key role in SF.

---

[93] 2003, p 80

With time, military SF became an established sub-genre. It was an example of expanding the SF field horizontally, into new themes and topics, and not vertically, by language and style *per se*. This was the way ahead: 1960s SF, in allowing the study of themes like psychology, environment interaction, history, sociology and philosophy, instead of merely focusing on engineering, exploitation and imperialism in Golden Age fashion, was the enduring achievement – again, this being a kind of "horizontal expansion" of putting new land under the plow, and not "vertical expansion" in the form of literary experiments. Because, writers like William Burroughs and Ballard continued writing their idiosyncratic kind of fiction even after the 60s, this supposed era of epoch-making literary revolution, while the *comparatively* less advanced talents of Delany, Zelazny, Ellison and Spinrad continued to work within the genre, enlarging their respective fields horizontally.

As intimated, in the 1960s *New Worlds* editor Moorcock declared the SF genre dead. But it lived on. And it will live on, not by experimenting itself beyond recognition, but by incorporating new, previously untried themes. In the 2010s, this would mean to start writing speculative fiction about volitional mental trance, astral projection, ascension and the like, going into parallel worlds by way of the mind. Finding stargates to higher dimensions, like in the TV series *Stargate SG-1*. Or returning to singular, esoteric SF achievements like *Lost Legacy* by Heinlein (*q.v.* chapter one), *Mythago Wood* by Robert Holdstock (*q.v.* chapter twelve) *The Coming Race* (1871) by Bulwer-Lytton and *A Dweller on Two Planets* (1905) by Frederick S. Oliver. This kind of spiritually elevated, esoteric SF, written with the attitude of "a good story, well told", is as a strategic way ahead for SF: thematically and conceptually advanced but not necessarily with the element of experimental prose.

Along with this SF may of course allow for some or other variety of space opera, planetary fiction, archeofuturist melodrama etc. etc. I'm not advocating a "one size fits all" concept. But to future speculative fiction a spiritual element is crucial. This is in sync with the emergent *Zeitgeist*. SF has to mirror this if it is to survive.

SF-ISH

Hereby some further deliberations on SF as regards style or the lack of it. You could say: the most advanced 60s SF was literary progressive, it was written in a different manner, having an experimental style (*q.v.* Ballard etc.). But in the long run, not every SF author could write in this mode, a kind of writing yourself out of the genre.

You could say: the less inventive a SF story is, the more it depends on style. And contrariwise, the more inventive a SF story is, the less it depends on style. Example. if you have a concept of a future space station the size of a planet, then you don't need to tell it in an advanced language. In fact, an advanced language would diminish the story, cloud its specificity, which is extra-literary. Again Lewis: "Describing odd things in an odd language is about one oddity too much".

Let's focus on SF *per se*, on texts deserving to be called SF, leaving out experimentation, God bless it. In order for a text to be labeled as "SF" it has to display some sign of genre consciousness. Often, this means being somewhat tangible, realistic and plausible in relation to some key concepts. Conversely, a text too self-conscious tends to evade the criteria a genre has to have. Case in point one, Doris Lessing's Shikasta series, though ingenious and entertaining sometimes tends to allegory, as suggested by Holmberg.[94] In metaphors and images her SF novels are satisfactory but some kind of tangibility and realism is lacking. She lacks the ability to convince the reader on a rational plane, and therefore she doesn't reach up to the level of "realistic speculation" that's the heart of SF. All this according to Holmberg and it's a point worth listening to. Speculation, but not all too free form; fantasies, but not too much out of the blue, might be a rule of thumb for creating SF worthy of the label.

Ernst Jünger, for one, was no stranger to speculative fiction (*q.v.* chapter seven). But he had the ability to frame his speculative worlds

---

[94] 2003, p 439

within reasonably realistic bounds. This can give you a memento as for how a mainstream, cutting-edge author might "make it" within the SF genre. Specifically, (or commercially), authors like Lessing, Lars Gustafsson or Ernst Jünger don't need the SF label for their speculative outings. But if he drifts into the field the mainstream author to a certain extent has to be relatable conceptually. And Jünger and Gustafsson (for the latter, *q.v. Det sällsamma djuret från norr*, 1989, a collection labeled as "SF") succeeds in being thus relatable. Conversely, I'd say that Lessing, in at least *The Marriages Between Zones Three, Four and Five* (1980) ends up in a conceptual never-never-land. This isn't "space fiction", it's a profiling of levels of consciousness in Sufi fashion, according to the author herself; interesting as such, but is it SF? I'd call it "metaphysical fiction". My point is, SF indeed demands speculation but you can't be too outré conceptually to stay within the confines of a genre.

Another author whose works are labeled as SF but often deviates from the SF idiom in a not fruitful manner, are The Strugatski Brothers (Arkadij & Boris Strugatskij). As intimated by Holmberg, some of their works seem merely to borrow metaphors and props from SF. For instance, *Piknik na obotjine* (*Roadside Picnic*, 1972) was slow and lacking in ideas, narrated in a lackluster way. However, one of the drafts of this story for the movie Tarkovsky made of it (*Stalker*, 1979), printed in the Swedish magazine *JVM* No. 401, October 1983, was more succinct. And that film is a classic, haunting in its narrative and imagery of a derelict industrial area. Tarkovsky made the film but the Strugatski Brothers deserve some credit as envisioning the framework story. However, bottom line is, you can't just label a text "SF" because it takes place in the future or on another planet; you have to give the SF setting meaning by way of extrapolation, ideas and innovative technology. Otherwise, don't say that you're writing SF. Exciting stories can be done by having them play on contemporary earth too. It's called "mainstream literature", I gather.

In the theme of "SF that isn't SF" you might also mention J. G. Ballard. However, his works exist in a kind of gray area that some call "Slipstream": not mainstream literature, not core SF either, but "something else" because of its speculative character. "Slipstream" may be something of a put-down but Ballard, for his part, had the advantage of being aware of the tropes and tricks of SF to make his stories vaguely recognizable, and satisfactory, to an SF reader. Ballard did, for instance, publish his works in *New Worlds* even before Moorcock became the editor; Ballard was allowed to experiment within the confines of the genre early on.

To sum it up, to label a story SF isn't easy. Even if you're a good mainstream author it takes a lot to fit into the genre. It's not merely about writing well. You have to be conceptually original. But not too original either. Metaphysics is a wide field and how to make a speculative, philosophically original story relatable might be the Philosopher's Stone of writing.

16. JORGE LUIS BORGES

After the above excursion of looking at SF as a genre, the study will now continue with the overview of writers. It's resumed with a brief detour to Latin America, the focus of interest in this chapter being Argentinian Jorge Luis Borges (1899-1986). His gray area fiction of riddles, ontological puzzles and archaic instances is a must in any study of speculatively traditional fiction.

LABYRINTHS

Politically, Borges was an anti-communist. This is seen in an interview with Richard Burgin in 1969. This political stance was rare for 20th century authors. What exactly Borges was *pro* is harder to define. But I don't think it's absolutely off the mark to call him "a man of the right".

Case in point: I can't find the source to it now but reportedly, Borges was awarded a prize from the right-wing Chile Junta in the 1970s. Borges went and received the prize. Later, it was said that this contributed to prevent Borges from ever getting the Nobel Prize in literature. He became controversial. The point is, a man of the left would hardly have accepted such a Chilean prize in the first place.

In a wider sense, Jorge Luis Borges might seem like a paragon of Tradition, a man steeped in ancient wisdom and learning. In truth, he was something of a nihilist veering towards absurdism – a quiet absurdism, uttered in studied poems and stories, but a nihilist nonetheless. For instance, in a foreword to *Labyrinths* (1964), André Maurois says that even though Borges likes metaphysics he doesn't acknowledge any system as true. Which would mean: all is just mind games, aesthetics and fantasy, like walking in labyrinths for the sheer intellectual pleasure, form being more interesting than content. This is post-modernism at its worst.

Overall, Borges is worth reading. I'll get to that. But he also has the traits of a snobbish agnostic. He stacks the deck towards ontological meaninglessness. And the reader, of course, is supposed to fall into a trance because of all the erudition and intricacy this nothingness is presented with. I, for one, am not so easily duped. I mean, what is Borges's "The Library of Babel" other than an intricate obsession: that of a library containing "all possible books", only randomly generating an intelligible book, the rest being collections of completely random series of signs. I don't see the meaning of this. It's a tale, told by a nihilist, signifying nothing.

And "The Circular Ruins", about a man trying to conceptualize a man by creating him out of thought, out of envisioning all his limbs, veins, organs etc. How materialist; ever heard of Logos, of man's spirit generating his body? In a Latin American context, the errant mysticism of "The Circular Ruins" makes you cry out for Carlos Castaneda. He at least acknowledged God (the Spirit), he knew about man's subtle bodies and he praised willpower in a way wholly compatible with Tradition. Borges, on the other hand, is the glorified nihilist.

NUANCES

There may be nuances in the Borges complexion. In Williamson's *Borges: A Life* (2004) it's reported about a trip Borges made to Japan in 1979. The encounters with Shinto, Buddhism, monks and temples made an impression, making the Argentinian acknowledge "agnostic mysticism". And, true, in the just mentioned "The Circular Ruins", the man trying to "dream a man", at the end experiences a dissolution of his self by feeling, in turn, how he's dreamed by some other operator. This is the kind of philosophical depth that nonetheless exists in Borges' opus, be he an agnostic, a nihilist or whatever. Like Lovecraft, he conveys rather a lot of mysticism even though he privately was no dyed-in-the-wool esotericist.

The stories I've mentioned so far in this chapter are to be found in *Fictions*, an English translation of *Ficciones* and *Artificios* (both 1944). Another notable instance from it is "Tlön, Uqbar, Orbis Tertius", about how the fictitious country Uqbar tends to become real thanks to an entry in an encyclopedia; voilà an example of text as the creator of the world, the author as the conceptualizer of reality. We also have "Death and the Compass" with its hieroglyphic murder mystery; the symbol of the *romboid* runs like a red thread through everything, first as a decoration on the wall of a paint store, then as a harlequin's costume and finally as a tile pattern in a mysterious house.

This is fiction written in hieroglyphics, with the sign retaining its individuality even after having been interpreted formally. This is not the flat representation of the phonogram, no, it's the ambiguous nature of the ideogram, that of both being a self-sufficient image and a signifier. For example, you can appreciate the Egyptian bird hieroglyph even after having gathered what it stands for, you can appreciate the pure image of a bird – but what to do with an "E" when you've uttered the sound it stands for?

WESTERN

The short story "The End" in *Fictions* has a spaghetti western feel:

> The plains in the last rays of the sun, were almost abstract, as though seen in a dream. A dot wavered on the horizon, then grew until it became a horseman riding, or so it seemed, toward the house. Recabarren could make out the broad-brimmed hat, the dark poncho, the piebald horse, but not the face of the rider, who finally reined in the horse and came toward the house at an easy trot.[95]

---

[95] Borges, 2000, p 139

This will represent Borges' sense of common stories, his feel for the common people and the gauchos and the knife fights, of which we get our fair share in *David Brodie's Report* (1972). According to the preface, Borges by now had accepted his fate to be Borges, he no longer needed to be so original in each story. Stories from Buenos Aires and its vicinity, heartwarming moralities told in the first person singular: they fly a little bit under the radar for a study of speculative fiction like this, however, in a general sense they prove that *"ars is artem celare"* – artistry consists in concealing your art. Art thrives in many forms but best in the simple.

But of course, there were fantastic stories even here and in *The Book of Sand* (1975). Like a Lovecraft pastiche, stories of mythical Nordic countries ("Undr", "The Disk") and the story of "David Brodie's Report," a Gulliver Travel among a strange people; a bit nihilistic that one, weird for the sake of weird. But I do appreciate the dramas from the academic and the artistic world, like "Guayaqil", "The Bribe" and "The Duel", the last of which is about a virtual stand-off between two female artists.

So in a formal sense, Borges has some relation to Tradition after all. He makes stories about researchers, historians and philologists seem viable; he takes us into the drama of reading, interpreting and conceptualizing reality by way of scripture. He's not an esotericist *per se* but he's not expressly anti-esoteric either. He opens a door to Mystery and Wonder, even though he himself isn't so starry-eyed all the time. But that's the condition of the author: "the author doesn't see the way he's pointing ahead", as Swedish poet Bertil Malmberg once said. If, in a glorified trance, the author sees The Truth this doesn't mean that he himself expressly embraces the same truth when he puts down the pen.

SHORTS

Borges' fiction demonstrates the power of the short story. The fantastic often comes into its own in short story form. Among the authors in this study he's comparable to Lovecraft, Bradbury and Ballard in having a predilection for the short fiction form. *The Book of Sand* illustrates this: it has ease and charm, it's an example of an author keeping his vigor into old age; he was about 75 when he wrote it. The volume has rather many outings into the fantastic. They convey a very peculiar sense of wonder. The fantastic is presented *en passant*, almost as afterthoughts. It's "magical realism" at its best.

To this, there's the condensation and concentration. "The Congress", for instance, reads like a novel. When you think back of it the whole staging, the figures and the plot, come through as a much more elaborate epic than the thirty pages it occupies in the book. I admit that the basic idea of the story, that of a Congress representing all men and consequently trying to be a reference point of all human knowledge, here gets ridiculed in a strawman fashion. The idea is presented as stupid and impossible as such. This attitude of Borges' is another example of his nihilism. It's like the Wittgenstein attitude of seeing general statements as impossible. Now, indeed they are if you reduce yourself into an imperfect human being gazing at your shoes. But *sub specie aeternitatis* we all can reach the causal sphere and the Eternal, Platonic Ideas enabling us to generalizations. So the idea of a Congress being the essence of human endeavor and human knowledge isn't far-out *per se*. In the history of thought it's called the Primordial Tradition, the virtual congregation of minds like Plato, Plotinus, Shankara, Buddha, Eckart, Steiner, Jung and Jünger leading men to higher levels by way of introspection.

That said, Borges, in his subdued manner, has a field day in describing how the Congress of the story was started in Buenos Aires in the early 20th century, who the odd participants were, like the chairman and instigator, Don Alejandro Glencoe, on whose *hacienda* part of the action plays, and then the undramatic but inevitable decline of it all, this ambitious Congess – all very succinct, all in just one short story. In a way, it spares you of reading those thousand page "wondrous" epics of Latin American literature. I'm not saying that Fuentes, Marquez etc. are insignificant, I'm just saying that Borges can concentrate a world into a short. It's not merely thanks to the short form, it's thanks to having a fantastic approach. Having a speculative idea is what drives the SF short story and Borges, being also "able to write" (being no mere scholar out to prove a point), being able to convey the wonders and paradoxes of living into everything he writes, eminently proves this.

Borges also wrote poems and essays. The essays are collected in *Other Inquisitions* (1964). These literary reflections are like his fiction: concise and thoughtful. More SF authors should write essays. I mean, if their literature is so conceptual, why not completely step out of the epic role for a while and lecture us on the bare-bones ideas that drive you?

LITERATURE

- *Fictions* (1998, originally 1944)
- *Other Inquisitions* (1964)
- *David Brodie's Report* (1972)
- *The Book of Sand* (1975)

17. CARLOS CASTANEDA

In the previous chapter was briefly mentioned Carlos Castaneda (1925-1998). In comparison with Borges, Castaneda had a firmer ethical-ontological footing. Castaneda also presented his worldview as narratives, as relatable stories, sometimes classified as fiction. Therefore, Castaneda has a place in this study. Castaneda was born in Cajamarca in Peru, grew up and studied in the USA and then got embroiled in the shamanic wisdom of Mexico. He wrote in English but he had a Latin American strain in his opus; this is why this study groups him with the previous author, the Argentinian Borges. In the next chapter the study returns to the USA proper. And there it will virtually stay for the rest of the book.

FICTION

Those 'in the know' say that Carlos Castaneda made up everything. The self-styled anthropological reports bearing Castaneda's name, such as *The Teachings of Don Juan*, *Tales of Power* and *The Power of Silence*, allegedly were all make-believe, figments of the mind, fiction. I personally do believe that Castaneda did go to Mexico and did get initiated into a circle of shamans but the criticism regarding the authenticity should of course not be ignored. You can't see the books as all-out objective reports. Beyond that, they have a rather relatable style, rather subdued as such – then again, Castaneda is no author in the realm of real fictioneers, of high-profile prose writers. But if the books are to be labeled "fiction" (as they are in some libraries and bookstores) I have no problem with that – since then he can be subsumed into this study of fantasy with a traditional element.

The world-view Castaneda gives us is relayed by a Yaqui Indian guru, Don Juan. In this section I will put "Castaneda" as the source of it all. So what does Castaneda tell us, what's his creed? It's traditional, *mutatis mutandum*. Man is driven by Will. With willpower he can change his life, change his mind; it's all in the mind. A reflective, willpower-driven person can do almost anything. In a very general sense this active mindset is the same as the wisdom conveyed in "God helps the man who helps himself".

Man has a soul, his body has an aura, which equals subtle bodies. Man's soul is created by the Spirit/God. This is traditional knowledge, Indian variety.

Castaneda says: the individual has to *Assume Responsibility* for his thoughts and actions. This is akin to any conservative creed. A person can raise himself mentally with willpower, he can attain moral perfection. *Impeccability*, it's called in the Castaneda books, an overall ideal stressing eternal values like modesty, simplicity and lack of pride. Only with such an honest mind, and with *Inner Silence* reached by meditation, you can be a complete human being, a Man of Knowledge.

The Castaneda world-view contains a lot more than this. But in essence, this "Indian Existentialism" has a lot to teach any reader needing to shape up and become a man, needing to have willpower coming to the fore in his mindset, raising himself mentally and becoming a more assertive, harmonious, together human being.

INDIAN MAGIC

In Book One in the series, *The Teachings of Don Juan – A Yaqui Way of Knowledge* Castaneda becomes the apprentice of Don Juan, learning the ways of Indian magic. He ingests psychotropic drugs, he encounters disembodied spirits, he meets shamans in the form of huge wolves and death in the shape of silver crows. In states of heightened awareness and dreams Castaneda, throughout the series, sees sublime landscapes and impossible things. He talks with coyotes and lizards; he fights for his life against witches; he ventures into parallel worlds. This kaleidoscope of marvels is, as is often the case in fantasy fiction, presented in a rather basic language. In this respect it's true that the reportage style annoys you at times, there's a certain lack of telescoping and there's a tedious repetition at times. In Book Two and Three Castaneda comes through as rather sluggish.

The Castaneda series is nothing for the literary gourmet. Still, "good style is having something to say" and this Castaneda has. For instance, *Tales of Power*, Book Four in the series, is a wonder of concentration and drama, of succinct wisdom and awesome esotericist action. This is Dr. Johnson and Boswell in Mexican twilight; moreover, "these books may be the *Pilgrim's Progress* of our time", according to the *Sunday Times*. They do reward the reader, if he has stamina and perseverance. That is, the books always convey wisdom and drama and sometimes it's even done in a memorable way, in a convincing style. Overall the books are fairly easy to read; conversely, they don't have the excruciatingly bare-bones style of Swedenborg's tomes, if you should compare with another high-profile esotericist. At best, Castaneda can give you a fairly ordinary chapter about a conversation with Don Juan, and then a mystical atmosphere arrives, and then Weird Stuff happens followed by this: "And then a windlike force blew the world away".[96]

SUGGESTIVE

There are literary, suggestive instances to the Castaneda books, if only now and then. But this has a great marginal effect. Conversely, not even renowned fantasy authors give you mystery and drama in every paragraph. The wondrous has to be mixed with the ordinary to be digested, to be relatable to the reader. This Ernst Jünger once

---

[96] Castaneda, 1985, p 315

observed, in the case of E. A. Poe's stories; they convince us because of the framework of everydayness they are set in. The same goes for Castaneda's narrative style. To begin a chapter with Castaneda and Don Juan sitting on the ramada, conversing about the look of the clouds, may be the opening for a scene of magic, wonder and terror. Like Borges' fiction you're tempted to classify Castaneda as magical realism.

The back cover blurb of *The Fire From Within* (Black Swan, 1985) has a fine metaphor: "Each of Carlos Castaneda's books is a brilliant and tantalizing burst of illuminations into the depths of our deepest mysteries, like a burst of lightning over the desert at night, which shows us a world that is both alien and entirely familiar – the landscape of our dreams."

SOLITARY BIRD

The Castaneda books contain some choice poetry, quoted poetry, vivid illuminations of the moods and wisdoms conveyed. One such quote is given at the beginning of *Tales of Power,* the book summing up Castaneda's apprenticeship and Don Juan's teachings. It's a prose poem by 16th century Spanish mystic John of the Cross, originally found in "Sayings of Light and Love". And here it is, "The Conditions of a Solitary Bird":

> The conditions of a solitary bird are five:
> The first, that it flies to the highest point;
> the second, that it does not suffer for company,
> not even of its own kind;
> the third, that it aims its beak to the skies;
> the fourth, that it does not have a definite color;
> the fifth, that it sings very softly.

This, to me, sums up the Castaneda world: mystery, piety and wonder.

THE WORKS

In the essential, epic, narrative sense there are ten books by Castaneda to be read.

The first is *The Teachings of Don Juan,* an overall classic, for an esoteric book rather tight and fast-paced, with lots of instances of psychotropic drugs and magical encounters. At the end of the book Castaneda quits the apprenticeship, he has had enough. In the next book, however, *A Separate Reality,* he returns under the auspices of Don Juan and learns of *Memento Mori* (your physical body has a limited lifespan, draw the conclusions; seek and see the wonders around you while you live). It's about Indian magic but also a lot of everyday, common wisdom is conveyed. The same goes for the next book in the series, *Journey to Ixtlan;* in holistic fashion "everything" is covered, there are repetitions (such as the constant stressing of *Memento Mori*) but we also get some lessons in dreaming. And what fantasy and SF reader doesn't like to venture out into the dreamlands? Lovecraft and Jünger did and so did Castaneda.

The next book, as intimated, is another classic: *Tales of Power.* Here, Don Juan repeats all the things he has taught, not in a scholarly fashion but in poignant one-liners and aphorisms. It's a non-literary, non-bookish doctrine and as such a little unsystematic but overall it's very enlightening. Remember your mortality, live life operationally, like a warrior, also, live in wonder and awe. This is the Don Juan creed. At the end of *Tales of Power* Castaneda performs his examination work and in the next book Don Juan is gone, Castaneda himself has to be the new leader of the ring of magicians Don Juan taught and led. Castaneda has met these other figures before but he has some hard times in growing into the role of master magician. Of this, we get our fair share in *The Second Ring of Power* and *The Eagle's Gift.* These books have their weird character, weird both as in "strange happenings" and "a specific vocabulary being used". However, Castaneda's writer's approach of "steady workman" guarantees that the reader doesn't have to solve riddles as to what every scene means, at least not superficially. There are weird goings on, this is magic, but the reader is brought along fairly well narratively. It should be mentioned, though, that *The Second Ring of Power* is a bit indulgent as to negative happenings. The story is about dealing with a company of sorcerers being adverse to him, distrusting him.

As for general atmosphere, the next two books, *The Fire from Within* and *The Power of Silence*, aren't exactly "feel good literature". However, the presence of Castaneda's first teacher, Don Juan, at times can create a somewhat merry atmosphere. For these two titles go back in time and return to dialogs Castaneda previously had with Don Juan, meetings he hasn't told of before. Dramatically this is a plus, Don Juan is always a stimulating acquaintance. On the back cover blurb for *The Power of Silence* (Washington Square Press 1991) it says that now he's back, Don Juan, "wise, infuriating, capable of working miracles and playing practical jokes, but always seeking the wisdom of the warrior".

Book Nine, *The Art of Dreaming*, is about dreaming systematically, about dreaming as a magical means. As such it can be a little esoteric but there are scenes in this surpassing many a good fantasy novel.

And then we have Book Ten, *The Active Side of Infinity*, which is a sort of summation of Castaneda's magic journey. In all, I can't say that any single book in the series is redundant. All of them have wisdom, exciting scenes and then some. So instead of reading a lackluster SF novel or magazine, read a Castaneda book and then exclaim, for real: Astounding! Amazing! Fantastic! And to the reader longing for horror and weird fantasy, I'd say: "Go thou to Carlos Castaneda and shudder"...

LITERATURE

- *The Teachings of Don Juan – A Yaqui Way of Knowledge* (1968)
- *A Separate Reality* (1971)
- *Journey to Ixtlan* (1972)
- *Tales of Power* (1974)
- *The Second Ring of Power* (1977)
- *The Eagle's Gift* (1981)
- *The Fire From Within* (1984)
- *The Power of Silence* (1987)
- *The Art of Dreaming* (1993)
- *The Active Side of Infinity* (1999)

18. EDGAR RICE BURROUGHS

THE STUDY IS NOW back in America. Thus, a look at Edgar Rice Burroughs (1875-1950) is a logical stopover. His fantastic fiction about Mars is a shining beacon for *archeofuturism*, this promising sub-genre mixing old with new.

MARS

The Edgar Rice Burroughs opus might be "an inch deep and a thousand miles wide", it might be a tad superficial or, at best, an object of antiquarian sentimentality. However, as it stands his debut *A Princess of Mars* (1912) is still worth reading. Apart from the solid workmanship and the charming narrative the main character has some depth.

It's like this: lost in the wilds of Nevada, Virginian John Carter finds himself in a strange cave, struck by a trance that gives him a sort of out of body experience. Looking out over the desert lands his gaze is captured by Mars, named after the patron deity of this trade, that of being a soldier. And by power of Will-Thought he wishes himself off to that planet and in the next moment finds himself standing there, under the chasing moons of Phobos and Deimos. The planet is called Barsoom by its inhabitants, five meter tall, four-armed lizards called "green men" or Warhoons. Carter is captured by them and he's kept as an amusing animal, he can come and go rather freely and soon he asserts himself in duels. Thus he becomes a Warhoon chieftain.

SAVAGES

It's a "life among the savages": the Warhoons are brutal yet honest nomads, they live to fight and fight to live. Carter, as the paragon of heroism he is, having fought in the Civil War and elsewhere, teaches his new allies compassion – compassion for a beaten foe, compassion for your mounts; compassion within the framework of duty, honor and courage.

Things like this elevates *A Princess of Mars* to a minor classic. It isn't merely about adventure; Carter narrates his story with elaborate detail, with zest and flair. The language may lack the atmospheric charm of a Howard or a Bradbury but the story is well told. It might not come through as wholly plausible, this action story with a thin SF veneer; still, the conceptualization is there, this is Mars with its plethora of people, customs, technology and landscapes. The story has its value secured by the meticulous detail work.

To live among the Warhoons is about riding a thoat, shooting straight and speaking the truth. The Warhoons, Carter says, are happy in that they have no lawyers. Their judiciary system is governed by common law and customs. These green lizards are a bit grotesque; even Carter admits it. Luckily, there are humans on Mars too, "red men", one of which is the lovely Dejah Toris. Carter becomes her husband and eventually a prince of her land, Helium, a human kingdom. This gives the story – *A Princess of Mars* – some relatability, even though these Martian humans aren't related to earthly humans, these red men being oviparous and rather long-lived, up to 1,000 years.

In his inventiveness Burroughs becomes a wee bit grotesque, even though, as intimated, his narrative style has its undeniable charm. It's got the allure of a naive piece of art. But more than this there's a solid tangibility to the novel; that it lacks any higher stylistic elevation is rather a plus, for, as C. S. Lewis said, "describing odd things in an odd language is about one oddity too much". The reader can digest this Martian grotesque because of the simple, meticulous style.

DESERT PLANET

In chapter fourteen of *A Princess of Mars* Carter has to duel with a native, a certain Zad who has struck another human prisoner, the native Dejah Toris. Carter challenges Zad to a duel – and wins, of course. Specifically, where have we seen this before: a man coming to a desert planet with ancient customs, he learns of them and becomes accepted in their ranks, he fights a duel and wins etc.? In Herbert's *Dune* of course, with Feyd Rautha taking the place of Zad. Overall, Burroughs seems to have been a pioneer in depicting a planet with some detail as to its ethnography, history and biology – a desert planet to that, with its variety of advanced science. Alex Raymond may also have learned something from Burroughs: swords and high-tech co-existing amicably.

Along with inspiring Bradbury, Heinlein and Jack Vance, Burroughs is the spiritual father of *Dune*, Flash Gordon and all the other archaic futures, holding a promise for us all. I'm not meaning this sentimentally; I mean it essentially. The future of man won't see atheists discussing space drives in sterile technotopias – not solely. It will also see adventure, passion and beauty, as Burroughs showed us in his Mars series.

BIO

You might have heard that Burroughs created Tarzan, the jungle hero with noble ancestry. This he did, but he also wrote a lot of speculative fiction too. Except for the John Carter series he wrote novels playing on Venus and in inner earth, the latter called *Pellucidar* in the Burroughs mythology.

Burroughs was an author rather "in spite" of himself, much like Heinlein: we see the pattern of the hands-on doer finding himself without means of subsistence and then resorting to writing, rather excelling in it. Burroughs was born in 1875 and first served in the military. Having failed the entrance exam for the US Army Military Academy at West Point he became an enlisted soldier of the 7th Cavalry in Arizona, seeing something of the still Wild West. Because of a heart problem he was discharged on medical grounds in 1897. Now he tried on a variety of jobs to support his family of wife and two children. Having at one time a lot of spare time he read pulps and he even started writing himself. He sent his attempt to *The All-Story Magazine* and had it accepted, serialized as *Under the Moons of Mars* in 1912. This story was the selfsame *A Princess of Mars* treated in this chapter.

At about the same time Burroughs created Tarzan and all the franchises in this realm (comic book, films) made Burroughs rather well off. Symbolic of this is that Burroughs soon bought a large ranch north of Los Angeles which he named "Tarzana". Then a community sprang up around the ranch and in 1927 the citizens voted to call it this, "Tarzana" when the municipality was formally founded.

LITERATURE

- *A Princess of Mars* (1912)
- *The Gods of Mars* (1914)
- *The Warlord of Mars* (1918)
- *Thuvia, Maid of Mars* (1920)

19. H. P. LOVECRAFT

Howard Phillips Lovecraft (1890-1937) was a man steeped in Tradition. He yearned for old times, he was an amateur antiquarian and he favored the English language of the 18th century. He has become something of a symbol for conservatism – for *paleoconservatism*, studied variety.

ANTIQUARIAN

"History exists – and it's all that exists." This H. P. Lovecraft meant. A more vocal statement of historicism, of living in the past, is hard to find. To find solace, yea, even salvation and a direction in life by reading old books, studying old architecture and meditating on bygone times: this, to me, seems to be the Lovecraft way of life, the passion for the olden-old as a more or less viable creed.

Lovecraft was an amateur antiquarian, an armchair researcher occupied with the history of old buildings, legendary sites and traditions of the American Colonial Times. In S. T. Joshi's biography, we read of Lovecraft's knowledge of worthy sights in his residential Providence, Rhode Island, and of trips Lovecraft made into the countryside in the search of Colonial remains. Such a road trip is mirrored in the Lovecraft story "The Shadow Over Innsmouth" where the protagonist is out to survey classical architecture for his own pleasure and possible research: "I was celebrating my coming of age by a tour of New England – sightseeing, antiquarian, and genealogical..."[97]

OLD SCHOOL

Lovecraft was old school. His stylistic ideal was Dr. Johnson and his dictionary, an 18th century endeavor promoting words like "incandescent", "effervescent" and "fulminate", a wide-scale anglification of Latin words. English written with many such terms is called "Johnsonese" and Lovecraft excelled in it – a style reveling in elaborate words and long sentences, a style signaling "erudition" to those who haven't attended university. But Lovecraft's style can't altogether be reduced to word fetishism and showing off. "L'homme et la style, c'est la même" (the man and his style is one). And many have tried to copy the Lovecraft style, without success.

Reportedly, Lovecraft had read Oswald Spengler's *Decline of the West* (1918-1922), an outline saying that the Westworld is doomed, having its best days behind it. Decadence rules and this Lovecraft for instance conceptualized in his New York stories ("He", "Cool Air", "The Horror at Red Hook"). He cherished the Colonial times when white Anglo-Saxons ruled America and he resented the large-scale, 20th century-style immigration; *q.v.* the short story "The Street," catching *in nuce* the sociological development of America. Lovecraft was pretty much against the modern lifestyle and embraced old-school and archaic attitudes aplenty. This we find in his correspondence, which is rather vast.

So for all intents and purposes, Lovecraft formally was a paragon of Tradition. How, then, does this translate into his fiction at large? How does stories of supernatural horror and cosmic fright mirror the archetypal image of the conservative drinking tea in his parlor admiring his bookshelves of classics in half-calf? Indeed, in Lovecraft's fiction you can find the Conservative Man going about New England

---

[97] Lovecraft, 1990, p 384

and encountering these cosmic horrors. But more fruitful than searching for the model antiquarian attitude in otherwise rather nihilistic stories ("man is doomed, powerful gods coming to suck his soul away"...) is to look at Lovecraft's more positive stories, his so called Dream World fiction.

DREAMS

Lovecraft had many strings to his bow. He could do more than convey panicky horror and hopelessness. He also envisioned dreamy, sublime sceneries in stories such as "The White Ship", "Celephais", "Polaris" and the novel *The Dream-Quest of Unknown Kadath*. You must be dreaming intensively to be able to sail in this more unknown Lovecraft-world, having to operate in "conscious unreality" to reach the blessed islands.

Lovecraft designated himself as a pragmatist and an atheist. There are letters of his hand proving this. But his literary work speaks of more than such reductionism. In it we find traces of perennial philosophy and thoughts about the true nature of reality beyond our mundane senses, like this:

> Men of broader intellect know that there is no sharp distinction betwixt the real and the unreal; that all things appear as they do only by virtue of the delicate individual physical and mental media through which we are made conscious of them; but the prosaic materialism of the majority condemns as madness the flashes of super sight which penetrate the common veil of obvious empiricism.[98]

Thus from the short story "The Tomb". There's a sliding scale between the real and unreal. Some inspirations can get us to see into the "unreal" which in fact is the essentially real: the reality of higher, eternal realms compared to everyday reality: the lands of wonder, the astral world, the eternal dreamland. You have to educate your eyes, see the prototype in the image and the essence in the ephemeral; to

---

[98] Lovecraft, 1994, p 18

venture out into the Mythago Wood, take a walk in fairy tale and legend and see primeval characters and archetypes. "I do not think that what I read in these books or saw in these fields and groves was exactly what other boys read and saw there..."[99]

ESOTERICISM

There's a discreet presence of esotericism in the Lovecraftian stories. For instance, the narrator in "The Book" is swept off to unseen landscapes and breathtaking views, just by reading this book. And the protagonist of "The White Ship" is a dreamy lighthouse keeper who listens to the stories of the sea, gets into a trance and sees a white ship stopping by the lighthouse; he embarks on a moonbeam and sails away to the dreamy countries. And in *The Dream-Quest of Unknown Kadath* the fairyland is reached by a certain Randolph Carter experimenting with his sleep; he finally goes the 711 steps down to the realms of the collective unconscious, wanders happy away across flourishing meadows and sees how everything is a little better, a little brighter, a little more real than the everyday gray:

> The sun rose higher over gentle slopes of grove and lawn, and heightened the colors of the thousand flowers that starred each knoll and dingle. A blessed haze lies upon all this region, wherein is held a little more of the sunlight than other places hold, and a little more of the summer's humming music of birds and bees; so that men walk through it as though through a faery place, and feel greater joy and wonder than they ever afterward remember.[100]

The dream quest: Carter encounters darker countries too, he must go through a creepy underground – "the subconscious" of unwelcome shadows and ghouls; however, as such, in a Jungian sense, needed for gaining spiritual fulfillment. So he meets and evades the ghosts, and so he reaches fairer dreamlands again, and eventually he comes upon his goal: the sought-after Kadath. Or does he? The story ends

---

[99] Lovecraft, 1994, ibid.
[100] Lovecraft, 1993, p 414

where it began, in Boston, Massachusetts, but the feeling of the quest nonetheless having been real is the lingering feeling: "... to the organ chords of morning's myriad whistles, and dawn's blaze thrown dazzling through purple panes by the great gold dome of the State House on the hill, Randolph Carter leaped shoutingly awake within his Boston room."[101]

The sun on distant rooftops is the road to essential reality, to the lands of wonder. To look at something that shimmers, shining in the sun or glowing in the fire, is also said to be the path to the higher reality in Castaneda's *A Separate Reality*.

The Dream-Quest of Unknown Kadath is about dreaming. To dream consciously in this way is no irresponsible occupation. As intimated earlier in this study, the Castaneda books are full of systematic dreaming. And Ernst Jünger, that informal teacher on esotericism, in *Eumeswil* said: "We're not defeated because of our dreams but because we haven't dreamed intensely enough." He also said: "Dreams are streams – from infinity."

The active esotericist has to take responsibility for his dreams. Observations like these are in sync with the mind of Lovecraft's Carter, who was skilled in the art of dreaming: "He was old in the land of dreams..."

There's an atmosphere of esotericism in Lovecraft's opus. However, his attitude toward the astral world isn't wholly commendable. To meet the Shadowland you need willpower and a lodestar in the form of acknowledging your Inner Light, and this attitude isn't so prominent in Lovecraft's reports from this realm. His tendency of indulging in Fear of the Dark is not to be recommended. Affirming the Light and meeting the spooks with stern Will-Thought is a better way of roaming the Shadowland.

THE POET

Lovecraft wrote some poetry in his day. Traditional in content they were, and metrically correct in the formal sense, yet lacking some life. Overall, Pound and Eliot have more to give as regards 20th century

---

[101] Lovecraft, 1993, p 486

traditionally inclined poets, and among relevant 19th century names Poe, Keats and Coleridge were a grade better bards than Lovecraft. The Lovecraft collection *Fungi from Yuggoth* presents a variety of scenes and instances, like "horror poetry" ending in a monster appearing, as such maybe interesting from an antiquarian point of view. Then we have the more ambiguous pieces, like "Continuity", capturing that longing, yearning mindset also seen in Lovecraft's Dream World fiction:

> There is in certain ancient things a trace
> of some dim essence – more than form or weight;
> a tenuous aether, indeterminate,
> yet linked with all the laws of time and space.
> A faint, veiled sign of continuities
> that outward eyes can never quite descry;
> of locked dimensions harbouring years gone by,
> and out of reach except for hidden keys.
> It moves me most when slanting sunbeams glow
> on old farm buildings set against a hill,
> and paint with life the shapes which linger still
> from centuries less a dream than this we know.
> In that strange light I feel I am not far
> from the fixt mass whose sides the ages are.

Admittedly, the last line isn't poetic at all. Poetry has to sing and have rhythm and melodically "from the fixt mass whose sides the ages are" is strained. However, another Lovecraft item overall worth quoting is this, "Alienation," about being an outsider. More on the short story with that title – "The Outsider" – later.

> His solid flesh had never been away,
> for each dawn found him in his usual place,
> but every night his spirit loved to race
> through gulfs and worlds remote from common day.
> He had seen Yadith, yet retained his mind,
> and come back safely from the Ghooric zone,
> when one still night across curved space was thrown

that beckoning piping from the voids behind.
He waked that morning as an older man,
and nothing since has looked the same to him.
Objects around float nebulous and dim –
false, phantom trifles of some vaster plan.
His folk and friends are now an alien throng
to which he struggles vainly to belong.

THE FESTIVAL

A certain short story by Lovecraft, "The Festival" (1923), astounds me every time. Maybe it's because of its musical quality, its character of being "a poem in prose". Anyhow, in this yarn the protagonist comes to a mysterious village with customary gabled houses, stained glass windows and murmurs in the corners of unnamable horrors, of "feastings unhallowed and old". Then it's suddenly time to go to an assembly in a temple on a hill, apparently for a "Yule-rite" in a church – but it doesn't end there – for next the congregation, in the church hall, heads for a staircase leading down into ancient crypts and tunnels. After a certain descent they reach an underground river.

They stand by the river, and then what? Indeed, they see this sight out of the baroque, something truly arabesque and grotesque:

> Out of the unimaginable blackness beyond the gangrenous glare of that cold flame, out of the tartarean leagues through which that oily river rolled uncanny, unheard, and unsuspected, there flopped rhythmically a horde of tame, trained, hybrid winged things that no sound eye could ever wholly grasp, or sound brain ever wholly remember. They were not altogether crows, nor moles, nor buzzards, nor ants, nor vampire bats, nor decomposed human beings; but something I cannot and must not recall. They flopped limply along, half with their webbed feet and half with their membranous wings; and as they reached the throng of celebrants the cowled figures seized and mounted them, and rode off one by one along the reaches of that unlighted river, into

pits and galleries of panic where poison springs feed frightful and indiscoverable cataracts.[102]

My comment on this is that I have no comment. This is so way-out that I'm amiss for words. As it stands, the passage might be devoid of deeper meaning but the craftsmanship gives it a lasting quality, like you admire a finely wrought embroidery or tracery.

Another Lovecraft story having made some impression on me is "The Music of Erich Zann" (1921). At the climax we see the musician, Erich Zann, warding off an attack by unseen monstrosities by playing music on his cello – weird music, music that the narrator has heard from afar at the beginning of the story, wondering what this might be. It's true that a remark by Brian Aldiss about this piece can make you smirk, like noting how the cellist has the instrument "between his legs" and that during the playing his "forehead was perspiring heavily"; something for the Freudian scholars out there to delve on. That said, the story begins rather stirringly – subdued yet with an unmistakable feel, capturing the mood perfectly, a mood of puzzlement and wonder, symbolized in what might be Paris but essentially comes to portray Any City or Anytown, the symbolic city within us all:

> I have examined maps of the city with the greatest care, yet have never again found the Rue d'Auseil. (...) The Rue d'Auseil lay across a dark river bordered by precipitous brick blear-windowed warehouses and spanned by a ponderous bridge of dark stone. It was always shadowy along that river, as if the smoke of neighbouring factories shut out the sun perpetually. The river was also odorous with evil stenches which I have never smelled elsewhere, and which may some day help me to find it, since I should recognize them at once. Beyond the bridge were narrow cobbled streets with rails; and then came the ascent, at first gradual, but incredibly steep as the Rue d'Auseil was reached. I have never seen another street as narrow and steep as the Rue d'Auseil. It was almost a cliff, closed to all vehicles, consisting

---

[102] Lovecraft, 1994, p 223

in several places of flights of steps, and ending at the top in a lofty ivied wall. Its paving was irregular, sometimes stone slabs, sometimes cobblestones, and sometimes bare earth with struggling greenish-grey vegetation. The houses were tall, peaked-roofed, incredibly old, and crazily leaning backward, forward, and sidewise. Occasionally an opposite pair, both leaning forward, almost met across the street like an arch; and certainly they kept most of the light from the ground below.[103]

The function of this passage is not merely to serve as atmosphere. It's about painting a psychological landscape, the emotions being symbolized in the odd nature of the street, the buildings etc.

Lovecraft externalizes his inner mind. That said, he can also mention specific thoughts outright. Such as, "my metaphysical studies had taught me kindness".[104] This is said about his relation to Erich Zann as he gets to know him, seeing that the old man is suffering from nervous strain. That "kindness" line has always struck me as appropriate, it gives the story some moral elevation; a rare word indeed in the Lovecraft universe, "kindness," an affirmation of the primeval force of Compassion.

OUTSIDER

The last fiction quote of this chapter will be from the beginning of "The Outsider" (1921). This might be something of a signature Lovecraft story, about being just that – an outsider. Colin Wilson named a whole study after this – *The Outsider* (1956) – about odd figures like Kafka, William Blake, Hesse and Nietzsche, focusing on their separateness, of being outside of polite society. The Lovecraft story in question is impossible to relate, this prose-poetic outing in lands unseen, of the narrator trying to break free from his isolation. I will only quote the beginning. Let it be clear: I don't endorse the kind of self-pity displayed but the passage has more than that, it has a timeless musicality:

---

[103] Lovecraft, 1990, p 335-336
[104] Ibid., p 340

Unhappy is he to whom the memories of childhood bring only fear and sadness. Wretched is he who looks back upon lone hours in vast and dismal chambers with brown hangings and maddening rows of antique books, or upon awed watches in twilight groves of grotesque, gigantic, and vine-encumbered trees that silently wave twisted branches far aloft. Such a lot the gods gave to me – to me, the dazed, the disappointed, the barren, the broken.[105]

PROVIDENCE

As time goes by I note that I'm not always so amused by mere fantasy and marvel as I used to be. It's the ordinary traits that capture me; I want *meaning*, in whatever form it appears. So as for Lovecraft I'd say that his correspondence still is viable in some instances; he wrote long letters to friends like C. A. Smith and Robert E. Howard and selections of this is in print.

The Lovecraft figure might live in the collective memory as a despondent recluse, fearing the advent of numinous cosmic forces. However, that selfsame Lovecraft used to sign his letters, "I am Providence", a word-play on his Rhode Island hometown but nonetheless, he willfully signed them so, no one forced him to do it. And he didn't just write "cosmic horror", he also wrote of his Dream World. Authors of stature have a level of complexity in their works, a character of not being able to be reduced into a simple formula. And while Lovecraft may be hard to like for a willpower-driven esotericist, this Lovecraft does also have an unmistakable, spiritual allure, a sunny disposition that isn't completely overclouded by his more commonly known, "defining" aspects of doom and gloom.

On Lovecraft's gravestone on Swan Point Cemetery it reads, along with his name and years of birth and death, "I Am Providence". It's a fine epitaph, better than "I'm off to the Ghooric zone" or something more "Lovecraftian".

---

[105] Lovecraft, 1990, p 11

LITERATURE

- *Fungi From Yuggoth.* 1982
- *H. P. Lovecraft Omnibus 1: At the Mountains of Madness* (1993)
- *H. P. Lovecraft Omnibus 2: Dagon and Other Macabre Tales* (1994)
- *H. P. Lovecraft Omnibus 3: The Haunter of the Dark* (1990)

20. CLARK ASHTON SMITH

THE PREVIOUS CHAPTER was about H. P. Lovecraft. Lovecraft, in turn, knew Clark Ashton Smith (1893-1961), fellow American author and fantasist. A feature to compare them by is this: reportedly, Lovecraft stopped writing poetry when comparing his endeavors with Smith's. And Smith may have been a more accomplished poet, at least in the formal sense. Like Lovecraft Smith wrote about faraway vistas in an antiquated way. The question is, does the aestheticism of Smith allow him to be called a traditionalist or does his opus border too much on nihilism for him to deserve that label?

MUSIC

In chapter one I mentioned the musical traits of Robert Heinlein. The activities of the Muses, the Greek goddesses of song, dance, poetry etc., exert some presence in Heinlein's works. But does he really come through as a musical man, a *musische Mensch*, as the Germans say? Well, not exactly. Heinlein was also rather titanic, praising technology and imperialism. But among the authors presented in this study Clark Ashton Smith surely deserves to be called a *musical man*.

In 2014 I published a biography of Ernst Jünger. There, I elaborated upon Jünger's embracing of the musical mode. For instance, I said the following:

During the visit to the eastern front Jünger spends the new year in an army HQ. The festive spirits are absent, both here and there this time. Festive joy isn't possible these days he says. (Kutais, December 31, 1942) So what then is a feast, what is joy? True joy has got to have *music*; the Muses, goddesses for arts like dance, music and epic poetry, is the etymological root to "music". In German they have the word "musisch" along with "musikalisch," the latter having to do with music specifically and the former – *musisch* – with the joy of art in life in general, a glorified, creative sense of mirth. English doesn't have this distinction, only having the word "musical". Jünger often talks about *die musische*, of the need for *musische* joy, *musische* living. From his brother Fritz (in "Griechische Götter", 1943) he had learned of the Olympian gods having parties which the titans didn't, the latter only having work and toil: all work and no play made the titans dull. In short: the titans had no music, they weren't *musisch* but the Olympian gods were. This becomes something of a sub-theme in Jünger's later works: the difference between gods and titans, and especially how our technological times often seem titanic in nature. And the symbol for the anti-titanic, olympian lifestyle is music, the talent for being musisch. We have the word in Swedish too – *musisk* – and it says a lot more than simply "cultural", and especially "working with culture" as the jargong goes – for against this Jünger would say that it's a contradiction to "work with culture". The musical soul of art has got nothing to do with work and toil, it's about divine inspiration and Apollonian ease. Apollo for example is said to build a city with the tones of his harp.[106]

So then, I'd say that Clark Ashton Smith was musical in this sense. I don't know if he could build cities with his harp but he sure could sing:

> Who has seen the towers of Amithaine
> swan-throated rising from the main
> whose tides to some remoter moon

---

[106] Svensson, 2014, p 227-228

flow in a fadeless afternoon...?
Who has seen the towers of Amithaine
shall sleep, and dream of them again.

These are words by Smith the poet, "Amithaine". Even his prose had musicality to it. For instance, this can be seen in *Out of Space and Time* vol. 2, telling about demons and gargoyles, brownies and fairies, charnel-dungeons and stupendous vistas, a truly mind-boggling journey through thick and thin.

Rememberest thou? Enormous gongs of stone
were stricken, and the storming trumpeteers
acclaimed my deed to answering tides of spears,
and spoke the names of monsters overthrown –
griffins whose angry gold, and fervid store
of sapphires wrenched from mountain-plunged mines –
carnelians, opals, agates, almandines,
I brought to thee some scarlet eve of yore.[107]

The collection also has prose-poems like "From the Crypts of Memory," about a shadowy existence in a dying land Beyond the Beyond. This is rich, creamy poesy with words you don't even find in the Longman Dictionary. The piece ending the book, "The Shadows," is as rich, with all its "fretted windows," "the undesecrated seal of death" and "a meaningless antic phantasmagoria". I read them again and again these jewels of literature: neither stories nor versified poems but *poems in prose* in the vein of Baudelaire. Being about two pages long they have just the right length for a prose poem.

Even the more conventional sides of the book are alluring, like "The Monster of The Prophecy", "The Death of Ilalotha" and "The Vaults of Yoh-Vombis". These outings aren't overly deep, not profound in any sense of the word – but fun in a quiet way, fun in a "oh-how-he-can-adorn-his-language-with-obsolete-words"-way. There's that personality you can't mistake, that jewelry tinge to it all that makes me come back for more, longing to dwell forever in the purple shadows and the hyaline shimmer of the Smith magic.

---

[107] "In Lemuria"

> For trumpets blare in Amithaine
> for paladins that once again
> ride forth to ghostly, glamorous wars
> against the doom-preparing stars.
> Dreamer, awake! ... but I remain
> to ride with them in Amithaine.[108]

HIEROGLYPH

Smith "could write", he knew the craftsmanship of words. His prose and poetry sang. But did his text ever mean anything beyond mere atmosphere? I'd say, sometimes his stories had meaning. As in the present collection, *Out of Space and Time 2,* in "The Last Hieroglyph", where a certain astrologer, Nushain, casting his own horoscope evokes a numinous mummy from the shadows. The mummy tells him that he, Nushain, has to go on a quest through the elements to meet Vergama, Lord of Hieroglyphs. On his quest Nushain is led by successively the mummy, a merman and a salamander, and eventually Nushain stands before the god Vergama. In his book are seen the symbols guiding his quest.

"In my book", says the god, "the characters of all things are written and preserved. All visible forms, in the beginning, were but symbols written by me; and at the last they shall exist only as the writing of my book."[109] What, then, is this? God controlling the Platonic World of Ideas? God with The Book of Life? Here I come to think of what Borges intimated in *Other Inquisitions*, namely, that the world is a text that we read and write, and in which we ourselves are written. For indeed, the story ends with this, the figure of Vergama disappearing in a swirl before Nushain, and:

> Then the god was lost in sight; and Nushain was a weightless and exile thing, the withered skeleton of a lost leaf, rising and falling on the bright whirlwind. In the book Vergama, at the end of the

---

[108] "Amithaine"
[109] Smith, p 31

last column of the right-hand page, there stood the hieroglyph of a gaunt astrologer, carrying a furled nativity. Vergama leaned forward from his chair, and turned the page.[110]

Perennial philosophy in the framework of a story, told with poetical prose, what more can you ask for? This is Tradition, highlighted in a 20th century fantasy.

DOOM AND GLOOM

Smith had his moments but overall, he was something of a nihilist. Dying worlds, dying cultures, and nothing to save us from doom and gloom, from annihilation and a non-existence in the dark recesses of the abyss, utter oblivion awaiting us in the bottomless void. So in all fairness, there's nothing to gather ethically from Smith's world, nothing to guide you, nothing to enrich you existentially. It's an empty gesture, aestheticism in the face of the downfall. Style isn't about building cathedrals of words; it's about having something to say. However, with that in mind, if you don't expect any profound lessons from Smith's stories it's no crime to read him and enjoy him. For example, in itself this is a credible description of a spent culture:

> We were a somber, secret, many-sorrowed people – we who dwelt beneath that sky of eternal twilight, pierced by the towering tombs and obelisks of the past. In our blood was the chill of the ancient night of time; and our pulses flagged with a creeping prescience of the lentor of Lethe. Over our courts and fields, like invisible sluggish vampires born of mausoleums, rose and hovered the black hours, with wings that distilled a malefic languor made from the shadowy woe and despair of perished cycles. (...) Vaguely we lived, and loved as in dreams – the dim and mystic dreams that hover upon the verge of fathomless sleep. We felt for our women, with their pale and spectral beauty, the same desire that the dead may feel for the phantom lilies of Hadean meads.[111]

---

[110] Smith, p 32
[111] Ibid., p 190

Tradition is about Higher Values and Higher Truths and these Smith didn't convey to any notable extent. But as intimated, he had his moments, his poetry is exquisite and in sheer craftsmanship of words he's a paragon. The purple prose and flowery language may remind you of Lovecraft but Smith overall has a brighter tone than Lovecraft, the programmatic sense of doom and gloom notwithstanding.

Smith along with Lovecraft and Robert E. Howard formed "the Three Musketeers" of *Weird Tales* in the 30s, being its most popular authors. In the same decade Lovecraft died of illness and Howard shot himself. Lovecraft felt alienated from mankind ("I am an outsider; a stranger in this century and among those who are still men", said in *The Outsider* and maybe reflecting what the author himself felt) and Howard saw no reason to live on when his mother had died. You shouldn't be judging either Lovecraft or Howard as persons but you can feel somewhat alien to their alienation. Smith, on the other hand, seems to have "accepted membership in the human race" (otherwise said by Kuttner about Heinlein, quoted in chapter one). Smith barely eked out a living as a fruit picker and gardener but he lived on into old age, dying in 1961.

Smith was born in 1893 and early on showed a gift for poetry. In his thirties he began writing prose, being published in *Weird Tales, The London Mercury, Mencken Smart Set* and others. From the mid-thirties Smith's interest in writing seems to have waned; he had said all he didn't have to say. Instead he turned to painting and sculpting. As for his sculptures, August Derleth has this to say in the foreword to *Out of Space and Time*:

> His sculptures, which are especially powerful and fascinating, are cut largely from strange and unusual minerals and have been compared to pre-Columbian art. While not widely circulated – they are never cast, but each one is original and has no copy – Smiths's sculptures have found numerous purchasers, not limited to the coterie of fellow writers with whom Smith is in constant touch.[112]

---

[112] Smith, p 8

This sculpting might have been an oddity and Smith might have been something of an odd writer – but still, there's a curious light shining over his opus, the "jewelry prose" having some life beyond mere aestheticism.

LITERATURE

- *Out of Space and Time*, 1971
- *Lost Worlds*, 1971

21. ROBERT E. HOWARD

"When a nation forgets her skill in war, when her religion becomes a mockery, when the whole nation becomes a nation of money-grabbers, then the wild tribes, the barbarians drive in." This is a quote by Robert Erwin Howard (1900-1936), American, author of westerns, historical fiction and fantasy. He's famous for creating the Conan stories, about a barbarian in a fantasy world. The words "Tradition" and "Barbarian" might not go well together but as the opening quote shows Howard did have some depth in his outlook.

URGENCY

Robert E. Howard created the Hyborian age, an era said to have taken place between the fall of Atlantis and the dawn of recorded history. Reportedly, Howard found it easier to write about fictitious countries than historical ones: voilà an example of "fantasy as artistic necessity". And the Conan stories, along with their character of historical pastiche and make-believe, are driven by some sort of urgency, having some kind of credibility and authority in them.

Conan the Cimmerian is the main character, a northern barbarian roaming the lands of Hyboria as a mercenary, a thief and a pirate. This doesn't sound as anything near Tradition. For instance, piracy and plunder are praised by Conan at the end of "The Pool of the Black One". But having said that, there are traits of eternal values even in this brute. Like, "there was an innate decency about him".[113] And in "The Pool of the Black One" we get this rather convincing view of the man. Conan has just been taken along in the crew of a pirate ship and even among pirates there has to be a sense of order. This quote has some general psychological insight along with acknowledging the higher values that govern any society. Again, it's about pirates, but *per se* this tells about responsibility and magnanimity, about archaic straightforwardness in the form of a glorified noble savage:

> Conan (...) mixed with the crew, lived and made merry as they did. He proved himself a skilled sailor, and by far the strongest man any of them had seen. He did the work of three men, and was always first to spring to any heavy or dangerous task. His mates began to rely upon him. He did not quarrel with them, and they were careful not to quarrel with him. He gambled with them, putting up his girdle and sheath for a stake, won their money and weapons, and gave them back with a laugh. The crew instinctively looked toward him as the leader of the forecastle.[114]

The age Conan finds himself in is in decline. The Hyborian world is about to meet its end, its lands having gone soft due to affluence and loose living. Conan, as the noble savage, looks unfavorably upon this. He doesn't just accept it fatalistically, like Poul Anderson's hero Dominic Flandry, seeing the space empire he lives in beginning to decline – no, Conan reacts: "Himself as cleanly elemental as a timber wolf, he was yet not ignorant of the perverse secrets of rotting civilizations."[115] Further, in "The Slithering Shadow" he comes upon a city of lotus-eaters, people happy with living in a drug-induced trance. "Damned degenerates"[116] he calls them. And approaching the

---

[113] Howard, 1986, p 107
[114] Ibid, p 170
[115] p 178
[116] p 105

city, suffering from thirst, this is the Conan condition: "A barbarian of barbarians, the vitality and endurance of the wild were his, granting him survival where civilized men would have perished".[117]

Conan knows self-restraint, he knows how to lead. In all this, he's driven by something more elemental than mere values studied and acknowledged: he's driven by Will. The Conan stories are a sort of "Nietzscheanism in motion". Fittingly, the first Conan movie (1982) had a Nietzsche quote for starters: "Whatever doesn't kill you makes you stronger." So Conan goes along in the world, searching for booty and women, not just for enjoyment but to test his strength against the elements, conducting operations as ends in themselves, as works of art.

Conan is a Nietzschean: he's anti-metaphysical, expressed as being opposed to any dealings in the occult. He "lives dangerously", shaping his life positively by venturing out in the world. It's true that Conan believes in a God, Crom, but otherwise he has the traits of a glorified nihilist. As we've seen, his outlook is coupled with some sense of Tradition; Conan is definitely not a representative of what Nietzsche termed "the Last Man", the person ignorant of beauty, passion and grandeur; on the contrary, Conan lives life to the full, meaningless or not. "Bring it on" seems to be his implicit motto, like Nietzsche affirmed the perspective with a seemingly endless walk in samsâra with a hearty, "Okay, once around!"

INSTINCT

Mostly, Conan goes by instinct. There might not be anything especially noble in this, there might be no lesson *per se* in seeing this predator stalking his prey, but the feline similes in this quote have some plausibility, some justification:

> [Conan] rose with the quick ease of a panther, drawing his saber, facing the doorway from which the sound had seemed to come. (...) His outthrust head was sunk between his giant shoulders, he glided forward in a half crouch, like a stalking tiger. He made no more noise than a tiger would have made.[118]

---

[117] Howard, 1986, 91
[118] Ibid. p 96

The Conan stories have a fair share of wise-cracking. Like, "[S]urely this is Hell and that was the Devil?" "Then Hell needs a new devil".[119] And there's general wisdom, like what the pirates of "The Pool of the Black One" call themselves: they "... dignified their profession by calling themselves Freeboters, while they dubbed the Barachans pirates. They were neither the first nor the last to gild the name of thief."[120] In other words, the Conan stories are a treat, a rewarding read generally. They are more than mere action stories. My three favorites are "The Pool of the Black One" (1933), "Shadows in Zamboula" (1935) and "The Slithering Shadow" (1933).

The first of the triad tells about a pirate raid to a remote island. Venturing inland Conan finds a deserted castle where a species of black giants lives, a structure centered on a dark pool wherein they throw their human prisoners, the waters transforming the victims into miniature statues which the giants keep on a shelf. Searching the castle when the giants are out looking for prey Conan finally sees this, the mysterious pool:

> Approaching the placid green disk, he stared into the glimmering surface. It was like looking through a thick green glass, unclouded, yet strangely illusory. Of no great dimensions, the pool was round as a well, bordered by a rim of green jade. Looking down, he could see the rounded bottom – how far below the surface he could not decide. But the pool seemed incredibly deep – he was aware of a dizziness as he looked down, much as if he were looking into an abyss. He was puzzled by his inability to see the bottom; but it lay beneath his gaze, impossibly remote, illusive, shadowy, yet visible. At times he thought a faint luminosity was apparent deep in the jade-colored depth, but he could not be sure. Yet he was sure that the pool was empty except for the shimmering water.[121]

At last, Conan gets help from the ship crew in slaying the giants, most of the party including the lovely pirate lass Sacha escaping from the

---

[119] Howard, 1986, p 181

[120] p 167

[121] p 180

island by the skin of their teeth. It might sound cliché when told like this but the whole is well crafted and credible given the conditions at hand.

SHADOWS

Another favorite is "Shadows in Zamboula", about an encounter with kidnapping cannibals in a desert city. The plot aside Howard gives this portrait of the city and its inhabitants, an ambiguous painting of a mixed society:

> Conan shifted his broad sword-belt to his liking and calmly returned the searching stares directed at him by the squad of watchmen as they swung past. They eyed him curiously and suspiciously, for he was a man who stood out even in such a motley throng as crowded the winding streets of Zamboula. His blue eyes and alien features distinguished him from the Eastern swarms, and the straight sword at his hip added point to the racial difference. (...) With a hillman's stride he moved through the ever-shifting colors of the streets, where the ragged tunics of whining beggars brushed against the ermine-trimmed khalats of lordly merchants, and the pearl-sewn satin of rich courtesans. Giant black slaves slouched along, jostling blue-bearded wanderers from the Shemitish cities, ragged nomads from the surrounding deserts, traders and adventurers from all the lands of the East. (...) The babel of a myriad tongues smote on the Cimmerian's ears as the restless pattern of the Zamboulan streets weaved about him – cleft now and then by a squad of clattering horsemen, the tall, supple warriors of Turan, with dark hawk-faces, clinking metal, and curved swords. The throng scampered from under their horses' hoofs, for they were the lords of Zamboula. But tall, somber Stygians, standing back in the shadows, glowered darkly, remembering their ancient glories. The hybrid population cared little whether the king who controlled their destinies dwelt in dark Khemi or gleaming Aghrapur. Jungir Khan ruled Zamboula, and men whispered that Naftertari, the

satrap's mistress, ruled Jungir Khan; but the people went their way, flaunting their myriad colors in the streets, bargaining, disputing, gambling, swilling, loving, as the people of Zamboula have done for all the centuries its towers and minarets have lifted over the sands of the Kharamun.[122]

I'd call this an archetypal portrait of a fairytale town, Mid-eastern variety, perhaps even more symbolic than the symbolism of the Baghdad of *A Thousand and One Nights*, the implicit model of this kind of scenery. Howard was a Texan, his familiarity with the subtropical climate putting its stamp on most Conan stories.

The best Conan story I've read so far is "The Slithering Shadow". I can't believe how Fritz Leiber[123] called it "repetitious and childish, a self-vitiating brew of pseudo-science, stage illusions, and the 'genuine' supernatural." As Howard stories go I see nothing especially inferior about it. Instead, the alleged pseudo-science is a clever invention indeed, of gems exuding light when rubbed one way and extinguished when rubbed the other way. Also, the people of the city in question can "manufacture food out of the primal elements," as the wonderful scientists they are. This adds plausibility to this archetypal desert city – a seeming mirage, offering a haven for Conan and his companion Natala, as the fugitives they are.

DESERT

Everything you put upon the stage becomes symbolic. And in grand scale, the desert is like a stage: what happens in a desert becomes eminently symbolic. A desert city is like the ultimate, archetypal city. Ballard was on to something similar when he, in a 1993 comment to *The Atrocity Exhibition*, said:

> Deserts possess a particular magic, since they have exhausted their own futures, and are thus free of time. Anything erected there, a city, a pyramid, a motel, stands outside time.[124]

---

[122] Howard, 1974, p 42-43
[123] *Fantastic*, May 1968, p 143
[124] Ballard, 2001, p 138

This symbolic character is demonstrated in the city of Xuthal, being the stage for "The Slithering Shadow". The first sight of it draws up the framework for all to come:

> He [Conan] halted suddenly, stiffening. For out on the desert to the south, something glimmered through the heat waves. At first he thought it a phantom, one of the mirages which had mocked and maddened him in that accursed desert. Shading his sun-dazzled eyes, he made out spires and minarets, and gleaming walls. He watched it grimly, waiting for it to fade and vanish. Natala had ceased to sob; she struggled to her knees and followed his gaze. "Is it a city, Conan?" she whispered, too fearful to hope: "Or is it but a shadow?"[125]

However, it is a real, tangible city, offering a safe haven for the pair. They meet people curiously asleep, as if dead. Then the corpses suddenly gain life; this was because they were in a drunken stupor, as it were, a drug-induced sleep. Then the numinous god ruling this town appears, the Slithering Shadow himself, Thog, snatching off humans to feast on so as to gather energy for a continued existence on this earthly plane.

The plot gives us more than this. I will only try to show the artistry of it all with two additional quotes, giving the kind of deathless atmosphere that Howard, C. A. Smith and Lovecraft were able of, "the Three Musketeers" of the magazine *Weird Tales* in the 1930s, the venue of their best writings. In the form of "The Slithering Shadow", this was offered in the September, 1933 issue of *Weird Tales*:

> Dusk had fallen, filling the strange city with purple shadows. They entered the open doorway, and found themselves in a wide chamber, the walls of which were hung with velvet tapestries, worked in curious designs. Floor, walls and ceiling were of the green, glassy stone, the walls decorated with gold frieze-work. Furs and satin cushions littered the floor.[126]

---

[125] Howard, 1986, p 91
[126] Ibid., p 94

Having escaped all the perils inside the city Conan and Natala plan to go south, to an oasis they've learned of. The end of the story is a rather masterful fade-out; Howard could write more than mere action: "Taking her hand with a thoughtfulness unusual for him, Conan strode out across the sands, suiting his stride to the shorter legs of his companion. He did not glance back at the silent city, brooding dreamily and ghostily behind them."[127]

BIO

Robert E. Howard was born in Peaster, Texas, January 22 and died in Cross Plains, Texas, June 12, 1936. When his mother Hester Howard died of TB Howard lost all will to live and shot himself in the head. Maybe the deed as such was planned, maybe Howard didn't kill himself on the spur of the moment. The bottom line is, that he seems to have lost an existential support in life with his mother gone. Howard left a note behind him with these lines, from the poem "The House of Caesar" by Viola Garvin:

> All fled, all done, so lift me on the pyre;
> the feast is over and the lamps expire.

This, of course, was a first-rate tragedy. It puts its stamp on everything preceding it, as in retrospect. Nothing can lift the constant moll-chord hovering over Howard's life story. Everything in it becomes tragic: at fifteen deciding to become an author, sending stories to the pulps and, in the 1920s, being published in *Weird Tales* along with magazines for fight fiction and westerns; in the 1930s being rather well paid because of his writings, like being able to buy a car, a thing setting him off in his Cross Plains neighborhood.

All this becomes tragic. Like Howard being interested in history, being an avid if somewhat unsystematic reader. And his love-affair with the teacher Novalyn Price, depicted in The Whole Wide World, the 1996 film with Vincent d'Onofrio as Howard and Renée Zellweger as Price. I won't try to erase the sense of tragedy in all this but in

---

[127] Howard, 1986, p 121

essence, the gist of Howard's life, being a gifted literary phenomenon with additional interests in boxing and roaming the land in his car, listening to and retelling stories of the Wild West and along with this concocting stories of his fictitious Hyboria – must all this, from the biographical point of view, be so immersed in tragedy and tears?

I just don't know.

On the biographical side I now only come to think of this, that in having the above mentioned film made of him Howard is unique among fantasy authors – he along with C. S. Lewis, of course, who had the excellent *Shadowlands* (1993) made about him.

WEIRD TALES

In chapter fifteen I told a rhapsodic story of the American SF magazine from *Amazing* and on. But before *Amazing* was a twinkle in Hugo Gernsback's eye there were other pulps around, the chief among them, from the viewpoint of fantastic fiction, being *Weird Tales* where most if not all seventeen Conan stories by Howard were published. And since this and the two preceding chapters have depicted "the Three Musketeers" of *Weird Tales*, its topmost author troika of Lovecraft, C. A. Smith and Howard, some lines about this magazine could come in handy.

Weird Tales was founded in 1923 by J. C. Henneberger. Although issued on a strictly commercial basis it did showcase some interesting talent from the start, like Lovecraft, Seabury Quinn and Smith. After some editorial turmoil a new editor took charge, Farnsworth Wright, seemingly having the ability to make *Weird Tales* into the "unique magazine" the caption on the cover said. *Weird Tales* ran everything from fantasy and SF to horror and exotic, earthly adventures. In 1932 the series of trademark covers with scantily clad women began, paintings by Margaret Brundage. A quote with unknown source that I've salvaged says this about these covers: "A sensuous blend of the exotic and the erotic which typified the magazine's appeal".

The 1930s was *Weird Tales'* heyday, with Lovecraft and Smith being joined by authors like Howard, space opera author Edmond

Hamilton and science fantasy author Catherline L. Moore. But when Howard and Lovecraft had died, 1936 and 1937 respectively, Smith had stopped writing and Farnsworth Wright had stepped down as editor, the "uniqueness" of *Weird Tales* got somehow lost even though it, in the 1940s, did publish notable authors like Henry Kuttner, Robert Bloch, Ray Bradbury and Fritz Leiber. Fantasy was still read but the Zeitgeist was now more in favor of the technological modernism *à la Astounding*. *Weird Tales* ceased publication in 1954 although its legacy never died out – its legacy of weird fantasy, sword & sorcery and romance. It was the archetypal venue of "dreaming science fiction" that Aldiss mentions in *Trillion Year Spree*, stories of the Burroughsian kind stressing atmosphere and feeling in contrast to the "thinking science fiction" of Wellsian origin, the kind of fiction promoted in *Amazing* and *Astounding* etc., stories using the fantastic in a more transparent fashion, focusing on science and invention.

LITERATURE

- *The Slithering Shadow* (1933)
- *The Pool of the Black One* (1933)
- *Shadows in Zamboula* (1935)

22. A. E. VAN VOGT

As stated in the introduction, this book is about SF adhering to Tradition in some form – to the primordial, holistic train of thought – a study of SF with a sounding board in The Eternal Natural Law, SF acknowledging an esoteric aspect of reality. And the esoteric strain is vividly present in the fiction of A. E. van Vogt (1912-2000).

HOLISM

A. E. van Vogt's most famous novel is *The World of Null-A* (1948). It's a story about a man having false beliefs about himself. He must be freed from these, "go sane", from which his name is constructed. The hero's name is *Gosseyn*, first name Gilbert.

Gosseyn has to reach enlightenment and mental clarity. van Vogt later said of this: "This is true of all of us. Only, we are so far gone into falseness, so acceptant of our limited role, that we never question it at all."[128]

Gosseyn's mission in *The World of Null-A* is to help people conceive the problems they face as complex, non-linear situations. This intimates a holistic mindset, a way of thinking outside of the dualistic box.

---

[128] van Vogt quoted after Aldiss, 1986, p 221

It's a known fact that van Vogt based this book on the theories of Alfred Korzybski (1879-1950). Indeed, quotes of Korzybski are to be found at the chapter heads, along with quotes of Aristotle and other metaphysicians. So what to say about Korzybski? For instance, he spoke about *time-binding*, an esoteric practice seemingly to be studied in psychology. According to Alexei Panshin in "Heinlein and the Golden Age",[129] "time-binding" [is] a Korzybskian term that meant the making of mental projections into time-to-come as an exercise of preparation for future change."

Korzybski said that time-binding is a human way of remembering, going beyond the sensuous reflex of an animal. The animal memory is conditioned, the human memory and thought are essentially unconditioned.

Thought can go beyond space and time. Thought, being free from the constraints of time, can bind it – both future time and past time.

CONCEPTUAL DREAMING

If indeed this is to be found in *The World of Null-A* then it deserves its status as an esoteric-holistic classic. It's true that van Vogt had a tendency for "gosh-wowery" and showing off, of telling stories with a lot of action and less thought, but I can't discard the first *Null-A* novel completely. It lives forever in a gray area of esoteric fiction, of dreamlike conceptualization and conceptual dreaming.

Hereby a further clue to van Vogt's holistic thought from Panshin. In "Man Beyond Man"[130] we read that van Vogt, according to himself, was "a system thinker and a system writer". Panshin labels him, not as a downright spiritualist, but as an "organic holist, a pattern-perceiver". In the Space Beagle novel this was called nexialism, defined as "applied holism". The short story "See-Saw," for its part, exhibited " a Whiteheadian sense of the holistic interconnection of things".

---

[129] http://www.panshin.com/critics/Golden/goldenage4.html
[130] http://www.panshin.com/articles/vanvogt/vanvogt4.html

With this in mind you could say: for a Campbellian author van Vogt wasn't altogether transparent, linear and reductionist in his thinking. Intuitions, immediate insights and heurekas led the way, in *Slan, Null-A* and elsewhere. "[H]olistic, organic, environmental and evolutionary" was the thought of van Vogt, a frame of mind not a million miles from the realm of Tradition, ontologically and metaphysically speaking.

NON-LINEAR

As intimated, van Vogt in the Null-A novel advocated to experience problems in a non-linear fashion: not to formally and analytically reduce them in the Aristotelian way but try to see the big picture, see wholes beyond the deceptive superficiality of concepts. This was what the Baron de Korzybski taught, the man who launched the non-Aristotelian semantics, "general semantics". The name of van Vogt's novel, *Null-A*, is to be interpreted as "non-Aristotelian". As we've seen, the holistic attitude is also inherent in the above mentioned nexialism of Eliot Grosvenor, hero of *The Voyage of the Space Beagle*. This exploring space ship has many experts in their respective fields – physics, biology, sociology etc. – but Grosvenor is a sorely needed generalist in this congregation. Like Hamilton Felix in Heinlein's *Beyond This Horizon* he's the *synthesist* as a hero which should be praised in this time of "people who know almost everything about almost nothing".

PANSHIN

van Vogt was an oddity, being like nobody else hooked to the Infinite. His style wasn't exclusive or highbrow as such, it was "ordinary" but the approach of van Vogt was different. For instance, he says this on his "dream prose" strategy, quoted after Panshin's "Man Beyond Man":

Each paragraph – sometimes each sentence – of my brand of science fiction has a gap in it, an unreality condition. In order to make it real, the reader must add the missing parts. He cannot do this out of his past associations. There are no past associations. So he must fill in the gap from the creative part of his brain.

Dream strategy: in an interview with Charles Platt, van Vogt said that a certain story was written by having the alarm clock set in the middle if the night; when waking, van Vogt would force himself to think of the story and note a possible continuation. Then back to sleep for another hour, then wake up again and note what he came to think of. I'd say, truly original. The resulting story was "The Human Operator" and the interview in question even got this title, to be read in *Pulsar* 2, 1979.

ENIGMA

Alfred Elton van Vogt was an enigmatic man. He wrote technical tales of spiritual strength. He knew the power of the symbol. Hereby some notes on the symbolic side of the man in question, his hieroglyphs and emblems that pointed beyond themselves.

As for symbols, van Vogt as a writer consciously knew about their power: "Form doesn't bind. It frees." he meant, according to Panshin.

When reading van Vogt you get the feeling that the book is about something other than what's described. You seem to be facing something mysterious, something inexplicable when entering the universe of a van Vogt novel. It's the symbolism that haunts you, hieroglyphics speaking to your subconscious. In the best of van Vogt's writings, we meet environments, objects and plot threads pointing beyond themselves, in true symbolic fashion.

Among the entirely readable van Vogt books are *Slan*, *The Universe Maker* and *Destination: Universe!*, the latter a collection of short stories. And, possibly, *The World of Null-A*. This novel was published in hardcover in 1948 and then followed a French translation by Boris Vian. It was a success; surrealist painter Vian gave prestige to van Vogt, like Baudelaire in his time rendering some additional mystique to Poe when he translated the American into French. The French Fantastic literature was given a new lease of life with this van Vogt edition, perhaps this was even the first use of the term "science fiction" in this country.

Brian Aldiss gives some attention to van Vogt in *Trillion Year Spree* (1986). According to Aldiss, the typical SF writer in the 40s was a master who knew the answer to everything; van Vogt however, "proceeded to beat your brains into scrambled eggs."[131] van Vogt floods you with enigmas and mysteries, mostly a great feeling, but sometimes it's mysteries and complexity for its own sake. "The Null-A serials (...) appeared to be saying something profound – no one has yet discovered what."[132] This might capture some of the obscurantism in van Vogt's opus but as we've seen, it wasn't totally devoid of meaning, like Panshin pointing to the holistic strains of it.

van Vogt could feed his plot with preposterous ideas just to keep it going, which in successful cases gave the text a dreamlike quality. Then it didn't matter that the prose was simple and the personal portraits superficial; all lived on its own terms, in true symbolist fashion. The reader's subconscious had to work shifts – like at the end of *The Universe Maker*, with speculations Beyond the Beyond rendered in sober magazine prose.

A variation on the art of throwing in strange things in the plot is given in the last Isher novel, whose very last words are: "Here is the race that shall rule the sevagram".[133] This is the first time ever in the novel that this "sevagram" is mentioned – so you stand there like a question mark, or perhaps with a sense of the sublime, a "sense of wonder" and amazement up over dharma-chakra.

van Vogt had the irritating habit of taking successful short stories, then fuse them, merge them and unite them by way of adding the needed transitions, and iron out some inconsistencies – and *voilà* he had a novel, more marketable than separate shorts. Unfortunately, this seldom succeeded artistically. For while shorts like "Far Centaurus" and "The Search" (both in *Destination: Universe!*) are masterpieces

---

[131] Aldiss, 1986, p 221
[132] Ibid.
[133] van Vogt, 1970, p 141

in their own right, merged together in *Quest for the Future* with a third story ("Film Library") they become less than what they were as separate works. Also, the short "See-Saw" for its part may be the most mind-boggling SF story ever, about a man trapped in a cosmic swing that will make *him* the origin of the universe, the story ending:

> Quite suddenly it came to him that he knew where the seesaw would stop. It would end in the very remote past; with the release of the stupendous temporal energy he had been accumulating with each of those monstrous swings. He would not witness, but he would cause, the formation of the planets.[134]

This the end that made Clarke, in *Astounding Days*, exclaim: "*Si monumentum requiris circumspice* indeed!" If you want to see his monument, look around.

However, as for fix-ups, van Vogt makes it all pointless when he forces this story to form the beginning of *The Weapon Shops of Isher*, where the man in question is just left swinging for a while and then ignored.

So beware of the van Vogt fix-ups. Instead, read the shorts and read novels written from beginning to end as novels, like *Slan* and *The Universe Maker*. True, the latter grew out of a 1950 short story, "The Shadow Men". But it grew organically from this, it wasn't that idiotic mix of three separate stories glued together, like *Quest for the Future* which was conjured up from the elements of "Film Library," "The Search" and "Far Centaurus," seemingly making up a novel but the gaps are visible, conceptually tearing it apart. The glue joints are cracking.

So much for *Quest for the Future*. However, and as intimated, the novel *The Universe Maker* is an artistic and dramatic triumph. In it, Morton Cargill unwittingly kills a woman in a car accident. Then, he's moved to the future and brought to justice, about to be sentenced to death by the very woman he killed – but he escapes and ends up in a larger scheme in this future world, facing three warring groups: the Shadows, the Tweeners and the Planiacs. The first live in

---

[134] van Vogt quoted after Panshin, "Man Beyond Man", ibid.

their soaring vessels, the other dream of world domination, and the third is people who can make themselves invisible. Each group will in turn claim Cargill for their schemes.

As always in van Vogt melodramas the plot is complicated. Suffice it to say that van Vogt delivers in this novel. The style is lucid and clear, the environments are varied and the dialogs have a natural feel. This is a truly metaphysical novel, truly speculative, truly breathtaking.

To merely stage a dreamlike plot isn't easy, it's rather the hardest thing there is, but van Vogt at least succeeded with his surreal project in this one. Surrealism may benefit from a touch of realism. *The Universe Maker* indeed has dreamlike atmosphere but in depicting this future we even meet mundane elements. Like when the Korea veteran Cargill to one of the warring factions describes principles about air support, and when he in a different context reflects that the birth rate rises in war, not vice versa.

Fantasy without any touch of realism may be indigestible. Contrariwise, one or two everyday elements in the plot rather enhances the sense of wonder; it provides a contrast, a stereoscopic effect. Too original environments and intrigues can make the reader a bit *blasé*, making him ask in what way this really concerns him – while the odd, realistic detail in the midst of all this can have a catalytic effect, can give the make-believe a foothold in the everyday.

CANADIAN

Alfred Elton van Vogt was born in Winnipeg, Canada, by Dutch parents. The year was 1912. Alfred eventually moved to the US and became a writer. The Dutch word "vogt," incidentally, means "bailiff".

A maybe interesting fact is that van Vogt sued the makers of the movie *Alien* (1979), because it was too similar to his short stories "The Black Destroyer" and "Discord in Scarlet". Both of these were about such a spacecraft haunted by monsters as in the movie. Reportedly, the thing was settled in van Vogt's favor.

When van Vogt worked for Hubbard's Scientology movement in the 50s, his main occupation was opening envelopes with 500-dollar bills, the fee for courses in "auditing". van Vogt became something of a poster child for the movement; for instance, in the 80s the Swedish branch sold copies of *Slan* as a relevant document. Which in some way it is, this story of a mental superman, and Scientology teaches of raising yourself mentally.

van Vogt subsequently left the movement but he remained a good friend of founder L. Ron Hubbard. So when the latter published his *Battlefield Earth* in the 80s van Vogt was immediately there and praised it as "a masterpiece", quoted on the cover. Later he admitted that he hadn't even read the book.

DICKIAN CONNECTION

In his History of SF, *Trillion Year Spree*, Brian Aldiss says:

> van Vogt was Philip K. Dick's spiritual forefather. Dick admitted as much. His emotional impact, his complexities, were what Dick took from him.[135]

This has to be noted for the record. And of course you see it yourself when you compare the two, van Vogt and Dick, both having a predilection for complex metaphysical novels. And most fitting, Philip K. Dick is the subject of the next chapter, depicting an author taking the esoteric strain of van Vogt into more acknowledged, traditional realms like those of Gnosticism and Christianity.

LITERATURE

- *Slan* (1946)
- *The World of Null-A* (1948)
- *The Voyage of the Space Beagle* (1950)
- *The Weapon Shops of Isher* (1951)
- *The Weapon Makers* (1952)
- *Destination: Universe!* (1952)
- *The Universe Maker* (1953)
- *Quest for the Future* (1970)

---

[135] Aldiss, 1986, p 220

23. PHILIP K. DICK

Hereby a story about a man who met God. It's the American SF author Philip Kendred Dick (1928-1982). He started out as a skeptic, making fun of the concept of God. Like writing about they having recently found the corpse of God, drifting in space... By this he got the mainstream of SF readers with him. How great, God is dead and now we get to hear it in an SF mode...! No God, no meaning, no higher values exist; relativism and passive nihilism is all we can adhere to, laughing ourselves to death. This was what the early Dick signaled. But in time his basic message in this respect changed. The novels of Dick and his own biography tell us of a man touched by God.

NUMINOSUM

Philip K. Dick was no stranger to the concept of God. Reportedly he was oriented in Western esotericism already as a student, having some knowledge of Plato and idealist ontology. And in his fiction he treated religious themes early on, in the 1950s, like in *The Cosmic Puppets* with its Zoroastrian battle in a small town and *Eye in the Sky* with a virtual visit to heaven and a meeting with the intimated All-Seeing Eye of God.

This was no ordinary, merciful God archetype. It was a *numinosum*, a fearful God image. Another such we meet in *The*

Three Stigmata of Palmer Eldritch, with a transformed space-traveler returning from an interstellar mission and having the ability to appear in the dreams of the users of his drug, Chew-Z.

Palmer Eldritch was a transformed man, a humanoid god, an avatar, a god reaching down to man, for better or worse. Another more-or-less relatable god was the Glimmung of *Galactic Pot-Healer*. Here we meet a dejected everyman of the future, one Joe Fernwright, planning to kill himself because of his difficulties in life. But a wonder occurs: he gets messages from a strange alien, the Glimmung, hiring him to come to his planet. The pot-healer Joe is eventually brought along in the Glimmung's project to raise a cathedral from the bottom of the sea.

This is some enigmatic novel. On the surface it's "trademark Dick" with a reasonably swift narrative, a dejected main character and a dismal future. In its 189 pages it runs along rather well with the cathedral raising project and voilà, it isn't totally nihilistic as such, as a novel about a man meeting a bizarre god and helping him in an artistic-spiritual endeavor. The ontology is kind of complicated but there's some symbolic quality to it all that stays with you. Dick wasn't an aesthetically accomplished author, he was more of a draughtsman than a painter, but he knew his limitations and he wrote effectively. And in the image of the finally raised cathedral we get this, a sketchy picture not without its symbolic beauty:

> Before him Heldscalla lay. Its pale turrets, its Gothic arch, its flying buttresses, its red-stained glass made from gold – he saw it all from a dozen eyes. It was intact, except for the engineering divisions, from another time, when he had planned to raise it externally. Now, he thought, I will enter you; I will become a part of you and then I will rise. You will go up with me, and we shall die on the shore. But you will be saved.[136]

What kind of spirituality does *Galactic Pot-Healer* display? The approach of the divine in the opening chapters, what should this be labeled as? I'd say, it might be "passive idealism". In all of Dick's theophany, admirable and illuminating as this "beholding of God" is,

---

[136] Dick, 1987, p 171

one element seems to be lacking: willpower. Dick receives the visions in a certain passive way.

Joe Fernwright is unhappy. Then a god reaches down and calls for his help, enabling Joe to leave his dismal everyday reality and join a project of artistic grandeur, that of raising a cathedral from the bottom of the sea. Specifically, the Glimmung needs Joe's skill as a pot-healer, a man mending broken pots. The element of pottery plays a heartwarming role in Dicks fiction and I'll return to that.

A God reaches down and touches a man. Then, to me, the lesson is: this isn't merely about receiving grace, living happily ever after. Man isn't a machine, merely needing to be recharged with divine power. He has to acknowledge and affirm that energy in an active way. But Dick, in this novel and in his experience of March, 1974 didn't have that active aspect. He was unhappy before he met God, he was unhappy after it, judging from the novel *VALIS* (1981) where he depicts his legendary, personal theophany.

So, briefly, this is amazing: an author, Dick, having written novels about meeting God, about interacting with God, about God reaching down to a man, like the Glimmung in *Galactic Pot-Healer* – this Dick suddenly, in real life, in 1974, receives visions, sounds and information that can only be interpreted as "having met God".

The doubter gets a lot of ammunition in *VALIS* itself. Were the visions really of God? Was "Horselover Fat", Dick's alter ego, not just mad? But also, Dick can rein in some of the useless bickering and lift the narrative above dialectics. As intimated he knew about esoteric matters even before the 1974 event and in the novel he interprets this mystic experience in a most enlightening way – enlightening for the studied esotericist. This is in the mainstream of spirituality, Gnosticism and Western idealism with a tinge of Taoism too.

VALIS

VALIS may be a bit straining to read but in the end it's rather rewarding. Not just for giving clues to Dick's esoteric sides. It educates you in Gnosticism, the mystic version of Christianity that wasn't well known until 1945 when a lot of ancient documents were found in the Egyptian village of Nag Hammadi. *VALIS* mentions this too, Dick stating that the uncovering of the Nag Hammadi texts was an event waiting to happen, a landmark event changing our times for the better. *VALIS* contains a lot of these esoteric aspects and quirks. But overall, it gives you a vision of God. The following is what I find most sublime in *VALIS*. Along with all the junkie jargon and the dismal every day of Fat, there are elements of profound wisdom and sublime esoteric beauty, like this:

> During his religious experience in March of 1974, Fat had seen an augmentation of space: yards and yards of space, extending all the way to the stars; space opened up around him as if a confining box had been removed. He had felt like a tomcat which had been carried inside a box on a car drive, and then they'd reached their destination and he had been let out of the box, let free. And at night in sleep he had dreamed of a measureless void, yet a void which was alive. The void extended and drifted and seemed totally empty and yet it possessed personality. The void expressed delight in seeing Fat, who, in the dreams, had no body; he, like the boundless void, merely drifted, very slowly; and he could, in addition, hear a faint humming, like music. Apparently the void communicated through this echo, this humming. "You of all people", the void communicated. "Out of everyone, it is you I love the most." The void had been waiting to be reunited with Horselover Fat, of all the humans who had ever existed. Like its extension into space, the love in the void lay boundless; it and its love floated forever. Fat had never been so happy in all his life.[137]

This is authoritative esotericism. This is Swedenborg in his Dream Diary, "The Ecstasy of Saint Teresa", Esiah seeing "new heavens and a new earth". It's incomparable in its vision of the divine, of Being, of That Which Is, that which ontologically can't be questioned. It's supreme bliss and rest.

---

[137] Dick, 2011, p 49

And it's conveyed by a man who could write, who could put words to his unusual experience. It's true that *VALIS* doesn't fully cohere. In this respect, the words of Thomas M. Disch in *The Magazine of Fantasy and Science Fiction*, July 1981, sums it up rather fine, saying about *VALIS* that "...as a novel, as a whole novel... it went off the rails sometimes. But the first half holds together wonderfully, considering how much there is to be held together".

Dick was an experienced writer. But he wasn't a word-smith in the realm of Lovecraft, Bradbury or Mervyn Peake. And maybe we should be glad of that in this case. As Disch intimates, there's so much to be held together in *VALIS* – the vision, the chaotic every day, the differing aspects of what's happening – that it's amazing how the narrative per se is transparent and understandable in every word.

Then there's the objections you can have. As I noted above, the overall spiritual attitude of Dick has a passive character. The way to God is, in his fiction, depicted as something passive, something to wait for and receive – an attitude of course not entirely condemnable, you can receive such a gift, but willpower is also a spiritual force to be used by the individual. But Dick ignored Will. Differences aside, this connects him to the religious attitude of C. S. Lewis, *q.v.* the end of chapter three.

Dick was a passive idealist. A telling line from *VALIS* is: "They ought to make it a binding clause that if you find God you get to keep him. For Fat, finding God (if indeed he did find God) became, ultimately, a bummer, a constantly diminishing supply of joy, sinking lower and lower like the contents of a bag of uppers."[138] This is an astonishing quote, astonishing in its stupidity. As underlined earlier in this study, God isn't a machine recharging the man-machine with grace. God, like man, is a dyad of Will and Thought, and in meeting God – as in everything else – we have to apply our Will. Suppose you meet God and like Fat / Dick become thrilled of the sensation. And then the next day you wake up and everything is as before. What to do then? Cursing God, saying "come back and do that magic you just did"? Or muster one's Will-Thought, steering one's mind to think of the experienced theophany and rejoicing in its afterglow?

---

[138] Dick, 2011, p 29

The word "Will" is conspicuously absent from *VALIS* and this drags it down, as it does all of Dick's fiction. There's the element of junkie carelessness, angst and nihilism all along the way. In *VALIS* it's touched upon when Fat undergoes psychological treatment, with a Dr. Stone pointing out Fat's problems as "fear, helplessness and an inability to act"[139] but this isn't elaborated upon. I'm not holding Dick's own text against him personally but as a moral example, the Dick life project was lacking in willpower.

EXEGESIS

The March 1974 experience spawned a lot of writing. Beyond the 271 page *VALIS* novel Dick wrote thousands of pages, labeled as "The Exegesis". There are different selections of this in print. Personally I've looked into Lawrence Sutin's *In Pursuit of Valis: Selections From the Exegesis*. Overall, this is more rewarding than the *VALIS* novel which in a sense comes through as dismal and dejected, even in the first half with its rays of brilliance. Reading the *Exegesis* itself brings you the wisdom directly. There's the element of junkie jargon ("Aristotelean two-way logic is really fucked") but as an esoteric document this is wholly successful. The essay form, of fairly short passages and paragraphs with succinct meaning, has its literary merit. SF is about fiction but the SF reader should venture out into the realm of essays and monographes sometimes since it's equally rewarding as reading stories.

VALIS / Exegesis conveys wisdom. What I found especially enlightening in *VALIS'* dedicated paragraphs of formal ontology (numbered quotes from the *Exegesis*) was that of coupling the yin-yang model of "the active force of light struggling with the passive force of the dark" to be fully compatible with the Gnostic worldview. In schoolbook Taoism there's a supposed balance between *yin-yang*, light and dark, spirit and matter etc. but essentially, Dick tells us, *yang* is Reality and *yin* is Un-Reality; Light is the supreme Being and Dark just moves along, countering the influence of Light, trying to avoid to be depolarized but being unable to do so.

---

[139] Dick, 2011, p 59

This is, *mutatis mutandum*, Dick's "two source cosmogony". Then there's the talk of the relation between the everyday world and the astral world, of our world and the world beyond, the dream-time, the dreamworld – the world where we can move in time as well as in space, unhindered in every direction. It's the realm where "time turns into space," a quote from Wagner's *Parsifal* that Dick often returns to in *VALIS*. In the *Parsifal* opera Guremanz describes the magic quality of the Grail Castle by showing Parsifal that here you can move through space in an instant. This is the way we move in dreams – for in dreaming we visit the astral world and there the limits of space-time are removed, we can move anywhere with the power of thought.

Dick, in elaborating upon the dream-time of the Australian bushmen and the *Parsifal* quote, that of "here time turns into space", then comes to the vision of unlimited space and God saying that he loves him that I quoted in the beginning of this chapter. Dick was astral tripping, more efficient than any drug.

WAVERING REALITY

In the March 1974 experience Dick is virtually invaded by God. He sees a pinkish light pervading his world, he gets information downloaded into his system, like the ability to read and understand koine Greek, the language of the New Testament. And he's invaded by the personality of Thomas, a Christian of Roman times. In one word: Dick's reality is slipping, the fabric of spacetime is ripped apart. He lives in a wavering reality – just as his fictional characters has been doing for 20 years...!

As I've shown you, the God element in Dick's novels is present long before March 1974. And so is the element of wavering reality, the fictionally staged questions of "what is real".

The early stories of this ilk had a kind of fundamental stability. Like *Eye In the Sky* from 1956, something of a metaphysical comedy of manners. It starts in the normal world, the approved, everyday world we all agree on is "reality". A group of people visits the company Bevatron to be showed its "proton beam", a nuclear device that somehow fails during the demonstration they get. The eight people of the group because of this incident fall into a sort of coma – and during this coma, they are subsequently translocated into each other's psyches, all of them living in each person's reality for a while. They thus come to live in the world of the prim secretary, the world of the devout Christian, the world of the left-winger and the right-winger etc., rather fun given the whole show.

As a comedy and a satire it works nicely. And in the end we get back to the living world, everything that happened was just the subjective, inner worlds of the participants (*idios kosmos*) and everything can return to normal, to the *koinos kosmos*, the agreed, communal everyday reality we all share. The food is on the table and the world is good, "the world as it is" will be there even when we close our eyes.

This was true even in the ontology of *Time Out of Joint* (1958). Ultimately, this scenario plays in a world common to all, even if there's the element of wavering reality for a while. The well-ordered world we're introduced to starts to fall apart, only to be replaced by another objectively validated reality.

But the parallel worlds continued to knock on the door to Dick's study, they had a prevailing authority, they had something to say. As in *The Man in the High Castle* from 1962 where we meet a parallel world inside a parallel world, and no one can tell which one is real. This is a "wavering reality" tour de force in Dick's fiction since the whole of this novel is rather transparently told. It's not jumbled and fast-moving like many of his others, therefore, in this instance, making the ontological element stand out in relief.

And so we have *The Game-Players of Titan* (1963) where you after a while question what you read but still, it's a rewarding read; Dick drags the reader along and tells a relatable story, but after a while the reality of this future world wavers. Who are the Titans, "the vugs"? Who is Dr. E. R. Philipson, is he an alien or Pete Garden's confidant psychologist? At the end some of the protagonists are moved to Titan, the Saturn moon, to play the game mentioned in the title, meeting up with the aliens themselves and to challenge them to play to make them disappear from earth – but does this takes place, or is it like Pete Garden dreaming?

In fact, the story convincingly conveys that all happens as it's told. But doesn't the world in question waver for a while? Indeed it does; the doors to other worlds and realities, and to mental collapse, are wide open. This is even more the case in *The Three Stigmata of Palmer Eldritch* (1964), in which the protagonist is hunted by an evil god through changing levels of consciousness, different worlds. A nightmare whose nature was true for Dick, as Brian Aldiss has pointed out. An ontological confusion, aggravated by the intake of drugs.

Flow My Tears, the Policeman Said (1974) also has a world that ontologically falls apart around the protagonist, already in the beginning. But in the end, he makes it back to his bourgeois, well-ordered world – or does he? I haven't yet wholly understood the declarations provided; let it suffice to say that there are sown doubts, doubts about what is real, which of the realms encountered has true being. But alongside the doubt grows a sense of compassion, of kindness – a kindness that may show a way out of this drug chaos, this roller-coaster ride through parallel worlds and diverse levels of consciousness. A sense of balance and moderation, of sanity, of "accepting membership in the human race": "Stretch out your hand, and build a bridge, a bridge of life"... A sense of the idea of compassion being a fundamental of existence, as I sketched it in the Introduction.

This is a pervading feeling of many of Dick's novels. A sense of compassion is brought along, one of the hardest thing to convey in fiction, according to Dostoyevsky. Evil we can all portray but good, how to credibly portray the good? Dick somehow mastered it. So in this respect you'll have to live with the typical elements of "lovable loser", "dismal future" of Dick's novels. I do dislike these aspects but all things considered, he had a heart and his best novels mirror it without it becoming syrupy.

ONTOLOGY

Many Dick novels examined the nature of reality. Then he met God and the mythological turning point was reached; all in time became different, I imagine. Dick linked up on a large, active system that improved his life: VALIS, a "Vast Active Living Intelligence System". He met all the worlds' metaphysical guarantor, God, and the reality was once more real.

The world was substantial again. What you think and feel is real, and if you feel like living in a world of sunlight seeping through the trees and wind blowing in your hair, well then, this world is real.

Actually, this persistent, "inner mind" – acknowledging of God isn't there, at least not in *VALIS* as the novel stands. There's the instant, sublime joy and fulfillment in meeting God but then there's mental illness again: Fat is sick, then he's cured, then he goes down the drain again. I can only say: maybe Dick's own life did improve after this. I don't know about his late novels; I haven't read them. But to me, *VALIS,* all things considered, crowns the Dick opus both ontologically and artistically. It makes sense of his earlier novels, and if only in this respect, *VALIS* is a triumph.

SENSE

In *Exegesis* there's a passage of Dick himself giving opinions of his own novels in view of his recent theophany. For instance, he acknowledges *Galactic Pot-Healer* in a general sense but he has nothing positive to say of the conveyed god image. This withheld me from reading *Galactic Pot-Healer* for a while – but now that I've read it, I love it. This Glimmung novel is enjoyable from beginning to end, it's fictionally relatable, while *VALIS* as a novel is jumbled and strange, although not structurally and narratively "weird".

VALIS is narrated by "Phil", telling of Horselover Fat's experience. So this Phil / Philip K. Dick can also mention his own novels in it, as in *Exegesis*. As a minor quirk one special Dick novel is mentioned in paraphrase: *Do Androids Dream of Electric Sheep?* (1968), occurring in *VALIS* as *The Android Cried Me a River,* a cheap SF novel Fat is said to have read. Never mind the disguise; here Dick comments on his actual 1968 novel, the one which became the film *Blade Runner*. He for instance says that it portrays the world as the Iron Prison of Gnosticism, this material world being a prison for those unable to ontologically see beyond it, unable of seeing the traces of God in it, seeing how God still tries to reach down to us. The Roman Empire officially suppressing Gnosticism becomes a symbol for this Iron Prison: "the Empire never ended" is the Dickian *VALIS* leitmotif, and specifically as concerns his 1968 novel it reads in *VALIS*:

> Once, in a cheap science fiction novel, Fat had come across a perfect description of the Black Iron Prison but set in the far future. So if you superimposed the past (ancient Rome) over the present (California in the twentieth century) and superimposed the far future world of *The Android Cried Me a River* over that, you got the Empire, the Black Iron Prison, as the supra- or trans-temporal constant.[140]

Ever since seeing the vista of the future Los Angeles in *Blade Runner* it has haunted me: a city in constant *ciaroscuro*, jumbled and with harsh living conditions but also with luxury comfort and instants of ordinary friendliness and humanity. The vision in Dick's *Do Androids Dream of Electric Sheep?* isn't artistically so sublime but in the end, the film enlivens the book and vice versa. In his vision Dick (and Ridley Scott) created a timeless symbol in the shape of an SF scenario, the just intimated "Gnostic" element giving it that extra depth.

ANDROIDS

For its part, *Do Androids Dream of Electric Sheep?* tells us about androids. For instance, we get to know that androids can commit suicide by holding their breath. That's an odd remark yet fully plausible.

Men can feel empathy, androids not. Pets need a caring human to look after them, androids are not in the practice of needing that kind of sympathy. This we also learn; rather poignant I'd say. The police officer Garland, an android, confesses that androids lack empathy. But we also meet the android Luba Luft, a trained opera singer and art lover. How can that be, how can a machine appreciate art? She

---

[140] Dick, 2011, p 48

likes the Munch picture "The Scream", also she likes the one called "Puberté". She, although a robot, can relate to the feelings conveyed in them. Or can she? In depicting robots Dick, according to himself, was concerned with the inhumanity of humans, not the humanity of machines, and as a reader you might have to skip the plausibility of things like "art-loving androids" and try to see it philosophically, what it represents to "us, the living".

We also meet the police officer Phil Resch, figuring if he's an android, guessing that the authorities could have given him fake human memories. "Fake memories," artificially induced memories, for their part were a secret agent practice in WWII. This could lead into the "wavering realities" Dick otherwise examined.

In the novel we also have the ever-present "Joe Schmoe" character of John R. Isidore who happens to meet and help the group of fugitive androids the novel is about. He feels compassion for the androids Pris, Roy and Irmgard Baty, and they, in turn, are amazed at the way he protects them. Pris tells Isidore that he's a great man, an honor for his species. Apart from this Isidore feels that the androids are different, they're so intellectual. That particular scene could highlight how ordinary humans behave: imagine a group of academics by chance meeting a car mechanic and occupying his kitchen, talking. In watching and listening to them the mechanic might surmise that they are of a different breed entirely.

Do Androids Dream of Electric Sheep? is a rewarding read. But it does get a little bit confused with the "wavering reality" element on top of the more relatable android theme, the police procedural story and the depiction of life in a future West coast sprawl. Dick puts in religion, a media messiah and actual "rupture of the fabric of reality" at the narrative denouement. This, luckily, was absent in the movie.

In the Dick circus, it gets a little too much sometimes. Conversely and in retrospect, you may come to think of these ideals: "go all the way, then step back" as Harley Earl said. And Goethe: "Restraint is the mark of the master".

POTTERY

Dick was steeped in Tradition in the form of Gnosticism and Taoism, in idealist ontology and religious outlook. He also had a keen eye for handicraft in the form of pottery. It's there in *VALIS*, *Galactic Pot-Healer* and *Flow My Tears, the Policeman Said*. A handicraft has to be taught by a master. True craftsmanship can't be mastered in a three-week course. The figure of the master is a lifetime concentrate of prowess and skill, his operational presence embodying the practical wisdom of ages. Of course, there are cunning electricians and bicycle repairmen too, they are also valuable for the running of a society, but a craftsman in the trades of cooking, carpentry, smithery, pottery etc. are "more traditional", their occupations going back several hundreds of years.

Pottery may go back even thousands of years. From ancient civilizations the oldest remains are shards of pottery. And this trade Dick has a predilection for. The love of material and techniques is present in *Galactic Pot-Healer*:

> His father had been a pot-healer before him. And so he too healed pots, in fact any kind of ceramic ware left over from the Old Days, before the war, when objects had not always been made out of plastic. A ceramic pot was a wonderful thing, and each that he healed became an object which he loved, which he never forgot; the shape of it, the texture of it and its glaze, remained with him on and on.[141]

In *Flow My Tears, the Policeman Said* the main character is talk show host Jason Taverner, a symbol of the inauthentic life, of mass media as the realm of superficiality; Taverner is a modern titan, an easy-going, smiling monster. He's set in contrast to Mary Anne Dominic, a woman pursuing a life far away from TV studios and luxury condos, a potter by trade. The pair meet, serendipitously, and some sort of sympathy evolves but Taverner plays her the wrong way. He wants to put her on his TV show, making the audience believe that she can make a pot similar to early Chinese pottery. Taverner:

---

[141] Dick, 1987, p 7

We'll show them; we'll make them believe. I know my audience. Those thirty million people take their cue from my reaction; there'll be a pan up on my face, showing my response.[142]

But Mary Anne will have nothing of it:

"Does everything have to be on a great scale with a cast of thousands? Can't I lead my little life the way I want to?"[143]

It's true that sermons like these aren't unusual in 20th century literature but Dick makes it all the more efficient by also depicting the Jason Taverner figure with some insight, a high society hustler proud of being who he is. Dick had the constant theme of "sympathy for poor people stumbling around in their everyday" but he regularly balanced it with the lives of high rollers, operationally minded people getting things done, and this makes his novels enjoyable. The emotional manipulation threatening in depicting Joe Schmoes, with the implicit command of "pity him", is balanced by having policemen, millionaires and doers alongside them in the plots. In this way you could, involuntarily, even feel pity for the high rollers, like police chief Felix Buckman in *Flow My Tears, the Policeman Said*.

WU

The subject of handicraft as traditional symbol is present also in *The Man in the High Castle* (1962). In this future scenario the axis powers have won the Second World War. The Germans have occupied Eastern USA; the Japanese, the Western. The plot focuses on doings on the West coast where the Japanese become the symbol of Tradition. Like the element of an object having *wu*, a Taoist concept. In the process, occupation government official Paul Kasoura talks to American antiques businessman Robert Childan about some current American artwork he has discovered, an amulet. Questions of authenticity are discussed. Don't mass produce is the Taoist lesson; in mass production the *wu* of an object is lost.

---

[142] Dick, 1986, p 163
[143] Ibid.

WRITING

As intimated, the model Dick novel used to have one high and one low character. To this, there was usually some dystopia future setting. And there were ideas, the more the better; Dick at his best could feed the plot with ideas. He was a bit manic in his writing habits, he had one novel going all the time, it seems. It's been said that this stressed him out. Maybe it did. The private person Philip K. Dick wasn't a mentally stable, healthy person in the 1960s and 1970s. That said, I don't think that we should pity him for having to write SF novels for DAW and Ace for a living. Would he have been happier as, I don't know, a journalist or a teacher? Instead, a writer goes mad by not being able to write. Dick's life was an example of drifting off course but you couldn't say that his writing practice made it worse.

It's like the move director Rainer Werner Fassbinder (1945-1982), who reportedly always had one film project up and running. Making movies was his way of life. Did this lifestyle make him unhappy, ruin him, kill him? Like Dick Fassbinder died rather early but you couldn't say that an artist doing his thing is essentially unhappy because of this. On the contrary...!

Dick's *Modus Operandi* in writing: improvise, feed the intrigue with ideas, have one high and one low character and then maybe a wild card. Then, have a dystopian future. And when you're almost through, tie up loose ends – and *voilà* a classic Dick novel. Dick thrived in the SF mode. When he wrote mainstream fiction his attitude became somewhat strained. Admitted, any book labeled "Philip K. Dick" carries artistic weight. But you who have read some of his SF novels, imagining that his mainstream work is The Thing, that object Beyond the Beyond worth striving for; be warned, because Dick's best writings was in SF.

To get some overall characteristic of Dick's SF, the qualities of his fiction was there during all of his career, from the early 1950s to the 1980s: seriousness coupled with humor, esotericism coupled with contemporariness and pop culture. And so the presence of Tradition, not only in the form of pottery but also in his knowledge of classical music. All this we get throughout the Dick opus. Unlike, say, Heinlein, Dick wasn't "married to the *Zeitgeist*", not in the same way.

BEYOND WAVERING REALITY

As we've seen, "wavering reality" was a major theme of Dick's fiction. He questioned the universe, he questioned reality. And this wavering, "psychedelic" aspect of reality came forth in works like *The Man in The High Castle*, *The Three Stigmata of Palmer Eldritch* and *A Maze of Death*. In the first of these, the apparently solid-but-alternate future of Japan having won WWII is ripped apart when a Japanese of the occupation force suddenly finds himself standing on a San Francisco street with Japanese driving rickshaws for the service of Americans. In the second, one of the main characters is chased by the demi-god Eldritch through successive parallel worlds; everyone he meets assumes the figure of Eldritch in a nightmarish, hallucinatory experience. And in the third a computer simulation with a recurring Christ figure at the end has this figure appear outside the simulation.

Wavering realities indeed. What is real? Does a reality common to us all even exist? You could say that, ontologically, most of us share a common description of the world. If we're set on this, we see the same reality. If not, if by some catalyst (a drug, a self-induced trance) we stop seeing the common reality, we may see "something else".

This can be described as the difference between an *idios cosmos* (Greek, personal reality) and *koinos cosmos* (shared reality). As I've already shown, this is displayed in *Eye in the Sky* where the main characters successively visit each other's *idios kosmos*, all the time thinking that it's a *koinos kosmos*. But at the end they're all back in the shared, everyday world which equals an alleged superior *koinos kosmos*.

The idea of separate realities existing in parallel is disconcerting. So then, is everything essentially a jumble, chaos and confusion? I'd say, the higher you get in the ontological levels the more real they get. The everyday reality is a hologram, above it is the astral world which is the dream world, but "the fifth dimension" is one of order and beauty, not of chaos. Reality seeps down from higher to lower by way of *influxus*. And the person blind to this influxus may at times get lost in dimensions of wavering reality.

If lost in a wavering, psychedelic hell, muster your Will and Thought and will yourself out of it. Realize your intentions, envision order and beauty. That's the esoteric power of will.

These deliberations aside, not all Dick stories of seeming wavering reality are really about reality coming apart. Instead, the koinos kosmos is affirmed at the end, as in "Retreat Syndrome", *Eye in the Sky, Time Out of Joint* and *The Game-Players of Titan*. The advice to the prospective Dick reader is to start with these and then venture out further into Dickian realms where reality literally wavers, stories even affecting your own everyday reality afterwards, engendering thoughts like, "is this real or am I dreaming this...?"

LITERATURE

- *The Cosmic Puppets* (1957)
- *Eye in the Sky* (1957)
- *Time Out of Joint* (1959)
- *The Man in the High Castle* (1962)
- *The Game-Players of Titan* (1963)
- *The Three Stigmata of Palmer Eldritch* (1965)
- *Do Androids Dream of Electric Sheep?* (1968)
- *Galactic Pot-Healer* (1969)
- *A Maze of Death* (1970)
- *VALIS* (1981)

24. LARRY NIVEN

LAURENCE VAN COTT NIVEN (1938-) is an American fiction writer, specializing in high-tech futures, space travel and cosmology. He has also written archaic fantasy, this making him into some sort of archeofuturistic phenomenon. However, this study will focus on his SF.

SHAKESPEARE

Do you create viable, traditionalist SF by captioning it with a Shakespeare quote? Not necessarily. Still, for the record, Larry Niven's short story *There Is a Tide* borrows the title from a line in William Shakespeare's *Julius Caesar* (1599): "There is a tide in human affairs", symbolizing the shifting fortunes in politics. Niven's story in question has got nothing to do with politics, it's about a gravitational tidal wave playing a crucial part in a standoff between a man and an alien in a galactic backwater. The old game of heads or tails also plays a part in this. You see, being steeped in traditional customs can be of help even in deep space...!

As for Shakespeare lines becoming SF titles I've gathered the following:

- "Something Wicked This Way Comes" (a 1962 Bradbury novel; quote from Macbeth)
- "All Our Yesterdays" (a history of 1940s SF fandom by Harry Warner; quote also from Macbeth)
- "Bid Time Return" (a 1975 Richard Matheson novel; quote from Richard II)
- "All My Sins Remembered" (a 1977 Joe Haldeman novel; Hamlet quote)
- "In Memory Yet Green" (volume 1 of Asimov's 1979 autobiography; in Hamlet, we have the line, "the memory be green")

Shakespeare has influenced SF films and TV series also. That *Forbidden Planet* from 1956 is a faraway-planet translocation of *The Tempest* is well known. In itself, the initial framework of *Forbidden Planet*, with an earthly spaceship sent out to explore the cosmos, is said to have given Gene Roddenberry the idea for his TV series *Star Trek*. There, as for Shakespearian influences, the episode "Catspaw" (1967) lends some traits from Macbeth. And the episode "Elaan of Troyius" (1968) reportedly has some traits from *The Taming of the Shrew* and then some.

Niven's story that got me started on this Shakespearian digression, "There is a Tide", is included in the collection *Tales of Known Space*. With this and other books, such as *Neutron Star* and *Ringworld*, Niven has chronicled the future from now to the year 3000. Beyond that year drama is implicitly absent because all the people then have "the Teela Brown gene" that brings the carrier luck. In the framework at hand earth in the 2000s was overpopulated. The right to have babies was earned in lotteries; only winners in these did bear children and Brown was a dominant figure in the competition, she became the first mother of the new humanity – a humanity that's "always lucky", luck being genetically determined. Children of winners automatically become winners. As such, this is something of a skewed logic since luck may be a relative phenomenon, but overall Niven's vision of an immanently lucky humanity has some allure. A golden age awaits mankind and stories with a positive disposition has a part in building that.

RINGWORLD

SF stories are a sort of modern fairy tales. They are similar to old fairy stories in that their essence is extra-literary, the essence being conceptualized in symbols. "Everybody" can tell of Snow White, Briar Rose and Cinderella because the plot is condensed into symbols (the seven dwarfs, a castle overgrown with thorns, the glass shoe).

As for SF it's true that you can't retell, say, *Dune* in a flash but the essence of it can be conveyed with the support of symbols: a galactic empire, a desert planet, giant sandworms. The same deathless, symbolic quality is the case with Niven's novel from 1970, *Ringworld*. This tells of a glorified artifact in space, the Ringworld, shaped like a hoop and with the diameter of millions of kilometers, circling a sun. On the inner side of the hoop, on the sunward-facing side of this ring-formed band, there's a landscape, you can live there. For all the engineering background and plausibility this, to me, primarily become something more than simply "hard SF", "a 20th century generic novel" or "a Niven book" – it's something archetypal and symbolic, a space-age fairytale that everyone gets the gist of directly: the tale of a journey from earth to Ringworld, this mysterious artifact seemingly just sitting there waiting for its discoverer, enigmatically circling its sun.

Ringworld is the modern version of the journey to The Promised Land, to a distant Shang-ri-la, cast in space form. A lot of American SF is said to portray such paradise myths, the dream of better worlds out there, like Heinlein's *Farmer in the Sky*, Varley's *Titan* and Williamson's "The Highest Dive". And why not; there must be a wealth of paradisaical worlds out there populated by humanoid aliens, our brothers.

Along with this we also have the SF stories of "venturing out and exploring enormous artifacts", spawned by Clarke's *2001* (*q.v.* chapters nine, thirteen). There we had the fairly manageable artifact orbiting Saturn (Saturn in the novel, Jupiter in the movie). I guess, without proof, that this 1968 novel inspired Niven for his spatial artifact. If so, then Clarke replied with *A Rendez-Vous With Rama* in 1973, about a 50 km long cylinder spontaneously entering our solar system. Then another British subject (specifically, an Ulster Scot), Bob Shaw, made the greatest artifact of them all in *Orbitsville*, a 1975 novel about a so-called Dyson Sphere, a spherical object completely surrounding a star creating a habitable environment on the inside, as such probably the Mightiest Machine ever imagined.

Ringworld had about the same diameter as Shaw's creation. But Niven's world was only a hoop, Orbitsville was a sphere. That said, the vision of Ringworld will live forever, it speaks to your subconscious in a truly symbolic sense. This artificial paradise, this artificial satellite shaped like a barrel hoop with a diameter of millions of kilometers, will forever orbit its sun out there somewhere in the galaxy, driven by its sheer mythical power.

WAYS

Niven has written many a good story. Like "Cloak of Anarchy", *q.v.* chapter thirty. And "All the Myriad Ways" (1968; eponymous collection in 1971). Like the anarchy tale this is another future-on-earth story, not space fiction. It begins with a policeman sitting in his office, cleaning his gun. He must solve the riddle surrounding a wave of unexplained suicides. He begins to suspect that it's due to the inherently carefree attitude that evolved when man managed to arrange trips to alternative worlds.

Anything goes, nothing matters – so why not killing yourself when your parallel world self lives on...? And then, in the story itself, everything branches out into possible alternative worlds, one where the policeman puts down the gun and tells the station that he's arrived at the solution, another where he tiredly remains sitting, the solution would not in itself stop the wave of suicides, a third in which he takes up the gun, fires and has the striker hit an empty chamber, a fourth where he puts the barrel to the temple... and so on. The actual narrative illustrates this branching out into parallel realities, a sort of mirror-to-infinity-but-with-subtle-differences-in-every-world – and this executed with no fanfare or stylistic bravado, instead, it's rather toned down but all the more efficient that way. SF is seldom emotionally gripping, not essentially, but this one has some existential angst to it, demonstrated with engineering precision.

LITERATURE

- *Neutron Star* (1968)
- *Ringworld* (1970)
- *All the Myriad Ways* (1971)
- *Tales of Known Space* (1975)

25. JERRY POURNELLE

In the previous chapter we wrote about Larry Niven. An author having co-operated with him is Jerry Pournelle (1933-), as in *The Mote in God's Eye* and others. Being something of the model right-wing SF author Pournelle deserves a chapter of his own. If the Pournelle opus should be condensed into two traditional values, they could be these: courage and faith. The element of courage, and its adjoining properties of determination, duty and responsibility, is covered in Pournelle's military SF, like *The Mercenary*. The faith element is covered in his writings on space, both fictional and factual, like *Exiles to Glory* and *A Step Farther Out*. Details aside, Pournelle had the ability to envision a viable future for man even in the defeatist sentiment of the 1970s.

MERCENARY

This study will treat military SF in more detail later, in chapter 32. Here we'll touch briefly on Jerry Pournelle's outings in the genre. As a Korea veteran he basically knew what he was talking about in these matters. Also, the level of military technology he depicts in his futures has a slant towards 1950s technology (as in the use of bolt action rifles, artillery and tanks). This might seem odd. But overall, the conceptualization with faster-than-light travel in an interplanetary future with different peoples and planets makes the not-always-cutting-edge-weaponry blend in rather well with the whole.

There are some highlights in the Pournelle epics. Such as the beginning of *Janissaries* (1979), with a platoon of mercenaries fighting a commie-style dictatorship in Africa getting abducted by an alien space ship, just when the unit was about to be overrun by Cubans. This is some archetypal event, like New York being transformed into a spaceship in Blish' *Cities in Flight:* the symbolism of it is etched into one's subconscious, making it eternally memorable in itself, beyond the mere story.

The mercenaries then have their adventure Beyond the Beyond. Another novel in the same vein is *The Mercenary*, first published in 1977, later incorporated into *The Prince* (2002). In its original configuration this was a succinct SF adventure, however, not anything for the faint-hearted. Duty, honor and mayhem, portraying "the muddy, bloody business of fighting on the ground". This is one for the grunts, basking in "the everlasting glory of the infantry". This is serving, this is loyalty, this is bonds of friendship, tied in blood; a gust of wind from the archaic, staged in the future. Thus, we again have the archeofuturist strain that often seem to accompany right-wing SF.

OPTIMISM

"He who marries the Zeitgeist soon becomes a widower". Thus in the German TV series *Heimat*. And didn't some of the Golden Age pundits become rather lost in the 1970s, in the hangover after the Apollo and moon euphoria of the late 60s...? Heinlein, for instance, in the 70s didn't have the same zest in his writings as before. Indeed, he was older now, but who can deny that in the 40s and 50s he was bristling but not so in the 70s. And this might have had something to do with identifying too much with the times.

But Pournelle kept the standard flying, even in the dark ages. He wasn't married to the Zeitgeist of doom and gloom. "A pessimist is always right", they say, but the case of Pournelle disproves this. He's an *optimist* proved right.

Here's the case. It wasn't just the meager aftermath of the moon missions that put its stamp on the era in question. In the 1970s we had something called the Club of Rome, a high-profile congregation speaking about "The Limits of Growth". It's true that earth can't sustain every kind of industrial exploitation. But the whole mood of the era was one of dejection, the party's over, make do, expect less. In this context Pournelle still had faith in human endeavor and science, and in the West against the Communist bloc. Not many high-profile commentators in those days did show much faith in the West. As for the science-and-technology part I know that I'm treading a fine line in saying that I don't really believe in old-school, big science-style colonization of the solar system any more, an element highlighted in Pournelle's books. But we do need a modicum of faith in the future and Pournelle symbolizes this with his assembly of essays, articles and science columns, collected in *A Step Farther Out* (1979).

OPTIMISM

This chapter is about the author Jerry Pournelle. However, for maximum clarity I here have to state my personal, overall creed – which is one of Willpower, Faith in the Light and Optimism. And in taking sides between bleak politicians speaking of the limits of growth and an author being able to envision a future of a reasonably positive, constructive kind, then I choose the latter.

The bright tone of *A Step Farther Out* is seen in this quote, conveying about everything that an operational-existential optimism stands for – to be able to go somewhere, to plan for something else, and having the mere notion that it's possible. *Mutatis mutandum*, I agree with the following:

> Mankind needs frontiers. We need new worlds to conquer, impossible odds to overcome, a place of escape from bureaucracy and government; a place where life is hard but the problems are simple, requiring no more than courage, determination, and hard work to win great rewards. Even for those who will never go chasing out to the frontier there's a great comfort in knowing

it's *there*: that you could, if you chose, pull up stakes and try your hand at making a new life. For the warriors and dreamers among us a frontier is so vital that if there isn't a physical one, we'll create an internal problem and fight that. I suppose that man's need for a frontier is a debatable proposition, in that somebody might question it; but I doubt that many science fiction readers would dispute the point. To a very great extent this is what science fiction is all about.[144]

EXOPOLITICS

Pournelle writes scientifically plausible SF and *A Step Farther Out* mirrors this in having sections about space travel, black holes and the energy crisis. But Pournelle also knows how to speculate. For instance, he devotes a few lines to the Dean Machine, once advocated by John Campbell as a means to a cheap space drive, this machine which transformed "circular acceleration to linear". The machine as such might have worked and Pournelle offers no definite answer on the question, he just delves into it as a subject worthy of consideration. The same goes for flying saucers which gets its own chapter. Pournelle duly mentions how SF fans and authors seldom even discuss this, it's considered weird and taboo. Still, Pournelle maintains, we have at least to be able to discuss this, the phenomenon as such is rather hard to avoid for a speculative mind interested in space. He's leaning towards the theory that the UFOs might be extraterrestrial spaceships. I can only say, I personally have the same attitude towards this phenomenon; the extraterrestrial hypothesis is worthy of examination. And Pournelle's payoff is sound:

> If the "unimaginative" experts of Big Science can take UFO's seriously, while we [SF writers, the SF community] won't even discuss them, what happens to science fiction writers' reputations as speculators? Not that we need contests on how many impossible things we can believe before breakfast; but can

[144] Pournelle, p 89

we not at least *speculate* consistent with the observations? Do we, of all people, *dare* ignore UFO's now that study of them is respectable?[145]

My personal reflection is this: if SF writers and fans dared browse internet pages on "exopolitical issues" and what they say of space drives etc., then they would get that Sense of Wonder-kick they so eagerly seek. There you can find speculative reasoning, with plausible premises. Like ships structurally, like a capacitor, containing the energy they need to go, generating a magnet wave, or ships riding gravity waves, for example. The rift between esoteric minds and SF minds needs to be healed. I'm not opting for esoteric material in SF magazines, SF should be about fiction, but a more speculative attitude in the science column could be needed. Pournelle isn't exactly an esotericist but as we've seen he can sometimes lift the veil to The Unthinkable.

BUILDING

An interesting chapter in *A Step Farther Out* is "Building the Mote in God's Eye". *The Mote in God's Eye* (1974) is an interstellar adventure Pournelle co-wrote with Larry Niven. Specifically, it's about a future where man has colonized space and then meets aliens, having that legendary "first contact". And in the chapter at hand Niven & Pournelle tell us how the novel was written, an interesting insight into how SF authors construct ships, planets and cultures and everything else a novel about a complex future needs to be plausible.

It's a *conceptual* text: a text about a text, as such rather rewarding since SF of this kind to a great extent depends on the things told being plausible per se, since neither Pournelle nor Niven writes in a style you could call elaborate or alluring. They write conceptual SF of the kind established since the days of Jules Verne, a narrative mode where ideas and constructs are more important than mere style, as is also demonstrated in the writings of Dick, Herbert, Heinlein, Asimov and Clarke, the classics of SF.

---

[145] Pournelle, p 111

Narratively, Niven & Pournelle have an exemplary style. In the chapter in question they also give us an excerpt from a prologue that was cut out from the published novel. I personally like this scene from a space war seen from the surface of a planet: "These nights interplanetary space rippled with the strange lights of war, and the atmosphere glowed with ionization from shock waves, beamed radiation, fusion explosions..."[146] The matter-of-fact tone generates a strange kind of beauty.

CONFIDENCE

I'm not forming a Pournelle fan club here and I don't support everything he says in *A Step Farther Out*. For instance, I could do without some of the tendencies of simplification, and some of the approaches to technocratic titanism. Still, the mere optimism and "confidence in confidence" the book exudes is striking. To believe that man could solve The Problems That Be and that the pessimists are essentially wrong, isn't a usual stance – not among writers in general or SF writers specifically, neither in 1979 nor now. The words of the introduction to *A Step Farther Out* are *not* standard fare as "policy documents" go: "I want to show you marvels. Dreams, in Technicolor, with sharp edges."[147] And:

> Over the years I have written of the fascination and excitement of science, and I have hoped to convey some of the sense of wonder – the conviction that we live in a generation of wonders – that I have felt. Perhaps that is the more important part of the book; yet I cannot help thinking that it is a worthwhile effort to show that we are not faced with doom; that the West need not close down; that we will survive.[148]

In 1979, those were prophetic words. Ten years after this, the Communist bloc and godless Bolshevism had crumbled. The West

---

[146] Pournelle, p 114

[147] Ibid., p 1

[148] Ibid., p 3

lived on and today man faces a better future than ever, even though there still are problems around. But in the vein of the optimism conveyed in this chapter I know they will be solved and that we're heading for a Golden Age. There's no risk for major war, for instance, despite what the remnants of the doom-and-gloom crowd says. This faction is hard to check but a fine groundwork was made back in the day by Jerry Pournelle, having a great symbolical value, a great marginal efficiency.

LITERATURE

- *The Mercenary* (1977)
- *Janissaries* (1979)
- *A Step Farther Out* (1979)

26. RAY BRADBURY

WE ALL KNOW that Ray Bradbury (1920-2012) was a man longing for years gone by, for the American 1920s with T-Fords, striped cotton suits and ice-cream sundaes. But this kind of sentimentality can't be tolerated in a study like this. Tradition isn't about being sentimental, it's about acknowledging Eternal Values, values that still can lift us, inspire us and guide us, offering an alternative to the current materialism and nihilism. For in essence, sentimentality is a form of nihilism. Therefore, it takes some time to sort out the Bradbury stories having to say something to us even today, stories about Faith, Musicality, Awareness and Courage.

IDEALISM

It may be that Ray Bradbury in the short story "The Pedestrian" showed us a dismal future where everyone sits inside watching TV. And where the cultured, musical citizen choosing to take a walk at nights is viewed with suspicion; a grim future, may we avoid it. But the tenor of this story is a bit too defeatist to me. At the end the pedestrian gets arrested for loitering: symbolically apt but it all gets kind of depressing.

This is passive idealism: the titanic forces win, culture is trampled underfoot. Personally, I need more of an *active* idealism. And this I get in the Bradbury novel *Fahrenheit 451*. In a discreet fashion we here find a belligerent conservatism, a conservatism ready to fight back, if only in chance remarks, in the odd acerbic passage. Like in part one, with the main character, firefighter Montag, speaking with his neighbor mentioning the pleasure to burn Millay on Monday, Whitman on Wednesday, Faulkner on Friday: "burn 'em to ashes, then burn the ashes. That's our official slogan."[149]

I find this irony rather efficient, this way of depicting a future where the fire department's task is to burn books. Books are forbidden for they stop people from being brainwashed by mass media. As for efficient, elegant remarks we also have the novel's part three. Montag has left his job and fled to the woods, to a copse inhabited by cultured refugees. One of these bums has been a holder of the Thomas Hardy chair in Cambridge before it turned into an Atomic Engineering School; this remarks just kills it, very apt.

In their wood the bums have memorized famous books. How, then, is this done? "All of us have photographic memories", the bums having only perfected the technique. In itself, that seems plausible. One of the bums says that when they take over they will build a mirror factory, having to look at ourselves, remembering – being sure that the works existed, that they themselves existed... Seeing yourself in the mirror is the evidence that God exists, seeing that divine spark in the eye. This sounds simple but the simple is difficult, as Clausewitz said.

In joining this odd group Montag too memorizes books, he becomes Ecclesiastes and Revelations, and quoted from the latter is this, at the very end:

> And on either side of the river was there a tree of life, which bare twelve manners of fruits, and yielded her fruit every month; And the leaves of the tree were for the healing of nations. Yes, thought Montag, that's the one I'll save for noon. For noon... When we reach the city.[150]

---

[149] Bradbury, 1979, p 13
[150] Ibid., p 157-158

Fahrenheit 451 combines a feeling for culture and musicality, of the activities inspired by the Muses, with a satirical touch. It's true that even today Grand Old Men might say that reading books is good, watching TV is bad. Now, TV may be educational and inspirational too but what Bradbury was after was the thing that TV generally *represents*, that of mindless entertainment and propaganda. And in the *Fahrenheit 451* story he said it efficiently and with flair.

THE MAN

One peculiar Bradbury story is "The Man". It was written in 1949 and is included in the collection *S Is For Space*. It's about the concept of faith, of having something within you responding to what an elevated guru may teach you. In the story we meet a space crew. They're roaming the spatial vistas, "always on the go, always searching" – for what? Now they've reached a planet where the population is in a state of bliss. They have namely been visited by an enigmatic guru, a Jesus figure, maybe the Saviour himself. He has healed people, he has fought hypocrisy and dirty politics. People are basking in the glory of his presence, believing he's still there. The ship crew also starts to believe it. But the captain will have nothing of it; deeming the rest of the crew fools he leaves with the ship, to keep on searching.

The mayor of the planet, upon the news of the captain having left, has this to say about it all:

> Yes, poor man, he's gone. (...) And he'll go on, planet after planet, seeking and seeking, and always and always he will be an hour late, or a half-hour late, or ten minutes late, or a minute late. And finally he will miss out by only a few seconds. And when he has visited three hundred worlds and is seventy or eighty years old he will miss out by only a fraction of a second, and then a smaller fraction of a second. And he will go on and on, thinking to find that very thing which he left behind here, on this planet, in this city.[151]

---

[151] Bradbury, 1968, p 103

Then they head for the city to meet The Man himself; "we mustn't keep him waiting".

You have to seek the Inner Light in order to be "saved". You have to have something inside responding to that which you seek in the outer world. This is the lesson of "The Man". In a wider sense this is a memento to those believing in "the second coming of Christ". In the story Jesus is indeed on the planet in question but his presence is only intimated. This eminently fits our age – for Jesus, according to esoteric theory, won't return in the flesh. "The return of Christ" is a metaphor for men having received the Gospels spiritually, having elevated themselves to Christ Consciousness, as such fairly similar to Buddha Consciousness and / or Krishna Consciousness. When people, without surrendering their everyday being, without having to accept mass immigration and the whole multicultural agenda, acknowledge the brotherhood of man – then "Christ has returned".

"The Man" approaches the same fundamental truth. That of having a sounding board within yourself, in order to evolve spiritually. That of being an esotericist.

If we can imagine peace, then we have peace. This is esotericism: to seek it within. This we see several examples of in "The Man". Like when the captain's ADC wonders what the captain will ask The Man if he finds him. Then, then captain says after some hesitation, he will ask him for a little peace and quiet; it's been a long time since he relaxed. And when asked why he doesn't try to relax himself, the captain doesn't understand the question.

This might seem a bit contrived but this is how it is for many people. They don't realize the power of Will – like the Will to Relax, the Will to Power Over Yourself, in Nietzschean terms. Will is needed both in the *vita contemplativa* and the *vita activa*.

Another fine moment in "The Man" is when the captain questions a local about this "wonderful man". She says that he walked among them and was very fine and good. And asked about the color of his eyes she says: "The color of the sun, the color of the sea, the color of a flower, the color of the mountains, the color of the night."[152]

---

[152] Bradbury, 1968, p 96

This confirms the captain's skepticism, this is nothing to go by, this might just be some sweet-talking charlatan. In sum, the story portrays the glorified doubter, the one always having yet another reason to doubt that The Words of Inspiration are being taught by a divine avatar. The doubter, the one being unable to look within for the truth.

Put differently, the model doubter is a victim of the Perfectionist Fallacy. This fallacy is expecting too much, expecting the expected to be Just Perfect, giving you everything you dreamed of in an instant, without yourself having to meet it halfway by mentally allowing change to take place.

SENTIMENT

"Sentimentalism is nihilism", I said at the beginning of this chapter. There are indeed sentimental nihilists around. But there might also be sentimental idealists. And Bradbury might inhabit a gray area of sentimentalism that you can interpret this way or that.

Put differently, the Bradbury fiction project has a tendency towards metaphor, allegory, simile. The focus is on moods, sentiments, symbols. When you're into this attitude he can be a wonderful writer, he's a discreet guide through the lands of Mars, of childhood, of times gone by. Conversely, the reader needing some statement, some tangible idea, some edge, often returns empty-handed from the Bradbury experience.

So I accept the sentimental side of the Bradbury fiction, there are indeed stories of this kind worth to read. And quote. Like Lovecraft, Moorcock, Tolkien and Howard he's a quotable author. That means: he writes a poetical prose. And indeed, the quotable element in prose is poetic (and the quotable element in poetry is prosaic).

A story that integrates the sentimentality rather well is "The Day It Rained Forever". It's about a dry season, a boarding house and a woman stopping by. Rain comes. And the lady plays the piano:

> She played and it wasn't a tune they knew at all, but it was a tune they had heard a thousand times in their long lives, words

or not. She played and each time her fingers moved, the rain fell pattering through the dark hotel. The rain fell cool at the open windows and the rain rinsed down the baked floor boards of the porch. The rain fell on the roof top and fell on hissing sand, it fell on rusted car and empty stable and dead cactus in the yard. It washed the windows and laid the dust and filled the rain barrels and curtained the doors with beaded threads that might part and whisper as you walked through.[153]

This is how the artistry of Bradbury plays out in a restrained way, the sentimentality (and the often occurring dejection) kept in check by the narrative structure. The story is to be read in *A Medicine For Melancholy*.

From the same collection I'll end with this, from "The Town Where No One Got Off". I remember seeing this on TV once, as a Twilight Zone story or some such. And I won't comment on the quote. Riding a train a man wonders about all these little towns you pass by, towns where no one seems to get off. So why not get off and experience the wonders of it all, of a Never-Never-Land city, a zero place in a zero existence. In doing this, getting off at a random place, the passenger also has an ulterior motive, as has a local man stalking him, "the old man". They have a stand-off. Then they part. At last, the passenger boards another train:

> Only when the train was pulling out of the station did I lean from the open Pullman door and look back. The old man was seated there with his chair tilted against the station wall, with his faded blue pants and shirt and his sun-baked face and his sun-bleached eyes. He did not glance at me as the train slid past. He was gazing east along the empty rails where tomorrow or the next day or the day after the day after that, a train, some train, any train, might fly by here, might slow, might stop. His face was fixed, his eyes were blindly frozen, toward the east. He looked a hundred years old. The train wailed. Suddenly old myself, I leaned out, squinting. Now the darkness that had brought us

---

[153] Bradbury, 1960, p 181-182

together stood between. The old man, the station, the town, the forest, were lost in the night. For an hour I stood in the roaring blast staring back at all that darkness.[154]

LITERATURE

- *Fahrenheit 451* (1954)
- *A Medicine For Melancholy* (1959)
- *S Is For Space* (1966)

---

[154] Bradbury, 1960, p 72

27. AYN RAND

AYN RAND, 1905-1982. Novelist and philosopher. Her name is like a trigger word, generating wild exclamations of pro or con. This chapter won't be playing that dualist melody. Instead, it takes a look at some fruitful traits in an early Rand story, *Anthem* – traits like taking responsibility, praising the creative individual and being anti-collectivist. In other words, relatable right-wing ideals.

PARADISE

In this study I've presented SF authors having some affirmative relation to Tradition. But as for Ayn Rand in general she was rather anti-tradition. This I admit. She was a pro-choice modernist atheist. According to Conservapedia she had "Hollywood values". And I don't support the slightly manic preacher Rand became in *Atlas Shrugged* (1957). And *The Fountainhead* (1943), for its part, praises the works of a modernist, anti-traditional architect. Instead, this chapter focuses on the Rand novella *Anthem*.

Born in Russia in 1905, Rand fled from the USSR in 1925. She eventually arrived in the USA. Her literary debut came in 1936 with *We, the Living*. This is a mainstream novel of people oppressed by the Bolshevik regime. Her second work was *Anthem*. This was reportedly written in 1937 and marginally revised for the re-issue in 1946.

Anthem continues the anti-communist theme of the debut. But now the setting is mythical and anti-utopic, telling of a world that formally never was, but we all understand the urgency of the story. This is about freedom versus slavery, written by a person who had seen the Bolshevik "paradise". *Anthem* is a political myth in the best sense of the word. The seeming simplicity of the plot is what gives it strength. Everything becomes symbolical. The story isn't mere bare-bones preaching, as the title might suggest. Rand gives her world just the right amount of *mimesis*. But still it doesn't count more than 100 pages. This is a masterpiece of stringency and concentration.

STAGNATION

In *Anthem* Rand is advocating "the right to difference" like French *Nouveau Droite*-thinker Alain de Benoist. And the story could be seen as an example of "the romance of progress and increasing insight," according to Spinrad a defining feature of SF.

In *Anthem* Equality 7-2521 is the narrator, 21 years old at the time of writing. He's too inquisitive, too learned for The Totalitarian State ruling the world. So on graduating he must become a street sweeper, living in the Streetsweeper Home and toiling from 9 to 5 clearing the streets. In this world the word "I" is forbidden. Since The Great Awakening (symbol for "the Communist Revolution") mankind lives as a collective; no individuals exist, only "a great WE, one, indivisible and eternal".

Life in The Totalitarian State is without love, color and emotion. It's about toil, sweat, mediocrity and leveling. Stagnation is praised; candles, window glass and sailing ships are approved technology but not much else. Electricity is unknown and forgotten, an invention of The Unmentionable Times preceding The Great Awakening.

TARGET: BOLSHEVISM

An episode showing that Soviet Russia is the target of the satire is the following. In chapter one the narrator goes outside town with two of his friends. On the outskirts they find a grate over a hole in a hill. Can they go inside? is the question. One of the friends says that The Council can't know about this hole, thus no law can exist allowing us to venture inside, "and all that isn't allowed by law is forbidden". Reportedly, this was also the philosophy of law in Soviet: "nothing is allowed and all is forbidden". This according to a juridical wisdom, according to which, further, the West supposedly had the motto, "everything is allowed but some things are forbidden". And, ultimately, in an Anarchy, "everything is allowed and nothing is forbidden…"

In spite of the legal doubt the narrator goes inside. And eventually he makes the cave he finds beyond the grate into his secret hideout, a place for experiments. He goes there in the evenings; the sweepers are namely entertained in a theater tent every night for three hours and he can easily sneak out from there. After the specific time has passed (measured with an hourglass) he can sneak back to the venue and inconspicuously join the throng as it leaves the tent. With stolen candles, knives, paper, metals, powder and acids the narrator conducts experiment in his cave. With bricks he builds an oven for melting. He also has manuscripts on science and nature, leftover from The Unmentionable Times. In these exploratory doings he finds a previously unfamiliar joy. The research for its own sake ultimately gives him peace.

THE GOLDEN

The narrator finds more than peace. In meeting with a woman working the fields a love starts to grow. He calls her The Golden. He also witnesses the burning alive of a criminal, a person having uttered the forbidden word. It isn't said here but the word is "I", the symbol of identity and self-hood, the uttering of which is the confirmation of the individual being an independent creature, a free spirit endowed with willpower and a sense of the Self.

In the next chapters the narrator conducts experiments in electricity, like re-discovering the electrical qualities of copper, zinc and a salt solution and how a rod of iron can conduct a lightning strike. In the end the narrator by this rediscovers electric light, an invention he surmises has been around before The Great Awakening. In chapter five he has succeeded in making a sort of light bulb, demonstrating electric light in a glass box. The parts, like copper thread, are essentially leftovers from Unmentionable Times. Then he's caught, his sneaking out of the theater tent has been discovered, but when whipped by the authorities he only says "the light, the light," this carries him through. He doesn't say where he has been. In time he manages to escape. And when returning to the cave the nest is intact with its candle, its oven and its glass box. Now he plans to go to The Home of the Wise and share his new invention.

He eventually does this. He comes before them and shows them his glass box – but the wise are scared by this. He tells them not to be, instead this is a gift to them and to mankind – "the force of heaven, the key to the earth". Take it and let's work together for the enlightenment of mankind. Leave torches and candles behind, this is the new Light for mankind...!

But the wise will have nothing of this. The narrator has broken the law by being inventive – and threatening to force the workers producing candles into unemployment – and ruining the planning of The World Council, it having spent fifty years to decide how to produce candles. So they want to seize him and imprison him but he escapes, glass box in hand. Now he heads for The Uncharted Forest into which no one of The Totalitarian State dares venture.

BACKWOODS HICK

Walking in the woods the narrator longs for his amour, The Golden. Will he ever see her again? At the same time, he cherishes being free as a bird. The unbound existence makes him discover his willpower, the free life releases creative thoughts: "Triumph to live, triumph to breathe, triumph to exist" as Swedish poet Edith Södergran said. He even discovers laughter, like Michael Valentine Smith in *Stranger in a Strange Land:* what defines man is that he's the "animal risible," the animal that can laugh, as Aristotle said. In The Totalitarian State no one laughed.

The narrator bows down to drink in a brook. When he sees his face mirrored in the waters he discovers his own beauty, suppressed by the regime he previously lived under. He discovers his personal specificity, something eventually leading to the discovery of his own Self, his I. This, namely, is forbidden in The Totalitarian State: to affirm and enjoy oneself, enjoying solitude; togetherness in a collective is the norm. Now the narrator discovers the basics of self-hood and self-reliance.

In chapter nine he reunites with The Golden. She followed him at a distance when he escaped. Now, at their reunion, she admires him for his firm countenance and upright posture, so different from how her fellow brethren back home look, the subdued citizens of The Totalitarian State. She will rather be doomed with him than blessed with her brothers, she says.

SUNSHINE

The narrator and The Golden find happiness together, another first along with self-hood, creativity and willpower. The pair lives in the wilds, surviving by hunting game with bow and arrow. The narrator muses on self-hood and joy, a joy stemming from creative work following a unique, inner vision, not by working in a group.

In chapter ten the pair has reached a mountain range beyond the woods. And in that range they find an empty two-story house with big windows. In this abode of light, a leftover from the previous, Unmentionable Times, the light plays on colors the likes of which the narrator has never before seen, having only known white, brown and gray. The house also has a library with printed books, another novelty to the narrator. All his previous documents were handwritten manuscripts.

In the next chapter the story culminates. The narrator discovers the word "I" – as in, "I am, I think, I will". In essence this is the answer to everything: "I am the meaning", "I am the one I've been waiting for". The quest that led the inquisitive narrator from his earliest days is over. The perception, discernment and will of an individual is the beginning and end of existence. Succinctly Rand says that an individual is no means to an end, no tool for others, no sacrifice on someone else's altar. The Self is a goal in itself.

The tone of the rest of this sermon is slightly egoistic. Now it's as if the narrator is the only man on earth, not willing to share anything with his fellow men. You could say, after his trials and deliberations the narrator doesn't come out as a lovable hippie type, ready to embrace all of mankind – instead, he's wary and on the guard against his environment, ready to share of what's his only if the other guy is worthy of the gift.

Such an egotism is socially if not morally justified. But in the context of the narrator, as a citizen in The Totalitarian State, having been virtually obliterated as an individual, this might be excusable. The closing anthem to individual freedom could be needed as a statement against The Powers That Be, always bent on intruding on the inborn independence of beings – of beings, human beings, once by The Savior given the motto, "I Am". The narrator essentially rediscovers this motto and this is a worthy aim for a philosophical story.

THIS

In *Anthem* the sermon goes further in literally putting the Self on a pedestal, worshiping it as a god, the only god. This, however, is taking it too far. To totally obliterate "we" from the language is extreme but the narrator intimates this.

Only because you've experienced the worst collectivist regime ever doesn't mean that you should go to the other extreme, worshiping the "I" and eradicating all aspects of the "We," like togetherness and meeting the "you" of another person. Totally neglecting the collective is impossible. For example, to totally think yourself out of your nation and culture is rather difficult – indeed, it's undesirable in the current era of an NWO flooding the West with remote immigration. But having said this, Rand in her stressing the reality of the individual was needed in times of nihilist collectivism, in the East and the West. She opposed the enslavement of the creative individual in an era focused on efficiency and utility. It was an essential message when she wrote it and it's important now.

MOUNTAIN PREACHER

Anthem closes with chapter twelve – fittingly, for a prophetic story, on the house on the mountain. The story started in the city of convention and dejection, continued in the cave where the narrator was transformed, and finally he ventured out into the woods and up in the hills, elevating himself beyond the everyday and becoming an Inspired Messiah. Prophets should preach from a lofty place, like Jesus Christ in Sermon on the Mount and Nietzsche among the Swiss alps where he got the vision of Zarathustra, becoming his mouthpiece in *Thus Spake Zarathustra*. Another remarkable feature of *Anthem*, for 20th century novels, is that it ends on a positive note. The narrator for instance says that he plans to sneak back to the town where the story began and bring along some friends that had shown signs of being misfits of The Totalitarian State. He will become a lodestar for everyone having some inner sense of Will and Self-hood. Along with his recruits he'll write the first chapter of the rest of human history.

This is an unusual ending for a story in the genre of dystopias. As shown previously in this study, *Nineteen Eighty-Four*, *We* and *Brave New World* all end dismally, or at best ambiguously, as in *Kallocain*. Only *Metropolis* has a degree of optimism in its stressing that "the mediator between head and hand must be heart". In this company *Anthem* is even brighter, stating the power of "the sacred word, I" as a bastion against all the attacks on personal freedom by The Powers That Be.

ANTHEM CONTRADICTING OBJECTIVISM

For the record, the following strain of *Anthem* seems to contradict the philosophy that Rand later developed, Objectivism. *Anthem* intimates a different ontology, that of subjective idealism.

In chapter eleven the narrator says that he wanted to know the meaning of things but then discovered that "I am the meaning". He says that he wanted a warrant to exist – but now he states that he doesn't need that to exist, he needs no confirmation of being alive since he himself is the warrant and the confirmation.

He says that his eyes are seeing, and the sight of his eyes give beauty to the world – his ears hearing gives the world its song. His consciousness is thinking, and the discernment of his mind is the only searchlight that can find the truth. His will chooses: "I want it" are his only holy, guiding words. Ontologically speaking, all this to me sounds like Schopenhauer's *"die Welt als Wille und Vorstellung"*. The environment is dependent on an observer; an objective reality doesn't exist. The world is our presentation. Reality is realized by our Will.

LITERATURE

- *We, the Living* (1936)
- *The Fountainhead* (1943)
- *Anthem* (1946)
- *Atlas Shrugged* (1957)

28. THREE AMERICAN SF NOVELS

IN A PREVIOUS CHAPTER was examined three stand-alone British fantasy novels. Here the same is done with three American SF novels, novels with some or other relationship to Tradition. They are written by Roger Zelazny (1937-1995), Lafayette Ron Hubbard (1911-1986) and Jack Williamson (1908-2006).

JACK OF SHADOWS

Jack of Shadows is a 1971 fantasy by Roger Zelazny. It's a bit hard to categorize. But it's a masterpiece, an other-worldly fairytale with succinct narrative and archetypal characters. It tells of a shadowy existence making his way in the world, a world with a heliostationary orbit – a world *tidally locked*, always facing the sun with the same hemisphere. On the dark side magic rules, on the bright side science rules. Drawing his strength from shadows the hero, Jack, has some advantage of the darkness.

He settles for a quest, a quest for a key that will doom or save him. As intimated, this is commendable because of the seemingly archetypal setting, although I've never read anything like it before. If it's about "new", previously unseen characters, how can they be symbolic? If so, the author has to have some myth-making skills. Also, the language is lucid and resilient. We get no oceans of words, no cathedrals of overwrought prose-poetry, which the poetically gifted Zelazny otherwise might have succumbed to. Making his debut in the 60s with reportedly way-out storytelling Zelazny remained a dark horse in fantastic literature, like giving us a succinct and alluring epic fantasy in the Amber chronicles (1970-1991). It's equally commendable, each installment being fairly short (circa 200 pages) but giving the reader everything he needs in the form of wonder and glory, told in an efficient yet poetic manner.

Zelazny knows Tradition. Maybe he went too far in *Lord of the Light* (1967), about people on a distant, future planet transforming themselves to gods with some ad-hoc scientific means, making them long-lived and strong-willed. Specifically, they impersonate Hindu gods. Conceptually, this sounds just awful. I'd rather read the Bhagavad-Gîtâ than some modern yarn of "Hindu" gods strengthening their will artificially, which is impossible.

RETURN TO TOMORROW

In chapter 32 of this study I touch upon Heinlein's *Starman Jones* (1953), about a young man going off into space, with time learning the ways of the merchant marine of the future. Physically and mentally demanding, interstellar travel becomes a rite of passage. Heinlein's novel has everything you could ask for – except for artistry. In the usual manner it's efficiently told but there are no memorable interiors, scenes, impressions etc. Heinlein knows his fortes (dialogue, ideas, lecturing) and focuses on them. It works – but when you read a similar story by a man having some artistic skills along with plotting and ideas, it's like a revelation.

Return to Tomorrow (1954) by L. Ron Hubbard is such a novel. From the very first paragraph, with a certain Alan Corday seeing an interstellar ship taking off, its exhaust flame casting a fiery glow over the surroundings, through the meeting with the captain Alan will serve under, to the ship interiors, the planets they visit and the climactic return to earth, Hubbard gives us just the right amount of details, milieus, color and depth. In short, this is a masterpiece. Just my ideal: succinct yet with a modicum of style.

The novel also underlines the alienation a traveling man can get when returning home. There's the case of Relativity Effects: put simply, one day elapsed on a ship traveling at velocities near the speed of light equals a week elapsed on earth; a week on the ship equals months, months on the ship equals years, and so on. So when returning after such a voyage everything the traveler knew is gone, he's a complete stranger, a man seemingly from nowhere, and chapter nine portrays this well with Alan's first homecoming, barely finding a trace of his relatives. So Alan returns to the ship, having found his real home among these nomads of the long, interstellar route.

As intimated, in the beginning of the story Alan meets the captain. It's in a tavern, a spacer tavern. Alan comes in and sees the man sitting by a piano playing. This gives it that musical feeling I've sometimes highlighted in this study. And music or not, it's such a heartwarming detail, that of a scarred veteran being something more than a Competent Man lauded by the Campbell era SF.

This is also a novel about taking responsibility, praising the traditional values of the service life: duty, courage, self-restraint and self-determination. Memorable is a scene at the end where Alan has become the captain himself. A navigator comes onto the bridge and sits down by the plotting table, putting a whiskey bottle on it. He's an alcoholic and the former captain tolerated this drinking while on duty. But now Alan grabs the bottle and throws it into the wall, shattering it. There's a new regime on deck – Alan's regime. That's a symbolic scene of responsibility and leadership, credible as such, mirroring the life at sea that Hubbard knew as a naval officer. Smashing the bottle might not be a paragon of self-restraint *per se* but it brought the message home, that of the Responsible Man taking charge.

LEGION OF SPACE

Jack Williamson's *The Legion of Space* (1934) also tells of serving, of being a man of courage and responsibility. It's true that it lacks the

"Analog-Astounding" credibility in this respect, that of Heinlein, Dickson and Haldeman, whose service novels I treat in chapter 32. But Williamson's novel decidedly isn't anti-tradition. It's heroic and well-told, rather artistic at times. It has a crisp narrative seasoned with telling detail.

It's the year 3000. John Ulnar, newly commissioned officer of the Legion of Space, gets his first assignment which is to guard a woman having knowledge of a secret weapon, AKKA. She's on Mars. John makes the journey there together with his cousin Eric who's also in the Space Legion, being something of a hero after a journey to Barnard's Star. There the man encountered various mysterious aliens, Eric being one of the few of the crew not becoming insane after returning home.

On Mars, Eric's real purposes are revealed. One night, a strange spaceship lands next to the Legion fortress and at the same time the commandant is found dead. John is persuaded to imprison the little garrison guarding the woman – Aladoree – because Eric is suspecting them of murdering the chief. But when the mysterious starship disappears the gruesome truth becomes clear to John Ulnar: Eric has abducted Aladoree, and with her the secret of AKKA, and brought her to Barnard's Star! He has gone over to the aliens, mankind is in danger!

John gathers himself after this debacle, not letting it crush him. He frees the legionnaires he previously had locked in and together they go to the Legion's headquarters on Phobos. There they become incarcerated by the Legion's supreme commander, another of John's relatives. After a series of trials and tribulations, they manage to get out of jail and steal a ship, setting the controls for Barnard's Star to free Aladoree. They succeed in this and eventually return to earth for a showdown with the alien fleet. The weapon AKKA plays a role in this.

SCENES

The scenes on the planet by Barnard's star are exquisite. Like the smooth walls of the alien city rising over the jungle like a mountain range, "a black town, built by giants". And the alien inhabitants themselves, soaring over the walls like green balloons.

The basics of the plot Williamson is said to have lent from Dumas' *The Three Musketeers*. Maybe he even based his main characters on Dumas figures, like the bucolic Giles Habibula, a sorely needed comic relief. Thus you can say: theft shouldn't be endorsed but all things considered, *The Legion of Space* stood out in 1930s SF so it has to be recommended. Williamson isn't a simple thief, he can portray, conjuring a space opera world in elegant shapes and forms. There were no aliens, and no AKKA, in Dumas' text. Williamson conceptualized the Dumas narrative to a new level of originality.

The politics of *The Legion of Space* are a bit odd. At first the ideal is anti-authoritarian, envisioning a certain Red Hall of a former solar-system empire standing empty, with a great throne of red crystal under a jeweled canopy, also empty. And on the throne is the emperor's old crown and scepter, seemingly waiting for an imperial resurgence. How do you sell such a dormant, possibly resurgent monarchy to a democratically imbued America?

At the beginning of the story the solar system is controlled by the Democratic Green Hall, which was preceded by the Red Hall's autocracy. John Ulnar, for his part, is prepared to defend the Green Hall at any price. But during an incident in the Phobos residence of the Supreme Commander, Adam Ulnar, John learns that this Adam Ulnar plans to restore the Red Hall Empire and persuades John to become the new emperor. John is namely a descendant in direct line to the last emperor. But he refuses obstinately; rather being prisoner for life than to betray the democratic ideals of the Green Hall…! However, in the end he does become the new solar emperor, he restores the Red Hall as if nothing had happened. Statism rules, the solar system is governed with authoritarian splendor. Graphically, this sits well with the cover of the hardcover edition of 1947, symbolizing Responsibility With Authority in its steel shimmering bastions.

Later in the 30s Williamson wrote *The Legion of Time*, despite the title not a sequel to the *Legion of Space*. It's not even about a legion. But this is also some kind of minor classic, a conceptual tour de force of two warring astral operators, the bright Lethonee and the dark Sorayina. Lethonee's realm is called Jonbar, a city of light, and Sorayina's is called Gyronchi. The hero Lanning gets involved in a plot where these two powers are potential realities to be realized, to be "collapsed" in the Heisenbergian sense. So what will it be: freedom and light or darkness and despair? Williamson stands us one better by merging the two in almost Jungian fashion, in the denouement integrating light with dark in fusing the Lethonee and Sorayina figures into one, thereby, beyond the personal happiness for Lanning in having both his dream women in one, resulting in a future promising for all, an era of spiritual growth and fulfillment uniting the opposites.

Williamson had some aces up his sleeve in this way, going on to write rather fine SF for many years (like "With Folded Hands" from 1947, about the societal consequences of perfect robots, later expanded into novels). Like Asimov, he remained mentally clear into old age, not veering off into senility like Heinlein and van Vogt.

LITERATURE

- Jack Williamson: *The Legion of Space* (1934)
- L. Ron Hubbard: *Return to Tomorrow* (1954)
- Roger Zelazny: *Jack of Shadows* (1971)

29. HISTORY

A DISCREET BUT NOTEWORTHY sub-genre of SF is the one dealing with history, like time travel to historical epochs and parallel worlds retaining some historical feature. This chapter focuses on "historical SF playing in antiquity". It's instant Tradition: these stories make us virtually walk the streets of ancient Rome and Constantinople, succinctly giving us a share of life in those days.

SCHOLAR

The SF I grew up with usually had heroes in the form of engineers, space pilots, statesmen and soldiers. But sometimes there figured this character: the history scholar. We see him both in L. Sprague de Camp's *Lest Darkness Falls* (1941) and Robert Silverberg's *Up the Line* (1969).

These two novels are the focus in the following. They're written in different eras and their main characters have different approaches but they share these similarities: it's about the late antiquity bordering on medieval times, it's about changing or not changing history, and, implicitly and explicitly, it's about being enthusiastic about times past, about yearning for "the glory that was Rome, the splendor that was Greece".

This we especially see in Silverberg's novel. Told in the first person this is a contemporary, classically trained scholar having some feeling for the specificity of 6th century Constantinople. The looming sentimentality is held in check by the extensive learning being portioned out, *en passant*, during the virtual tourist tour of the era the main character serves as a guide of. For instance, we get to love the Christian splendor of the Hagia Sofia; to Silverberg (1935-), the subsequent 14th century minarets added nothing to the structure.

Up the Line tells of time travel, of guided tours to times past. The visitors may not affect or alter anything they meet. But the visitors themselves, by merely being there, tend to crowd up the scenes successively, when more and more such tourist parties visit the scenes. You might think of Heisenberg here, of even a mere spectator affecting the scene he watches.

The lingering memory of having read *Up the Line* is the vivid depiction of 6th century Constantinople. These were the days of Justinian and Theodora. Theodora is worth some lines, being an example of "from rags to riches". In this instance we have figures like Joachim Murat who was the son of an innkeeper, Bernadotte who was the son of a lawyer, Hitler who was a day-laborer and the Hongwu emperor who was a farmer, and finally Theodora, who was a prostitute – humble beginnings all for these operators. Theodora, for her part, married Emperor Justinian and became Empress. And at the so-called Nika riots, she said to her husband to stand firm and hold out:

"There is no better sweeping than the imperial purple!"

This referred to the color of the mantle the emperors wore. As for the Nika event in 532 CE Constantinople was in an uproar; two groups, formed on the basis of the quadriga racing sport "blue" and "green" supporter teams, fought openly in the streets, and across the Black Sea northern barbarians came to interfere. But everything was put down on the Emperor's orders, specifically by General Belisarius who rounded up the rebels in the arena and killed them there.

NIKA

The Nika rebellion was put down and the empire recovered, this Eastern Rome that had a thousand years of history left to write. And in Silverberg's novel we get to visit the capital, Constantinople, during its heyday, with palaces and alleys and the Golden Horn glittering in the sun; imagine being able to go into Hagia Sophia, light a candle and praise the Lord. One who really gets his dream fulfilled in this respect is the time traveler Judson Daniel Elliott III, the novel hero who guides his party to the Nika riots and even falls in love with a Greek foremother in the process. But the latter he's doing on purpose, he expressly goes back in history to have sex with his foremothers; voilà the use of history to a 20th century dandy.

Having said that, Silverberg's novel does convey enthusiasm and wonder for times past. This is the remaining feeling of *Up the Line*, which has to be stressed. Because, enthusiasm and wonder, credibly conveyed, are not common instances of 20th century fiction.

In the novel a visit is also made to the assassination of Huey Long, Louisiana's alleged dictator in the 1930s, a controversial right-winger in his time. Silverberg doesn't add anything specific to the man's creed *per se*, he only relates of the man and how he died, assassinated in Baton Rouge, 1935, which is what the time travelers in question is out to see. However, in itself this is an elegant way of narrating history, it's "*historia in nuce*" (history in a nutshell) as Manuel Venator would say, the main character of Jünger's *Eumeswil* of which I told in chapter seven. As a novel reader in this way being told of someone called "Huey Long" gives you the impulse to look the man up and receive some useful information, an example of learning as entertainment.

GAP IN TIME

In *Lest Darkness Falls* by Lyon Sprague de Camp (1907-2000) an American by chance falls through a ripple in the time-space fabric, ending up in Rome of the early 530s; one moment he's out walking in today's Rome, then he gets struck by lightning and falls through a gap in time – and immediately he found himself in late antiquity, or should we say early medieval Rome (the ancient times formally, from the academic viewpoint, ended in 476 CE), just after the eastern Nika rebellion and before the Byzantine invasion of Italy. Being venturesome this Martin Padway engages in business; he founds a brandy distillery, he starts a newspaper and he establishes a semaphore telegraph. It all goes well and the money's flowing in but then the world of politics demands his attention, the Eastern Roman Empire is about to invade this rather quaint, Goth ruled Italy he finds himself in. In the process Padway gains the position as supreme commander of the Italic army and manages to stave off the threat of invasion.

As the historian Padway is he knows that this invasion in reality was devastating for this post-imperial Italy; there was an approximately thirty year period of war and devastation after which Italy was ruined, literally, to recover only slowly. But in the fictional framework, with the territory secured against East Romans and later Franks, as well as with industry revitalized with the innovations he has introduced, Padway as an advisor to the King can look to the future with confidence: the supposed "medieval darkness" will not fall upon Italy, perhaps the whole of Europe can be subsumed under some imperial hegemony again. Grand politics aside, the novel is a fine look into a bygone era, de Camp having a true feeling for 6th century Rome with its Vandals and Goths, overwrought Italian aristocracy and religious conflicts. You read about Gothic mercenaries and ordinary Romans, about Arian quarrels on wine taverns, of a businessman's problems in the contemporary environment and more. There's a plausible feel to the environment and the dialogue, it all comes through as believable even though it's about a time traveler who ends up in the past and manages to change this, which is rather far-fetched. But with his style and ease de Camp makes the reader willingly suspend his disbelief.

LITERATURE

- L. Sprague de Camp: *Lest Darkness Falls* (1941)
- Robert Silverberg: *Up the Line* (1969)

30. ANARCHY

Anarchy might be to politics what nihilism is to ethics: a necessary phase to go through. For in ethics nihilism, according to Ernst Jünger, is the phase from "common, exoteric idealism" to "true idealism, acknowledged by the inner mind". And he meant more or less the same about anarchism, intimating that every true politician has an anarchist phase in his ideological development. This chapter takes a look at anarchism in SF, in stories by Ernst Jünger and others.

RUSSELL

Anarchism seems to keep its allure through thick and thin, being the Gordian Knot answer to all political questions: how about no government and no laws, just citizens making mutual agreements? Eric Frank Russell, for one, maintains that this could work. But his novella *And Then There Were None* (1951) depends entirely on its otherworldly setting, the action taking place on a future space colony. Russell stages his anarchist utopia without common limitations such as ethnicity, traditions and scarcity of resources so it gets rather artificial. Russell's ideal society has no politicians, no laws and no money; it all works by the colonizers making mutual agreements and having obligations on each other.

Is it that simple? No money, just obligations? In a small society it might work. As such, depicting a tiny colony of people, Russell's story is rather witty and elegant, telling how this small-scale utopia is threatened by the forces of imperialism. It's a viable ideological experiment in fictional form, like Huxley's *Brave New World* or Zamyatin's *We*, which didn't pose any questions about ethnicity etc. either but were the settings for interesting discussions nonetheless.

Another work of short fiction dealing with anarchy is Larry Niven's "Cloak of Anarchy" (1972). In this short we have a future Los Angeles with the freeways turned into parks – free parks – since cars as we know them have been replaced by soaring vessels, hovering craft of the today generic SF type; this conclusion isn't explicitly made in the story but it's a viable guess. These enclosed parks with entry fees are a social experiment with some hippie connotations, places to be free, their only prevailing rule being "no violence". The parks are supervised by airborne cameras called copseyes; at the sight of any violence the police can arrive and uphold the law. The park's visitors practice micro-level anarchy like preaching for dumb-ass religions, wearing outrageous costumes or just hanging out, an anarchy that can exist as long as there's macro-level, state-executed violence to safeguard it.

UNSTABLE

This small-scale utopia is rather quaint and harmless but let's go with it for the sake of the narrative. Because, some day at LA's King's Free Park some genius takes down all the copseyes, as if on cue: they all drop to the ground thanks to the clever guy's hacking abilities. So what does that turn the park into? A small-scale hell. With no restraint, no threat of public interference the fabric of civility cracks. Among other things some heavies post guard around the drinking water fountain, only letting selected people come forth for a drink. The queues line up. And this is a perfect picture of what a collapsing society would mean: scarcity of necessities, violence, insecurity.

In time the copseyes come up again and everything reverts to normal but the central characters have a scary night behind them, depriving them of what delusions of anarchy they might have had. "Anarchy isn't stable"[155] is Niven's terse conclusion and I can go with that.

JÜNGER

Like Larry Niven, Ernst Jünger is skeptical about the common view of anarchism, giving eternal bliss to everybody as soon as it's installed, but Jünger doesn't discard anarchism altogether. In *Eumeswil* (1977) he redefines it in the role of the Anarch, being an antipole to the ruler but not (as an anarchist) bent on destroying him, just content with watching him. The Anarch can take action if he wants to, like fighting in a war or even killing the monarch, but he doesn't have to.

The Anarch is independent, a true sovereign. He's an equal to the monarch, neither a servant nor an enemy, not as such. The Anarch is his own land, his own state. As intimated he can serve the current land he lives in a war, by national service, but this doesn't make him a slave. The Anarch is free by default, as a reflecting, conscious human being. As any human, by his esoteric, divine nature he has Free Will and this can never be taken from him. This gives the Jünger way of anarchism a spiritual founding lacking in most other instances.

The Anarch wants to be free, not by changing society but by mentally seceding from it. In the figure of the Anarch Jünger may have given anarchism a new lease of life – an existential anarchism with possible feelers out to society. It may become a bit "too much and too little", the Anarch figure always having the right answer, always being free, as Jünger defines it in his elaborations in *Eumeswil*. Jünger is Anarch and the Anarch is Jünger; the Anarch in Manuel Venator's shape seemingly becomes the last court of appeal of politics, history and ontology. He's a preacher, a teacher, an interpreter of art, life, politics and everything in all ages. Uwe Wolf once called the Anarch figure "*Gottesunmittelbar*" (in direct connection with God), the individual having a direct line with the Creator, not needing priests, religion or anything to guide him. This is esotericism, not

---

[155] Niven, 1983, p 132

politics. But maybe a way of taking esotericism into the realm of politics, giving back to politics a sorely needed spiritual foundation. In days of old society was steeped in spiritual values, as Evola showed in *Revolt Against the Modern World.* Now society by definition is nihilist and materialist.

This reminds me of what I said in chapter one when discussing Heinlein's *The Moon is a Harsh Mistress,* that of solving the equation of personal freedom with societal demands, even societal freedom:

> [T]here may be societal rules around, you may have to follow them for the sake of practicality, but nonetheless you remain free in your essence, you can break the laws if your sense of freedom demands it – and in doing this you're still a responsible man, you're morally responsible for your acts, the very thing that makes you free. Only the responsible man can be truly free. Freedom obliges, you might say; that's the aristocracy of the soul that the best of Heinlein's heroes belong to. Bernardo's high-profile saying in question reads like this: "I am free because I know that I alone am morally responsible for everything I do."

This summarizes the conservative ideal of accountability, linking it to the timeless ideal of freedom; existential, personal freedom, from which societal freedom is derived.

MIRAGE

In chapter one Heinlein's *Coventry* was covered, which dealt with an alleged anarchist utopia. But in essence this was no anarchist heaven, just an ordinary state with taxation, courts and a national defense. It was anarchy as a mirage, a myth. And that's what anarchy will remain if it isn't footed in the individual's existential freedom, in the person acknowledging his inborn freedom in the shape of Free Will.

LITERATURE

- Robert A. Heinlein: *Coventry* (1941)
- Eric Frank Russell: *And Then There Were None* (1951)
- Larry Niven: *"Cloak of Anarchy"* (1972)
- Ernst Jünger: *Eumeswil* (1977)

31. NIHILISM

A PERSISTENT TRAIT OF 20th century literature is *nihilism*. All is lost, we're doomed, all we can do is to die in style; *voilà* the nihilist creed. The term is derived from Latin *nihil* (nothing). Nothing has any value, there's no meaning, no transcendent values exist. That is, the very opposite of Perennialism, of Idealism lauding the Eternal Values of faith, hope, self-reliance, duty and honor, the very basis of this study. Hereby a brief look at the other side, the "no future, no values, no meaning" aspect of SF.

PASSIVE AND ACTIVE

To be sure, nihilism isn't all that bad. For instance, the *active nihilism* of Nietzsche can be rather invigorating. It's like the "atheism as purification" of Simone Weil: to have the absence of meaning etc. as a mental exercise. Science fictional, active nihilist outings can be rather good reads, like William Gibson's *Neuromancer*. Overall this is a classic SF novel with ideas about computers and how to interact with them, about parallel worlds of the mind and how to conduct operations.

Neuromancer is a narrative feat, very rewarding. But to be sure, the outlook of the book is nihilist to the bone. The future world depicted has no governing states, only a jumble of major companies ruling like feudal lords. People live for material enjoyment only, like the criminals at the center of the plot. And the main character, Case, is a drug addict. Before the operation he's hired to participate in (to hack a master computer) his employer pays him for having surgery that stops him from enjoying drugs, putting in certain sacs in his body making him incapable of metabolizing cocaine and amphetamine. But when the mission is carried out and Case gets his monetary reward he pays for surgery removing the sacs so he can go on be a junkie. Overall, this might be a credible plot development but *per se*, this demonstration of a nihilist mindset can make you cringe.

BALLARD

As we saw in chapter eleven J. G. Ballard had his fruitful aspects, even from a conservative point of view. But he was also an incurable nihilist.

The first four novels of Ballard told about global apocalypse and downfall, by each of the four elements: air, water, fire and earth. The last, *The Crystal World*, reduces transcendence into a weird, "eternal" life for transmigrated souls in crystallized form. What a strange way of exemplifying the eternal, esoteric, immaterial qualities of the soul. At the end the hero, with a jewel-adorned cross, ventures out into the woods to join with The New Light. In itself, this is a fine fantasy image but essentially it becomes meaningless, given the nihilistic framework Ballard works within. No trance, no ascension into higher levels of reality is hinted at, no acknowledging of esoteric truths to be discovered Beyond the Beyond. This counts for all seemingly "enchanting" and "alluring" Ballard stories of transformation of nature, of everything becoming a jungle, as in *The Day of Creation* and *The Unlimited Dream Company*. A surreal vision of the world becomes sterile if the author doesn't have an opening into the esoteric and the eternal. In short, if he isn't steeped in the Perennial Thought of Plato, Plotinus, Eckart and Jünger.

In *The Burning World* fire was the element by which everything perished. The narrator Ransome has the line: "I've always thought of the whole of life as a kind of disaster area". This, to me, symbolizes nihilism. True, at the end of this, the last of Ballard's four apocalypses (along with *The Crystal World* the others were *The Wind from Nowhere* and *The Drowning World*), rain falls. That's the piece of hope leading away from nihilism into a more ambiguous state. That's why Ballard remains readable, even in his more somber moments.

NUCLEAR

I admit it: I can't read stories about nuclear disasters, nuclear energy or anything like that. These disaster stories to me seem like nihilism all the way, passive nihilism: we're doomed. Therefore, I will hardly ever open the pages of works like *On the Beach, Atomskymning, Dr. Bloodmoney* or *When the Wind Blows*. It seems so utterly pointless. I know that these authors were led by High Ideals, that of Warning Against an Unfavorable Development, but in the framework of the current study I just chose to bypass all this. And remember, there won't be a nuclear war, mankind is past this trial. To dwell on the theme of nuclear disaster is indulgence of the worst kind; the passive nihilist kind.

ANIARA

The ship Aniara leaves earth for Mars, carrying colonists wishing to escape our war-torn planet. On the way the ship has to evade an asteroid and comes off course, from then on helplessly heading out into the void. All is lost, the ship is doomed. The poem then elaborates on this until everybody aboard has died.

This is Harry Martinson's *Aniara* from 1956. It may be true that it has some artistic qualities, being as it is an epic poem of musical perfection. Not many such were written in the mid-20th century. Its major fault is the atmosphere and conceptual drift, which is passive nihilism. Again, good style is having something to tell. And to merely say that everything is lost, that "same old no tomorrow kicked in the face", this is a parody of a message.

Everybody dies, everybody falls to the floor to an eternal state of nothingness in the mirror halls of Aniara. True, from a general, dramatic point of view I have nothing against such dark endings. For instance, the similar fate in Poe's "The Masque of the Red Death" (an isolated castle is visited by undead infected with the plague; everybody dies) has always brought me some satisfaction as a reader: "And Darkness and Decay and the Red Death held illimitable dominion over all". And this, too, is a story showcasing some passive nihilism.

So I don't know. Maybe it's the undertext of *Aniara* that kills it for me, the not-so-subtle allusions that the ship and crew symbolizes man in the atomic age – man is doomed – now please reader, fall down in dejection and despair. Martinson comes through as a major manipulator of the reader's feelings.

ANTIHERO

In storytelling we have the phenomenon of the *antihero,* the case of a man being the opposite of a traditional hero. In the general sense and for narrative purposes, I have nothing against this. I praise "artistic freedom" as an ideal, as important as academic and journalistic freedom, the freedom of expression in general. And novels like Gene Wolfe's *The Book of the New Sun* (1980-1983), Sam J. Lundwall's *No Time for Heroes* (1971) and Harry Harrison's *Bill, the Galactic Hero* (1965) are all rather enjoyable, the first for its accomplished style, the latter two for their drive and wit.

That said, to have an executioner as main character (Wolfe) overall leads out into nothingness, as does the bantering of the other two, I figure. A hero is led by Will, Truth and Compassion; an antihero is a symbol of the opposite, of decadence, whose core concept is nihilism. If you accept that, then these books can be estimated at their true value. Just don't come and say that they're some kind of all-time, essential classics pointing the way ahead. For this some embracing of ideals is needed, some spiritual elevation.

ABSURDISM

The Harrison and Lundwall stories can make you think of absurdism. Stories telling about absurdities, ain't they funny? Of course you can have a good time with Douglas Adams' *The Hitch-Hiker's Guide to the Galaxy* (1979) and some of Robert Sheckley's stories (like "Ticket to Tranai"). Along with the nihilism they do convey some notable sense of wonder. But no one should convince me that they, or "absurdism" in general, have the answer to "life, universe and everything". Do you expect me to listen to your twisted way of looking at things, as if it were a revelation...?

Posing questions concerning the nature of reality is a viable practice. You get the answers by looking inside, by listening to the heartbeat of the universe. We're all sparks of the Eternal Light, here to affirm this selfsame lesson. But how to explain this to a confirmed nihilist?

SCREAM

The short story "A Boy and His Dog" (1969) by Harlan Ellison plays in a post-apocalyptic America. In this dismal future the boy Vic has a telepathic dog, Blood, who helps him find women. Vic in turn gets food for the pair. They eventually meet the girl Quilla June. The plot has some complexity to it but in the end it's intimated that Vic kills his new love and cooks her to save his dog. Nihilist? No, not at all.

Again, artistic freedom has to reign. I'm not using this "nihilist" chapter to succumb to mere name-calling and labeling. Ellison, for his part, might be the jester of SF, sorely needed as such. For instance, once (in the foreword to *Dangerous Visions*) he suggested that Disney's "Steamboat Willie" was the first SF story. A mouse steering a boat, how much more speculative can it get...?

So Ellison has his worth. I can also acknowledge the artistry of another of his stories, "I Have No Mouth, and I Must Scream" (1967), about a group of people trapped inside a cruel computer, hell as a psychological landscape. But I admit it, personally I can't bear myself to read it anymore. It's a notable piece of art, like a Francis Bacon painting, but not anything I can enjoy or praise, and this because of the searing nihilism. As a conservative, today I don't care about this, "A Boy and His Dog", *Aniara* or nuclear disaster stories. Still, I love "The Masque of the Red Death" and *Neuromancer*. And *Bill, the Galactic Hero* was rather fun as an anti-war piece aimed at *Starship Troopers*. Nihilism can't be ruled out from fiction altogether. I mean, take Shakespeare, whose *Macbeth* and *Richard III* are rather nihilist, with murder most foul and no spiritual element to ameliorate it. That said, you have to call things by their proper names and to me, the traits examined in this chapter are examples of nihilism, leading out into the desert: "This is the dead land. / This is cactus land" as Eliot said in "The Hollow Men".

LITERATURE

- William Gibson: *Neuromancer* (1984)
- J. G. Ballard: *The Wind from Nowhere* (1961)
  - *The Drowned World* (1962)
  - *The Burning World* (1964, also as *The Drought*)
  - *The Crystal World* (1966)
  - *The Unlimited Dream Company* (1979)
  - *The Day of Creation* (1987)
- Nevil Shute: *On the Beach* (1957)
- Katarina Brendel: *Atomskymning* (1953)
- Philip K. Dick: *Dr. Bloodmoney, or How We Got Long After the* Bomb (1965)
- Raymond Briggs: *When the Wind Blows* (1982)
- Harry Martinson: Aniara (1956)
- Edgar Allan Poe: "The Masque of the Red Death" (1842)
- Gene Wolfe: *The Book of the New Sun* (four novels, 1980-1983)
- Lundwall, Sam J.: *No Time for Heroes* (1971)
- Harrison, Harry: *Bill, the Galactic Hero* (1965)
- Harlan Ellison: *I Have No Mouth, and I Must Scream* (1967)
  - *A Boy and His Dog* (1969)

32. WAR

IN CURRENT SF there's something called *Military SF*. Hereby a look at three novels that to me symbolizes this sub-genre: *The Forever War, Dorsai!* and *Starship Troopers*. This chapter is about war and combat, about serving in the military, SF variety. It also deliberates on Heinlein stories about serving in tight organizations other than strictly military, like the merchant marine of the future, SF yarns learning us something about responsibility and decision making. This is the "duty, honor, courage" part of SF.

ARCHAIC

War stands for the archaic in the modern, it's been said. The ideals of "follow the leader," the emblems of flags and standards, the *pathos* that comes from risking life together in a unit, the willpower needed to sustain the hardships of an operation: all this is anathema to the modern lifestyle of passive nihilism, self-seeking, irony and relativism.

A soldier lives in earnest: every second in the combat zone can end in death. Then there's no time for irony. Combat is a crisis business. This has been depicted in literature at large and in SF specifically. The symbol of the soldier is the infantryman. And to me, an SF novel eminently capturing the uniqueness of being an infantryman is *The Forever War* (1974) by Joe Haldeman (1943-).

Haldeman had been in the Army, in Vietnam. Specifically, he was a combat engineer, not in the infantry proper, but all army men must learn the ways of the infantry. That's the basics and the *sine qua non* of every army. And Haldeman's story on modern war is an exquisite rendering of the infantry way of life. In this respect it's even better than Heinlein's *Starship Troopers*, which although depicting "mobile infantry" literally soars above ground all the time. And Heinlein had never been in a ground fighting unit, he was a naval officer serving on ships. This has got to be stated for the record. Then, as for the military SF discussed in this chapter, we have Dickson's *Dorsai!* Dickson had been in the Army but he hadn't, as far as I know, seen combat and this reflects in his novel, impressive as it may be. But Haldeman had seen war, he depicts the infantry of the future and it's simply the best in this respect.

I once served in the infantry myself, during my national service, so I can personally vouch for the credibility of Haldeman's story. This is how it should sound:

> We'll be advancing on a heading .05 radians east of north. I want Platoon One to take point. Two and Three follow about twenty meters behind, to the left and right. Seven, command platoon, is in the middle, twenty meters behind. Two and Three, Five and Six, bring up the rear, in a semicircular closed flank.[156]

The first part of *The Forever War*, given in *Analog*, June 1972 as "Hero", is what I base my praise of Haldeman on. I have indeed read all of the novel but this isn't commendable as a whole, veering off as it does into, let's say, libertine lifestyles and excessive modernism. But the *Analog* excerpt is just right in giving us the gist of the infantry way. For instance, we're treated with the unit in question being trained before it's sent into the field. Here the narrator, private Mandella, is given responsibility for a mortar. A grenade launcher isn't so high-tech per se but along with the protective suits, the "lasguns", the drones and the insights into how infantry units move through the land and how they're led, seasoned with some quaint but restrained army jargon, makes the whole into an exemplary narrative of military SF:

---

[156] Haldeman, p 42

I peeked out over the edge of the rock. My rangefinder said that the bunker was about three hundred fifty meters away, still pretty far. I aimed just a smidgeon high and popped three, then down a couple of degrees and three more. The first ones overshot by about twenty meters, then the second salvo flared up directly in front of the bunker. I tried to hold on that angle and popped fifteen, the rest of the magazine, in the same direction. [Next during this exercise the narrator is hit by low-effect laser and is out, and:] Since I was officially "dead," my radio automatically cut off and I had to remain where I was until the mock battle was over. With no sensory input besides the feel of my own skin – and it ached where the image converter had shone on it – and the ringing in my ears, it seemed like an awfully long time. Finally, a helmet clanked against mine: "You OK, Mandella?" Potter's voice. "Sorry, I died of boredom twenty minutes ago."[157]

This is how it should be done. This plus the expedition they later go on, raiding an enemy base, makes "Hero" (*The Forever War*) into a deathless classic of combat SF.

I rolled out onto the wing of the craft and jumped to the ground. Ten seconds to find cover – I sprinted across loose gravel to the "treeline," a twisty bramble of tall sparse bluish-green shrubs. I dove into the briar path and turned to watch the ships leave. The drones that were left rose slowly to about a hundred meters and took off in all directions with a bone-jarring roar.[158]

DORSAI!

Dorsai! (1960) was written by Gordon Rupert Dickson (1923-2001). Even without the military element it's a deathless classic, telling of a soldier advancing to become the ruler of all the solar systems man occupies in the 23rd century. In restrained, controlled stages and chapters the hero Donal Graeme comes through as a credible

---

[157] Haldeman, p 26
[158] Ibid., p 41

superman, a genius of tactics and strategy. It reads like a combination of Asimov, Herbert and Dickson. All the bravado and fierceness that characterized Heinlein's *Starship Troopers* is absent here, for better or worse. War is reduced into a sort of chess game. But still, Dickson's novel is altogether commendable, chess game or not. No military SF story conveys true tragedy anyway. If you want to depict war "as it is" then the realist way is best, like in Väinö Linna's *The Unknown Soldier* (1957) or Delano Stagg's *Bloody Beaches* (1961).

Dorsai! tells us of space battles and interstellar intrigue. Fighting on the ground only occupies a couple of chapters. But they do indeed show that Dickson has some insight into this phenomenon. It's restrained, it's like a game but in the context of the whole novel, this is just right:

> [T]hey began to move out. Dawn was not yet in the sky, but the low overcast above the treetops was beginning to lighten at their backs. – The first twelve hundred meters through the woods, though they covered it cautiously enough, turned out to be just what Lee called it – a Sunday walk. It was when Donal, in the lead with the first half-Group, came out on the edge of the river that things began to tighten up. "Scouts out!" he said. Two of the men from the Group sloshed into the smoothly flowing water and, rifles held high, waded across its gray expanse to the far side. The glint of their rifles, waved in a circle, signaled the all clear and Donal led the rest of the men into the water and across.[159]

You might disagree with the technological level of Dickson's army of the future. No beam weapons, no heavy support, just infantry with rifles firing flechettes and slivers. Operationally, this degenerates into a "cowboys and indians" type of warfare. In a wider sense, the traditionally minded reader might like the Dorsai planet of warriors that Donal Graeme comes from, a future world with some Scottish influences. The second chapter of *Dorsai!*, depicting Donal Graeme's coming of age-ceremony with some late-night small-talk among the men of the clan, reads like "a Dune before Dune". In a future-time

---

[159] Dickson, p 42

SF setting, this is about as traditional as it gets. It's about being a man, about assuming responsibility.

Dorsai! is an efficient *exposé* of Norman Schwarzkopf's dictum: "When placed in command, take charge." Donal Graeme takes charge for whom he is as a man, an infantry commander, a naval commander and, at last, as supreme commander of an interstellar coalition. It's a science fictional illustration of the old US Army motto: "Be all that you can be". In a subsequent novel in the series it's even intimated that Graeme with his mindset takes mankind to the next level of development, becoming the first "Responsible Man". With its brainy reflections, its elaborations in a tight but eminently readable framework, *Dorsai!* is an all-time lodestar, not just of military SF. It's *the* novel to read for the executive, responsible mind. Also, *Dorsai!* portrays a *human* interstellar culture (no aliens), thus forming a conceptual chessboard of grand-scale politics, strategy and technology.

Dorsai! burns with a quiet fire, a Dune before *Dune*, an Asimov with a sense of urgency.

CONSERVATIVE CLASSIC

I'll now move on to some topical novels by Robert Heinlein. *Starship Troopers* will be treated last. Before that I'll give you a review of some other stories he wrote about serving. First a look at *Space Cadet* (1948).

In chapter one of this study I delineated what *Space Cadet* has to tell about traditional values, like its stressing of qualities like responsibility, self-restraint, self-determination and nobility of character. Responsibility: as a ship commander you have to function as an absolute ruler, symbolizing The Law to your crew. Self-restraint: an officer must curb his ambition and greed. Self-determination: an officer has to exert cunning and bravery. Nobility of character: an officer must have a sense of justice to be a true and noble knight.

This is what Commander Arkwright of the Space Academy tells the cadets. I've said it before and I say it again since this passage is a paragon of conservative SF. Overall, *Space Cadet* is an excellent novel in the beginning, in the chapters about the main character, Matt

Dodson, coming to the Space Academy, signing in, getting tested in every possible way and seeing comrades getting eliminated (chapters one - three); a tough process indeed.

"Put up or shut up" is the implicit message. Like in showing us the spoiled cadet who arrives at the Academy with a lot of packages, expecting carriers to come and help him with it. Message: this man has no inborn sense of responsibility and is not officer material! Then we have one of the tests Matt performs, one of being blindfolded and putting peas in a bottle. Matt discovers that you can ease the blindfold and thus see directly when doing the test. He mentions this flaw to a functionary and by the answer Matt gets he learns that the real test was not to cheat.

Don't lie! That old ideal. Heinlein returns to it in *Starman Jones*, where a starry-eyed youth bluffs his way into the space-faring guild. Later he must admit that he cheated. A true leader of men must not be a liar and a cheater. That's the message Heinlein brings home with some efficiency.

OATH

Space Cadet and the service life. In the testing process, a short jump into space is also made and then Matt has his doubts whether he will persevere. Will Matt make it into becoming a space navy officer? He eventually shapes up and is there to take the oath (chapter four). Now the cadets are allowed to wear a proper uniform. Now they're also exposed to education by the cadets in the superior class, in subjects like table manners and general conduct befitting a future officer of The Interplanetary Watch. The novel in telling all this is very vivid and poignant. It's the epitome of story-telling, of good style in Matthew Arnold's sense: *having something to tell*.

BALANCE

In medieval times a knight should be "without reproach and fear". That is, exerting a balance between nobility and self-restraint on the one hand, and bravery and "get-up-and-go" on the other. I intimated this above. An officer must have both drive and self-control, being both determined to solve his tasks and to curb his worldly ambition while doing it. He must balance industry with modesty. In *Space Cadet* this argument is brought home at the end. Three cadets have become marooned on Venus. They eventually find a wreck of a ship from an earlier expedition. The process of recommissioning the ship is plausibly told and eventually the group succeeds in the task; they can blast their way home to the space station near Earth.

When this episode takes place the cadets have been in The Watch for about a year. They are petty officers and the like, NCOs, slowly but steadily advancing to become second lieutenants. To become an officer would take 2-4 years, but they figure, after this feat they might get their commissions right away...! Finally, back home, a talk with the Academy commander cuts them down to size. He mentions nothing of the salvaging of the Venus wreck, he just gives them critiques of their overall ship service, their apprenticeship "in the field". Matt eventually gets the orders to return to the Academy for his second year, for a term of theoretical studies, with the prospect to graduate after this has been completed. Matt then talks with his comrades to figure out why they weren't praised for their heroic feat of recommissioning the ship wreck. They eventually realize that this was merely what was *expected* of them; that's why the commander didn't mention it. It leaves them with a warm-cold feeling but eventually it makes perfect sense. It's a lesson in the realm of, "put up or shut up, do your duty, don't expect a gold medal for every act".

Even earlier, while on Venus and deciding to start to save the wreck, the cadets have no high hopes of succeeding but they get going anyway. For, as Matt puts it, The Watch would probably send a rescue ship to search for them and when it arrived the cadets should not sit on their butts waiting, no, they should be engaged in some activity showing that they're working on their own redemption – for this is what's expected of members of The Watch. *Space Cadet* is sprinkled with lessons like these, the wisdoms of a life in uniform. Wisdoms of the active life, the will-driven life, controlled by a stoic equanimity.

OPERATIONAL

There's something called *operational fiction*: stories about operations, about operational outings of the one or the other kind, with an author hopefully knowing what he writes about. In mainstream fiction it's works like *The Unknown Soldier* and *Bloody Beaches*. And in SF Heinlein was a master of this, not only as regards pure military conflicts (*Starship Troopers*, *Sixth Column*) but also more generally such as *The Puppet Masters*, about an insidious alien invasion, and why not pure civilian ventures like *Time for the Stars* and *Starman Jones*. In all of them the Heinlein experience of leading and / or being part of operations, acquired in the Navy, is portrayed.

A formality on how to operate is to have a *staff*, an HQ. Napoleon had a staff, General Lee had a staff, but in those days the staffs were relatively small. The system reached a higher level in Germany after Moltke the Elder's reforms in the mid 19th century. With this, a commanding general would have an extended management group at his disposal, with sections dealing with intelligence, logistics, support and even operations *per se*. How big these staffs were depended on whether they belonged to a whole army or just a division, but they were there and they began a new era of simplifying decision making in complex matters such as combat.

Heinlein often returns to the conceptual breakthrough of having such a staff. For instance, in *Sixth Column* the USA is invaded by "PanAsians", Sino-Soviet conquerers, and the only ones opposing them are six army men of diverse talents. But they have an underground laboratory facility, some gold bullion and a new beam weapon invention. They start to organize the counter-offensive. Having gotten the ship off the ground (like organizing churches only allowing white men and arming their priests with the new weapon) Major Ardmore after a while gets overworked: he has too much to do, too many responsibilities, too much to decide on. So he calls on his factotum, Jeff Thomas, who advises him to organize a staff. He says that Napoleon was "the last general" in that he held all the reins in his hand, deciding on everything. The new general staff devised by Moltke, an HQ beyond the collection of secretaries and orderlies Ardmore already has, is the operational paragon.

Ardmore holds the rank of Major but he hasn't received any higher military education, he's an ad man being called up and hastily given a commission in the intelligence service. But Thomas helps him devising the new staff by searching for competent men within the organization (by a search in the punch card files, a now *passé* system which when used actually did work), gathering a bunch of people with civilian administrative experience. From this group a chief of staff is designated and under him a brain trust of guys knowing "the principles of scientific administration".

Ardmore soon thrives as the head chief. He had always been something of a loner and now he has to work with people speaking on his behalf and even taking decisions in his name, *ex officio*. Sufficient control is maintained by having people working in his spirit and those who doesn't are dismissed, by suggestion on the chief of staff. Thus Ardmore is free to work strategically, perfecting the ways on how to defeat the PanAsians. Also, he now has a command group from which to take a stand-in if he himself should fall.

MOON

As for terms, the word "chief of staff" is important. In the US today, namely, this often means "top head of an organization". But properly speaking a chief of staff is only head of the HQ, as such a glorified aide to the executive commander. And the model of the leader having to have a chief of staff Heinlein returned to in *The Man Who Sold the Moon*. Industrialist D. D. Harriman is planning a trip to the moon – the first. Among other things, he has to build a ship for this. Having put his engineering chief Coster on the task Coster later complains, like Ardmore, of having too much to do. His most important task, engineering, has to be done in spare times, at night. So Harriman builds him a set-up to protect him against routine work; he creates a staff. Thus Coster, as chief engineer and top man, can concentrate on the strategic issue, how to build a rocket ship. His newly designated chief of staff, Jock Berkeley is "Lord High Everything Else". Poignantly Jock says to Coster:

> "[B]ypass me all you want to – you'll have to run the technical show – but for God's sake record it so I'll know what's going on. I'm going to have a switch placed on your desk that will operate a sealed recorder at my desk". "Fine!" Coster was looking, Harriman thought, younger already. "And if you want something that is not technical, don't do it yourself. Just flip a switch and whistle; it'll get done!"[160]

This is operational fiction par preference.

FORMALITIES

To lead is not merely to stand on a hill and point. You have to have a staff enabling you to do that pointing.

It might get a little technical with all these formal maneuvers. As if war or any operation is about discussing formalities. But Heinlein knew the whole gamut, from combat decisions in the front line to the above intimated discussions in higher echelons. So what more examples can I give? The Heinlein titles given in this chapter, operational stories from the 1940s and 1950s, all have a plethora of aspects and details on how to operate. *Sixth Column* for instance deliberates on how to lead, the need of having a deputy ready to take over and how to run radio communications, Heinlein's previous professional area. The novel is a bit melodramatic and unrestrained but it has a solid core of operational sensibility.

Before moving on to *Starship Troopers*, let's look at the space travel stories and glean some operational tidbits from them. They're about civilian ships but to sail a major ship is a kind of crisis business too, it's about obeying the commander, a thoroughly operational matter. For instance, when reading Heinlein we're taught the need for written orders. Like in chapter twelve of *Time for the Stars*. And chapters fourteen-fifteen of *Starman Jones*. It's the phenomenon of a guy having

---

[160] Heinlein, 1951 II, p 114

a hold on you, forcing you to do something operationally improper. But if you insist on having the order in writing it'll be recorded in the log. Thereby the order will be booked, there to be checked by the system. Thus the other guy comes under fire and you're off the hook, having forced his hand.

You have to obey the commander, even on a civilian ship. *Time for the Stars* brings this argument home in chapter sixteen. There has been discontent with a new captain, groups are formed, plans are discussed, but the narrator finally realizes what this is:

> Mutiny. It's the ugliest word in space. Any other disaster is better.[161]

And on the nature of running a ship, we are then given this reflection:

> [T]he Captain had better be right, you had better pray he is right even if you disagree with him... because it won't save the ship to be right yourself if he is wrong. But a ship is not a human body; it is people working together with a degree of selflessness that doesn't come easy – not to me, at least. The only thing that holds it together is a misty something called its morale, something you hardly know it has until the ship loses it.[162]

The worst hazard to a ship isn't machinery breaking down or attacks from hostile natives. No, "maybe the worst hazard was some bright young idiot deciding that he was smarter than the captain and convincing enough others that he was right."[163]

GLORY ROAD

In 1963 Heinlein published the novel *Glory Road*. I examined it in chapter one, deliberating on its theme of traditional values and how to embrace them today. Along with this, *Glory Road*, with all its tall-tale fantasy plotting, jargon and wise-cracking has some more

---

[161] Heinlein, 1973, p 170
[162] Ibid.
[163] Ibid., p 171

instants of seriousness. The first two chapters tell about the hero's life in the real world, in 1950s America. For instance, this Oscar Gordon has served in the Army. In those days there was national service, the draft, the potential obligation for any able-bodied male to serve in the armed forces.

This Gordon has to do. He's ambivalent about the whole thing. He compares doing military service to a lobster about to be cooked, customarily dropped alive into boiling water: it might be his finest moment but it isn't his choice... Still, the narrator is a patriot even though it's deemed old-fashioned in his time. He has forebears having served at Gettysburg and Korea. In school, Gordon argued for patriotism in Social Sciences but this served him no good, earning him a "D"; then he shut up and passed the exam.

For its part, the draft meant a form of selective service; the Army didn't need to put every man into the ranks like in WWII, a selection had to be made, still the system was a menace to young men of those days. You could avoid it by studying, marrying and getting children. In the context of the novel Gordon signs up nonetheless, he's sent to Southeast Asia – and after a tour of duty, suddenly, he doesn't give a damn about anything. The everyday world of suburbia, wife and kids seems paltry compared to his childhood dreams of wanting Roc's egg, Excalibur and the moons of Barsoom flying over his head.

In talking about the specificity of Army life Gordon also mentions Ian Hay's *The War to End All Wars*. There it says that all armies have a Unit for Surprise Parties, a Unit for Practical Jokes and The Unit of the Good Fairy. That would be an apt way of characterizing the nature of bureaucracy, in itself necessary for the massive organization a modern army is. Seen from the individual point of view army life might seem unfair and haphazard, indeed crazy at times. And, at times, as a Good Fairy giving you abilities to study free, travel free etc.

Glory Road is a lot about fencing. Gordon takes a fencing class in secondary school. And as for the jungle fights he's glad that he doesn't have *aichmophobia* (the fear of sharp things). So when he comes to the parallel fantasy world, hired to fight dragons, he's in his element. The sword he receives has the inscription, "*Dum vivimus, vivamus*" (while we live, let's live). *Vivamus* becomes the name of the sword.

The carrying of a sword makes Gordon feel like a man. At the end of the book, Gordon being back in the everyday world, the memory of the prophylactic feeling of wielding a sword makes him don the sword-belt again and head for adventure – just going out in the street, sword in scabbard, and getting in touch with Mrs Fantasy again. It's a slightly unnerving image, giving you ideas of the late-period Heinlein throwing ideals like self-restraint, reserve and impeccability out the window and like a parody of a Nietzschean living in "the impulses, the subconscious, the flesh". I mean, I can appreciate the feeling of "I want adventure" permeating *Glory Road* but to be an adventurer can't mean that you stop to think, merely living by instinct.

STARSHIP

Now for Heinlein's most infamous book, *Starship Troopers*. It isn't a perfect novel. For one, the gung-ho jargon is annoying. You might say, "but combat soldiers are like that, cocky" but then I say, not necessarily. For instance, Ernst Jünger managed to tell you of four years in the combat zone with a fairly low-key style (*q.v. Storm of Steel*). Overall, the Heinlein style has "drive, dash and guts" implicit and when it's toned down it gets rather efficient, more efficient than being exposed as open bravado.

The downsides of *Starship Troopers*: as intimated in the beginning of this chapter, Haldeman's *The Forever War* has more credibility in depicting the infantry of the future, of presenting an SF scenario of fighting on the ground. But having said that, *Starship Troopers* is commendable in almost every respect. David Weber, author of the Honor Harrington series, says this on the nature of Military SF and it reads like a characteristic of *Starship Troopers*, the novel spawning the genre:

> For me, military science-fiction is science-fiction which is written about a military situation with a fundamental understanding of how military lifestyles and characters differ from civilian lifestyles and characters. It is science-fiction which attempts to realistically

portray the military within a science-fiction context. It is not 'bug shoots'. It is about human beings, and members of other species, caught up in warfare and carnage. It isn't an excuse for simplistic solutions to problems.[164]

The specificity of war, of combat, is rather well captured in *Starship Troopers*. I earlier said that realistic novels are essentially better in capturing the tragedy of war – and to this we may add the specificity of war in general – the dangers, the hardships, the excitement. Having said that, the first chapter of *Starship Troopers* really grabs you, that I have to admit. The narrator sketches the situation of the unit being dropped onto a hostile planet for a raid, we are told of the squad leaders and get some knowledge of the special equipment used, and then the platoon leader holds his speech. After the usual jargon it comes down to this, that operational essence that reads like poetry:

> You'll be dropped in two skirmish lines, calculated two-thousand-yard intervals. Get your bearing on me as soon as you hit, get your bearing and distance on your squad mates, both sides, while you take cover. You've wasted ten seconds already, so you smash-and-destroy whatever is at hand until the flankers hit dirt.[165]

Hereby some more sample quotes on the operational viability of *Starship Troopers,* the *sine qua non* of this novel:

> There mustn't be any shadow of doubt when you give an order, not in combat...[166] The idea was to secure the entire target and allow the reinforcements and the heavy stuff to come down without important opposition; this was not a raid, this was a battle to establish a beachhead, stand on it, hold it, and enable fresh troops and heavies to capture or pacify the entire planet.[167] A week later we made rendezvous, coming out of drive and coasting

---

[164] Weber interviewed by Stephen Hunt, quoted after https://en.wikipedia.org/wiki/Military_science_fiction
[165] Heinlein, 1987, p 8
[166] Ibid., p 128
[167] Ibid., p 119

short of the speed of light while the fleet exchanged signals. We were sent Briefing, Battle Plan, our Mission & Orders – a stack of words as long as a novel – and were told not to drop.[168] Even a platoon leader should have "staff" – his platoon sergeant. But he can get by without one and his sergeant can get by without him. But a general *must* have staff; the job is too big to carry in his hat. He needs a big planning staff and a small combat staff.[169]

POLITICS

Basically, the political model of *Starship Troopers* is this: only those having held a job in public service – any official, not just of the military – are given the right to vote. And this right is to be executed only after they have completed their service. Thus a model *combining responsibility with authority* is to be secured. The model of 20th century style democracies is degraded as breeding irresponsibility, sometimes degenerating into tyranny. That could for instance be true of the *demokraturas* of the current Westworld, regimes ruling by brainwashing and conditioning the electorate using propaganda and a rigged language.

Westworld electorates are urged to vote for this and that party promising them peace, prosperity and a good will to all. But is this electorate responsible, even given age-limits? Against this we have the *Starship Troopers* model of government, presented like this, by a teacher in a History class at the Officer Candidates School the hero of the novel eventually attends:

> Under our system every voter and officeholder is a man who has demonstrated through voluntary and difficult service that he places the welfare of the group ahead of personal advantage. And that is the one practical difference. He may fail in wisdom; he may lapse in civic virtue. But his average performance is enormously better than that of any other class of rulers in history. (...) To

---

[168] Heinlein, 1987, p 186
[169] Ibid., p 177

vote is to wield authority; it is the supreme authority from which all other authority derives – such as mine to make your lives miserable once a day. *Force*, if you will! – the franchise is force, naked and raw, the Power of the Rods and the Ax. Whether it is exerted by ten men or by ten billion, political authority is force.[170]

But this isn't the whole picture. The teacher, Major Reid, says that along with authority must come responsibility:

> Both for practical reasons and for mathematically verifiable moral reasons, authority and responsibility must be equal – else a balancing takes place as surely as current flows between points of unequal potential. To permit irresponsible authority is to sow disaster; to hold a man responsible for anything he does not control is to behave with blind idiocy. The unlimited democracies were unstable because their citizens were not responsible for the fashion in which they exerted their sovereign authority... (...) Since sovereign franchise is the ultimate in human authority, we insure that all who wield it accept the ultimate in social responsibility – we require each person who wishes to exert control over the state to wager his own life – and lose it, if need be – to save the life of the state. The maximum responsibility a human can accept is thus equated to the ultimate authority a human can exert. Yin and yang, perfect and equal.[171]

The question of responsibility indeed has to be raised. It's not enough to preach freedom, as the current Westworld democracies are wont to do. Heinlein construed his system in a particular context (first the world is dragged down into global civil war, then war veterans institute the above model, and then the space war against "the bugs" break out). And for the constitutional debate of the 2010s we're dealing with different, more peaceful parameters. True, we live in a world seemingly on the way to major war, there are provocative maneuvers, "shady characters and dirty deals" in the east, but this will never become a major-league hot war, a global "hyper war," since we

---

[170] Heinlein, 1987, p 155
[171] Ibid., p 155-156

now live in Sat Yuga. Statistically, the scale and intensity of the wars of the world has gone down since 1945. 1990, with the end of the Cold War, was a breaking point for the better. In the 2010s the death rates of the wars fought have gone up a bit. For sources on this, see the reports of Uppsala University's UCDP led by Peter Wallensteen.

However, the trend is clear: major war is a thing of the past. So in that respect, Heinlein's "only war veterans can vote" model is something of a curiosity. But his coupling of responsibility and authority is worth considering as such. The governance of tomorrow must appeal to the electorate's responsibility – not enticing it with liberality and the prospects of a vegetative life, with people executing this kind of franchise only as a kind of religious rite. *Sat Yuga* means people affirming their Inner Light, their essence as divinely created beings, and in this framework the authority implicit in voting will be executed with responsibility as a matter of course.

SERVICE LIFE

Starship Troopers is an eminent novel about the service life, covering such subjects as what it means to lead, to obey, to protect and serve, to "go career" and to take responsibility. All in a plausible framework of the ways of a future Armed Force, with scenes from basic training, ship duty and combat. Plus, some discussions on philosophy and politics. In all, an impressive mixture of an action story and a novel of ideas.

You could say: what *Space Cadet* delineated, *Starship Troopers* exploited to the full.

LITERATURE

- Dickson, Gordon R.: *Dorsai!* (1960)
- Haldeman, Joe: *Hero* (1972)
  - *The Forever War* (1974)
- Heinlein, Robert: *Space Cadet* (1948)
  - *Sixth Column* (1949)
  - *The Man Who Sold the Moon* (1950)
  - *Starman Jones* (1953)
  - *Time for the Stars* (1956)
  - *Starship Troopers* (1959)

33. MARGINALIA

Under the caption of "Marginalia" this section is devoted to subjects that didn't make it into the other chapters.

There are some memorable right-wing SF not necessarily dealing with Tradition. One such would be Desmond Bagley's novelette "Welcome, Comrade" in *F&SF*, April 1964 (the author used the pseudonym "Simon Bagley"). It tells about how the Soviet Union takes over the USA by means of conditioning and hypnos, much like Cultural Marxism actually has done in the real world.

Bagley's story doesn't mention Cultural Marxism, the Frankfurt School or anything like that but it tells of a sociological project, "Project American", allegedly trying to map the Americans in a thorough ethnographic study. The study then becomes a cover for influencing men's minds, making them ripe for collectivist nihilism, pretty much like Political Correctness until now has triumphed, like having every opinion former along, "from Madison Avenue to Oshkosh Gazette"...

Throughout this book, here and there, I've referred to Norman Spinrad's idea of "the romance of progress and increasing insight". Spinrad's train of thought was part of an explanation of what made the so called cyberpunk stories by William Gibson and Bruce Sterling so appealing. Gibson's *Neuromancer* (1984) indeed is worth reading as an SF story, it has style, a tight, techno-saturated plot and memorable characters. However, the overall world-view is a bit nihilist (*q.v.* chapter 31) so I can't devote a chapter to that novel in this study of traditionally inclined SF. However, for the record, here's Spinrad's discourse in question given in some detail.

According to Holmberg,[172] this was Norman Spinrad's take on the specificity of SF. Spinrad meant that the greatest value of the cyberpunk movement of the 1980s and 1990s was that it again enabled the union of the romantic impulse with science and technology. Because, once upon a time SF was special in expressing intellectual progress in romantic terms. This can be exemplified with stories of space travel, a central theme for SF from the mid 19th century to the mid 20th century and beyond.

Spinrad's train of thought is this: traveling into outer space with ships employing some technical innovation isn't merely about faster communication, it's a mind-bending achievement, a striking experience and a challenge towards existence itself. As I personally would say, it's a metaphysical feat, not just a physical. It's about reaching another level of reality, a higher dimension. Spinrad talks about "the romance of progress and increasing insight" as the dominating feeling of SF literature. This was lost in the 1960s when cutting edge authors started focusing on inner space; a humanistic, anti-technological grouping disposed toward soft sciences (biology, sociology) versus a traditionalist camp deliberately neglecting the humanistic dimension that's needed in giving technological ventures a deeper dimension.

But in cyberpunk these two camps again merged into one, creating an amalgam of technology and humanity, of idea-driven stories and romanticism.

---

[172] 2003, p 81

Elsewhere in Holmberg[173] related ideas by Spinrad are discussed. In the Golden Age of the 1940s and 1950s, Spinrad maintains, SF unified speculation and humanism. The New Wave in the 1960s, for its part, focused on humanistic sciences and the workings of man's inner mind. Technology and its creations were deemed as unimportant and ventures into outer space became irrelevant. New Wave authors did indeed speculate about the everyday world, they didn't solely dream away into Lands That Never Were, and in doing so some technological inventions were deliberated upon, but the New Wave authors chose to play down this and instead focused on the stylistic, psychological and surreal qualities of the texts. But in doing this SF also lost some zest and flavor, Spinrad seems to mean. However, the spirit of science-married-to-romanticism was possibly regained by cyberpunk.

A book worth mentioning in this right-wing survey of SF is Rütger Essén's *De släckta metropolerna* (in Swedish only, the title meaning "The Darkened Metropolises," 1937). Essén (1890-1972) wrote this story under the pseudonym of "Leif Erikson". Essén was a Swedish nationalist. He was also, in some respects, pro-German and this has made him controversial. However, Swedish SF-scholars who call his novel racist are in the wrong. Race and ethnicity aren't mentioned at all in the story. Instead, *De släckta metropolerna* is an outing in the realm of Last Man-novels, a Robinsonade in an SF setting with the added element of ideological debate.

The novel tells the story of how an able-bodied engineer, Erik Ryding, after a catastrophe starts civilization anew with a working class woman and a female doctor. The trio eventually engenders a lot of kids and the man can plan the farming, the building of houses for them, the schooling of the kids etc. As for working with his body, it's said of Ryding that "the manual work kept him in good health and bestowed inner satisfaction,"[174] a true conservative ethic. A buffer

---

[173] Holmberg, 2003, p 186
[174] Essén, p 77

against hunger is the canned food they can salvage from the deserted city they live near, Stockholm. Everything seems fine. But there is also a conflict in this urban microcosm between the cunning heroes and some working class people in another part of town, another group of survivors. And this may be seen as a vague reflection of H. G. Wells' *The Time Machine* (1897) with its future conflict between ethereal upper-class people and troglodyte workers. More than that, *De släckta metropolerna* reads like a 1930s Robinsonade, hands-on and pragmatical. The beginning with the hero, Erik Ryding, seemingly all alone in a summery Stockholm somewhat echoes M. P. Shiel's *The Purple Cloud* (1901), about a man having become all alone in the world after a poisonous cloud has killed all of humanity. In Essén's novel mankind is killed by the volitional releasing of a gas by an American millionaire, a Mr. MacFarland having misanthropically become fed up with humanity.

De släckta metropolerna is rather well executed as a novel. The initial chapters of Ryding walking around in the deserted Stockholm have their desolate beauty. Generally, the plot moves on effectively and plausibly, several years being covered in the narrative without it being sketchy. And the discussions between Erik and his MD wife, about the ideological lines they're planning to build their new world along, are stimulating. Ryding here represents radical conservatism, his wife urban liberalism. And later on, Marxism is represented in the opinions of the adopted guy Ante. The symbolic difference between Berit's and Erik's outlooks is formulated like this, with Erik saying that to her life is a psychosis and a complex, to him, an adventure and a mystery.

Some quotes of the images of "magnificent desolation" could be given. First, the dead city, the summer Stockholm where everyone seemingly has fallen for the poisonous cloud:

> A tram had derailed and rolled over against the wall at the Hornsgatan Hump. Inside were a dozen morning passengers, all dead, all with the same surprised gaze. The conductor lay face down over the driver's seat. In the middle of the park a policeman lay dead. At a cab-stand on the left side three cars were sitting. All

three drivers were dead. Erik Ryding opened the first car, lifted the driver out and laid him on the grass. Both from detective novels and war experience, he knew that rigor mortis doesn't occur until after six to eight hours. All these people must have been alive for only a few hours ago. Most likely they had all died at once.[175]

Also, the view of the deserted world, seen from an airplane Erik and one of his sons eventually get ready and fly, has everything you can demand in the way of mimesis, of depiction of milieu, of sublime vistas. They get to see the "darkened metropolises" of Europe, Berlin, Paris and London etc., being slowly reclaimed by nature. This is how they, having had their fill of sightseeing, start from the aerodrome of Croydon, England, for the last leg home:

> Again, they filled up on petrol and controlled the propellers and the oil supply. Erik also wanted to throw a glance at the other British cities and therefore plotted a compass course towards the northwest. Everything went well, and soon the weather cleared. A velvety green and pleasant land spread out below them, with wild parks, oak groves and small sparkling waters, the England of *A Midsummer Night's Dream* having returned. First they descended on Birmingham, half an hour later on Manchester and Liverpool, then following the coast to the north all the way to Glasgow, a dull and gray urban desert, which also was visited at the height of one hundred and fifty meters. The fifty kilometers due east from Glasgow to the even in death striking Edinburgh took only fifteen minutes, and at 12:30 PM they could set a course straight out over the North Sea, towards the Skagen peninsula and Gothenburg.[176]

Mutatis mutandum, *De släckta metropolerna* is worth reading. Contrariwise, it doesn't deserve to be placed in the poison cabinet, covered with a sign saying "nothing to see here, move on"...

---

[175] Essén, p 37-38, translated by the author.
[176] Ibid., p 116

The Right is right, the Left is wrong. The Left has had its time. Both in society at large and in the SF community. Throughout the Westworld there has until now been a left-liberal hegemony. The repression is quite tight, regimentation and ostracism is brought to bear as soon as someone shows conservative, anti-PC opinions. But things are about to change now. The revolution is brewing, even in the microcosm of the American SF community.

It's called "the Hugo Wars", a controversy of nominations etc. concerning the prestigious SF prize Hugo, awarded every year since 1955 at the annual World SF Convention. Novels mentioned in this study having earlier received this prize are for instance *Ringworld*, *Dune* and *Double Star*.

Tactically, what the current battle is about is a counteroffensive. The SF world has long been dominated by left-liberals, Political Correctness and "Social Justice Warriors". These SJWs are attacking the slightest deviation from the norm. There are many details and instances in this. I personally don't support everything that the alleged right-wing in this business stands for. But the focus in the SF world has to be moved from PC-ism and overwrought leftism. And the raging "Hugo Wars" (they did at least rage in 2015 and before that) to me seems to be part of a trend, that of both SF grass roots and some profiles being tired of the regimentation, harassment and intolerance shown by left-leaning SF fans and critics.

Details aside, *mutatis mutandum* and all that, this counter-attack is a positive sign. The cultural PC dictatorship has gone too far. It has depleted the creativity of SF. To a large extent, SF isn't about captivating, creative, entertaining stories anymore. Critically highlighted SF has degenerated into Politically Correct statements.

Hence the need for this firebrand. It all has already achieved some success. The Hugo Awards in 2014 reportedly awarded what may be considered as right-wing writers. There were also some gains in 2015. Maybe it's a quiet revolution going on. A new generation of readers, critics, and writers taking back their genre from SJWs, globalists and cultural Bolsheviks. The resurgent Right wants to combat this, an oxygen-deficient, all negative force having squeezed the life out of a genre that still is a viable method to depict ideas, scenarios and ontological questions in symbolic form.

Historically, the "clerics" of the SF field (editors, critics, pundits) might have been left-leaning; none mentioned, none forgotten. Campbell, for his part, was influential in his day but such a clear-cut right-winger in the SF editor role is historically rare. However, many SF authors have been men of the right (see this study) and so have many readers; they're the silent majority, now coming out to feel the sun.

That's how "the Hugo Wars" might be interpreted. Therefore, critics, bloggers and readers of a right-wing inclination now should speak up and continue to roll back the frontiers of leftist nihilism. The Zeitgeist favors it and the foundation has been laid by the Hugo Wars' right-wing operators, none mentioned, none forgotten.

The Hugo Wars' right-wingers say they want a new "Campbellian revolution". Where have I heard that before? In the 60s. Then the New Wave said it was in for a "second Campbellian revolution" (mentioned in foreword to *Dangerous Visions,* 1967). New Wave aside, if the resurgent right-wing wants to change the face of SF it must be more than a change of superficial attitudes, more than a change of style and / or the embracing of some new topical subject. In order to survive SF will have to base its outlook on Tradition and Eternal Values. In order not be irrelevant SF must embrace the spiritual paradigm and stop being reductionist-materialist.

As shown earlier in this study, the Campbellian project had *faith*. The New Wave, for its part, was artistically interesting but ended up in philosophical nihilism. In this perspective, then, will the "resurgent right-wing of SF" have "faith" or will it be "just another nihilism"?

A rather odd right-wing novel is *The Iron Dream* (1972) by Norman Spinrad. It's an SF story allegedly written by Adolf Hitler, if he hadn't become a politician but instead had moved to the US in the 1920s. The book has "The Iron Dream" as title and Spinrad as the author, but when opening it the reader is met by the caption of "The Lord of the Swastika," a novel by Adolf Hitler. Then there's a short biography giving the parallel world setting, that of Hitler being an Austrian moving to America to become a pulp illustrator and author. Then the novel proper is given, "The Lord of the Swastika". And then, in line with the parallel world concept, we get an after-word by a fictitious scholar, "Homer Whipple," analyzing the novel for the contemporary, 1970s audience (according to the fiction it was written in the 1950s) but still in a parallel world mode, since the world Whipple lives in is the same where Hitler never became German Führer and thus, the Soviet Union, unhindered, could conquer all of Europe. This dire geopolitical state of things Whipple notes in his essay.

As for *The Iron Dream* it's been said that because of the double fiction, the novel in the novel, the ironic effect is doubled: in the fictitious world where Hitler writes "The Lord of the Swastika" the concept of a triumphant Germany becoming the master of Europe is fiction – but our reality (our reality up until about 1942, at least). We, the readers of Spinrad's novel, in a sense live in the parallel world that the novel-writing Hitler dreams about.

The Iron Dream indulges in violence and chauvinism. And I don't endorse that. The novel is a not so subtle distortion of the subject at hand. That said, it has its moments. The book relates how a certain Feric Jaggar (Adolf Hitler) rises to power in Heldon (Germany) along with his cronies Waffing, Boggel and Best (Goering, Goebbels and Hess). The final challenge comes in facing up to the Zind (Soviet) empire. The story of how Jaggar comes to power in Heldon by laying his hands on the Steel Commander, a mythical weapon wielded by former Heldon heroes, is rather original and elaborate as such.

As intimated, the double irony gives the story some power. Also, Carl Jung once said that "Mussolini is a man; Hitler is a myth". With that he hinted at the elemental, hard to define nature of Adolf Hitler. Spinrad, in conceptualizing Hitler as Feric Jaggar, somehow captures this mythical aspect of the subject.

Throughout this study, I've stressed the artistic aspect of SF. Like this: the gist of this book is conceptual, it's about SF having a relationship to Tradition and traditional values. But since the main subject is literary and artistic, treating novels and short stories, the artistic dimension has to be highlighted along with all the pragmatical lessons taught.

I mean, if some budding right-wing author reads this and thinks that "eternal values in fantasy fictional form equates with an instant classic", he's in the wrong. To succeed in telling a relatable story conveying some meaning isn't easy. But this study is no handbook in writing. This study focuses on the structural aspects of traditional SF.

As a general tip to the "budding right-wing author", I say: writing fiction is a complicated business, it's a way of saying things with a modicum of symbolism. The things you have to say, the specific messages and concepts, have to be brought forth with characters, milieus and a semblance of style. And not all have a talent for this kind of shaping. So if you have things to say in a traditional vein, maybe an essay or a lecture is a better way to convey your thoughts than a fiction story.

In the introduction I intimated that this book is an essay, a somewhat idiosyncratic view on SF with a traditional slant. In the process, I may have omitted some right-wing fantasist. One such omission I do admit, a guy that "should have been along" but which I gladly leave out: Poul Anderson (1926-2001).

Anderson may have been a Golden Age author and he may have written the traditional Nordic Fantasy *The Broken Sword* (1954) – and of course, this is a worthy number. And when interviewed once by Charles Platt in *The Dream Makers* (1980) Anderson noticed how few SF authors created societies having any form of traditions. The common future world in his day often seemed to be built on nothing, an implicit nihilism. This Anderson meant and it's a viable thought for a study like this. But otherwise I can't bear myself to read the man. I mean, he did know of Tradition and he was the Bard of

SF, having the ability to portray the spatial vistas with some zest and color, but the goody-good attitude he acquired from the 1960s an on, the attitude of treating Profound Subjects in a Humanistic Fashion, just kills it for me, as in "The Sharing of Flesh", "The Problem of Pain" and "High Treason". I may return to his authorship in some remote future but as for this study, I just can't approach his texts with any form of inspiration.

Reportedly, there was an SF story that Adolf Hitler personally liked: *The Tunnel* (*Der Tunnel*, 1915) by Bernhard Kellermann. To be fair Hitler hadn't, as far as I know, read this book about a transatlantic railway tunnel but reportedly he was aroused by a 1920s screening of the film based on this work. The biographer Alan Bullock relates how Hitler specifically reacted to a scene with an agitator firing the minds of a gathering of workers; Hitler was said to have been highly inspired by this. Speculative minds can ponder what this SF story meant for the creation of the Nazi movement, of Hitler speaking at rallies and beer halls and public squares, building a mass movement that subsequently controlled all of Europe.

If you want to get an idea of Kellermann's rare novel, you might read the pastiche *A Trans-Atlantic Tunnel, Hurrah!* by Harry Harrison (1972).

Robert Silverberg had his moments. I've already praised *Up the Line* in chapter 29. And his Nebula awarded *A Time of Changes* (1971) could deserve some lines.

As for serious, esoteric SF with a moral message this is a fine effort. It tells of a future planet where the word "I" is forbidden, as such a more exotic setting of the "don't say I, say we" strain also shown in *We* and *Anthem*. As for more similar SF novels we have Delaney's *Babel-17*, also into the element of a language devoid of first person pronouns. In his novel Silverberg delves into the angst related to not being allowed to say and conceive of yourself as an individual – and, conversely, of the liberation felt when allowed to say "I" in all its glory.

Silverberg's story might not be altogether perfect artistically. But still, it's a worthy example of SF dealing with psychology, with "inner space" and the existential aspect of being human. This isn't a lecture, it's a spiritual psychodrama ending in the words "go and be healed", a not very common valediction as 20th century novels go.

At the beginning of this "Marginalia" section I mentioned Desmond Bagley's "Welcome, Comrade" as a viable example of right-wing SF – right-minded SF, though not one specifically dealing with Tradition, as was otherwise the criterion for the stories treated in this study. That is, Bagley's story is an example of SF within the more everyday confines of the "right-wing, conservative" label. SF that is anti-communist, pro-enterprise, anti-collectivist and so on. Having delved into this, from the point of view of the current study, "uncharted territory," I get the urge to propose what could be an anthology of "right-wing SF, GOP-variety" or whatever. Viable right-wing SF not necessarily footed in Tradition. For such a potential collection I would choose these stories:

- "Coventry" (1940) by Robert Heinlein (*q.v.* chapter one), a story of political dreams versus reality.
- "See-saw" (1941) by A. E. van Vogt, or a similar excerpt sporting the Weapon Shop slogan of "Best energy weapons in the whole universe; the right to buy weapons is the right to be free".
- "Margin of Profit" (1956) by Poul Anderson, a heroic yarn of being a space-age merchant.
- "The Pedestrian" (1951) by Ray Bradbury, of the rebellious trait of being a studied recluse in a time of media-drugged zombies.
- "Cloak of Anarchy" (1972) by Larry Niven (*q.v.* chapter thirty), of anarchy as a fine ideal and a brutal reality.
- "Hero" (1972) by Joe Haldeman (*q.v.* chapter 32), the first part

of *The Forever War* once published as a novelette in *Analog*, about assuming responsibility in a modern combat situation.
• "Welcome, Comrade" (1964) by Desmond Bagley, on the dangers of Cultural Marxism invading us by conditioning.
• "The Hound" (1922) by H. P. Lovecraft, a warning against the nihilist-dandyist lifestyle of the Huysman and Baudelaire kind.
• "Birth of a Notion" (1976) by Isaac Asimov, about the entrepreneurial and conceptual daring of Hugo Gernsback creating science fiction.

How about that for a mainstream right-wing SF anthology? I'm not an editor and I have no tangible urge to edit such a book as the above intimated. However, if any reader thinks this sounds like a good concept for an anthology, go ahead, feel inspired. And if the need would arise to flesh it out and make it more substantial as to the number of pages, then you could add Heinlein's "The Man Who Sold the Moon" (entrepreneurial SF) and Rand's "Anthem" (spiritual individualism).

In chapter 23 I mentioned Philip K. Dick's *The Man in the High Castle* (1962). Hereby some additional notes on it. The Axis powers have won the war and split America between them, Japan taking the western part and Germany the eastern. Other than the parallel world theme the novel is fairly mainstream in its depicting Germans as brute animals and Japanese as art-loving stoics: this goes down well with any liberal critic. And the idea as such of the Axis powers physically occupying USA after winning the war is unrealistic as they in reality would have been satisfied with cutting down the American Army and Navy, leaving it as a harmless regional power. However, at times this novel has its allure. As intimated earlier, take the never-never-land feeling achieved in the scene where a Japanese occupant for a moment finds himself in a parallel world where the Axis didn't win the war; that's some *tour de force*, having an alternate future in an alternate future.

As for Dick's other political SF you could deliberate further on *Flow My Tears, the Policeman Said* (1974). This was written in post-Watergate times, giving the leftist Dick a chance to lambaste Richard Nixon and all that he stood for. In the novel the president is responsible for creating a dictatorship in America making all things bad, just plain bad with martial law, checkpoint queues and concentration camps. *Flow My Tears...* reads like a parody of a leftist vision of right wing America. And Dick actually wrote more in that vein, meant as an intentional parody, in *Eye in the Sky* in 1956, mentioned earlier, depicting as it does the successive journey through a group of people's minds after an accident in a nuclear facility. The radiation has made it possible for their minds to migrate in this way, and one of the chapters is dedicated to the rightist person's mind where it's all chauvinism, tanks and soldiers in the streets and whatnot. To be sure, Dick also parodies the leftist mindset in the same novel, about getting all sentimental over "Pete Seeger songs and memories of the International Brigade" ... in all, fair and balanced!

I don't want to endorse generic anti-right fiction; far from it. However, some additional lines could be dedicated to *Flow My Tears...* because it's such a good read. Dick was fairly good at giving his stories a human angle without manipulating the reader's feelings. In the novel in question he for instance gives a rather vivid portrait of a police chief that turns against the system; not that this in itself comes to mean anything, even though the system at long last is changed and more normal societal conditions are said to be restored. That's another plus of this novel: its unheroic and everyday atmosphere, coupled with the future setting and ontological speculations. That's the Dickian hallmark: he just knew story telling in SF – and had a special something in it. However, when he wrote plain realist, contemporary novels (*The Broken Bubble, In Milton Lumky Territory*) the magic wasn't there.

This study focuses on traditional aspects of SF. In the narrower sense, this is "right-wing SF", at least as regards the gist of authorship like

Heinlein, Herbert, Jünger, Lewis, Lovecraft, Howard, Dickson and Williamson etc. The books examined are all published before 1984, so how about the new ones? Looking at more contemporary right-wing SF you could mention titles like Randolph D. Calverhall's *Serpent's Walk* (1991, with post-1945 underground Nazis coming to the fore again with economic and metapolitical means) and William Pierce's *The Turner Diaries* (1978, about white nationalist guerrilla warfare). To be fair I don't endorse these books, at least not structurally. But they have their value in showing that SF can be the means of expression for oppressed and forbidden political ideas, ideas considered taboo in polite society.

Also, note that these novels are American. Could they have been published in Europe? US laws on freedom of speech seem to be more liberal than what we have in the Old World. The societal climate in Europe makes it easier for the regimes to repress inconvenient books (like, back in the day having Spinrad's *The Iron Dream* only sold "under the counter" in Germany).

Current right-wing SF: as for modern dystopias we for instance have Scott Wilson's *Utopia X* (2004), where America in 2048 is ruled by a totalitarian government disguised as a tolerant, anti-racist democracy. With mind control and the outlawing of "insensitivity" and freedom of speech the stage is set for a modern *Nineteen Eighty-Four*, only now there's a ray of hope in the form of a guerrilla movement that begins to take shape, intent to defend liberty and freedom for all. More stylistically elaborate is Alex Kurtagic's *Mister* (2009) with a sombre future characterized by political correctness, corruption, crime and globalism; the book has been lauded for its avant-garde style, erudition and humor. This could be labeled as contemporary right-wing SF for the educated man.

To make this survey complete you can mention two American race oriented dystopias, Kyle Bristow's *White Apocalypse* (2010), on the modern implications of the idea of whites having colonized America 17,000 years ago, and Ward Kendall's *Hold Back This Day* (2003), about the last white people on earth. A final dystopia, for better or worse closer to the mainstream, is Frenchman Jean Raspail's *The Camp of Saints* (1973), extrapolating on the theme of European mass immigration. By some critics it's said that third world immigrants are treated with silk gloves, hence the "saint" element of the title.

In other words, it's clear that SF lends itself to hot topics and non-PC narratives, to more or less controversial political discussions.

34. CODA

A SORT OF PAYOFF, conclusion or coda should end a book like this, I figure. I have conceptualized 100 years of SF into the above lectures – so how do I see on the times ahead? I have already intimated it, in the Introduction and elsewhere, and hereby some sort of summation of my views on the future of fantastic fiction. The keywords will be *Archeofuturism* and *Idealism*.

As for the archeofuturist strain, this is more than mere "swords and spaceships", more than mere action plots *à la* Flash Gordon. This is the conceptual fusing of "old" (the sword) with "new" (the spaceship). Conversely, to imagine that man's future will be "modernist", that it will be totally anti-tradition, anti-everything that preceded the "let there be light" of the atom bomb, is a misconception. Man's soul is made up of Will, Thought and Compassion, acknowledging the Light – and in this respect, to think that materialist nihilism is the way of the future is simply madness. Even though our times are characterized by hedonist liberalism and a denial of things spiritual, the children of tomorrow won't think so. Man is currently on the threshold of a Golden Age, an age of spiritual and esoteric acknowledgment. The realization of this depends on men peacefully wishing this, peacefully aiming to rid the world of the materialist nihilism governing it today, to replace it with a regimen of truth and justice; of co-nationalism and ethno-pluralism, giving every people, including Europeans, an assured existence; of spirituality, acknowledging eternal values.

Eternal values like duty, honor and courage, accountability, determination, vigilance, self-restraint, self-sacrifice, magnanimity, compassion and modesty, are still cherished, albeit not by our current "elites". But the values *are* being upheld, they are still remembered, by myself and others, and this assures their continued existence. Man has the worst behind him in terms of trials. We aren't living in paradise yet but the times they are a-changing – for the better. Ancient documents are still studied and lauded, alleged out-of-date attitudes and values like the above mentioned (duty, honor etc.) are still upheld to some extent and they will be even more cherished when people in general return to them, having been reminded by this book and others.

Old attitudes, still viable, will live on. As Frank Herbert has shown us the future may be archeofuturistic – the archaic traits in his fiction, and in fiction by Heinlein, Lewis, Tolkien, Lovecraft, Jünger, Howard, Borges, Castaneda, Pournelle and Bradbury, tell me that eternal values are still embraced by authors and readers. Stories about traditional values will continue to be written. Conversely, a literature imbued with nihilism and cynicism can't survive. You can't build a culture on nothing. Stories conceptualizing Tradition for a new era, will live on, be these stories labeled as SF, speculative fiction or whatever.

I said I would be speaking about Archeofuturism and Idealism. As for the latter, to even acknowledge ideals is to be an archeofuturist, it seems; to be an archeofuturist is to look at Tradition, getting to know its ideals and attitudes and adapt them to contemporary and future times.

As for the future of the speculative attitude in general, these times, to me, seem speculative in themselves. People speculate over space, time and aliens like never before. The MSM view on these matters, conveyed by documentaries on what official scientists think and propose, may still be on the level of "we'll never get the answers whether we're alone in the universe or not". But in essence, I'd say, exopolitical resources are already available. Contact with them has been upheld for ages by saints, seers and channelers. While I can't vouch for the authenticity of them all I don't, on the other hand, belong to the puzzled faction, the just intimated "we'll never know"-bunch of thinkers.

But if aliens are already around, if they make contact – will SF not die out then? Will SF literature not seem lame in comparison? Indeed, such a development would strain SF conceptually, challenging it to focus on essentials. But until the actual event of "first contact" arrives, I'd say that SF authors should keep on writing about such meetings but, in order to adapt to the coming age, do it more spiritually credible. Put differently, first contact will only come when mankind has raised itself to the level of the positive aliens now reportedly having the upper hand (case in point, the hostile "gray alien" has all but disappeared from sight, virtually; what does this tell you?). When all men are peaceful and harmonious inside out, then grand scale first contact may occur. And if SF wants to be along on this ride it has to step up a notch spiritually, acknowledge Will-Thought and man's Inner Light. If not, SF will become irrelevant.

In 1970 Alvin Toffler wrote *Future Shock*, about our lives changing dramatically during the 20th century, whether tangibly or more subtly. And to guard us against such future conceptual onslaughts, SF could play a part: Toffler allegedly held SF as a remedy for future shock. As you know my drift by now, I'd add a spiritual element to this: "become more spiritual", acknowledge the discreet forces in life such as Tradition, Will and Compassion, and you'll be better equipped for the times ahead, for possible "future shocks". The same goes for SF: the speculative literature of tomorrow must become more conceptual, cleverer, and within this framework of spirituality. "Spiritual SF": this mustn't, for that matter, degenerate into stories about "meditating adepts". But it has to take on the challenge of spirituality, of raising ourselves mentally to reach psychological lands of infinite possibilities. Conversely, to delve further into materialistic lands, exploring the realm of "man machine" (as in stories of body modification, implants, genetic engineering and the like), to me seems a dead end.

The SF of tomorrow must become more spiritual. If so, it may survive. If not, other literatures with this attitude will take its place.

This may be some play with words. I mean, I admit that I like SF as a label, I have some sentimental ties to the genre *per se* and to books labeled "science fiction". But as we've seen in this book I also acknowledge the conceptual viability of books not labeled as SF when published, such as the books by Boye, Zamyatin, Huxley, Jünger, Borges and Castaneda I've treated. And my own novel *Antropolis* (2009) didn't carry any generic label. So stories conceptualizing man's encounter with exopolitical forces, stories about parallel worlds and different developments in the times ahead, will still be written, be they labeled as SF, fantasy or whatever. Maybe "metaphysical fiction" of "mefy" may be a new label.

Be that as it may; we live in interesting times and there are still stories to be written: conceptual stories, brainy stories of the SF kind. Because, such a literature of ideas, of brainy reflections, today eminently seems to have a future since the level of erudition is going up. Computers and the internet have raised the mental level of mankind and this, among other things, bodes well for the kind of literature that SF is.

So then, a literature of "brainy reflections," is what I look forward to? What happened to art, dreams and enchanting vistas? You could say: the conceptual element, the ideas and speculative angles, is the defining feature of SF. "Having something to say" is the *sine qua non* of all literature. With that in place, the artistry (alluring language, vivid imagery etc.) tends to come along as an epiphenomenon. I know that you can't expect art to be created out of nothing. I merely want to say, to primarily ask for "artistry" in a literature of ideas such as SF is a little odd. The prime directive of the SF operation is to have something to say, to make sense, to be relevant to the times ahead. And since those times will be spiritual SF must become more spiritual to survive.

As for survival in a more general sense, that of mankind, SF could indeed play a part in this. I just mentioned the concept of "Future Shock" and the idea of SF as a remedy against it. This also makes me think of Dr. Isaac Asimov who once said: "Individual science fiction stories may seem as trivial as ever to the blinder critics and philosophers of today – but the core of science fiction, its essence, the concept around which it revolves, has become crucial to our salvation if we are to be saved at all".

SOURCES

NON-FICTION

Aldiss, Brian: *Trillion Year Spree: The History of Science Fiction*. London: Gollancz, 1986
Ashley, Mike: *The Time-Machines: The Story of the Science-Fiction Pulp Magazines From the Beginning to 1950*. Liverpool: Liverpool University Press, 2000
- *Transformations: The Story of the Science-Fiction Magazines From 1950 to 1970*: Liverpool: Liverpool University Press, 2005
Asimov, Isaac: The Second Revolution in Ellison, Harlan (ed): *Dangerous Visions* (orig 1967). New York: New American Library, 1975
Bergman, Ingmar: *Laterna Magica*. Stockholm: Norstedts, 1987
Borges, Jorge Luis: *Other Inquisitions* (orig 1964). Austin: University of Texas Press, 1975
Burgin, Richard: *Jorge Luis Borges: Conversations*. New York: Holt Rhinehart Winston, 1969
Campbell, John: Introduction in Heinlein, Robert A.: *The Man Who Sold the Moon*. New York: Signet, 1951
Campbell, Joseph: *The Hero With a Thousand Faces*. New York:

Pantheon Books, 1949
Carpenter, Humphrey: *J. R. R. Tolkien – A Biography*. London: George Allen & Unwin, 1977
Clarke, Arthur C.: *Astounding Days*. London: Gollancz, 1990
Disch, Thomas N.: *Talking With Jesus in F&SF*, July 1981
- *The Dreams Our Stuff Is Made Of – How Science Fiction Conquered the World*. London: Touchstone, 2000
Dugin, Alexander: *The Fourth Political Theory*. London: Arktos, 2012
Edwards, Folke: *Den barbariska modernismen*. Malmö: Liber, 1987
Edwards, Folke: *Futurism in Berefeldt*, Gunnar (ed): Bild och verklighet. Uppsala: A&W, 1972
Evola, Julius: *Revolt Against the Modern World*. Rochester, VT: Inner Traditions, 1996
Faye, Guillaume: *Archeofuturism* (orig 1998). London: Arktos, 2010
Foss, Chris: *2000-talets Foss* (British original same year as *20th Century Foss*). Stockholm: Carlsen If, 1979
Guénon, René: *The Crisis of the Modern World* (orig 1927). Hillsdale NY: Sophia Perennis, 2004
Herbert, Frank: *The Illustrated Dune*. New York: Berkley Books, 1978
Holland, Steve: *Sci-Fi Art – A Graphic History*. Lewes, GB: ILEX, 2009
Holmberg, John-Henri: Inre landskap och yttre rymd. 1. *Science fictions historia från H. G. Wells till Brian W. Aldiss*. Lund: Bibliotekstjänst, 2002
- Inre landskap och yttre rymd. 2. *Science fictions historia från J. G. Ballard till Gene Wolfe*. Lund: Bibliotekstjänst, 2003
Humphreys, Richard: *Futurism*. Malmö: Fogtdal, 2000
Joshi, S. T.: *H. P. Lovecraft – A Life*. West Warwich, RI: Necronomicon Press, 1996
Jünger, Ernst: *Typus, Name, Gestalt*. Stuttgart: Ernst Klett Verlag, 1963
Kranz, Gisbert: *Ernst Jüngers symbolische Weltschau*. Hamburg:

Pädagogische Verlag Schwann, 1968
Kuttner, Henry: The Innocent Eye in Heinlein, Robert A.: *Revolt in 2100*. New York: Signet Books, 1955
Lagercrantz, Olof: *Tretton lyriker och Fågeltruppen*. Stockholm: W&W, 1973
Lundwall, Sam J.: Startpunkt: 1851 in *Science Fiction Nytt* 65/1981
Miller, Russell: *Bare-faced Messiah*. London: Penguin Books, 1987
Moorcock, Michael: Starship Stormtroopers in T*he Opium General*. London: Harrap, 1984
Platt, Charles: *The Dream Makers*. Ann Arbor: Berkley Books, 1980
Spinrad, Norman: *Science Fiction in the Real World*. Carbondale: Southern Illinois University Press, 1990
Sri Dharma Pravartaka Acarya: *The Dharma Manifesto*. London: Arktos, 2013
Stableford, Brian: *Algebraic Fantasies and Realistic Romances*. Rockville, MD: Wildside Press, 1995
Sutin, Lawrence (ed): *In Pursuit of Valis: Selections From the Exegesis*. Novato, California: Underwood-Miller, 1991
Svensson, Lennart: *Ernst Jünger – A Portrait*. Melbourne, Australia: Manticore Books, 2014
Williamson, Edwin: *Borges: A Life*. London: Viking Books, 2004

FICTION

Aldiss, Brian W.: The Day We Embarked for Cythera in *New Worlds Quarterly* 1, September 1971
Ballard, J. G.: *Super-Cannes*. London: HarperCollins, 2000
- *The Atrocity Exhibition* (orig 1970, annotated edition 1993). London: HarperCollins 2001
- *The Complete Short Stories*. London: HarperCollins 2002
Borges. Jorge Luis: *Fictions*. London: Penguin Classics, 2000
Boye, Karin: *Dikter – Kallocain – Kris*. Stockholm: Bonniers, 1992
Bradbury, Ray: *Fahrenheit 451*. London: Granada, 1979

- *A Medicine For Melancholy*. Bantam: New York, 1960
- *S Is For Space*. London: Pan Books, 1968
Castaneda, Carlos: *The Fire From Within*. London: Black Swan, 1985
Dick, Philip K.: *Flow My Tears, the Policeman Said*. London: Grafton Books, 1986
- *Galactic Pot-Healer*. London: Grafton Books, 1987
- *VALIS*. New York: Mariner Books, 2011
Dickson, Gordon R.: *Dorsai!* London: Sphere Books, 1978
Essén, Rütger (writing as "Leif Erikson): *De släckta metropolerna*. Stockholm: Saxon & Lindström, 1937
Haldeman, Joe: *Hero in Analog*, June 1972
Heinlein, Robert A.: *Assignment in Eternity*. New York: Signet, 1954
- *Beyond this Horizon*. Riverdale, NY: Baen Books, 2007
- *Revolt in 2100*. New York: Signet, 1955
- *Starship Troopers*. Dunton Green, Kent: New English Library, 1987
- *The Green Hills of Earth*. New York: Signet, 1951 I
- *The Man Who Sold the Moon*. New York: Signet, 1951 II
- *Time for the Stars*. London: Pan Books, 1973
Howard, Robert E.: *Conan the Adventurer*. London: Sphere Books, 1986
- *Conan the Wanderer*. London: Sphere Books, 1974
Jünger, Ernst: *Auf den Marmorklippen*. Berlin: Ullstein, 2006
- *Eumeswil*. Malmö: Bo Cavefors förlag, 1981
- *Heliopolis*. Stockholm: Natur & Kultur, 1954
Lewis, C. S.: *The Magician's Nephew*. London: Collins Publishing Group, 1989
Lobsang Rampa: *The Third Eye*. London: Secker & Warburg, 1956
Lovecraft, H. P.: *Fungi From Yuggoth*. West Warwick, RI: Necronomicon Press, 1987
Lovecraft, H. P.: *H. P. Lovecraft Omnibus 1 – At the Mountains of Madness*. London: HarperCollins, 1993
Lovecraft, H. P.: *H. P. Lovecraft Omnibus 2 – Dagon and Other*

Macabre Tales. London: HarperCollins, 1994
Lovecraft, H. P.: *H. P. Lovecraft Omnibus 3 – The Haunter of the Dark.* London: HarperCollins, 1990
Moorcock, Michael: *The Jewel in the Skull.* St Albans: Mayflower, 1973 I
- *The Knight of the Swords.* St Albans: Mayflower, 1973 II
- *The Sailor on the Seas of Fate.* London: Grafton Books, 1981
- *The Sleeping Sorceress.* London: Quartet Books, 1975
- *The War Hound and the World's Pain.* Dunton Green, Kent: New English Library, 1983
Niven, Larry: *Tales of Known Space.* New York: Del Rey, 1983
Pournelle, Jerry: *A Step Farther Out.* New York: Ace Books, 1979
Smith, Clark Ashton: *Out of Space and Time, Volume 2.* Frogmore, St Albans: Panther Books, 1974
Tolkien, J. R. R.: *The Fellowship of the Ring.* New York: Ballantine Books, 1988 I
- *The Two Towers.* New York: Ballantine Books, 1988 II
van Vogt, A. E.: *The Weapon Makers.* London: New English Library, 1970

ABOUT THE AUTHOR

LENNART SVENSSON (born 1965) made his English language debut in 2014 with *Ernst Jünger – A Portrait*. The following year he published a bio of another controversial German, Richard Wagner. In Swedish Svensson has written novels and essays and he's currently working on several projects in English, his adopted language. He has a BA in Indology and lives in Härnösand on the northern coast of Sweden. He blogs at The Svensson Galaxy.

www.ingramcontent.com/pod-product-compliance
Lightning Source LLC
Chambersburg PA
CBHW022100150426
43195CB00008B/207